CISTERCIAN STUDIES SERIES: NUMBER TWO HUNDRED TWENTY-ONE

David M. Goldfrank

Nil Sorsky:
The Authentic Writings

Early 18th century miniature of Nil Sorsky and his skete
(State Historical Museum Moscow, Uvarov Collection, No. 107. B 1?).

CISTERCIAN STUDIES SERIES: NUMBER TWO HUNDRED TWENTY-ONE

Nil Sorsky:
The Authentic Writings

Translated, Edited, and Introduced

by
David M. Goldfrank

Cistercian Publications
cistercianpublications.org

LITURGICAL PRESS
Collegeville, Minnesota
litpress.org

A Cistercian Publications title published by Liturgical Press

Cistercian Publications
Editorial Offices
161 Grosvenor Street
Athens, Ohio 45701
cistercianpublications.org

Nil Sorsky, 1433/1434–1508

© Translation and Introduction, David M. Goldfrank, 2008
Published by Liturgical Press, Collegeville, Minnesota. All rights reserved. No part of this book may be used or reproduced in any manner whatsoever, except brief quotations in reviews, without written permission of Liturgical Press, Saint John's Abbey, PO Box 7500, Collegeville, MN 56321-7500.

Library of Congress Cataloguing-in-Publication Data

Nil, Sorskii, Saint, ca. 1433–1508.
 [Works. English. 2008]
 Nil Sorsky : the authentic writings / translated, edited, and introduced by David M. Goldfrank.
   p. cm.—(Cistercian studies series ; no. 221)
 Includes bibliographical references (p.   ) and indexes.
 ISBN 978-0-87907-321-3 (pbk.)
 1. Spiritual life—Russkaia pravoslavnaia tserkov,. 2. Monasticism and religious orders, Orthodox Eastern—Russia—Rules. 3. Nil, Sorskii, Saint, ca. 1433–1508—Correspondence. I. Goldfrank, David M. II. Title.
 III. Title: Authentic writings.

 BX597.N52A2 2008
 248.4'819—dc22   2008008410

'Εστίν ἐν ἡμῖν νοητὸς πόλεμος τοῦ αἰσθητοῦ χαλεπώτερος.
Єсть мысла рать, внасъ самѣх, чювьственыа лютѣйши.

— Philotheus the Sinaite —

Within our very selves is a war of the mind fiercer than of the senses.

Фк 2: 274; Eparkh. 344: 343v

TABLE OF CONTENTS

Author's Preface   xi
Table of Bibliographic Abbreviations   xvii
Transliteration from Cyrillic Letters   xx
Technical Abbreviations in the Footnotes   xxi

Part I: Toward a Study of Nil Sorsky

I. THE LITTLE WE KNOW   3
   Omega as Alpha   3
   The Shadows of the Kremlin   4
   The Northern Beacon   8
   The Holy Mount   13
   The Quiet Kelliot   18
   A Busy 'Abode of Stillness'   20
   Publish Lest They Perish   23
   Four and Twenty Saints Lives   24
   The Church at Large   30

II. A TENTATIVE TOP TEN   33
   The Maybe Mentor   33
   The Congenital Connection   36
   The Compatible Companion   37
   The Best of the Bookmen   39
   The Loose Cannon   42
   The Man in the Middle   44
   The Ardent Ascetic   46

The Unexpected Bedfellow   48
The Colonizing Coenobite   55
Once a Boyar . . .   58

III. THE WRITTEN LEGACY 62
Texts and Structures   62
Centrality of Sources   68
The Acolyte as Adapter   80
Literary Devices   83
Technical Terms   86
A Bit on Nil's Hesychasm   95
Further on Nil's Non-Possession   97
Nil's Nil in a Nutshell   100

Epilogue: WIN SOME, LOSE SOME   101
Love's Labors Lost?   101
Making It   102

PREFACE TO THE TRANSLATIONS 105

Part II: Nil Sorsky's Original Texts

THE *PREDANIE* 113

THE *USTAV* 124
Exposition of the Chapters   125
Foreword   126
1. On the Differences of the Mental Campaigns   131
2. On Our Combat . . . Prayer and Stillness   137
3. On How to Fortify Oneself   154
4. On Control of Every Activity   158
5. On the . . . Eight Principle . . . Urges   162
   1. *On Gluttony*   163
   2. *On Fornication*   167
   3. *On Avarice*   172
   4. *On Wrath*   173
   5. *On Sadness*   175
   6. *On Despondency*   177
   7. *On Vainglory*   182
   8. *On Pride*   184

Table of Contents ix

    6. In General, Against All Urges   189
    7. On Remembrance of Death   191
    8. On Tears   202
    9. On the Guarding of These Things   210
    10. On Detachment and True Carefreeness   213
    11. On Appropriate Measures   219

THE THREE EPISTLES   229
    To Vassian Patrikeev   231
    To Gurii Tushin   238
    To German Podol'nyi   245
    A Little Epistle   250

THE *SOBORNIK* APOLOGIAI   251
    Foreword   251
    Postscript   253

THE TESTAMENT   255

Appendices

Appendix I. The Nil Polev / Nil Sorsky Codex   259
Appendix II. The Predanie *Addenda*   270
Appendix III. The Zavĕt *of Innokentii Okhliabinin*   273
Appendix IV. Index of Biblical Citations   277

Bibliography   281

Index   324

AUTHOR'S PREFACE

Let us start by clearing the air on two issues. First, this volume contains as its centerpiece the ninth published translation, or alleged translation, to date of Nil Sorsky's theoretical-practical treatise for monks, known as his *Ustav* (Typikon). Only three of the other eight are, however, genuine translations: Fairy von Lilienfeld's German (1963), *monachos* Vasileios Grolimund's modern Greek (1985), and Gelian Prokhorov's modern Russian (2005). Hélène Izwolsky's English (1948) is free and also incomplete. The French text of Sr Sophia Jacamon OSB (1980) is a translation, with some recourse to the original, of the modern Russian explicated adaptation by Archimandrite Iustin (1892). Marusja Galmozzi's and Lisa Cremaschi's Italian (edited by Enzo Bianchi, 1988) seems for the most part to translate Jacamon. Finally the English rendition of George Maloney SJ (2003) is a free translation and somewhat metaphrased version of Iustin, perhaps mediated by Jacamon or Galmozzi/Cremaschi, and again with some recourse to Nil himself and also to Izwolsky. Hence the need, as well as utility, of this volume's faithful English translations.[1]

Second, consider a situation where virtually everyone believes a paradigm on the basis of anachronistic documentation which came to light a century and a half ago—a paradigm diametrically opposed to what actually happened. Such is the case with Nil Sorsky (1433/34-1508), medieval Russia's outstanding master and teacher of stillness or hesychasm. Since the 1850s most people

[1] See further below III. 'Preface to the Translations.'

with any knowledge of Nil have viewed him through the lens of the later struggle between so-called 'Nonpossessors' or Transvolgan Elders and 'Possessors' or Iosifites (Josephites). The analysis since the 1950s of the genuine paper trail has led to a different historical picture, one which, for sure, not all specialists accept, but whose crucial evidence has yet to find a serious rejoinder, much less a refutation. Accordingly, in the most pressing religious issue of Nil's day, the conflict between traditional Orthodoxy and dissidence, Nil Sorsky collaborated with Iosif Volotsky (1439/40-1515), the master-pen behind Russia's inquisition, coenobitic reorganization, and rationalization of commemorations for departed souls. Nil's and Iosif's different life styles, reflected in their respective monastic teachings and rules, did not lead in Nil's lifetime even to a literary debate, much less to a public, politicized struggle between them over the propriety and fate of monastic estates and wealth or anything else.

I am therefore asking the readers, if they have any preconceptions of Nil based on the traditional paradigm, to lay these aside and let Nil speak for himself from his authentic works. As a teacher, writer, and, so far as we can tell, practitioner of traditional Orthodox monastic spirituality and of the newer methods of mystical prayer, Nil enjoyed the acclaim of Orthodox contemporaries and future generations of all stamps. His Sora hermitage flourished as such for well over two hundred years as the model small, individualistic cloister. His writings are a unique witness to how Orthodox stillness was taught and practiced in the late fifteenth and early sixteenth centuries, perhaps in the Balkans as well as Russia. They also are major cultural and historical, as well as religious documents from the Russia of his time, but not of the nineteenth century with its quite different spiritual agendas.

As with my translation and analysis of Iosif Volotsky's Rules for this series, I have attempted, while making no concession to the strictest standards of scholarship, to do justice to Nil as a bearer of a great sacred tradition and to let his voice be heard. Two other scholars, von Lilienfeld (1963) and Maloney (1973), each far more qualified than I, have elucidated where Nil stands within this dynamic ongoing tradition of mystical prayer. In so doing, they—the first as rigorous professor, the second more as zealous pastor—have used Nil to present the fundamentals of this tradition to the contemporary reader. Their adherence to the Nil-vrs-Iosif paradigm does not detract from the value of this aspect of their books. Since prayer is such an individual experience, I leave it to interested individuals to sort out in their own way the devotional matters. My introductory chapters, rather, should serve, for everybody, to contextualize Nil and his writings on the basis of the available documents, the latest scholarship, how people thought in his time, and how we can imagine his world in today's terms.

My source work with the Old Slavic translations, as well as the Greek originals, if the most ambitious concerning Nil to date, suffers from my concessions to quotidian needs. I thereby utilized mainly the available photocopies of microfilmed Hilandar Serbian recensions and the microfilms of Iosifov Russian versions, both at Ohio State University, rather than the Saint Petersburg-housed, Kirillov-Belozersk and Sora manuscripts—ones most likely to contain the precise recension, maybe even the very codex Nil studied. Still, my experience with these papers leads me to believe that the manuscripts I consulted are close enough for my purposes. Hopefully, a future, critical Russian edition of Nil, by consulting the most useful Russian manuscripts, will complete the collective *Quellenforschung* presented here.

As author-translator, I would like to thank this series editor, E. Rozanne Elder, for suggesting that I produce this volume. It has been an illuminating, intellectual adventure. I never imagined that I could do justice to such a powerful spiritual figure as Nil, and am not at all certain that I have done so.

I would also like to single out four library complexes for special appreciation. As usual, the Dumbarton Oaks Center for Byzantine Studies and the Woodstock Library at Georgetown University have been invaluable, as has been the regular Georgetown Lauinger Library's Interlibrary Loan and Reference staffs. At Dumbarton Oaks, Professor Ned Keenan, Alice-Mary Talbot, Nancy Hinton, and Deborah Brown, and at Georgetown, J. Leon Hooper SJ, Pamela Anne Noyes, and Susan Karp have been especially helpful. A genuinely new experience for me, supported by travel grants from Georgetown's Center for Eurasian, Russian, and East European Studies, was the Hilandar Research Library at the Ohio State University. Working there seems like being in three or four fine medieval Slavic monastery book depositories and simultaneously a modern, reference-rich, reading room, within a major research library and with an expert and generous staff, that is the team under Predrag Matejic and Mary-Allen 'Basha' Johnson. Moreover, thanks to photocopies of some of its Serbian codices and to the Georgetown library stacks, my home office became my own 'Little Hilandar.' Finally, unexpected delays due to pressing family matters postponed my submission of this manuscript and other business in Saint Petersburg, allowed me to consult some key manuscripts, locate several more sources, and examine first hand Nil's collaboration with Iosif. I am thus most grateful to Elena Shevchenko and to the entire helpful and friendly staff of the Manuscript Division of the Russian National Library (RGB) there. In addition, the Library of Saint Vladimir's Orthodox Theological Seminary kindly supplied me with maybe North America's unique available copy of Grolimund's annotated translation, and the Library of Congress, the New York Public Library's Slavic and Baltic Division, Harvard's Widener Library, and the Slavonic Collection of the National Library of Finland (University of Helsinki) proved welcoming and useful.

To their credit, the free and adapted translations are replete with inspired renderings, which I have mined, of various turns of Nil's speech. Likewise, I owe a great debt of gratitude to other past and present professional colleagues and scholars, including some whose conclusions I sometimes dispute—among them, the late John Meyendorff and Iakov S. Lur'e, Tomáš Špidlík SJ (created Cardinal on 21 October, 2003), Fairy von Lilienfeld, Boris M. Kloss, Gelian. M. Prokhorov, Andrei Pliguzov, Elena Romanenko, Tamara Lënngren, and Jennifer Spock. While she was located in Saint Petersburg, Erika Monahan sent me invaluable information about some Kirillov manuscripts. Similarly, my old close friend and colleague Richard Stites dispatched useful photocopies from Helsinki, and Marcello Garzaniti of Rome and Florence supplied me with a copy of the Bianchi volume. Francis Butler, Henry Ronald

Cooper, Bill Darden, Michael Flier, Ann Kleimola, George Majeska, Olga Meerson, and William Veder responded to my urgent request and shared thoughts concerning some vexing translation problems. My Georgetown colleagues and former students, in this case, Elizabeth Zelensky, Catherine Evtuhov, Jo Ann Moran-Cruz, Dennis McManus, David Collins SJ, Argyrios Pisiotis, and Isaiah Gruber, provided excellent sounding boards for ideas.

I wish to thank Donald Ostrowski and Robert Romanchuk for their comments on my introductory chapters, and the latter singularly for his most careful reading of my translations. If this work is good deal less flawed than it might have been, these two, along with Polyvia Parara of Georgetown, who proofread the Greek, and Ludwig Steindorff of Kiel, who pointed out some German-language and other flaws, deserve a large share of the credit. Moreover, without Ostrowski's pioneering source criticism and Romanchuk's brilliant analysis of pedagogy and hermeneutics in fifteenth-century Kirillov, this work would have far less that is new to offer the reader.

Penultimately, Princeton Ph.D. candidate Ilya Kharin, a 2005 graduate from Georgetown who was planning at that time to specialize on the development of Russian-introduced Orthodoxy in Meiji Era Japan, proved an invaluable assistant to me under the Georgetown University Undergraduate Research Program, especially in the spring and summer of 2003, when I started this project. The identification of a fair number of Slavic sources and some excellent choices of words in the translation, as well as the avoidance of all sorts of mistakes, are due to his acumen, labor, and devotion to Orthodoxy. I, of course, bear responsibility for all of the shortcomings.

Finally, I must not neglect to mention once more (the now, unfortunately, late) M. Basil Pennington OCSO (1931-2005), founder of this series, and such a generous and exemplary teacher, pastor, and ecumenist, to whose memory I happily dedicate this volume.

D.M.G.

March, 2008

TABLE OF BIBLIOGRAPHIC ABBREVIATIONS[1]

ANSSSR	Akademiia nauk USSR (now RAN)
ASEI	*Akty sotsial'no-ekonomicheskoi istorii Severo-Vostochnoi Rusi* (9)
BLDR	*Biblioteka literatury Drevnei Rusi* (3)
BMFD	Byzantine Monastic Foundation Documents (3)
ChOIDR	*Chtenie v Imperatorskom obshchestve istorii i drevnostei rossiiskikh*
CMMHRL	*Catalog. Manuscripts on Microform of the Hilandar Research Library* (Matejic) (4)
CS	*Cistercian Studies* (3)
DRIU	*Drevnerusskie inocheskie ustavy* (3)
EO	*Echos d'Orient*
Eparkh.(GIM)	Eparkhal'nyi Fond (5)
FC	*Fathers of the Church* (3)
GBL	Gosudarstvennaia biblioteka imena Lenina, Moscow. (now RGB)
GIM	Gosudarstevennyi istoricheskii muzei, Moscow

1. Numbers in parenthesis refer to divisions in the Bibliography.

GPB	Gosudarstevnaia publichnaia biblioteka, Saint Petersburg (now RNB)
HM	Hilandar Monastery
HUS	*Harvard Ukrainian Studies*
KB	(GPB/RNB) Kirillov-Belozerskii Fond (5)
IRI	*Istorii Rossiskoi ierarkhii* (Amvrosii) (1a)
Ios.	(GBL/RGB) Iosifo-Volokolamskii Fond
KTsDRIVM	*Knizhnye tsentry drevnei Rusi. Iosifo-Volokolamskii monastyr'* (4)
KTsDRRAI	*Knizhnye tsentry Drevnie Rusi. Raznye aspekty issledovaniia* (7)
MKVZ	*Monastyrskaia kul'tura. Vostok i Zapad* (7)
MMR	*Monashestvo i monastyri v Rossii XI-XX veka* (7)
MRC	*Medieval Russian Culture* (7)
MRKIS/CIM	*Moskovskaia Rus' (1359-1584): kul'tura i istoricheskoe samosoznanie* (7)
MRIV	*The Monastic Rule of Iosif Volotsky* (2nd ed) (Goldfrank) (9)
NPNF	*A Select Library of the Nicene and Post-Nicene Fathers* (3)
NSA	Τοῦ ἐν ὁσίος πατρὸς ἡμῶν Νείλου Σόρσκυ (Grolimund) (10a)
NSE	*Nil Sorskij e l'esicasmo* (Bianchi, et al.) (7)
NSSS	*Nil Sorskij und seinen Schriften* (von Lilienfeld) (10a)
NSTRM	*Nil Sorskii i traditsii russkogo monashestva* (Romanenko) (10c)
OCA	*Orientalia christiana analecta*
OCP	*Orientalia christiana periodica*

Ostr.	*The Ostroh Bible 1581* (6).
PB/SB	*Palaeobulgarica / Starobŭlgarskita*
PDP	*Pamiatniki drevnei pis'mennosti (i iskusstva)*
PG	Patrologiae . . . graeca (3)
PL	Patrologiae . . . latina.(3)
PNSIK	*Prepodobnyi Nil Sorskii i Innokentii Komel'skii.* (Prokhorov) (1a)
PSRL	*Polnoe sobranie russkikh letopisei* (9)
PSW	*The Philokalia.* Edd. Palmer, Sherrard, Ware. (3)
RAN	Russian Academy of Sciences
RGB	Russian State (formerly, 'State . . . Lenin') Library, Moscow
RH	Russian Hesychasm (Maloney) (10a)
RH/HR	*Russian History / Histoire russe*
RNB	Russian National (formerly, 'State Public') Library, Saint Petersburg
SC	Sources chrétiennes
Sinod.	(GIM) Holy Synod Fond (5)
SKKDR	*Slovar' knizhnikov i knizhnosti drevnei Rusi* (2)
SMS	(HM) Slavic Manuscripts (5)
SNS	*Sobornik Nila Sorskogo* (1a)
Sol.	(RNB) Solovetskii Fond (5)
TODRL	*Trudy otdela drevnerusskoi literatury*
VMCh	*Velikiia Minei chetii.* (Makarii) (3)
VMCh-M	*Velikie Minei chet'i . . . March . . .* (3)
VPS	*Vassian Patrikeev i ego sochieniia* (Kazakova) (10a)
Φκ	Φιλοκαλία τῶν ἱερῶν νηπτικῶν (3)

TRANSLITERATION FROM CYRILLIC LETTERS[1]

a	а	o	о, ѡ
b	б	p	п
ć	ђ (Serbian only)	ps	пс, ѱ
ch	ч	r	р
d	д	s	с
e	є, е; also э	sh	ш
ě	ѣ	shch	щ
f	ф, ѳ	sht	щ
g	г	t	т
i	и, ї, i also й	ts	ц
ia	ꙗ, ѧ, я	u	оу, ꙋ, у, ѵ
iu	ю	ŭ	ъ (Bulgarian)
k	к	v	в
kh	х	y	ы
ks	ѯ, кс	z	з
l	л	zh	ж
m	м	ъ (brief ŭh)	ъ
n	н	ь (brief ĭ)	ь

1. The original Cyrillic alphabet kept or transformed all of the Greek letters, including the obsolete digamma (F -> s) and koppa (ϙ -> ч), necessary for the letter-number system (here 6 and 90). Besides creating some new letters and combinations, it also directly or indirectly took two Hebrew letters (צ -> ц), (ש -> ш).

TECHNICAL ABBREVIATIONS IN THE FOOTNOTES

[ ]	contains the numbered paragraphs of this discourse
' '	the text within the quotations
1st	first person
2nd	second person
3rd	third person
abs.	the absolute construction (with dative in Old Slavic)
acc.	the accusative case
act.	active voice
adv.	adverb
affrm.	affirmative
alt.	alternative
aor.	aorist (simple past)
dt.	dative case
Gk	the (printed) Greek original
fm.	feminine
fut.	future
gn.	genitive case
gram.	grammatical(-ly)
imprv.	imperative

ind.	indicative case
inf.	infinitive
instr.	instrumental (quasi-ablative) case (in Slavic)
msc.	masculine
MS(S)	manuscript(s)
nt.	neuter
nm.	nominative case
orig.	original
pl.	plural
prp.	prepositional case (Slavic)
prs.	present tense
prtçpl.	participle
pssv.	passive voice
pst.	past tense
sg.	singular
subj.	subjunctive
transl.	translation
v	the *verso* side of a book or codex page, numbered on one side only
var.	variant

. . . Father Nil, who was at the Sora Hermitage in Beloozero, courageously struggled physically and mentally against the devil in our years of the last generation. That he was a virtuous man is intelligible from . . . his divinely-inspired and soul-profiting writings. And having raised them out of the vineyard of his heart, he departed to his loving Christ, leaving for us, as a specific deposit or loan, his divinely inspired and soul-profiting writings, not hiding Christ's talent, which were of sweat and toils.

— Nil Polev —

PART I
TOWARD A STUDY OF NIL SORSKY

I
THE LITTLE WE KNOW

Omega as Alpha

> I beg you, cast my body in the desert, so that beasts and birds consume it, since it has sinned greatly before God and is not worth a burial. If you do not do this, then, digging a pit in the place where we live, bury me in total dishonor.[1]

Thus implores Nil in his *Testament,* and thereby invites us to start this brief, *ersatz* biographical sketch of him with his death. For his manifest opposition to having his relics serve as a miracle cult likely slowed its development, with the result that his *de facto* local canonization occurred well after any eyewitnesses could supply details of his life.[2] We thus hardly know more about him than his extant writings allow us, and what little turns up is mostly literary or theological, with a sprinkling of a few unconnected autobiographical facts. Paradoxically, Old Russia's greatest writing spiritual figure is almost a hagiographic cipher. We do not even know his original first name.[3]

---

1. See below, *Testament* 2.
2. Romanenko places these events in the 17th c.: NSTRM, 188–194.
3. To my knowledge, the claim found in SNS I (p 10), that Nikolai was Nil's baptismal name lacks a reliable source.

The Shadows of the Kremlin

> Can any good come to us from Moscow? Do we not already obtain from there burdens, heavy tributes, oppression, stewards, informers, and bailiffs?[4]

The hagiographer Epifanii the Wise weaved words well, as he placed this celebrated if fictive rhetorical question and provincial gripe into the mouth of a Finnic shaman a few decades before Nil's birth year, 1433/34. Epifanii also clouded a most important fact about our subject's home town. For sure Moscow's commoners also faced their share of 'burdens . . . oppression, stewards, informers, and bailiffs'. But they enjoyed the advantages of an ecclesiastical and political capital, which skimmed off for itself a generous share of Russia's 'heavy tributes', officially destined for the Qipchak Khanate (Golden Horde).

Moscow at that time was a stone-walled kremlin, which dated from 1367 and covered almost its present area. A patchwork of palace and boyar estates and stables, cloisters, apiaries and other productive enterprises, and plebeian faubourgs containing modest artisans' homesteads with vegetable gardens and orchards surrounded this rather large citadel. Within the ramparts stood the Grand Prince's and the Metropolitan's palaces and the homes of the boyar and mercantile elites—all of wood—along with at least eight masonry construction churches, two of them monastic. None of these edifices approached in any dimensions a respectable Western cathedral. A few other masonry churches lay outside the walls, but there too wood predominated. A network of roads, waterways, and portages provided Moscow with links in all directions: to the fur-rich Russian North; to the cattle- and horse-raising steppe to the southeast; to the ancient Rus 'mother-city' Kiev and further to the original Byzantine and Balkan founts of Rus Orthodoxy to the southeast; to Lithuania and its half of Old Rus to the west; and to the flourishing Russian republics of Novgorod and Pskov and then the Baltic lands beyond to the northwest. Samples of

---

4. *Zhitie Sv. Stefana Permskogo*, 40/*Slovo o zhitii . . . Stefana*, 180.

virtually all regionally produced goods or ideas eventually reached this city of destiny on the River Moskva.

A literal reading of Nil's tropological '. . . I am an ignoramus and a rustic'[5] prompted his first monographer, A.S. Arkhangel'skii, to hypothesize peasant family origins.[6] Other scholars assumed that Nil's hearsay Moscow origin and Maiko/Maikov family name meant that he sprang from the 'well-born'.[7] In my opinion, a middling pedigree of some type, service gentry, mercantile, even clerical, seems likely, as it allows for the education and career of his brother Andrei Fëdorovich. In any case, their parents or guardians provided a literate education for the boys, Andrei, moving up the scribal ranks to finish as a state secretary (*diak*) and diplomat.[8] The Sora 'tale' from the 1660s claims that Nil was at first a judicial clerk,[9] so maybe he did follow his brother into the world of Moscow's chancery scribes before the momentous decision renounce the secular kingdom for that of the Divine Writings.

The records allow us to present the great events that someone born in Moscow around 1433/34, or who moved there soon thereafter, would have experienced, if only indirectly. A certain degree of disorder as well as order prevailed all over Rus. Moscow's throne was in dispute until 1452. So was that of the Church until

---

5. *poselianinb*, literally, *villager*; see below, *To Gurii* 16; also Fedotov, *Russian Religious Mind* 2: 265, and others, but rightly criticized by von Lilienfeld, NSSS, 71, note 79; this trope is in Nikon, *Taktikon*, Fwd. 8, more precisely, within the source of Nil's Confession of Faith: see below, *Predanie* 2.

6. Arkhangel'skii, *Nil Sorskii i Vassian Patrikeev*, 3.

7. The oft-used term 'noble', as in a good deal of scholarship, clouds this issue, since Russia had no legal 'nobility' until Peter the Great, but rather the vague status of 'princes', 'boyars', and various 'servicemen', and the descriptive 'well-born'.

8. See below, under II, 'The Congenital Connection.'

9. *sudiiam* (dt. pl.) *knigъchiiu* (dt. sg.) *chinomъ* (instr. sg.) *emu* (dt. sg.) *byvshu* (dt. sg., as dative absolute)—literally, *his having been by rank/profession a bookman/scribe for the judges* (most of whom would have been illiterate then): Prokhorov, 'Povest' o Nilo-Sorskom skite', 161; PNSIK 388, 395; The author Ivan Pleshkov (see below, III. 'Making It') or his source seems to have made a singular out of the Old Slavic rendition of the LXX Dt 1:15 *knigchia*=γραμματοεισαγωγεῖς (nm./acc. pl.) *sudiiam*=τοῖς κριταῖς (dt. pl.) of Dt 1:15, as in KB 3/8: 384, rather than combined the *knigchia* and *sudii* of Dt 1:15 and Jsh 8:3: cf. Prokhorov, PNSIK, 10.

1448. The Greek Photius (or Fotii, r. 1410–1433) was the last metropolitan to preside uncontested over the Orthodox of Moscow-dominated eastern Rus (part of what we call Russia), Polish-Lithuanian western Rus (future Belarus and Ukraine), and Great Novgorod (northwest Russia), which enjoyed a precarious independence between the two. Also in disarray was the longstanding regional suzerain, the Qipchak Khanate, now split among rival successor states, with some of these Tatars having recently moved north from the steppe into the forested borderlands.

Our young Nil would observe in succession the capture of Grand Prince Vasilii II (r. 1425–62 with interruptions) by a Tatar band outside of Suzdal in 1445, his extorting a large ransom from his Russian subjects, and their subsequent dethroning of him in favor of his cousin Dmitrii Shemiaka. As Vasilii had earlier blinded Dmitrii's rebellious elder brother, now Dmitrii in turn deprived the deposed ruler of his sight. But the tide of elite Russian opinion soon turned against the usurper, and by 1447 Vasilii II was back on his throne. Soon he was able to stabilize relations with his former Tatar captors by granting them a buffer vassal khanate in the eastern part of his domains, another sign of Moscow's rising power. Finally, in 1456, he imposed a treaty on Great Novgorod, whereby the latter promised to subordinate its foreign policy to Moscow.

By now, Nil was twenty-two or twenty-three years old and may have heard how a decade earlier the hegumen of the elite Troitsa-Sergiev (Trinity-Saint Sergius) Monastery had sided with Shemiaka, while the hegumen of the rising Kirillov-Belozerskii cloister lifted Vasilii's oath of submission to the former. Early in 1462, if Nil was still a layman, he would have noticed the high stakes of political intrigue, when the retainers of one of the moribund Vasilii II's disgraced cousins tried to free their prince from prison and, during Lent of all time, suffered spectacular tortures, dragging 'by horses through every town and market place' before their beheading.[10] Later that year, the reputedly very intelligent, twenty-two year old Ivan III (r. 1462–1505) ascended the throne and set the

---

10. Alef, *The Origins of Muscovite Autocracy*, 15–16.

realm on a determined course of eastern Rus unification, westward expansion, technological imports from Europe, and the rebuilding of the Moscow kremlin as would befit a regional great power under a mighty monarch, cut out to be the first of Russia's three 'Greats'.

Ecclesiastical affairs, if less violent, provided their own drama. In 1441, Nil would have been only about eight when the last Greek metropolitan of all Rus, Isidor (r. 1436–1441), returned from Italy to Moscow as a cardinal and papal legate. Two years earlier, in Florence, he and the accompanying Russians, as well as the Greeks there, had agreed under pressure to Church Union with Rome. The Byzantines, however, not to say the other Eastern patriarchates, never formally ratified or acknowledged this rapprochement, as huge opposition prevailed among the Orthodox masses, monks, and a few bishops. The Russians themselves soon pulled back from this decision by what they derisively termed the 'Eighth Council', where 'Greek, Church Latin, and Philosophy' (i.e., Western Scholasticism) were spoken.[11] Placating the Russian faithful, but avoiding a diplomatic scrape, Vasilii II shortly expelled Isidor and later promoted the local candidate for metropolitan, Iona of Riazan (r. 1448–1461).[12]

Nil would have been about twenty when the news reached Moscow that Constantinople had fallen to the Ottoman Turks, an event often interpreted in Russia as divine retribution for the recently attempted Church Union. While Moscow welcomed the Greek patriarchate's return to strict Orthodoxy under the conquering Sultan Mehmet, and Russians continued to regard a pious and learned Greek as a source of spiritual wisdom, they would not countenance a return to their former hierarchical subordination.

---

11. *grecheskii, friazskii* (literally, *Frankish*, which might also mean *Italian*), *filosofskii*: PSRL 8: 102.

12. This act led to Moscow's jurisdictional separation from Kiev and Orthodox Western Rus, which lasted, depending upon how and what one counts, for two-to-five centuries, and has resurfaced since the break-up of the Soviet Union in 1991 among some Orthodox of Ukraine, not to say the revived Uniat, that is, Eastern Rite Catholic Church there. The Orthodox still recognize as valid Ecumenical Councils only the first seven.

Henceforth their church would be autocephalous. Religious-patriotic notions such as 'New Israel', 'New Jerusalem', 'New Constantinople', and 'Third Rome' were logical next steps in Russia's transformed, if not yet articulated, self-image. But our future Nil would reside outside of this process.

The Northern Beacon

> And of Saint Kirill, why should I write and speak out? His traditions and teachings, now kept in his cloister, which shines like the light of a candelabrum in the present times, are a witness . . . .[13]

So wrote Iosif Volotsky, maybe in the early 1500s, of what he had seen first-hand twenty-odd years earlier, and he ought to have known what he was talking about. But even assuming, as we have no right to do, that he was not consciously skewing events to promote his pedagogic and political purposes, his sense of history was the victim of hagiography hiding how much Kirillov's celebrated coenobitic rigor developed after the death of the founder. Nil's Kirillov of the 1470s may have shone 'like . . . a candelabrum', but due to later innovations as much as to 'the traditions of Saint Kirill' (d. 1427).

What is our story here? Thanks to the recent, meticulous research of Robert Romanchuk, we have a reasonably good picture of Kirill's cloister, starting as a smallish hermitage on a lake about five hundred kilometers north of Moscow in 1397, but, after the death of his second disciple-successor Khristofor (r. 1428–1434), developing into a property-holding coenobium with masonry structures.[14] If, as one of Kirill's encyclopedic miscellanies shows, he arrived in Beloozero equipped with the authoritative canonical, penitential, ceremonial, calendrical, and doctrinal texts to serve, if needed, as an episcopal vicar and prince's advisor in this frontier

---

13. MRIV 10.13:229.
14. Romanchuk, *Byzantine Hermeneutics*, 94–104, 128–136.

region,[15] the manuscript evidence shows him chiefly as the personal, ascetic-hesychastic *abba* to maybe fifteen monks. Externally guided by the *Scete Typikon,* which hearkened back to a disciple of the latest, highly influential master of stillness, Gregory the Sinaite (c. 1263–1346),[16] Kirill and his literate acolytes apparently immersed themselves in the asceticism of the Desert Fathers and the classics of hesychasm.[17]

This orientation changed in Nil's boyhood under Khristofor's successor, Trifon (r. 1435–1448)[18], the very hegumen who lifted Vasilii II's oath to Shemiaka. Not only did Trifon introduce the coenobitic rule and acquire property for the monastery. He also mobilized some of the intellectual resources of the better established, coenobitic Spaso-Kamennyi (Savior-of-the-Rock, on Lake Kubenskii, north of Vologda) and Troitsa-Sergiev monasteries to establish a more sophisticated grammar or reading curriculum. Such training went beyond the ascetic and ethical concerns of the original Christian monastics and grounded the more mentally agile adepts in contemplating the real world, as then knowable, with categories from John of Damascus's watered down Aristotelianism.[19] For reasons we can only surmise, the Kirillov elders, including Trifon's learned Troitsa recruits, deposed and replaced him with another Spaso-Kamenny trainee, Kassian (r. 1448–1464/5, 1465/6–1470), under whom Romanchuk sees greater balance between what he calls the traditional 'desert' pedagogy and (for

---

15. Prokhorov, *Entsiklopediia.*
16. E.V. Beliakova, 'Russkaia rukopisnaia traditsiia Skitskogo ustava'; 'Skitskii ustav i ego znachenie v istorii russkogo monashestva'; 'Ustav pustyna Nila Sorskogo'; and below, Appendix I.
17. At least that is what the surviving MSS would indicate: Prokhorov, 'Keleinaia isikhatskaia literatura . . . v Kirillo-Belozerskogo;' Keleinaia isikhatskaia literatura . . . v . . . Troitse-Sergievoi'; 'Knigi Kirilla Belozerskogo. Egorova argues that the Slavic 'ascetic miscellany', which figured so heavily in cell life, originated in the mid 1300s under these same influences: 'Russkie asketicheskie sborniki', 182–183. (The earliest extant such Greek miscellany is from the tenth century.)
18. Corrected from 1435–1447 of MRIV (2000), 94.
19. Romanchuk, *Byzantine Hermeneutics,* 138–140, 149–150, 172–173; and below, under III, 'Technical terms', note 132 and text thereto.

Russia) the newer 'academic'. It was Kassian who presided over the great Serbian immigrant Pakhomii Logofet's ('the Logothete') composing the Life of Kirill, which paints the founder essentially as a hesychast, coenobiarch, and healer.[20] Kassian also was possessed of diplomatic talents, and headed missions on Metropolitan Iona's behalf, to Constantinople in 1448 and to Western Rus a decade later.[21] So under the able Kassian, Kirillov 'shone' in more than one way.

Why Nil resolved to become a monk and when he actually did so is not known. If quantity counts for something and if Nil's later treatise contains a clue to his character, then, among the dangerous moral failings for laymen that could have led him to repent, he was more concerned with pride, lust, and gluttony, in that order, than with vengeful wrath or avarice.[22] In other words, he was normal as a lay youth, but neither especially 'macho' nor particularly ambitious for glories of this world. If, however, quantity and quality together are what counts in this regard, then it was the positive attraction of prayer that drew Nil into monasticism.[23] Either way, this surely occurred after he was fifteen and before he was thirty-six, that is, under Kassian.[24] In extant land documents dated 1460–1470 and 1470–1475, a 'Nil' is listed as an elder of the monastery, in the latter case as the junior-most member of the hegumen's inner council of five.[25] One hint of a *terminus ad quem* of the early 1460s is a Kirillov manuscript written under Pakhomii's direction with some orthography, which our leading specialists on Nil's manuscripts provisionally detect his hand.[26] Whenever it was that he joined the brotherhood, he probably

20. *Pachomij Logofet. Werke in Auswahl*, ix–xlix.
21. Toucas-Bouteau, 'Nil Sorskij e il monastero di Kirill di Belozero', 77–78.
22. Note the space devoted to each of the 'eight urges', *Ustav* 5.
23. See *Ustav*, Fwd, 2.
24. The murky period around 1465, when Trifon, now Kirillov's suffragan archbishop of Rostov, tried unsuccessfully to impose his brother Filofei as hegumen, seems an unlikely time for anyone as intelligent as Nil to join this brotherhood.
25. ASEI 2.173:109, 215:139, 290:234; or Lur'e, 'K voprosu ob ideologii Nila Sorskogo, 189.
26. Lënngren SNS 1:15; Prokhorov, PNSIK, 13.

relinquished a promising proto-bureaucratic career in the rising, but potentially dangerous Muscovite court and state for possibly Russia's most successful cloister in integrating communal life, stillness, and the mentalities of the extreme ascetic and the moderately curious, if disciplined, monk-intellectual.

The most impressive such thinker was the hieromonk and master editor-copyist, bibliographer, and pedagogue Efrosin (d. 1511–1514). This quite rare figure abstracted chronologies for framing hagiography and secular history; he de-allegorized the fanciful zoological descriptions from bestiary-influenced Old Testament stories; he de-tropologized geography from a pilgrimage to the Holy Land; and in doing all of this, he produced new, serviceable texts for students. He also collected semi-secular literature, such as perhaps the earliest known *Dracula Tale* and Russia's earliest extant *Alexander the Great* narrative, in ways that no countryman before him or for another century would do. Taking a cue from recent scholarship on the medieval West, Romanchuk sees in Efrosin the peak of 'Byzantine Humanism' in Russia.[27]

Nil's *in situ* education, however, may have commenced under a third graduate of Spaso-Kamenny, Paisii Iaroslavov (d. 1501), considered one of the most learned and able elders of his era. We shall return to Paisii and his source problem a bit later,[28] since our interest now is the substance of Nil's training. This had to commence with obedience and the daily routine of the community Matins and liturgy, the refectory meal, one's assigned labor, chanting the Hours, Vespers, a light supper, Compline, and silent handicraft, reading, psalmody, prostrations, and stillness in one's cell before sleep.[29] Even if Nil had already acquired certain monastic

---

27. Compared to Western philosophical developments, this humanism is 'pre-Scholastic'. On Efrosin, Lur'e, *Ideologicheskaia bor'ba*, 70–72; 'Literaturnaia i kul'turno-prosvetitel'naia deiatel'nost' Efrosina'; Kagan, et al., 'Opisanie sbornikov XV v. knigopistsa Efrosina'; Romanchuk, *Byzantine Hermeneutics*, 197, 202–203.

28. See below, II. 'The Maybe Mentor'.

29. Cf. MRIV, the provisions of *Extended Rule* 1–9, which, while omitting the Hours and individual cell rule prostrations and psalmody, ought to give a picture of life in a cloister consciously modeled on the Kirillov of Pakhomii's early 1460's *Life of Kirill*, plus what Iosif himself experienced there in the late 1470s.

tastes while a layman, he surely would have developed his interactive love of the liturgical hymnographers during the long daily services, his desire for eloquent hagiography at the daily refectory readings, his penchant for patristic metaphrasis in the course of spiritual conversations, and his longing to replicate the mystical feats of the hesychastic masters, as he engaged in his evening and nocturnal devotions.

As we already noted, Nil eventually became involved in the monastery's administration, specifically in the legal titles of its land holdings.[30] Perhaps, given his presumed scribal background, this is no surprise: he probably knew the ins and outs of official paper work as well as anyone in the cloister. Nil's writings, as we shall see, also exhibit some of the marks of Kirillov's 'academic' environment, and since its leading epistemological source, John of Damascus, was also revered for his liturgical hymns and his defense of Orthodoxy,[31] Nil would have had no pious grounds to reject the available 'academic' analytical tools, which included systematic thinking, a conscious grasp of literary-rhetorical devices, and a sense of the scientific as then understood. Nil's special *métier* at Kirillov may have been book-copying, but we lack any authenticated codices or even pages by his distinct hand from this period.[32] It is likely that he also acquired some experience with saints lives, which a certain Kiprian, a contemporary fellow Kirillovian, would also compile, if not redact in Nil's later manner.[33]

At any rate, Nil's two chief interests turned out to be hagiography and prayer, the future focus of his literary talents. Elena Romanenko has recently suggested that his selection of Nil as his monastic name reflected an early commitment to hesychasm, as Neilos the Sinaite (d. c. 430) was then credited with the *Chapters in Prayer* by the earliest of the theoreticians of stillness, Evagrius

---

30. See above, note 25.
31. See below under III, 'Centrality of Sources'.
32. On Nil's orthography, Prokhorov, 'Avtografy', 44 (the letters ѣ, ц, щ), and Kloss, 'Nil Sorskii i Nil Polev', 159 (the letter ж).
33. Romanchuk, *Byzantine Hermeneutics*, 202, 242–243, which offers manuscript-based corrective to Romanenko's assertion that such collections were produced in Kirillov during 1458-1470: NSTRM, 8; also SNS 1:15.

of Pontus (346-397).³⁴ In one of Nil's rare, later, autobiographical moments, he claimed that while in the cloister, he became an expert in his own right in the 'Divine Writings' and, accordingly, avoided 'worldly entanglements'.³⁵

We can be reasonably certain that Nil advanced at Kirillov from discipleship and acquired at least one like-minded acolyte, Innokentii Okhliabinin.³⁶ Then at some point Nil, or maybe both of them, became restless. He/they could have left to found his/their own community—what each of them eventually did. Before that, however, in the 1470s or possibly the 1480s,³⁷ he/they set out from Kirillov for Mount Athos on a quest for Orthodoxy's spiritual holy grail.³⁸

The Holy Mount

A stone / hurled by one of the gods³⁹ / fell into the sea / and was transformed / into the Church of God. / The wilderness / scented by incense, / the desert / in blossom; / here one cannot tell apart earth from heaven. / The garden / planted / for the Mother of God. / The

---

34. Cf. Romaneko, NSTRM, 7-8, which does not mention the generally accepted attribution of 'Neilos the Sinaite's' *Chapter on Prayer* to Evagrius: see below under III, 'Centrality of Sources.'

35. *To German* 4.

36. We have no sound evidence that Innokentii traveled with Nil, just part of a suspect invented tradition that first appears in known, extant writing as hearsay in 1784: ChOIDR 1887.4. 'Materialy istoriko-literaturnye', 123–124; Prokhorov, PNSIK, 399. Yet it makes sense that Nil did not travel alone; further on Innokentii, see below, text to note 46 and II. 'The Compatible Companion'.

37. Prokhorov, PNSIK, 3–24: note here from Prokhorov, Sergei Bolshakov's unsubstantiated 1465–78, Irina Dergacheva's guess of their accompanying Mitrofan Byvaltsov (MRIV 10.37) with the surmised nine years of 1470–1479, and von Lilienfeld proposing between 1455 and 1475: 'Der athonitische Hesychasmus des 14. und 15. Jahrhunderts', 442: Nobody knows!

38. On the prestige of Mt. Athos as the model for Russian monastic practices, MRIV 10.31.

39. Poseidon/Neptune, according to legend.

mountain / crowded with fugitives; / mystified / by
the ultimate enigma / they find the answer / here.⁴⁰

Thus divined the poet, professor, and Serbian Orthodox priest
who personally microfilmed many medieval Slavic manuscripts
for his brainchild and foundation, the Ohio State University's
remarkable Hilandar Research Library. And as he so toiled, he
reflected upon those pre-Edisonian copyists, 'at the light of a candle
. . . gradually losing their sight' to 'enable others to see'.⁴¹

For us, though, pious and romantic musings about the venerable
monastic republic on the roughly 20-x-5-mile Euboeian peninsula
known by its highest peak Mount Athos (2039 m) will not solve
the mystery of what Nil (and perhaps Innokentii) actually did
there. In this sphere we know even less than we do about Nil's
origins, his Kirillov experiences, and later life. When did he/they
go? What route(s) did he/they take? Where else did he/they travel
besides the environs of Constantinople, as he reported?⁴² Who
financed the journey? Did he/they undertake any special mission
for Moscow's church or state authorities? Where did he/they stay
at Athos? Did he/they interact with Greeks as well as Slavs—or,
should one ask, with Slavs as well as Greeks? What did Nil learn
that he did not already know or could not imbibe at home?

We can only try to imagine some answers. This pilgrimage
would have occurred between the early 1470s and the late 1480s,
coinciding with the second and last upsurge in Russian copying
of 'hesychastic cell literature'.⁴³ Nil/They may have taken an over-
land route through Kiev and modern Romania, and Bulgaria past
Constantinople. More likely, the voyage included some sea travel,
because that is the easiest way from Constantinople to the base of
Mount Athos off the Aegean Sea, and because Nil used some

---

40. Fr. Mateja Matejić, bi-lingual author, *Holy Mount/Sveta Gora*, in *Hilandar Manuscript/Hilandarsko rukopis*. Belgrade: Raška škola (1998), 6–7.
41. *Scribes of Hilandar/Pisari Hilandarskih Rukopisa*, in Ibid., 42–43.
42. See below, *Ustav* 11.12
43. Prokhorov, 'Keleinaia isikhastskaia literatura . . . v biblioteke Kirillo-Belozerskogo monastyria s XIV po XVII v.'; 'Keleinaia isikhastskaia literatura . . . v biblioteke Troitse-Sergievoi lavry s XIV po XVII v.'

imagery of waves and maritime storms in his writings.[44] Moscow's generally good relations at the time with the Crimean Khanate also would have facilitated the voyage down the Don River to the Sea of Azov, the Black Sea, and thence to Constantinople. The Ottomans would have posed little problem, as they had ruled over the region since the early 1400s and generally left the monks to their own devices in return for the taxes and periodic extraordinary contributions imposed upon non-Muslims.[45] Perhaps inspired by Nil's comments on more temperate climes,[46] a later tradition from the Sora hermitage has him visiting Palestine too[47] —a suspect jaunt which would have almost doubled the distance he is known to have covered.

Athos in the 1470s–1480s had several thousand monks and nineteen or twenty major cloisters in various states of repair, disrepair, and inhabitation, and headed by the founder Athanasius's Laura. Among the other leading monasteries were a second Greek establishment, Vatopedi, and then the Serbian Hilandar, the 'Rus Pantaleimon', and the Bulgarian Zograf.[48] All of these served at various times as loci of the efforts of Greek-reading Slavs to amplify and modernize the original literary corpus of *Slavia Orthodoxa*. Scattered among the large abbeys were various dependent kellia and scetes of one or several brothers, at least some of whom, according to Nil's testimony, practiced stillness.[49] Hilandar's Karyes Kellion had possessed an elite scriptorium, which played a central

44. *Ustav* 1.19, 2.26, 5.6.68, 6.4, 11.10, of which, however, only the first has not been identified as taken from a patristic source.
45. Kastorskii, *Sostoianie pravoslavnogo vostochnogo monashestva so vremeni zavoevaniia turkami*, 5, 41; Zachariadu, "'A safe and holy mountain;'" Speak, *Mount Athos*, 113–120.
46. *Ustav* 5.1.16.
47. NSTRM, 10; Prokhorov, PNSIK, 399; for a purported Rus pilgrimage itinerary escalating in the fourteenth century literary imagination from Athos to Mt. Sinai, see Goldfrank, 'Vojšelk', 54.
48. Diakon Zosima, 'Kniga glagolaema *Ksenos*', 126; from various data, Kastorskii gives 2200–6000 ascetics for the sixteenth century: *Sostoianie*, 146.
49. See below, *Ustav* 11.12; Kastoskii, *Sostoianie*, 141–142; the latter's descriptions of *kalivy* (houses with 1–3 monks and postulants) and scetes correspond respectively to what Nil called *kelia* and to what his foundation became, with a small church.

role in the diffusion of hesychastic texts a century earlier. As in Russia, the major monasteries were generally supposed to be coenobitic, with a central role for the council of leading elders, but paths actually diverged. State support in this era facilitated the conversion of Russian cloisters from the 'separate-life',[50] where monks fully supported themselves and rarely dined together, to the communal type. Harder times for Christians under the Ottomans produced at Athos an individualistic move in the opposite direction.

The extant manuscripts give us scant information on the intellectual life of the resident Slavs around when Nil sojourned there, or of what he would have gained from their libraries. The three dozen or so surviving Balkan Slavic codices from the 1450s–1490s are almost exclusively liturgical, scriptural, and hagiographic. The only purely monastic text from the period is an *Alphabetic Patericon*.[51] If the Slavic Athonites were recopying their century-old codices of the hesychastic masters, these books are outside the Balkans or lost—except for one copy of Climacus from about 1500.[52] The few extant writings that would qualify as 'academic', such as the *Chronicle* of Gregory Harmartolus or the *Physiologus* (a Christian bestiary), had been copied earlier and were no more sophisticated than what Efrosin glossed and reworked in Kirillov.[53] An observant Slav at Athos in the 1470s might have noted an interest in canons of Andrew of Crete,[54] and the *Life of John of Damascus*,[55] both of which Nil later shared. A Slavic visitor could also have been introduced to the creativity of Dimitur Kantakuzeni (b. 1435), who composed prayers modeled on those attributed to

---

50. *Osobozhitie*, not necessarily the full *idiorrhythma*, which may be thoroughly individualistic; Sinitsyna, 'Tipy monastyri', 116–129, notes the fluidity of these terms.

51. Panteleimon (Pan.) No. 15: CMMHRL 2: 816, dated 1485.

52. A systematic manuscript search outside of the Balkans might invalidate the thrust of this paragraph.

53. Panteleimon (Pan.) No. 17, 22: CMMHRL 2: 818, 821, dated 1381, 1410s.

54. Great Lavra (GLZ) No 7: CMMHRL 2: 111, dated 1470s.

55. Hilandar (HM SMS) No. 465: CMMHRL 1: 555, dated 1450s.

Ephrem (Ephraim) of Syria—a practice not foreign to Nil's future activities.[56] Nil could not have missed the veneration of Sava (1169–1237), the renovator of Hilandar and the founder of the autocephalous Serbian Church, and perhaps it is no accident that Nil's disciple or devotee, Gurii Tushin, copied down Russia's earliest known copy of Sava's Life.[57] Nil also might have run into some rather questionable prophesying, such as predictions for the years 1452–1459 embedded with a number table in a Book of Hours.[58] Everything here is hypothetical.

The greatest puzzle regarding Nil's stay at Athos remains his interaction with his Greek counterparts. If the extant codices with Symeon/Pseudo-Symeon the New Theologian are any guide, then the half dozen which stem from Athos before 1500, despite the vicissitudes of Ottoman domination, would indicate some serious interest in stillness, but how intensive or widespread is anybody's guess.[59] We also lack an indication that a first-rate Greek or Slavic practitioner was present for Nil to encounter. He certainly met no one capable of being the writing teacher that he turned out to be, only, maybe, some seasoned adepts. As he recounted:[60]

> . . . just as we were eye-witnesses at the Holy Mountain of Athos. . . . If a spiritual elder is found anywhere having a disciple or two, and, when need be, three, and if any nearby are engaged in stillness, by coming at the proper time, they are enlightened by spiritual conversations.

Perhaps some future scholar will make the necessary investigation of all of the texts associated with Nil's works to ascertain if and where one can determine that Nil bypassed the Slavic versions available in Russia and relied on those found only in the Balkans

---

56. Novi Sad (NS) No. 158: CMMHRL 2:801; *Ustav* 5.8.96, 7.22, 29.
57. See below under II, 'The Best of the Bookman'.
58. Hilandar (HM SMS) No. 357: CMMHRL 1: 484, dated 1450s.
59. Krivochéine, 'Introduction', 67–112.
60. *Ustav* 11.12.

or on the original Greek—and for the latter, where these might have been located. For now, however, we must be content with the conclusion that while at Athos Nil either learned or finished learning how to read Greek, even if he might have ignored the diacritical marks.[61] He undoubtedly mastered stillness as it was then practiced there and does not seem to have worried about its fourteenth-century detractors or the hot debate instigated by Barlaam of Calabria.[62] Nil certainly did not become a proponent of Gregory Palamas's more philosophic and natural-scientific defense of hesyschasm or doctrine of divine light.[63] Further than this into such matters we dare not go, except to propose that Nil may have already been thinking about his future collection of monastic saints lives, and even checking his Slavic texts against the available Greek originals.[64] Some language study, some hagiographic *Quellenforschung*, and an advanced practicum in Athonite stillness is as good a guess as any to why Nil went, but it could be 'none of the above'.

The Quiet Kelliot

> Then, with the departure for my pilgrimage, upon returning to the monastery, I made a cell outside near the monastery and so lived in keeping with my power.[65]

This next autobiographic tidbit by Nil recounts his attempt to emulate the Athonites who sought the best of both the anchoritic

---

61. See Gurii Tushin's copy of the Slavic-influenced Greek signature of 'Sinful and Witless Nil' in Prokhorov, *Avtografy*, 39/PNSIK 47, and below, *Sobornik Postscr.*: the signature employs one or two ligatures.

62. Von Lilienfeld, 'Der athonitische Hesychasmus des 14. und 15. Jahrhunderts', 442, 447–448.

63. This is clear not only from Nil's writings, but also from his ignorance or rejection of Palamas's anachronistically didactic redaction of the Life of Peter of Athos in favor of the original version. Cf. Lake, *Early Days of Monasticism on Mount Athos*, 17–39; Gregory Palamas, *Oratio in . . . Petri*, PG 150:996A–1040C; SNS 1:227–268.

64. See below, under I, 'Four and Twenty Saints Lives'.

65. *To German* 4.

and cœnobitic. The late 1470s–early 1480s, after Nil's presumed return from Athos, moreover, would have been the logical time and place for him to acquire more disciples, followers, and lay devotees. If, for example, Gurii Tushin (1452/5–1526), who took the tonsure in 1478/1479, was indeed such an acolyte before his brief tenure as Kirillov's hegumen in 1484, we ought to place Nil's kelliotic period at least a few years before that.

At this point Nil could have remained nearby Kirillov as the resident master-teacher of hesychasm, and thereby, with the more worldly Efrosin, co-directed the equivalent of a two-chair collegium. For all we know, Nil tried this, for he later wrote:[66]

> . . . those who lived in monasteries . . . and . . . were in cities, like Symeon the New Theologian, and his elder Symeon the Studite in the middle of the Imperial City, in the great cloister of Stoudion—in such a populous city—shone like heavenly lights with spiritual gifts; and similarly were Nicetas Stethatos and many others.

What worked in Constantinople five centuries earlier, however, proved not to Nil's liking—maybe due to his character, maybe due to the politics of Kirillov's administrative or intellectual leadership, or maybe due to the Russian customs of day and the annoying penetration of secular habits into the great cloisters.[67] Certainly the circumstances of 1483–1484, when Kirillov's 'fifteen major elders', staged a demonstrative departure until hegumen Serapion resigned,[68] even if Nil might have sympathized with their discomfort, would have appeared incompatible with his saintly models.

> And Isaac says to those who wish truly to practice stillness and purify the intellect in prayer: withdraw far from the visions of the world, and sever conversations, and do not wish habitually to host friends in your cell,

---

66. *Ustav*, Fwd. 8.
67. See below, *Ustav* 5.8.95, 10.5, 11.17.
68. MRIV, 95.

not even in good form, except for some, who are like-minded, harmonious, and fellow-initiates.⁶⁹

In other words, the genuine hesychast must reside in a place dedicated to stillness and only to stillness. Nil's academy would have only one chair *in situ*—his. Only time and events would tell how quiet it would be.

A Busy 'Abode of Stillness'[70]

> Now I have relocated far from the monastery, because, with the grace of God, I found a place pleasing to my knowledge, since it is little traveled by children of the world, as you yourself have seen

With these words, and, by present standards, this run-on sentence, Nil finished explaining his move to a distraught devotee.[71] It turns out that about twelve miles of dense and mossy spruce forest, with various berries but no other edible plants,[72] constituted 'far from the monastery' for Nil, as he settled north of Kirillov near the little Sora River and Lake by the name. It was also about twelve miles to the west of Ferapontov, the other prestigious cloister of the defunct Beloozero principality. Not too distant from either for useful contacts, Nil was less likely to attract unwelcome visitors by the Sora than in the vicinity of Kirillov.

Nil's 'many reverent brothers come to me wishing to dwell with us', is tropological, adapted from the encyclopedic Nikon of the Black Mountain. We do not know how Nil gathered resident disciples 'of his ethos' and ready to live strictly by 'the traditions of the Holy Fathers . . . according to the Divine Writings',[73] as he

---

69. *Ustav* 10.11: partially adapted from Isaac the Syrian.
70. Cf. below, *Ustav* 11.14.
71. *To German*, 4; see below under II: 'The Loose Cannon'; Nikol'skii dates the founding of the scete 1486: *Kirillo-Belozerskii monastyr'* 2: 416.
72. Prokhorov, *'Povest' o Nilo-Sorskom skite'*, 16.
73. See below, *Predanie* 3, 4, 6.

put it. But he seems to have established something like Kirill's original hermitage, with about a dozen residents clearly subordinate to one superior, while they followed the *Scete Typikon*. Kirill's version of it, faithful to the original, provided for illiterate monks, who defaulted to the Jesus Prayer when they did not know the required psalms of the standard cell rule.[74] Nil, however, omitted that provision,[75] as if, in the manner ascribed to the ancient Athenian Academy, he had inscribed outside 'our scete', as he termed it,[76] 'The Unlettered Shall Not Enter'.[77] On the economic side, he forbade ethical transgressions, such as exploitation of others labor, acceptance of ill-gotten gains as charity, or even bargaining over prices. Adornments were out of the question, and only seasoned elders were to speak to visitors.[78]

The mid-seventeenth century 'Tale of the Arrival of Nil Sorskii' and the later descriptions and sketches of the hermitage indicate, perhaps *de rigueur*, that Nil himself dug the well, made the pond for watering the garden, and constructed a mill for his hermitage. The cells were small log cabins, sitting apart from each other, with trees still standing for full privacy, and housing one monk only.[79] Well away, perhaps two hundred fifty yards, from the housing complex, Nil personally made a hill of dirt over a swamp and there raised a little wooden church dedicated to the Presentation

---

74. Prokhorov, *Entsiklopediia*, 162. Accordingly, the entire Psalter was equivalent to 6000 recitations of 'Jesus Christ, Son of God, have mercy upon me' or '. . . have mercy upon me, the sinner'; cf. MR IV 13.2.1, where Iosif has his monks who are ignorant of Psalm 144/145 recite the Jesus Prayer.

75. See below, *Scete Typikon* 33, note 61; also Prokhorov, 'Avtografy', 50, an PNSIK, 28, and Elena Shevchenko's forthcoming 'Neizvestnyi avtograf Nila Sorskogo', concerning another copy in Nil's hand of this recension of the *Scete Typikon* (personal communication in the Manuscript Division of the Russian National Library, 20 July, 2006).

76. *Predanie* 41.

77. Plato allegedly had stipulated that one unschooled in geometry (ἀγεωμέτρητος) could not study philosophy—at least with him.

78. *Predanie* 29, 31–34.

79. *Povest' o Nilo-Sorskom skite*, 398–399: see the frontispiece illustration of the skete.

(Candlemas).⁸⁰ Elena Romanenko claims from an early sixteenth-century manuscript that Nil composed the Vigils service.⁸¹

The extant copy of Nil's *Predanie* by his hand contains a supplement providing for communion via consecrated bread without a priest.⁸² However, by the time of death in 1508 his scete may have already had a regular hieromonk-superior, as definitely would be the case by 1515.⁸³ In the 1670s, the hermitage also had a 'guard', who heated the narthex of one of the churches in winter, checked daily for the superior on the health of the monks, and cared for the ill.⁸⁴ Whether such held under Nil is impossible to ascertain.

Romanenko also argues that Nil was consciously transposing into the forest the description of such 'scetes', found in the ancient monastic Lives, which he redacted and copied.⁸⁵ This point is moot and quite possibly true, but it is clear Nil's established his as a place where he could pray, write, and teach. Curiously, so far as we know, none of his major or writing disciples or followers stayed with him and remained to continue this work at his foundation. Rather, his literary legacy indicates that he kept up his connections with genuine acolytes like Innokentii and with Kirillov, attracted talented elders from elsewhere to establish their own kellia or hermitages in the vicinity, and employed scribes to do some of the copying. Nil's two most important literary colleagues, Gurii Tushin, who remained at Kirillov, and Nil Polev, who moved nearby from Iosifov without severing his ties with the latter, were master-copyists and codex-publishers employing their own scribe-assistants, yet taking credit for the resultant books.⁸⁶ So 'far from the monastery' was no hindrance to solid networking with Russia's most productive cloistered scriptoria.

---

80. Prokhorov, 'Povest' o Nilo-Sorskom skite', 12; NSTRM, 136–137.
81. Romanenko (E. Kolkutina), 'Nil Sorski e il suo "skit"', 113; NSTRM, 152.
82. See below, Appendix II.
83. *Akty Arkheograficheskoi ekspeditsii* 1: 161.
84. *Povest' o Nilo-Sorskom skite*, 397.
85. NSTRM, 133–138.
86. See below, II. 'The Best of the Bookmen' and 'The Man in the Middle'.

Publish Lest They Perish

> But in his mercy God has caused grace to diminish from the saints for a while, so that they may accomplish the provisioning and the care of the brothers with a discourse of ministry, that is, instruction in piety, as Saint Macarius says of those who have attained perfection.[87]

This abstraction and paraphrase from Byzantium's model metaphraser provides a clue to Nil's activities at his scete. The ultimate goal may have been the praxis of *theoria*, that is, well trained mystical contemplation and communication with the divine, but Nil saw himself as part of a chain of instruction originating with God.[88] The bulk of his literary creativity was didactic, his original works serving for hesychastic 'distance learning' as well as on-the-spot pedagogy.

Furthermore, as a comparison with his epistles shows, his *Ustav* could and did serve as a didactic source book. For example, in response to an alleged request for a remedy for the *logismos* ('urge') of blasphemy, Nil cribbed from the corresponding section of the *Ustav* that identifies despondency, via ingratitude, with blasphemy, and from related passages.[89] Thus the recipient or other reader of the epistle would have on hand, besides the advice contained therein, an example of how to use the *Ustav*, or anything like it, to instruct on his own. In this case, the nominal addressee, Gurii Tushin, certainly knew Nil's writings as well as anyone other than Nil himself and hardly needed the epistle for his own instruction, but could gain from its construction for his edification of others.[90] As we shall see in the next part of this book, Nil's writings are

---

87. Nil Sorsky, *Ustav* 2.39, inspired by Pseudo-Macarius via Symeon Metaphrastes.
88. Nil Sorsky, *Predanie* 1; *Ustav*, Fwd. 1, 13–14.
89. *To Gurii* 7–9.
90. Gurii's Sof. 1468: 166v contains the brief 'On the Blasphemous Urge', which most likely is partially streamlined from *To Gurii* 8, or its source, *Ustav* 5.6.78.

replete with explicit and implicit advice and paradigms for the teaching and writing elder.[91]

Didactic purpose and hence intended audience, moreover, can serve as the key for our grasping the essential difference between the formal structures envisioned by Nil's two chief original compositions, his *Predanie* and his *Ustav*, also to be examined further on.[92] The *Predanie* provided for a community of disciplined and supervised lavriotes, who confessed monastic infractions to their superior. Though specific to his scete, the *Predanie* was available, with modifications, for others.[93] The *Ustav*, focusing on the linked struggles against passions and for stillness, was, theoretically, for all monks, and thus could abstractly treat 'two or three' as the royal road between solitude and the coenobium.[94] Nil's contemporaries and literary executors did not see any of these ideal types as the sole route to Orthodoxy's monastic nirvana, and neither should we.

Four and Twenty Saints Lives

> I have written from various manuscripts, striving to find the correct ones. And I found in those manuscripts much uncorrected, and as much as was possible for my meager knowledge, I corrected them. And what was impossible, I left be, so that someone having more knowledge than we correct the uncorrected and fill in the lacunae.[95] . . . And—what is not readily knowable—this, with simplicity of speech, have I placed within knowledge.[96]

Employing Gregory the Sinaite's analogy of a 'sluggish monk' to 'a ship . . . at standstill' in need of 'oars or a galley', Nil advised his

---

91. See below, II. 'Literary Devices'.
92. See below, III. 'Texts and Structures'.
93. See below, under II, 'The Compatible Companion', and Innokentii, *Zavět*.
94. *Ustav* 11.8.
95. *Sobornik, Forew.* 1.
96. *Sobornik, Postscr.* 2.

disciples to 'read the . . . Lives of the Fathers'.[97] But, as this extract from his *Foreword* indicates, he did more than that. Using his linguistic and metaphrastic skills, he created his own three-volume *Sobornik o Boze* (Collection in God) of twenty-four Lives of monastic saints, who lived from the third to the tenth centuries. According to Prokhorov, the watermarks on the paper Nil used indicated that he may have been working on this collection as early as the 1480s.[98] Tamara Lënngren, who has taken it upon herself to publish this work and provide a verbal concordance, treats it as important as the *Predanie* and *Ustav* for understanding Nil's overall outlook.[99] If any precise gaging with respect to such a comparison may be impossible, still the *Sobornik* affords us a unique peek into what Nil most valued and gives us another glimpse at how his mind operated.

True to liturgical principles, Nil structured his *Sobornik* in order by feast days, starting with 1 September—then the beginning of Russia's calendar year—and with one undated saint attached to the last one (Paisius).[100] By using our own chronological, geographical, and analytical criteria, however, we can see that Nil devoted about a third each to the early history of monasticism in Egypt and Palestine, both eremitical and coenobitic, and the rest to Syria and Greece.

Commencing in Egypt with the murky Paul of Thebaid (?228–341), who had fled imperial Roman pagan persecution, Nil moves next to Paul's pre-death acquaintance, the central monastic figure of Anthony the Great (251–356), and then on to a loosely linked cluster of fellow anchorites, Hilarion (291–371/372), Paisius the Great (d. 400), and Arsenius the Great (c. 354–c.450). The person of Patriarch Athanasius the Great of Alexandria (r. 328–373), not the Life, provides the connection from Anthony to Pachomius the Great (290/292–346/348), the founder of coenobiticism and

97. *Ustav* 2.26, metaphrased from Gregory.
98. Prokhorov, PNSIK, 33.
99. SNS 1:11–17; 'Nil Sorskii i ego "Sobornik"'; also NSTRM, 63–98.
100. According to the annual calendar commencing 1 September, Lënngren's 'Part 1', with Lives for 24 May, 12 June, and 5 July (two), as well as Paisius's, would have been Nil's third volume, her 'Part 2' his first, her 'Part 3' his second.

initiator of the black garb, and thence to the ex-coenobite Onouphrius the Hermit (d. 400). Implicitly, Paisius's alleged biographer John Colubus ('the Dwarf', 339–?405) and Onouphrius's —Paphnutius the Recluse, Abbot of Scetis—also figure in Nil's panorama of the foundation figures of desert monasticism.

Nil's parallel presentation of Palestine's pristine asceticism commences with another refugee from persecution, Chariton of Iconium (mid 3rd–mid. 4th c.), at whose Pharan Monastery Euthymius the Great (377/8–473) later settled. After the latter come two celebrated Cappadocians, Theodosius the Coenobiarch (423–529), and Euthymius's disciple Sabbas the Sanctified (439–532), whom Patriarch Sallust of Jerusalem appointed as supervisors, the one over the regional coenobia and the other over the laurae. Nil also included Euthymius's disciple Cyriacus the Recluse (447/9–554/6), Sabbas's disciple Bishop John the Hesychast (454–559), and a free floating anchorite Martinian (d. c. 400). Numerous references in the *Life of Euthymius*, moreover, point to the close ties between Palestine and Egypt.[101]

Palestine links up with Syria and its pillar sages, as Theodosius, en route to Palestine, had visited Symeon Stylite the Elder (390–459). From the top of his column, Symeon appears as well in the *Life of Euthymius*. Symeon's Life, celebrated on 1 September, commences the *Sobornik*. Nil similarly redacted the Life of that Syrian's namesake, Symeon the Stylite and Thaumaturge of the Wondrous Mountain (521/2–592)—the longest piece in the collection. The latter's monastery, we might note, figured in the real life and writings of one of Nil's most important sources, the eleventh-century Nikon of the Black Mountain.[102] Nil also ties Palestinian monasticism to the Levantine and Byzantine defenders of icon-worship in the eighth and ninth century via the Saint Sabbas Laura theologian-hymnographer John of Damascus (c. 675–750). The historic scene now shifts to the

---

101. SNS, 3: 272–273; Cyril/*Kirill*, 21; Cyril Scythop., *Lives* 30. Cyril of Scythopolis also composed the originals of the Lives of Sabas, John the Hesychast, and Cyriacus, but not Nil's version of Theodosius.

102. SNS 3:30, 288; see below under III, 'Centrality of Sources'; also MRIV13.9. This Symeon was also the purported recipient of an Epistle (Slavic version, *Slovo* 55) of Isaac the Syrian, another of Nil's key sources.

great coenobitic cloister of Stoudion in Constantinople and the Lives of Theodore (759–826) and his kinsman and successor abbot Nicola (d. 847–50). In the Greek sphere, Nil has already included two unconnected anchorites: Isaac of Dalmatia (d. 383) and Theodore of Sykeon (d. 613), and for the later period adds a third—Ioannikios the Great (752–846).

Nil finally takes us a bit further westward to his era's and his personal monastic Mecca, Mount Athos. He gives us first the model ninth-century, ex-soldier anchorite Peter, and then its tenth-century pedagogue and coenobiarch, Athanasius. So for Egypt, Palestine, Byzantium, and, specifically, Athos, Nil does not discriminate among the recluse or the non-communal laura, on the one hand, and the coenobium on the other hand. In fact, Athanasius or his acolytes, by calling his communal cloister a laura, symbolize Sorsky's sense of the sanctity of all modes of monasticism.

The style and content of Nil's *Sobornik* still require extensive monographic treatment, though some excellent, if conflicting work has already commenced. Comparisons with the earlier Slavic translations clarify that Nil was essentially a talented editor, making grammatical, syntactical, lexical, and even interpretative alterations for the sake of consistency and his readers' comprehension.[103] Whether he had recourse to Greek originals, no trace of which remain from his era in Russia, is a mystery. The pioneering imperial Russian hagiologist Ivan Pomialovskii, unaware of Nil's hand here, was sure that the redactor of his Slavic version did not check the Greek *Life of Sabbas*, and Nil's lacunae would back this position. The team of T. Helland and Tamara Lënngren, though, are convinced that Nil did so for his *Life of Symeon the Stylite of the Wondrous Mountain*, even if he privileged the available Slavic.[104] This question for sure remains open.

We still, however, can say a few useful things about the portée of these Lives. Virtually all of them combine healing and other

---

103. Romanenko, NSTRM, 69, building upon K.V. Pokrovskii, 'K literaturnoi deiatel'nosti Nila Sorskogo'; Lur'e, *Ideologicheskaia bor'ba*, 325–331; Kloss, 'Nil Sorskii i Nil Polev', 164–166.

104. Lënngren, 'Zhitiinii tekst', also citing Ivan Pomialovskii, *Zhitie sv. Savvy Osviashchennogo*.

miracles (some by relics), the prerequisite for sanctity, with the three essential elements of Nil's specific spirituality: consistent renunciation-poverty, dogged seeking of solitude-stillness, and energetic prayer, especially against demons. Nil's coenobiarchs hardly spurned hesychasm. Where solitude completely takes a rear seat, the Stylite pursuit of the public good or the Studite battle with heresy strides to the forefront.

In fact, a majority of Nil's subjects defended Orthodoxy, a half-dozen of them—such as the lone Isaac of Dalmatia who won over the Emperor Valens's top 'boyars'—at serious risk to their own necks. Characteristically, at the behest of their supreme bishop, the Patriarch of Jerusalem, both the ceonbiarch Theodosius and the lauraite Sabbas interrupt their abbatial superintendency to battle the Monophysiticism of their day. Similarly, Anthony aids Athanasius against Arianism, and the later Stylite heads the successful opposition to Manicheanism and astrology in Antioch. Meanwhile Cyriacus and John the Hesychast fight Nestorianism and also Origenism, which is still kicking around, at least as a straw horse, in the fifth and sixth centuries. Even some obscure heresies, which never make the Church History headlines, appear to be fought, such as the denial of the hypostatic equality of the Holy Spirit, faced by Paisius. In the pro-active sphere, Euthymius, an opponent also of Manicheanism, and the elder Symeon Stylite converted many nearby Arabs.[105]

Nil may have included his unconnected monk-saints for just one lesson or two. The recluse Martinian's Life has a series of fantastic escapes from the lures of lust, before he dies at an unseemly young age for an ascetic of that time.[106] Theodore of Sykeon, first a bordello offspring, next a protector of female virtue, and always an avid advocate of the cult of the martyr Saint George,

---

105. SNS 1: 127–129, 419–420; 2: 30–32, 37, 76, 508; 3: 99–100, 209–210, 255–261, 373, 434–439. Nil retained from the original *Life of Euthymius* the characterization of Nestorians as 'Jewish-reasoning' (*zhidovomudreni*) and of the Monophysite Theodosius as 'precursing the Antichrist'—terms also applied against contemporary Russian dissidents: SNS 3: 281, 282; Cyril Scythop,, *Lives*, 37, 38; Cyril/*Kyrillos*, 26, 27; AfED, 425, 428; and below, I. 'The Church at Large', and II. 'The Unexpected Bedfellow'.

106. SNS 3: 337–365.

upbraids the tyrant-Emperor Phocas to his face for murdering his subjects.[107] The ex-heroic warrior ('Second David'), extreme ascetic, and wonder-worker Ioannikos can levitate, walk over water, and make himself invisible to rescue prisoners under the noses of their guards.[108] Were there any spiritual fortresses that these ascetic athletes for Christ could not storm?

If we take into account the fact that Nil utilized for his original writings the corpus of only two of these monk-saints, John of Damascus and the Theodore the Studite, but neither very much, and otherwise only a few instructive episodes from the *Sobornik*,[109] we can see how this collection meshed with his reading-teaching curriculum. The major spiritual masters, with their own collections of discourses, brief chapters, or apophthegms, spoke for themselves and constituted a different set of courses in the theory and practice of asceticism and stillness. The *Sobornik* contained not so much the abstract word as living history and models, for which Nil's editing and his glosses of hellenisms, as Lënngren and Romanenko have shown, could only aid his reader.[110] They have also demonstrated how the *Sobornik* amplifies what we already know of Nil from his writings and book-copying.[111]

One of the strangest accusations leveled at Nil—and it may have been part of a polemical pommeling of prelates and Iosifites in the 1550s—is Pseudo-Vassian Patrikeev's placing in the mouth of the long-gone Iosif the charge that Nil 'deleted miracles' from the Lives of the 'ancient . . . wonder-workers'.[112] To the contrary, some of these Lives are so full of miracles as to muddle the modern mind with incredulity over the credulity of yore. Almost a century ago, Konstantin Pokrovskii, agreeing with Nil's mid-sixteenth

---

107. SNS 3: 341.
108. SNS 2: 165, 171, 178–180.
109. For example, Pachomius's pulling down his lovely church and Arsenius's burial instructions: *Predanie* 34; *Testament* 2.
110. NSTRM, 77–80; Lënngren, 'Zhitiinyi tekst', 28.
111. NSTRM, 80–98; Lënngren, 'Nil Sorskii i ego "Sobornik"', *et al.*
112. Pseudo-Vassian Patrikeev, 'Prenie s Iosifom', 280; on it's late date, maybe the 1550s, see Ostrowski, *Fontological Investigation*, 186–239; Pliguzov, *Polemika*, 253–77; for the text, see the citation, below, commencing the Epilogue.

century defender, argued from two of the Lives that our hero did not tamper with content and only corrected from originals,[113] but this story may be more complex. For all we know, by resorting to his 'meager knowledge',[114] Nil may have incorrectly 'corrected'. In other words, formally speaking, Nil may have corrupted a text, though I doubt that any suggestion of subverting substance could survive serious scrutiny of this sumptuous ascetic smorgasbord.

The Church at Large

> Would you please write to Paisii and Nil and consult with them over this: 'As soon as three years shall have come, the seven thousand will terminate'. . . and please write back to me, if Paisii and Nil can visit me to talk . . . about these heresies, and whether you have at Kirillov and Ferapontov and Kamennyi these books: *Pope Sylvester of Rome, Athanasius of Alexandria*, . . . and *The Logic*, and *Dionysius the Areopagite*, because the heretics have them all.[115]

In these words Novgorod's energetic and inquisition-seeking Archbishop Gennadii (r. 1484–1504, d. 1505) implored his former Rostov colleague Ioasaf (from the Princes Obolensky, r. 1481–1489, d. 1514) in 1489—an excellent starting point for our inquiry into Nil's involvement in public life. At this time the archbishop was not only launching an offensive against purported, learned dissidents in Novgorod and Moscow (the so-called 'Judaizers'), he was also trying to limit Grand Prince Ivan III's confiscation and bestowal of archepiscopal and monastic lands in his recently acquired Novgorodian domains upon loyal and often needy warriors. According to the older scholarly paradigm, Nil should have been the

---

113. Pokrovskii, 'K literaturnoi deiatel'nosti Nila Sorskago, 33, approved by Lur'e, 'K Voprosu ob ideologii Nila Sorskogo', 199–201; NSTRM, 66.

114. *razum*: for the difficult choice of English words here, see below under III, 'Technical Terms', text to notes 152–156.

115. AfED 318, 320.

Grand Prince's ally, not someone to whom Gennadii would turn, since the prelate's proclaimed preference regarding 'heretics' was, consciously *modo iberico,* to 'burn and hang them'.[116]

How did Nil stand on these two issues that so troubled this admirer of Spain's budding inquisition? If the *Sobornik* is a guide, Nil would not have shed any tears over lost monastic wealth, though he might not have approved of the Grand Prince's high-handed measures which apparently caused the deaths or impoverishing displacement of thousands of Novgorodians.[117] On the other hand, if asked by the church leaders, Nil himself would have been in the thick of the fight against heresy, and, like Anthony, Theodosius, Euthymius, or Sabbas, ready to lend all talents to the cause. However, more than one scholar has credited the reluctance of the Moscow Synod of 1490 to execute the accused heretics to (Paisii's and) Nil's presence there and influence,[118] though not a shred of paper, authentic or pseudo, points directly to Nil here. We shall see later on that the *Sobornik* Nil is the real one, not the Nil of some wishful-thinking modern admirers.[119]

Here we turn to what would become another burning public issue: a cycle of documents from the 1550s and 1560s see Nil at the epicenter of the moral and theological backing of Ivan III's purported attempt at a synod in 1503 to terminate monastic landholding.[120] This not being the forum to present the pros and cons regarding the evidence, suffice it to say that the opinion of the most knowledgeable, source-based Nil scholars, who still accept the historicity of such a conclave and debate, envision his giving only a personal opinion against monastic property and not presenting a

---

116. AfED, 381; on the inspiration from Spain's persecution of Jews, relapsed *conversos,* and other heretics, see Goldfrank, 'Theocratic Imperatives', 34, 290, note 20.

117. Skrynnikov, *Tragediia Novgoroda,* 12–21.

118. Von Lilienfeld, NSSS, 67–68; Skrynnikov, *Gosudarstvo i tserkov',* 181; *et al.*; Nil's brother Andrei was definitely there as one of Ivan III's representatives: AfED, 385: see below II, 'The Congenital Connection,' text to note 15.

119. See below under II, 'The Unexpected Bedfellow'.

120. Note Alekseev, Sinytsina, and Skrynnikov against Ostrowski and Pliguzov: Prokhorov and Romanenko do not enter this debate at all.

principled political pose.[121] What is certain, from about thirty per cent of Nil's *Predanie* and the occasional statement in the *Ustav*, is that on paper he was a consistent 'non-possessor' in the organization of his scete, and that in his teachings he considered worldly attachments to be pernicious. He implored monks to:

> recognize by what wretchedness we are enveloped and to what mindlessness we surrender ourselves, striving for participation and success in this world, acquiring perishable objects, and on their account marching into clamor and fights, and effecting a loss for our souls.[122]

But he never, so far as can be ascertained from his writings or reliable sources, summoned the state to manage or confiscate monastic properties, so that, free from worldly concerns, monks might practice *theoria*.[123]

Perhaps a more fruitful approach here is not to argue over what we do not and cannot know about any synodal activity in 1503, but rather take a look at Nil's relations with his attested closest companions, collaborators, and devotees and see what such evidence may tell us about him, his public life, and his influence.

---

121. Prokhorov, PNSIK, 27–28; Romanenko, NSTRM, 124; contrast Nikol'skii, 'Obshchinnaia i keleinaia zhizn', 177–178; Moiseeva, *Valaamskaia beseda*, 20–32; Lur'e, *Ideologicheskaia bor'ba*, 412–417; Zimin, *Krupnaia feodal'naia votchina*, 67–72, and *Rossiia na rubezh*, 197–209; Kazakova, *Ocherki*, 68–86; Sinitsyna, 'Spornye voprosy'; 'Tipy', 133; Alekseev, *Pod znakov kontsa vremeni*, 245–68; and the old emigré and religious scholarship, such as Meyerdorff, 'Partisans et enemis', 38–41, or Špidlík, *Joseph de Volokolamask*, 161. Writing before Ostrowski and Pliguzov challenged the older paradigm, von Lilienfeld, NSSS, 167–174 and Maloney, RH, 44–45, as well as Lur'e and also Goldfrank for the first edition of MRIV, 10–11 (contrast the revised ed., 37–39), assumed the validity of the later sources.

122. *Ustav* 2.45; see below under III, 'Further on Nil's Non-Possession'.

123. 'When the synod on widower-priests was concluded, the elder Nil started to say that monasteries should not have villages, and monks should live in hermitages, and they should feed themselves via handicrafts, and the Beloozero hermits were with him'. Thus wrote the unknown author of the 1550s–1560s (Prokhorov would date it 1540s) 'Pis'mo o neliubkakh' (Writ of Emnities), PIV, 367. This same source has the dead Paisii Iaroslavov also in attendance at this synod. See Ostrowski, *Fontologicial Investigation*, 107–120; Prokhorov, 'Skazanie Paisiia Iaroslavova', 143.

II
A TENTATIVE TOP TEN[1]

The Maybe Mentor

The Grand Prince began to consult with Paisii . . . and
desired him for the metropolitanate, but he wished not.
The Grand Prince had forced him earlier to be the

1. Excluded from this list is Prince Constantine-Kassian of Mangup (d. 1504), a Greek who came to Moscow in the suite of Ivan III's second wife Zoe/Sofia Palaiologa, entered the service of Archbishop Ioasaf of Rostov (r. 1481–1489), and then founded his own monastery (contrast here, from 1981, Goldfrank, 'Nil Sorskii,' *Modern Encyclopedia* 25: 12). Ioasaf himself was a former hegumen of Ferapontov near Beloozero, to whom Gennadii appealed regarding Paisii, Nil, and the dissidents. Both Kassian and Ioasaf fit the profiles of possible intimates of Nil, but Ioasaf left no literary traces, and, as Ostrowski and Prokhorov have pointed out, the basis for attributing Nil's supposed Epistle to this Kassian is flimsy at best. The style of this 'From the Divine Writings to a Suffering Brother' has almost nothing to do with Nil; his name does not appear on the MS (GBL/RGB MDA, Fond 185); and it stems from the second half of the 17th century. The 16th-century MS with pp. 23–26 noted by Arkhangel'skii (GPB/RNB Q. XVII.50), contains no such item at all, though it does have two pseudo-Nil pieces (58–61v): Arkhangel'skii, 55–56; PIV 109–112; Lur'e, *Ideologicheskaia bor'ba*, 301–302; Prokhorov, *Poslaniia* 129, and PNSIK, 34–36, 210–213; and Ostrowski, 'Towards Establishing', 47–48. The last two, though, may go too far in identifying thematic dissimilarities: for example, the *Ustav* 5.4.60, like this pseudo-Nil letter, does analogize the Judaeans' treatment of Christ. My own argument against such attribution is that, as in the case of the *Prayer and Thanksgiving* to be discussed below, (see II. 'The Best of the Bookmen', note 35), Nil composed known works on this theme which were textually connected to his other authentic works. For translations of it into German, English, Greek, and Italian: NSSS, 276–81; Maloney, RH, 256–62, and *Nil Sorsky*, 128–135; NSA, 247–255; and Bianchi, 152–160.

Also excluded from this list is Nil's brother's 'friend', Ivan Gavrilov, the son of a Zabolostkii prince: Nikol'skii, *Opisanie*, XXXVIII, of whom we know nothing else, and Archbishop Gennadii of Novgorod, whose relationship with Nil, like Ioasaf's, is in no way clear.

hegumen at Troitsa-Sergiev Monastery, but he was unable to turn the monks to the divine path, to prayer, and to fasting, and to abstinence, and they wanted to kill him. For boyars and princes had taken the tonsure there and did not wish to submit, so he abandoned the hegumenate and thus did not want the metropolitanate.[2]

Although the occasional chronicle entry indicates the high regard in which Ivan III held Nil's purported preceptor, Paisii Iaroslavov (d. 1501), he remains our mystery man. The source for Paisii's serving as Nil's teacher is one of those suspect later documents.[3] Nil himself is reticent in this regard and defaults to 'the divinely-inspired writings' in place of the 'reliable teacher' recommended (so far as he knew) by the Great Basil.[4] Rather it was Archbishop Gennadii, who coupled Paisii and Nil as the resident all-around theological experts in the Belozersk region, and not necessarily as mentor and ex-disciple. German Podol'nyi sort of linked them by noting down Paisii's death as well as Andrei Maiko's.

How close Paisii and Nil were to each other is anyone's guess, but, assuming they had at least a few things in common, we might pause for a moment on Paisii. Presumably from Spaso-Kamennyi, where he could have met the twelve-year old future Ivan III in 1452,[5] Paisii first appears on the historic scene in 1479 as the baptizer of Ivan III's first son by his second wife (Sofiia Palaiologa), that is, the future Vasilii III. Under pressure from the Grand Prince, Paisii became at that time the hegumen of Russia's richest and most prestigious cloister, Troitsa-Sergiev, and in 1480 he was litigating over land against none other than Kirillov. He also played a mediating role that year in Ivan's dangerous, cold civil war with his brothers, at a moment when Russia's overall military-diplomatic situation was especially tenuous. The next year Paisii resigned from his hegumenate, as indicated above, over disciplinary

---

2. PSRL 6: 236.
3. 'Pis'mo o neliubkakh', 366.
4. *Ustav* 11.13; cf. Basil/Pseudo-Basil, *Ascetic Discourse*, 63.
5. Prokorov, 'Skazanie Paisiia Iaroslavova', 160.

issues and returned to the north. Three years later he flatly refused Ivan III's offer of the office of Metropolitan, whose incumbent Gerontii (r. 1463-79) irked the sovereign, but would not resign.[6]

Evidently Paisii was an erudite and commanding character, capable of awing the elite. But he preferred his principles over prestige and proximity to power. A later, random morality tale attributed to him in the *Volokolamsk Patericon* about a fatally incorrigible monk deceived by a demon posing as the Apostle Thomas would indicate that Paisii's sagacity was legendary.[7] He was residing some place within or near the triangle defined by Kirillov, Ferapontov, and Kamennyi, when Gennadii's urgent questions to Pasii and Nil regarding the calendar and invitation to Novgorod appeared in 1489.

The codices provisionally associated with Paisii—nothing is certain—indicate the usual library of a serious monk of his time: some monastic Lives, some hesychastic cell literature, a book of Hours, and a Gospel with patristic glosses which he donated to Iosifov(!).[8] As Lënngren points out, the hagiography suggests a possible pedagogical relationship to Nil on Paisii's part,[9] but this is still conjectural. More interesting may be Paisii's one known work, the *Genuine Account* (*Skazanie izvěstno*) of the *Foundation of Kamennyi Monastery*, which he was commissioned to compose after the monastery burned completely in 1476. This tasking indicates that he did have some personal memory stretching back to eyewitnesses of its renovation a century earlier. The *Account* is a half patericon, half chronicle, and all hagiography of a place. It combines the activities of a early prince-explorer and the asceticism and stillness of some randomly settled hermits; the careers of the Athos-trained Greek abbot Dionisii and of his disciples, the local hermit Alexander and the ceonobiarch Dionisii Glushitsky; and the activities of Kirillov's abbot Kassian and the young prince-monk Andrei-Ioasaf. Dead by

6. PSRL 6: 236; cf. Gonneau, *La maison de la Sainte Trinité*, 186–190.
7. *Drevnerusskie pateriki*, 103–104.
8. Prokhorov, 'Skazanie Paisiia Iaroslavova', 143–149; for the Troitsa-Sergiev miscellany of the time associated with a 'Paisii', R.P. Dmitrieva. 'Chet'i sborniki XV. v kak zhanr', 156; for the donated Gospel, KTsDRIVM, 50.
9. Lënngren, 'Nil Sorskii i ego "Sobornik"', 2–5.

the age of seventeen, Andrei-Ioasaf's body remains whole until the fire. Miracles and healings abound—in general, if not specifics—and in Alexander's hermitage as well as Kamennyi–chiefly due to several wonder-working icons, to Alexander's and Ioasaf's relics, and perhaps (the Greek) Dionisii's tomb in the church.

Paisii makes no secret of a cloister's need for material support. In return for political backing in civil strife and for commemorative prayers for the souls, both Vasilii II and his widow Maria grant a named village to Kamennyi.[10] Not at all in keeping with Nil's principles, Kamennyi's glory under the Dionisii derives from a multitude of brothers and fine church adornments.[11] Somewhat closer to Nil's *Sobornik* than to his original writings, Paisii's *Account* combines asceticism and hesychasm with miracle cults and gifts. A hesychast? Partially. Our mentor? Possibly. But no principled 'non-possessor' was he.[12]

The Congenital Connection

> . . . then a year later or less Nil's big brother Andrei died.[13]

Surely German Podol'nyi, an admirer of Nil, would not have noted the passing of Andrei Maiko had the siblings lost contact after Nil's tonsure. A few other random extant jottings may elucidate. For almost a half century, the scribe and later state secretary 'Maiko' traveled in quite lofty circles, serving as agent with the holy and the profane and having at least one close and special aristocratic 'friend'.[14] Andrei handled Vasilii II's business with (Paisii's) Kamennyi in

---

10. Does this explain Andrei Maiko's mission there?

11. Cf. *Predanie* 31–34; *Ustav* 5.8.95; Prokhorov, 'Skazanie Paisiia Iaroslavova', 157: Paisii uses the same words or lexemes, *bratii mnozhestvo, ukrasiv,* and *slava,* which Nil criticizes.

12. Already in 1960, Lur'e saw this: 'Zametki k istorii publitsisticheskoi literatury kontsa, 460–465.

13. Nikol'skii, 'Opisanie', xxxvii - fac. (from KB 101/1078: 253v).

14. Ivan Gavrilov Zabolotskii, as recorded by German: Nikol'skii, 'Obshchinaia . . . , 181.

1453–55 and Troitsa-Sergiev in 1459. He arranged the tonsuring of Vasilii's widow Maria by Kirillov's hegumen in 1477, and also her large gift there. He was the state secretary, along with two boyars, representing Ivan III at the 1490 synodal heretical trial and then helped settle a land dispute of the leading boyar, Prince Ivan Iurevich Patrikeev in 1490/91, whose son Vasilii later attached to Nil. And in 1494–95, 1499–1500, and 1501, Andrei served on diplomatic missions to Ivan III's less than appreciative new son-in-law, Grand Prince Alexander of Lithuania (r. 1492–1506, as of 1501, King of Poland, too). The first two times Andrei was with the alleged leader of Moscow's 'heretics', the senior state secretary Fëdor Kuritsyn.[15] All that travel late in life may have hastened Andrei's death—according to Romanenko, as a recently tonsured Kirillov monk.[16] But if 'little brother' Nil needed to know a thing or two about the world he had so thoroughly renounced, or, for that matter, if he had required financing and a safe-conduct passport for a fact-finding trip to Athos, he certainly had the connections—with his well placed 'big brother' Andrei, who could help out from a distance.

The Compatible Companion

> O, Innokentii, if you be zealous in attending with love of labor to Divine Writing, you shall obtain three things: first, you will feed yourself from your labors; second, you will expel the demon of idleness; third, you shall converse with God.[17]

This sort of post-it-note reminder, placed in Innokentii Okhliabinin's 'academically' informed if 'desert'-oriented presumed codex

---

15. Likhachev, *Razriadnye d'iaki*, 67–68; AfED, 385; Iu. G. Alekseev, *U kormila Rossiiskogo gosudarstva*, 76, 170, 176, 189–194.

16. Romaneko, NSTRM, 6, who notes Andrei's registration in Moscow's Dormition Cathedral synodicon for commemorations.

17. Borovkova-Maikova, NSPU, 'Prilozhenie', xxviii, 24); Prokhorov, PNSIK, 299–300, 320: KB 25/1102, 162–162v.

of his own, of Nil's, and of other writings,[18] is a moniker for the master's message and its highest hopes. A scion of the princely Khvorostinin family with possible Byzantine origins, Innokentii took the tonsure in Kirillov and became Nil's disciple. The hellenisms on the codices associated with him, independently of the later traditions, suggest that Innokentii indeed did accompany Nil to Athos. Where Innokentii was during Nil's kelliotic period outside of Kirillov can be left to the imagination, but Innokentii may have co-directed the Sora scete before he established his own further to the east in the Komel forest and lake region. Tradition is silent as to when he left, but suggest that he kept a hand in Sora's governance after Nil died.[19] At any rate, Innokentii's regulatory *Zavět* (Testament) indicates that he considered the *Predanie* the basis of his rule too, and the *Ustav* maybe a foundation block of his spiritual instructions[20] His provisions for cell ownership and for monks who leave and return are consistent with what we know later for the great Solovki coenobium,[21] and may inform concerning Sora.

A few eighteenth- and nineteenth-century manuscripts contain three works attributed to Innokentii, with some markings of the laconic style of his self-instruction and of Nil's teachings. They are also perfectly consistent with the revived neo-hesychasm of Paisii Velichkovsky (1722–1792) and his followers and require a thorough study of their own.[22] Whatever the case here, Innokentii's life and writings bear witness to an inner corps of Nil's disciples,

---

18. Borovkova-Maikova, NSPU, 'Prilozhenie', xxviii, 25): Curiously, it follows soon after a long 'academic' glossary of about 600 historical names and terms (147–158v) and precedes a another brief one (162v–163v).

19. Prokhorov, PNSIK, 304–306, 399–400; this tradition is also suspect, converting Innokentii into a coenobite, and, rather, ascribing his regulations on individual cell ownership to the Sora scete. See above, I, texts to notes 36, 46.

20. See below, Innokentii, *Zavět* 7,15; also Bychkov, *Opisanie*, 96 (No. XVIII), where Nil's *Predanie* and *Testament* are followed by Innokentii's *Zavět*. My 1975 article mistakenly refers to Innokentii's rule as 'coenobitic': 'Old and New Perspectives', 298.

21. *Tipik Obiteli . . . Zosimy i Savatia chiudotvortsov*, Sol. 1059/1168: 94v.

22. Prokhorov, PNSIK, 323–383: in my opinion, the attributions to Innokentii here are tenuous as best.

who were, as he required, completely 'of his ethos', or at least almost so.[23]

The Best of the Bookmen

> And what you are attempting, how to withdraw from the world: this ardor of yours is good, but strive in deed so to perfect this in yourself. . . . Do not desire to receive the conversations of the usual friends, who reason in a worldly manner and exercise themselves with the irrational cares entailing profits of monastic riches . . . . And you, man of God, do not commune with such people. It is not proper even to go after such people with speeches, or revile or reproach, but leave all this to God.[24]

And in this manner Nil advised Gurii Tushin (c. 1452/5–1526), the greatest monk-publisher of day whose near half-century at Kirillov (from c.1479) included a brief, early tenure as hegumen in 1484. This was before he settled down into the book business and, so it seems, entered the monastic *Guinness* of his day by overseeing the production of thirty-seven codices.[25] Our accessing the accounting of this activity within the rubric of the rule of common property might further our fathoming of the financial mechanics of Muscovite monasticism. For now, however, we should assume that the entrance gifts of the wealthy permitted them a discretionary budget to promote the business of the cloister and do a little for the self as well. In other words, if one stemmed from the boyar Kvashnin family, as did Gurii, and one wished to be a master-copier and editor, *noblesse oblige*, but, as Nil insisted, avoid

---

23. *Predanie* 1 and *Testament* 1. The *Scete Typikon* in KB 25/1102 (216v ff.), unlike Nil's Eparkh. 349, contains the provision for illiterate monks.
24. *To Gurii* 11.
25. On Gurii, Nikol'sky, *Kirillo-Belozerskii monastyr'* 2: 155–157; Kazakova, 'Knigopisnaia deiatel'nost'; *Ocherki*, 244–276; Prokhorov, 'Gurii Tushin', and 'Avtofgrafy Nila Sorskogo', 37–49.

the spiritually 'irrational' attachment prompted by that most rational of entities—money.

The degree to which Gurii's training made him Nil's formal disciple is moot, as that term does not appear in the extant sources. Gurii did, however, serve as Nil's chief in-residence Kirillov collaborator and literary executor. The numerous copies of Nil's writings that now sit in the Kirillov, Novgorod-Saint Sofiia, and Solovetskii collections owe their origin at least partially to Gurii's activities. The present state of the scholarship affords no further elaboration.

Gurii's publishing menu of Holy Writ, liturgical works, hagiography, moralia, and master hesychasts—among them Isaac the Syrian, Symeon the New Theologian, and Gregory the Sinaite, and such others as John Cassian, Dorotheus, Peter Damaskenos, and the more general Theodore the Studite—as well as his brief piece on the 'blasphemous urge'[26] betray Nil's imprint. Also of note is Gurii's creative interest in chronicling, which, if not bearing the same fruit as the Iosifov Monastery historiographers,[27] shows a parallel development at a time of great uncertainty for the faithful. By 'not straying from the true path',[28] Gurii was in many ways just what Nil needed to counter Efrosin's more 'academic' orientation within the walls of Kirillov.[29] '*For writings are many*, but *not all are divine*', Nil had written, adapting from Nikon of the Black Mountain, but hardly adopting the intellectually 'critical' stance towards Scripture and patristics once attributed to him.[30] Gurii generally accepted Nil's rather narrow definition.

It might be said that after Nil died, his mantle of occupying the center and trying to reconcile monastic factions passed to Gurii,

---

26. See above under I. 'Publish Lest They Perish', note 90.

27. Kloss, 'Iosifo-Volokolamskii monastyr' i letopisanie', and *Nikonovskii svod*, 19-54, 81–88.

28. *To Gurii* 14.

29. On this, Romanchuk, *Byzantine Hermeneutics*, 204–205.

30. *To Gurii* 15; this nineteenth-century Russian Idealist notion of Nil's 'criticism' crystallized in Zhmakin, *Mitropolit Daniil*, 26–27, and Arkhangel'skii, *Nil Sorskii*, 276–281. More recently, in qualifying the notion of Nil's 'critical, scholarly approach to the sources of tradition', or treating his 'criticism' as 'so-called' (*sogenannte*), Father Maloney and Professor von Lilienfeld have seen in Nil a personal and independent approach to these sources: RH, 195–197; NSSS, 126–133.

who, in the words of one Iosif's biographers, was devoted to honoring of 'traditions and commands of Saint Kirill the Wonder-Worker'—the common turf of the serious-minded.³¹ At the same time, as a publisher, Gurii was looking for new items, and these included Russia's oldest copy of the Life of Sava of Serbia, and some of the writings of Iosif, Vassian Patrikeev, and the Renaissance-Italy-trained Maksim the Greek. As if compiling a Kinko's or electronic reserve reader of diverse opinions for students, Gurii included Iosif and his late-life opponent Vassian in the same codex, but again, as if heeding Nil's earlier advice, moderated Vassian's invective and radicalism.³²

Gurii's last codex contains an anonymous, penitent *Prayer and Thanksgiving*, traditionally assigned to Nil.³³ My preliminary literary analysis yields enough of Nil's thematic influence to admit the *Prayer* into his circle, but not enough of his style to credit it to him.³⁴ Nil composed prayers on this theme within his *Ustav*, and had he composed a special pre-departure supplication of repentance, surely Gurii would not have been so selfish as to await his own decline to circulate it along with the *Predanie, Ustav*, and Epistles. And just as surely, Nil's other co-workers, correspondents, and devotees would have pounced on it for themselves. My own hunch is that Gurii, either alone, or with the help of a disciple-assistant or two, was the modest author of this emotive piece, which seems to have occupied its own leaflet within the codex.³⁵

---

31. MRIV 46; Savva Chernyi; *Zhitie . . . Iosifa*, 497.
32. Sof. 451, but with '*Slovo* 12' misidentified as Iosif's by Abramovich, *Sofiiskaia biblioteka* 3: 211–215; Nikol'skii, 'Obshchinnaia i keleinaia zhizn'', 176; Kazakova, 'Knigopisnaia deiatel'nost'', 182–189.
33. N.K. Nikol'skii published the *Prayer and Thanksgiving* in *Izvĕstiia* ORIaS, 1897 2.1 78–79, the version used von Lilienfeld in her Geman translation: NSSS, 257–63; Prokhorov republished Nikol'skii's with a modern Russian translation: PNSIK 261–79; it has also been translated by Jacamon into French, 117–26, Grolimund (NSA) into Modern Greek, 247–55, and Galmozzi and Cremaschi into Italian: Bianchi, 123–133.
34. The use of extreme pleonasm (verbosity) and extended hyperbole are foreign to Nil.
35. Sof. 1468: 61–72 (72v is blank); Sov. 1451 mentions three disciples, two of whom died after Gurii: Nikol'skii, *Kirillo-Belozerskii monastyr'* 1.1, Appendix, 4: XLII–XLVI.

The Loose Cannon

And when in the monastery with the brothers, who, reckoning themselves in submission, shepherd themselves irrationally with self will, and similarly effect solitude without understanding, . . . of such John Climacus . . . says: 'With self-regulation rather than direction, they would sail by presumption', which is not for us to have. As for you, acting according to the Divine Writings and the life of the holy Fathers, with the grace of Christ, you will not sin.[36]

This was Nil's counsel to German Podol'nyi (d. 1533), another aristocratic follower, in this case a Kirillov bibliographer and teacher,[37] who had sought out the master 'in spiritual love', and received a precise reference to the patristic source.[38] Earlier they had been in the monastery together,[39] and later German had approved of the Sora location.[40] But at times Nil's harsh messages did not sit too well with this relatively independent type, who hosted fellow aristocrats in his cell,[41] and toward whom, as we noted earlier, Nil felt compelled to justify himself.

Indeed four extant letters—Nil's, another from an upended Kirillov kinsman or student,[42] and two from Nil Polev—indicate that German got into scrapes of some kind with all three of them and could have landed in some pretty hot soup.[43] The problem

---

36. *To German* 7–8.
37. On German, Nikol'skii, *Opisanie*, XIII-XL, and *Kirillo-Belozerskii monastyr'* 2: 163–165; Prokhorov, 'German Podol'nyi'; Romanchuk, *Byzantine Pedagogy*, Ch. 5.
38. *To German* 6–7.
39. *To German* 4.
40. Prokhorov, 'German Podol'nyi', 151.
41. Nikol'skii, 'Opisanie', XXXVIII.
42. It is difficult to discern the exact relationship here: the writer calls German *gospodin* (Lord), but also knows his family and addresses him by the diminutive *Yermanushka*.
43. *To German*; V. Zhmakin, 'Nil Polev', 185–99; Arkhangel'skii, *Nil Sorskii i Vassian Patrikeev*, 50–1, note 8.

with the student or kinsman arose over German's leaving the monastery without permission, thereby also abandoning his pupils and some resident relatives, and, in passing, shaming his parents.[44] We do not know when this happened or how it ended.

Around 1501, German established his own cell outside the monastery. He resided there for about eight years, faithfully recording the deaths of Paisii, Andrei Maiko, and Nil, and, perhaps, doing a little teaching on the side. Marginalia on German's copy of his Epistle, made from Nil's, indicates nothing but deep respect.[45] But the two did not concur on all important matters. German's codex, which contains Kirillov's (and Russia's) earliest extant library catalogues, virtually starts with three-stage advice for students' (or anyone's) reading: first concentrate on the known; second seek the advice of the wiser for the unknown; and where that does not work, hope for enlightenment from God. Was this a green light for the independent-minded to explore beyond the what the texts or the living sages could provide? It did not exactly square with Nil's insistence on keeping within the boundaries of the Divine Writings to avoid sin.[46]

Unlike Nil, so far as we know (though again we cannot be sure when this started), German eventually took a principled stand against severe repression of heretics and allegedly said:

> It is not proper to judge anyone, believer or nonbeliever; but it is proper to pray for them and not send them to prison.[47]

---

44. The student or kinsman was also caught in the contradiction of requesting silence about the private letter—which would also be an act of disobedience to one's superior and vow.

45. Prokhorov, 'German Podol'nyi', 151.

46. KB 101/1178: 4v, as cited and interpreted in Romanchuk, *Byzantine Hermeneutics*, 195–197, 206, but also, perhaps, as Nil, maybe from Gregory the Sinaite: *Ustav* 2:48.

47. Zhmakin, 'Nil Polev', 194; also Prokhorov, 'German Podol'nyi', 151; this was one of the positions which Iosif opposed first in his 'Epistle to Nifont' (1493–1494) in the 'Discourse on the Condemnation of Heretics', the future *Slovo* 13 of the extended *Enlightener*: AfED, 427, 430, 488–494; also AfED, 509, the germ of *Slovo* 15, where, presumably, Iosif, relying on Church canons and

Then, around the time Nil died, Iosif bypassed his local archbishop in a serious material matter and suffered excommunication by him—only to be exonerated by the Moscow synod of bishops under the Grand Prince.[48] German in turn joined with Iosif's critics, went out on a canonic limb, and claimed that all who had been tonsured by him were likewise excommunicated. This initiative may represent the first known stirring of an alleged disciple of Nil specifically against Iosif or his followers,[49] but in no way did anyone at that time implicate Nil in German's undertaking. Reproached by Nil Polev for opposing the Moscow synod, German apparently kept quiet and instead departed to another, maybe his own new monastery in the Vologda region. There, if he were true to his calling, he would have no choice but to follow the master and reel in himself, as well as his charges, who otherwise might 'sail by presumption' into perdition.

The Man in the Middle

> In this book, up to here, are the transcriptions of Elder Nil, the Recluse of the Sora Hermitage, which is in Beloozero.

With these few words at the end of the third volume of Nil Sorsky's personal, hand-written copy of his *Sobornik*, the Iosifov elder Nil Polev of Volokolamsk gentry origin completed a chapter from one of the most remarkable literary collaborations in Russian monastic history. How it came to be that Kirillov could not supply Nil Sorsky with the necessary assistants or material support is itself an intriguing question, but Polev's close work with Sorsky and possession of these manuscripts illustrate a striking fact. Nil Sorsky

---

the hierarchy, threatens monks who take independent positions against the Church regarding 'heretics and apostates'.
  48. See MRIV, 39–41.
  49. Cf. Lur'e *Ideologicheskaia bor'ba*, 426–449; the authorship and the timing of the written and verbal broadsides against Iosif after 1507 are impossible to sort out.

had not one, but two monastery-patrons, Iosifov as well as Kirillov, and not one but at least two literary executors-publishers, Polev as well as Tushin.[50] In modern parlance, this Nil was a senior research associate on an extended leave from his tenure home—a situation analogous to a hypothetical modern post-doc. from Cal. Tech. being on loan to an MIT Nobel Prize winner for a major project on particle physics. Polev's and Sorsky's hands are similarly present in what could be the earliest extant copy of the *Predanie* and *Ustav* together and in another important codex.[51]

Nil Polev served, so-to-speak, as Iosifov's mobile equivalent of Gurii Tushin, and could have been the latter's partner for a time. In addition to the five collaborative efforts with Nil Sorsky, ten other codices connected with Nil Polev's copying and/or entrepreneurship are known: three Scriptural, four hesychastic ascetica, two desert paterica, and one book of church canons.[52] According to Russia's specialists, the handwriting of the some of Nil Polev's secondary, commissioned scribes points to the Kirillov scriptorium, not to Iosifov. It also appears as if soon after Nil Sorsky died, Nil Polev, who just recently been at Iosifov, went to Kirillov with the master's manuscripts of the Lives and Epistles for Gurii's workshop to copy.[53]

The continued cooperative efforts with Gurii after Sorsky died explains why Polev was in Beloozero when Archbishop Serapion excommunicated Iosif, and German tried to extend this ban to the Iosifov tonsurees. Invoking the collective episcopal and abbatial authority of the Moscow Synod, Polev now revealed himself as a solidly researching, logically writing, spirited adherent of Iosif and

50. SNS 1: 467. In the private conversation mentioned earlier (note 75, above) Elena Shevchenko warned against restricting Nil's 'literary heirs' to these two, whom I see as having been most involved in his writing and book production.

51. Eparkh. 349: 9–14, 17–83v; see below under II, 'The Unexpected Bedfellow', and III, 'Texts and Structures'. Thus the report in the *Pismo o neliubkakh* ('Writ of Enmities'), that Nil Polev 'abandoned the promise of his tonsure without Iosif's blessing', (PIV, 368) is ridiculous.

52. Kloss, 'Nil Sorskii i Nil Polev', 152–154.

53. Kloss, 'Nil Sorskii i Nil Polev', 161–166; Prokhorov, 'Avtografy', 46; 'Poslaniia', 131–133; Iosifov papers show Nil Polev serving as a council elder in November, 1507, but not February of that year: AfZKh, No. 36–37.

lashed out against opposing any legitimate ecclesiastic decision. German's quick retreat and Gurii's silence at the time on these matters is telling. Around 1510, 'the Kirillov Monastery elders and all the Trans-Volgan elders', were not about to invoke their magistral mystic against one of his close collaborators and the latter's primary preceptor.[54]

Nil Polev soon returned to Iosifov, where he served as a council elder and donated eight fine books in exchange for memorial services.[55] Three of them fully and two partially represented Sorsky's work, while only one of them was mainly Iosif's. Moreover, at least four other Iosifov elders directly or indirectly copied from the Sorsky-Polev *Predanie-Ustav* codex or from another one related to it.[56] Now this says something about Nil Sorsky's repute in Iosifov, doesn't it?[57]

The Ardent Ascetic

And another one fasted with the father in the monastery,[58] Dionisii, who was of the Princes called Zvenigorodskii, exceedingly industrious. He suffered alone in the bakery to do two brothers' work, and, in addition, chanted 77 psalms and made fifteen hundred prostrations every day. He loved solitude and requested from the father to be released to Father Nil, who shined

---

54. This notwithstanding a polemic later composed in their collective name against executing any heretics or imprisoning the penitent: 'Otvet kirillovskikh startsev'; on the dating, Pliguzov, *Polemika*, 57–80.

55. MRIV, 118–119 (Int.(B).3–6).

56. Eparkh. 343 (1530, Simeon the Hermit/Choirman); Eparkh. 350 (Q2 16th c., Isaak Sumin, disciple of Epifanii Lenkov); Vol. 137/492 (by 1558, the writer Fatei, disciple of Kassian Bosoi); Vol. 139/497 (16[th]c.): Arkhim. Iosif, *Opis'*, 115–121; see below under III. 'Texts and Structures'.

57. Cf. Lënngren, 'Nil Sorskii i ego "Sobornik"', 15–16, where the content of Nil Polev's donations to Iosifov serve as irrefutable proof of 'a single complex of . . . ideas'. For the up to twenty identifiable (by manuscript collaboration, copying or ownership) Iosifov devotees of Nil in the sixteenth-century, see Goldfrank, 'Nila Sorskogo priverzhentsi.'

58. That is, with Iosif Volotsky in Iosifov.

like a candle in the hermitage at Beloozero. And the
Nil named Polev accompanied.[59]

So one more of Iosif's pedigreed proteges made the pilgrimage to
the Sora, established his own hermitage nearby, and matriculated at
the master's feet—possibly after having received Nil's 'Little Epistle'.[60]
But this physical and spiritual athlete was no Polev, that *macher extraordinaire* of the Kirillov-Sora-Iosifov triangle, but, rather, its German, more independent, and, eventually, having his own disciples.
Fingered by German in his quixotic sortie into canonic exegesis
that extended excommunication to the tonsured acolyte, Dionisii
duly dispatched the details to his senior colleague from Iosifov and
then dutifully recorded for posterity the latter's responses.[61] Back
home around 1511–1512, Dionisii did not hold a major administrative post, did not, so far as we know, join the formal council of elders,
did not associate with the cloister-sponsored writers' workshop,
could not avoid a painful tussle with his last hegumen there,[62] and,
unlike Polev, was not among the abbey's memorialized and interred
elite.[63] Dionisii's story does not end here.

Emblematic of an independent relationship with Nil Sorsky,
Dionisii brought back to Iosifov a slightly different version of the
Ustav, the recension copied there by the bibliophile and sometime treasurer Tikhon Zvorykhin and by Iosif's nephew Dosifei
Toporkov.[64] Tikhon's massive, six-hundred-leaf ascetic-hesychastic
miscellany placed obedience and patience in the beginning, repentance and the Terrible Judgment at the end, and Nil's *Ustav* close to
the middle—just one of numerous examples of how Iosifov's and

---

59. *Zhitie prep. Iosifa . . . neizvestnym*, 30.

60. It survives only in the late 15th-early 16th or 16th c. miscellany of Dionisii's disciple Anufrii Isakov: RGB Vol. 189/577: 22; Prokhorov, *Poslaniia*, 136, 143; Arkhim. Iosif, *Opis'*, 231.

61. RGB Vol. 235/661: 128–149, along with a canonical work and mainly sacred history: Arkhim. Iosif, *Opis'*, 314–315.

62. R.P. Dmitrieva, 'Dionisii Zvenigorodskii Lupa'; Dykstra, *Russian Monastic Culture*, 159–160, and elsewhere for individualism in Iosifov.

63. Nil Polev and some family members were buried in the main church there near the old altar: *Kormovaia kniga*, 123, 201, 372.

64. Eparkh. 351, 344, 342.

other monks integrated Nil into their reading and writing. Dionisii also probably had one of the earliest extant copies of Nil's Epistles, that which ended up at the front of the miscellany of his own disciple Anufrii Isakov.[65] Dionisii's personal library, for its part, included at least thirteen books of the usual monastic mix. One of them, however, stands out for including a version of the 'Debate Between Life and Death' (recently acquired from Germany), information about contemporary natural disasters in Italy and Hungary, and an attack by Maksim the Greek (né Michael Trivolis and soon to be confined in Iosifov for 'heresy') against the German court physician, astrologer, and promoter of Church Union, Nicholas Bulev.[66] Would Nil have seen Dionisii pushing the ascetic envelop of 'Divine Writings' for his interest in current external events and 'Latin' texts with an apocalyptic portée?

The Unexpected Bedfellow

> After Compline, . . . one should flee in silence into one's cell and not speak to anyone. And so one should apply oneself with stillness in prayer or handicraft or reading, be watchfully mindful of oneself with prayers and tears, and repent and confess all transgressions to the Lord.[67]

This is what Iosif Volotsky wrote in both redactions of his Rule, and it seems close to what Nil had in mind, when he stated:

> Gregory the Sinaite not only taught anchorites and solitaries watchfulness and stillness . . . but also directed those living in coenobia to attend and take care over this . . . .[68]

---

65. Vol. 189/577: 1–22; dating of end 15th-early 16th c., in Prokhorov, 'Poslaniia', 134–135.

66. Eparkh. 401; for the others, KTsDRIVM, 25, 26, 29, 31, 34, 35, 62, 73, 80, 82, 83 85, including Eparkh. 348, Basil's *Asceticon*, with, among other things, the Life of Gregory the Sinaite appended.

67. MRIV 6^B1, 3/4.1, 3; cf., below, Appentix I, *Scete Typikon* 33.

68. *Ustav*, Fwd. 8–9.

Not normally considered a hesychast, Iosif was the most versatile, forceful, and controversial monk of his day. One could easily write a book about him, and indeed the author of this book has already done so and published it in two editions for this fine series, and plans yet another book. But until said author started working on this one, he never realized the degree to which Iosif operated at ease within the world of stillness. One of Iosif's teachings on community prayer with an affinity to the hesychastic notion of divine light should have tipped off all concerned long ago:[69]

> For the light of prayer is just like the light of a candle. And if your train yourself to pray with precision, . . . God, without any mediator, enlightens your mind.

And the Soviet scholar Goleizovskii also noted that hesychasm influenced Iosif's understanding, even of iconography:[70]

> . . . those wondrous and most renowned iconographers, Daniil and his disciple, Andrei, always elevated intellect and thought to the immaterial and divine light, . . . would sit on their benches with their all-venerable and divine icons, . . . gaze fixedly upon them, and be filled with divine joy and illumination.[71]

Iosif himself, in composing his own brief history of native ascetics, did not neglect stillness:[72]

---

69. AfED 352–353; MRIV 1ᴮ.18/1.18, adapted from John Chrysostom (the English here altered according to the principles of this translation of Nil); it was so characterized, but without the source, by Goleizovskii, "'Poslanie ikonopistsu,'" 230–231.

70. Goleizovskii, "'Poslanie ikonopistsu,'" 233, referencing the following citation, but focusing elsewhere.

71. MRIV 10.29.

72. MRIV 10.23. Iosif also adapted from Isaac's linkage of practical ethics and stillness: *He who neglects/despises a sick man will not see the light*: MRIV 2.15; cf. Isaac 76: 379; HM SMS 179.55: 241; Gk: *Epst.* 4: 375.

> The blessed Varsonofii . . . lived in the hermitage for forty years and . . . had no work other than praying, chanting, and reading books . . . possessed nothing of his own, not even one copper coin. . . . Because of his great attention, silence, prayers, and reading, he was worthy of so much divine grace.

So maybe we should not be in the least surprised that the extant ascetic miscellany from the disciple days of the reputedly precociously 'experienced'[73] Iosif includes some of the hardest core hesychasm,[74] and that, as his new monastery was setting records for rapid development, he was in the position to lend Nil an able assistant or two. Characteristically, though, Iosif's inclusion of an equivalent of the *Scete Typikon* instructions for illiterate monks in his codex[75] indicates the same wider, quasi-*Mahayana* sweep of pedagogy in stillness that Kirill had evinced, rather than the more narrow Nil with his literacy requirement.

Still, if hesychasm and hagiography had delimited the collaboration within the Kirillov-Sora-Iosifov triad, then we might speak confidently only of Nil's expansive influence within the heresy-hounding citadel of Russia's coenobitic reform movement, but Iosif's *bon voyage* to Zvenigorodskii and Polev had another side, as illustrated below:

> If someone dishonors the image of the king (*tsar*), he is tormented with capital punishment. How much more worthy—these torments—is he who dishonors the likeness of the Heavenly King or his saints or churches? But here according to the divine canons he is punished with capital punishment and rendered an eternal anath-

---

73. Savva Cherny, *Zhitie* . . . *Iosifa*, 458.
74. Eparkh. 357. Besides Ephrem on stillness, Climacus on asceticism and fighting temptations, Patriarch Germanus's *Verses,* and a brief of Peter Damaskenos's guide, the codex has the mystical Hymns of Symeon the New Theologian found in his standard Slavic compilation and used by Nil: see below, *Ustav* 2:36–39, and also Part III.'Centrality of Sources'.
75. Eparkh. 357: 225–225v.

ema after death, with the Devil and the Judaeans, who crucified Chirst and said: 'His blood is on us and our children'[76]—condemned to the eternal fire.[77]

For over four centuries, readers of these words have attributed them to Iosif, and probably rightly so. At some time around 1502, according to the present consensus of the manuscript and orthography experts, however, Nil Sorsky copied (and possibly edited) this passage as part of his collaborative work on that other project: the carefully crafted and finely finished, first-edition manuscript of Iosif's celebrated *Prosvetitel'* (*Enlightener*), here in its brief, eleven-discourse redaction.[78] Can we then blithely deny Nil a share of Iosif's responsibility for the burning as heretics and apostates of Novgorod's Archimandrite Kassian, of the juridical expert and state secretary Ivan Volk Kuritsyn, and of several others in 1504–1505?[79] Ought we not question the modern fictive fancy that Nil and Paisii were able to limit the punishments of those indicted in1490, rather than having expressly sanctioned the terminal imprisonment of at least one culprit residing in Moscow and Gennadii's non-lethal *auto-da-fé* against others in Novgorod?[80]

---

76. Mt 27:25.
77. In Nil's hand in Sol. 326/346: 215v–216; cf. AfED, 344–345.
78. Kloss, 'Nil Sorskii i Nil Polev, 155; Prokhorov, 'Avtografy', 52–53, and PNSIK, 52–53; Lur'e, 'Unresolved Issues', 164–171, and 'Nil Sorskij et la compozitione', 101–103; Romanenko, NSTRM, 95–96; also Pliguzov, 'O khronologii', 1058. This is Sol. 326/346, up to p337v, where, unlike every other Slavic manuscript I have ever seen, each discourse begins on a separate leaf and hence could be a separately redacted leaflet.
79. Goldfrank, 'Theocratic Imperatives', 35, and 291, note 26.
80. On the 1490 proceedings, 'Burn Baby Burn', 24–25, and Pliguzov, 'Archbishop Gennadii', 270–277; on the standard postion regarding Paisii and Nil in 1490, see Arkhangel'skii, *Nil Sorskii*, 32–33; Kologrivof, *Essai*, 195; Fedotov, *Russian Religious Mind* 2:267; Fennell, 'The Attiudes of the Josephians and Trans-Volga Elders', 491; Von Lilienfeld, NSSS, 166, but questioned in 'A proposito', 67; Maloney, RH, 44; Bianchi, *Nil Sorskij*, 9; Pospielovsky, *The Orthodox Church*, 53; et al. According to Romenenko, this view was first aired by I. Panov in 1877, and the only serious challenge, which her data from Nil's hagiographic *Sobornik* support, came from Lur'e: NSTRM, 25, 86. For criticism of groundless attempts to link Nil to heretical thinking, see Lur'e, 'Unresolved Issues', 163–164, and note 32.

Indeed, the canonic opinion cited above represented, as Iosif stated elsewhere, the inclusion of 'gruesome' punishments from Byzantine Civil Law within the 'divine canons'[81]—curiously, a deadly serious stretching of the saintly examples in Nil's *Sobornik*.[82]

Nil's share in the penning of this work, which may well have circulated at the 1504 Synod,[83] amounted to about forty per cent. He created the elaborate title page and copied the initial part of the emotive and tendentious, introductory *Skazanie* or 'Tale of the Newly Appearing Heresy of the Novgorod Heretics,' whom we should 'hate with perfected hate' (pp 47–51). The first two regular discourses, explaining the Trinity and the Incarnation, and containing an invective 'myriad of anathemas' against the heretics, constituted his second section (pp 67–103v). His final contribution, the eight, ninth, and tenth discourses, perhaps part of his positive response to Archbishop Gennadii's earlier appeal for calendrical help (though the style is Iosif's), cogently abstracts Byzantine theological epistemology, elucidates the inscrutability of the second coming, and defends the consistency and authority of Scripture and patristics, despite some suggestions within these texts that the apocalyptic moment actually was at hand (pp248–287v).

Nil also copied the last two-thirds of the seventh discourse, which is a mini-handbook of Orthodox doctrine, rituals, devotion, and monasticizing ethics for laymen (pp 215–247v). Nil's portion of this contains the earliest version of Iosif's reworking of Chrysostom's theory of community prayer cited earlier,[84] and also an older version of the standard hesychastic advice to the pious regarding the Jesus Prayer:

---

81. MRIV 3.33, 8.2; also AfED, 491–492; and Freshfield, *Procheiros nomos*, 154: Nikon, well before Iosif and Nil, treated the 'civil law' (*gradskii zakonъ*) as canonic: *Pandekty* 4:36v.

82. As Romanenko points out, Nil's saints resolutely resisted heresy and Jews in various ways, including, in one instance, praying for their conversion: NSTRM, 87–92.

83. Lur'e, 'Unresolved Issues', 165–166.

84. See above, note 69.

And you, beloved one, wherever you be, either at sea, or on a road, or at home, either walking, or sitting, or sleeping, everywhere and continuously pray with a pure conscience, saying thusly: 'Lord Jesus Christ, Son of God, Have Mercy on me'.[85]

This compendium of *moralia* goes significantly beyond the usual demands for industriousness, forgivingness, prudence, chastity, charity, obedience, discipleship, penitence, tithing, and so forth. It also contains a unique call in original Russian letters for non-obedience to an impious king (*tsar*)—here a startling combination of classical political theory, Christian martyrology, and an adaption of the Orthodox notion of the eight principle, demonic *logismoi* to secular rulers:[86]

If there is a king reigning over men, but has, ruling over himself, passions and sins: avarice and anger, wickedness and injustice, pride and fury, and, worst of all, disbelief and blasphemy, such a king is not God's servant but the Devil's, and not a king but a tyrant. Such a king, on account of his wickedness, our Lord Jesus Christ did not call a king, but a fox: '*Go*', he said, '*and tell that fox*'.[87] And the Prophet said: '*An arrogant king will perish, for his ways are dark*'.[88] So you are not to obey such as king or

---

85. Sol. 326/346: 239v; cf. AfED 356; in the *Ustav* 2.7, Nil remarked: *Nowadays, the Fathers add a word: after they say 'Lord Jesus Christ, Son of God, have mercy on me'; they forthwith say: 'a sinner'*.

86. Sol. 326/346: 218v–219; cf. AfED, 346. On the eight *logismoi* or urges, see below under III, 'Technical Terms'. Of those mentioned here, avarice and anger are Nos. 3–4, pride No. 7, and blasphemy, as a deeper essence of despondency, No. 6. The others in this passage expand on these four. On part of the ideational etiology, Ševčenko, 'A Neglected Source,' especially note 26, and Goldfrank, 'The Deep Origins of *Tsar'-Muchitel'*.

87. Lk 13.32, part of a defiant message Jesus is giving a Pharisee to tell to Herod (i.e., the historic tetrarch, Herod Antipas—to whom Pontius Pilate later sent Jesus for the trial resulting in scourging—not Antipas's father, King Herod the Great, who reigned at the time of Jesus's birth.)

88. Cf. Ps 1:6, Prv 2:13, 22.

prince, who leads you to impiety and wickedness, if he torments, if he threatens death. The prophets and apostles and all the martyrs, who were killed by impious kings and did not submit to their command, bear witness to this.[89]

What do we make of this situation, in which Iosif teaches or directs his elite disciples to the equivalent of *Hesychasm 101* and then sends a couple of his best 'graduates' to the Sora for their advanced training, and Nil abets Russia's proto-inquisition? Do we not really have, in modern parlance, an under-staffed and struggling multi-campus collegium at which Nil held the Chair of Hesychasm, Hagiography, and Sacred Letters, Iosif served as the Dean of the Faculty of Coenobitism, Dogmatics, and Sacred History, Gennadii ran the Institute for Biblical, Latin, and Calendrical Studies, and all three resolutely opposed the inchoate Moscow Chancery School of Grammar, Natural Philosophy, Law, and Politics, with its tendencies towards freer thinking, interest in Judaica, dabbling in astrology, and also some direct access to the no-nonsense, growth-oriented, secular and ecclesiastical land-grabbing, crowned and ruthless CEO of the entire Muscovite conglomerate?[90] You want to know why Nil and Iosif were allies? This is why![91]

Fairy von Lilienfeld was certainly correct in the early 1960s in positing a 'crisis of tradition' as the backdrop to Nil's activities.[92]

---

89. Presumably, then, in this system a melancholy (No. 5) or vain (No. 7) glutton (No. 1) or lecher (No. 2) qualifies as a genuine and non-tyrannical, if sub-optimal king, so long as he be pious and not wicked: such a scheme more or less fits medieval Christian society as it operated. For Nil's explict reference to 'tyrants' and martyrdom, see below, 'To Gurii' 7.

90. For a creative reevaluation of the Judaic and quasi-rational input into the barely accessible dissident circles, see Moishe Taube, 'The Kievan Jew Zacharia'; 'The "Poem on the Soul"'; and 'Literature of the Judaizers or Literature for the Judaizers'; for recent caution regarding the dissidents' rationalism, see Romanchuk, *Byzantine Hermeneutics*, 22–25, and 'Reception of the Judaizer Corpus'; for a penetrating, comparative ideational analysis of Gennadii, Iosif, and Nil, see Thomas M. Seebohm, *Ratio und Charisma*, 484–493.

91. Cf. Lënngren, 'Nil Sorskii i ego "Sobornik"', 15–16.

92. NSSS, the title of the book and of the analytical first part.

What none of us knew then, but what intrigued Professor von Lilienfeld much later, was the evidence of Nil's collaboration with Iosif.[93] So until some orthography expert disproves the initial analysis of Kloss and Prokhorov, we cannot avoid the simple fact that Nil copied, edited, and adapted dozens of authors, but only one of them, so far as we know, was a Russian—the slightly younger Iosif Volotsky. Now that tells us something too.

The Colonizing Coenobite

> The Blessed Kornilie made a typikon for all of the brothers engaged in manual work and all the offices: to make no idle chatter, but continuously to psalmodize or say the Jesus Prayer, and to thank God and have love for one another . . . and for no one to do his own will, but everything by the command of the superior.[94]

So wrote the hagiographer of the remarkably energetic coenobiarch Kornilii Komel'skii (1455–1537/8), who at the age of forty-two may have in anticipated Innokentii in setting out with a few companions for the dense, bandit-infested Vologda forests, and yet commenced his own Rule almost *verbatim* from Nil's *Predanie*.[95] Kornilii's earlier career had crossed some of Nil's paths. And Kornilii's Life, written in the 1550s–1560s with an unknowable combination of realism and lip-service to the expected, paints him as a devotee of stillness.[96]

Born to landed Rostov gentry family in the service of the Grand Princess Maria Iaroslavna, who was also at least an occasional employer of Nil's brother Andrei, Kornilii went at the age of twenty with his uncle to Kirillov and became student-postulant

---

93. Von Lilienfeld, 'A proposito della ricerche', 68.
94. *Zhitie Korniliia Komel'skogo*, 34-35/BLDR 13:320.
95. Kornilii Komel'skii, *Ustav ili pravila*, Introd. 168; cf. *Predanie* 1.
96. A Slavic *bezmolv-* (= *stillness, hesychasm*) word appears no less than twenty-seven times in the Life: *Zhitie Korniliia Komel'skogo*, 86; also BLDR 13: 308, 322, 330, 332, 336; Konoplev, 'Sviatye Vologdskogo kraia', 87–94; Budovnits, *Monastyri*, 280–93.

of a sort.⁹⁷ Residing there from about 1475 to 1482, he may have met Nil (and also, in 1478, the allegedly incognito-touring Iosif, before he became 'Volotsky').⁹⁸ Kornilii next wandered as an unattached tonsured monk to various places, and ended up in Novgorod as an assistant, an ordained hieromonk, and eventually a valued suburban kelliot or scete-dweller serving Archbishop Gennadii.⁹⁹ Then in 1497, with the blessing of Metropolitan Simon of Moscow, Kornilii ventured northeastward and founded his Komel Forest cloister, dedicated spiritually to the Presentation of the Theotokos and materially to exploiting the region's natural riches. Some time after 1515, when the tonsured brethren and hired hands had constructed their stone church, refectory, infirmary and almshouse, two of his disgruntled foremen sought to murder him. Indefatigable at the age of sixty, Kornilii in turn entrusted his abbey to a dozen elders, and went off to found a hermitage advantageously located forty miles to the southeast. He hoped to build this one up too. Grand Prince Vasilii III (r. 1505–1533) honored Kornilii and granted him material support, but demanded that he return to his original foundation. At the time of his death, his main cloister had ninety monks. At least eight of his disciples founded their own monasteries.¹⁰⁰ So he was quite an influential figure, for whom Nil was one of several models. But how much?

As has been known for a long time, Kornilii took his regulations chiefly from Iosif, but such specialists as N. Konoplev more than a century ago and Father Maloney more recently claimed that the 'influence of Nil . . . was much stronger', in part because Kornilii did not accept or retain all the property offered to him.¹⁰¹ Such

---

97. So according to the printed Life of Kornilii: *Zhitie Korniliia Komel'skago*, ed. Gerd, 21 and BLDR 13: 306–307, both based on different late 16ᵗʰ c. MSS (Pogod. 787, KB 28/1267), not age twelve, as in Budovnits, *Monastyri na Rusi*, 281, based on an early 17ᵗʰ c. MS (Troitsk. 676/RGB f. 304.I).

98. MRIV, 26.

99. BLDR 13: 306–308: The historical-calendrical-ascetic Sof. 1474 contains the descriptive inscription: 'Miscellany of Gennadii's Hermitage.'

100. BLDR 13: 785.

101. Konoplev, 'Sviatye Vologdskogo kraia', 100–101; Maloney, RH, 232: Konoplev recognized that Nil's spiritual path was for the very few.

calculations are tricky and elusive at best, if for no other reason that Nil and Iosif both present themselves as 'sinful and unworthy'; both would expel an infidel to their 'traditions'; both demand obedience and confession to the superior and also his permission to leave the premises; both require only timely and useful conversations, silence at work, and continuous prayer; both link exterior behavior and interior attitudes, and both counsel memory of death. So arbitrarily to assign Kornilii's strictures on these matters to Nil's influence alone is rather questionable. In one place in the Konoplev-Maloney scheme, Nil even gets the credit for the standard coenobitic principle enunciated, not by him, but by Iosif–the prohibition of any personal property whatsoever.[102]

One should not belabor this point, but four considerations merit mention. First, the simple fact that a coenobitic rule borrows at all from Nil's *Predanie* is itself a striking testimony to his influence, but, to preview our coming analysis of the sources, what goes around comes around. The *Predanie* is itself mostly adapted from a coenobitic rule,[103] and Kornilii has merely applied his source back again to its own fount. Second, if statistics mean anything, then Kornilii's copying and adapting of the *Predanie*—perhaps by way of his regional neighbor Innokentii—represent, by my count, a mite over twenty percent of the entire Rule. On the other hand, Kornilii virtually neglects or contradicts Nil's strictures on nonpossession. For example, Nil opposed the very notion of monks acquiring in order to distribute alms, whereas Kornilii was determined that monastery's common treasury, not the individual monks, effect the standard monastic alms-giving.[104] Kornilii, moreover, lifted or adapted for his text a whopping sixty-three per cent from Iosif, that is, maybe three times more than from Nil.[105] Third,

---

102. Konoplev, 'Sviatye Vologdskogo kraia', 100; Maloney, RH, 232-33; this despite Konoplev's strange use of Iosif's Brief Rule (pp. 96–99), though the Extended Rule was available from the VMCh publication.
103. See below under III. 'The Centrality of Sources'.
104. Cf. *Predanie*, 21–23; Kornilii Komel'sky, *Ustav ili pravila*, 12: 183–184.
105. Nil and Iosif are equal sources for Kornilii's Introduction and Ch. 10 on labor. Nil virtually 'owns' Ch. 11 on leaving the monastery, and Innokentii and Nil predominate in Ch. 13 on alcoholic beverages; but Iosif solely governs Kornilii's

adaptations can be revealing, when the changes are significant. As if downplaying hierarchy within his stillness-seeking hermitage, Nil 'wrote . . . for myself and my genuine lord brothers. . . .'.[106] Kornilii juggled Nil's words, so that the 'brothers' are no longer 'lords', but men closer to Iosif's lower-ranking and deployable 'brothers in Christ'.[107] Fourth, Konoplev pointed to the hagiographic report of Kornilii's rejecting Vasilii III's offer of a village in favor of a some neighboring productive land and forest,[108] but neglected to add that the same text included the abstract of an immunity charter—a sure sign of 'possession'—and that Nil saw such outdoor labor as proper only for coenobites.[109]

Kornilii certainly bears witness to the wide applicability of Nil's writings, and not only for hermits, as well as to the principled proximity of Russia's prominent proponents of pristine asceticism. But in our critical revisiting from the vantage point of the venerable if outdated Nil-vrs.-Iosif paradigm, Kornilii, viewed by some as Nil's receptive acolyte, ends up as a deceptive coenobite.

Once a Boyar . . .

> God, having loved you, and taking you from this world, has by his mercy and plan placed you in the ranks of his service. Therefore you must most abundantly thank his mercy and do everything in your power towards his gratification and the salvation of your soul, forgetting the worldly past as useless, and reaching to the

---

words regarding communal prayer (Ch. 1), eating (Ch. 2–4, 9), and all sorts of possessions (Ch. 5-8), including the prohibition against monks' accepting any alms for themselves (Ch. 12). The last two chapters on new or returning brothers arriving with personal property (Ch. 14–15) are Kornilii's: they raise a theme found in Innokentii and then apply Iosif's supervisory principles.

106. *Predanie* 1.

107. MR IV, Extended Rule Title, Fwd. 1, 12.1. Iosif, however, calls his council elders and officials, 'my fathers and brothers' (13.3), which approaches Nil's level of social respect.

108. Konoplev, 'Sviatye Vologdskogo kraia', 100; *Zhitie Korniliia Komel'skogo*, 41/BLDR 13:328.

109. *Predanie* 16.

virtuous future as intermediary for eternal life. Rejoice, step onto the honor of the calling of the Most High, granted in the heavenly fatherland to former ascetics. . . .And may the God of all joy and comfort, comfort your heart and preserve you within his fear, with the prayers of the most pure Mother of God and all the saints. [110]

Such was Nil's advice of 1499–1500 to the erstwhile merry gentleman, Vasilii Patrikeev, now Vassian, the exiled and forcefully shorn heir to Moscow's fallen, preeminent prince-boyar, who along with his closest relatives, with one most unfortunate exception, had barely escaped, heads intact, the Kremlin's succession intrigues. Selecting Kirillov as his first monastic resting place, Vassian attached himself to Nil in some fashion, and requested advice regarding present 'terrors' and 'assailing *logismoi* of yore from the worldly life'.[111] But what this self-styled disciple was doing while the Sorsky-Polev-Volotsky ateliers were operating at full steam, producing *Prosvetitel'* and promoting a death-dealing inquisition, is another mystery, since Vassian emerged after Nil's death as a virulent opponent of executing heretics.

What is more, we have no sign of even a short-term interest in hesychasm on Vassian's part. Though he could manipulate with sting the discourse of stillness and mental warfare,[112] no one has discovered a hesychastic manuscript bearing his imprint or evidence of his having prayer-oriented disciples. Physical warfare, court politics, ecclesiastical law, and biting polemics were in his bones. More than a century before Russia's state apparatus was sufficiently staffed or so inclined, he wanted to shake up the Church and have bishops' officials manage all ecclesiastical properties.[113] So Nil's advice notwithstanding, Vassian cashed in on his monastic education, and as soon as political circumstances permitted,

---

110. *To Vassian* 4, 19.
111. *To Vassian* 2; MR IV, unlike this study, assumes actual discipleship.
112. See his 'Slovo otvetno', 260, 263.
113. 'Slovo otvetno', 269.

maybe 1509–1510, he was back in Moscow at Kirill's ancestral Simonov Monastery. From there Vassian polemized against Iosif and his disciples and sometimes acted as an unofficial advisor to Vasilii III (r. 1505–33).[114]

Vassian has been the subject of several books,[115] and to do any justice whatsoever to him here would take us well beyond the boundaries of this one. Hopefully these four observations can suffice for our purposes. First, Vassian's positive work with the ecclesiastical canons—the *Kormchaia Kniga*, Russia's *Pedalion* or *Rudder*—was built in part on the efforts of the late Ivan Kuritsyn, whom Nil's collaboration with Iosif had helped to turn to human ash.[116] Second, Vassian's savage and sarcastic assault on Moscow's ersatz inquisition[117] was, therefore, whether he knew it or not, also partially an attack on what Nil had done.[118] Third, the caustic tone of Vassian's polemics against rival Orthodox ran absolutely counter to Nil's *ad hominem* advice for handling the errant:

> Cleave unto the reverential fathers . . . . Stay away from those who are not such, and be on guard and endeavor not to reproach or condemn anyone over

---

114. Pliguzov, following Ankhimiuk, argues that Vassian's first such foray was the rather recently discovered *'Discourse against Iosif's Composition'*, an attack on Iosif's inquisitorial program, dated 1511–1512: Pliguzov, *Polemika*, 78–80; Ankhimiuk, 'Slovo na "Spisanie Iosifa"'.

115. Kazakova, *Vassian Patrikeev*, and *Ocherki;* Pliguzov, *Polemika*.

116. Begunov, Iu. K. 'Kormchaia Ivana Volka Kuritsyna', contested in part by Pliguzov, *Polemika*, 141–178; see below, note 117.

117. Goldfrank, 'Theocratic Imperatives', 35–36; specifically, and without examining the issue of recidivism, Vassian rejected executions of heretics ('Slovo otvetno', 270–271), if not also the Church's refusal to trust the repentance of the convicted (as in Pseudo-Vassian, 'Prenie s Iosifom', 7–8: 277).

118. In one sense Nil's Epistle to Vassian (*To Vassian* 17) contained a deadly jab at Ivan Kuritsyn, whom both Andrei Maikov and Vassian (earlier) most surely knew: *It is written that it is impossible for him who reasons (mudrьstvuiushchemu) rightly and lives piously to perish*. Around the time Nil composed this, he was also helping Iosif issue his book against '*the Novgorod Heretics, the archpriest Aleksei, the priest Denis, Feodor Kuritsyn, and the others who so reason (mudrьstvuiushchikhъ*: Prosvetitel', 27.). The three named culprits had already passed from the world when Nil copied these words, which contributed to the indictment, conviction, and execution of the allegedly objectionably reasoning Ivan Kuritsyn.

anything, even if something appears not good to you. Rather consider yourself totally sinful and unfit in everything.[119]

And finally, Vassian's canonic endeavors and crafty polemics to discredit Iosif and his followers lost out, but only in the short run. Vassian in turn was framed, it seems, as an adherent of an obscure heresy.[120] Accordingly, he finished his days as a prisoner in Iosifov.[121] But, thanks to some determined opposition to the Iosifites in the 1550s and 1560s, Vassian and Pseudo-Vassian ended up controlling the policy aspect of Nil's legacy and structuring the grand narrative of his life and times—that is, until the past half century, when the intellectual DNA code of the scholarship underwent some serious mutation, and what I see as a more realistic variety of *flos sorskiensis* started to bloom.

---

119. *To Vassian* 14.
120. Aphtharodocetism—that Christ's human body was incorruptible: 'Sudnoe delo Vassiana,' 298.
121. Kazakova, VPS, 76–77; Lur'e and Zimin, *Poslaniia*, 369.

III
THE WRITTEN LEGACY

Texts and Structures

Indeed we, the unknowledgeable, within the meager limits of our knowledge, have written these things as a reminder to ourselves and to those similar to me, who are in the rank of disciples, if they so desire.[1]

The intensity of toil entailed by the *Sobornik* is as good an explanation as any as to why Nil's output of original works is quantitatively, though not qualitatively meager. What did he actually write? Tinkering slightly with Ostrowski's excellent if perhaps too stringent criteria for assigning authenticity, we ought to accept that Nil composed the following extant works: the *Predanie*, the *Ustav*, the Epistles to Vassian, Gurii, and German (probably in reverse chronological order), the *Little Epistle*, the related *Forewords* and *Postscripts* to the *Sobornik*, and the *Testament*.[2] All other such attributions turn out to be hypothetical or downright wrong.[3]

---

1. *Ustav* 11.19.
2. All of these are textually interrelated, and only the *Testament* is not found on paper from or close to Nil's lifetime. The relatively low percentage of the *Testament*'s correlation to the 'inner corpus' is genre determined; Sections [1–3], if not the disposition of goods [4–5], correlate with the *Predanie*, the *Ustav*, and the *Sobornik Life of Arsenius*; cf. Ostrowski, 'Toward Establishing the Canon', 46.
3. From von Lilienfeld's list of works attributed to Nil (NSSS, 90–98) and using Ostrowski's principles ('Toward Establishing the Canon') as I modify them, we have thirteen likely spuria. In the publications and translations since 1980, two of these works still have proponents of authenticity. Jacamon, Grolimund,

Consequently, we should beware of (and so warn our students against) relying upon publications and secondary literature when they fail to be critical in this respect, lest they and we be led astray by a piece of Pseudo-Nil and then all 'sail by presumption' into the wrong port.

As for their approximate dating, Nil composed *To German* and also, in stages, the *Predanie* after founding the Sora scete. This could have been anytime from the late 1470s to the 1490s. A version of the *Ustav* preceded *To Gurii* and *To Vassian*, the latter penned no earlier than 1499, when the recipient was forcefully shorn. The *Forewords* and *Postscripts* to the *Sobornik*, as well as the *Testament*, pertain to the end of Nil's life or at least when he first had a sense of imminent death.

Nil's shortest works, the *Little Epistle*, the *Forewords* and *Postscripts*, and the *Testament*, ranging in English translation from sixty to three hundred ninety words, require little by way of introduction. The *Little Epistle* and the *Testament* survive in one copy each,[4] the *Forewords* and *Postscripts*, as part of the few extant *Sobornik* volumes. Dedicated to one theme only, they are simple, but elegant. Only the *Testament* divides into two parts, an ethical-hortatory *exordium-narratio*, and the disposition of Nil's few items. The others flow from one sentence to the next. As if following the standard principle for communicating to busy people, he was brief, he was clear, and he was gone.

Nil's three directed Epistles are another matter. They survive in at least thirty-two full and sixteen partial copies, mainly from the

---

Bianchi, and Prokhorov include the *Prayer and Thanksgiving*, which I provisionally credited to Gurii's circle (see above under II. 'The Best of the Bookmen'). Bianchi (tentatively) and Maloney include the longer *Epistle . . . to a Grieving Brother*, traditionally seen as addressed to Kassian of Mangup (see above, the first note to II. 'A Tentative Top Ten'). Recently Prokhorov has suggested a new one, a possible translation 'of elder Nil', of generalized prayers for the dead credited to Cyril of Jerusalem: PNSIK, 247–251.

4. The *Little Epistle* follows the three genuine ones in Anufrii Isakov's Vol. 189/577 (see above under II. 'The Ardent Ascetic', note 66). The *Testament* is placed after the *Predanie* and before the *Ustav* and the three Epistles in Troits.-Serg. 188/1576 (second half 16th c.): Arsenii and Ilarii, *Opisanie* (1878.2), 182, so dated by Prokhorov, 'Poslaniia', 135, and serving as the basis of the Borikova-M order of publication.

sixteenth and seventeenth centuries. The minuscule but identifiable textual differences led Prokhorov to conclude that the earliest Iosifov copies came from those Nil retained, while Gurii's workshop copied both these versions and those which the addressees had preserved. Some later scribes produced combinations.[5] *To German* is as long as a middle-sized *Ustav* item for Nil (some thirteen hundred words), and the other two like a large one (about eighteen hundred words). Each of them neatly divides into subjects which are handled as extensively as one of the smaller *Ustav* pieces. The body of *To Gurii*, which is more general, contains distinct sections on battling lust, opposing despondency-blasphemy, withdrawing from the world, and not straying the path. More personal, and commencing with a rhetorically clever *exordium*, playing on Nil's 'sinful' and 'unknowledgeable' state, *To Vassian* has sections devoted to joyful renunciation of the world, fighting his unclean *logismoi*, overcoming his fears, fulfilling his new duties, and holding proper attitudes. The divisions of the even more intimate *To German* speak of their personal relations, Nil's own guiding principles, extended advice to follow the Divine Writings, and further apologies over the past. Nil's care for symmetrical structure and his limiting to three quality Epistles illustrate of his sense of modesty as well as seriousness of purpose in writing for present needs and posterior use. Each Epistle stands alone, yet together they complement the *Predanie* and *Ustav* and illustrate the practical application of his principles.

The *Predanie*, as a functioning Rule, composed over time with some obvious additions, is more complex than the Epistles, if, at about twenty-two hundred words, less than a fourth larger than *To Gurii* and *To Vassian*.[6] The more literary initial two fifths of the *Predanie* can be divided among the personal introduction,

---

5. Prokhorov, 'Poslaniia', 130–136; in PNSIK, 220, he notes a total of 48, 47 are listed, but Sof. 1460 has them twice.

6. These are rough English-translation word counts, but proportional to what Russian bookmen of Nil's time would have considered to be separate 'words'. Iosif considered his 1300-word summary 'Rule in Brief' (*Slovo* 12 of his Extended Rule), appropriate to read aloud to the entire, assembled brotherhood, which included some illiterates: MRIV12.9.12. As a point of comparison, one

credo, and the principles of accepting brothers. Passing quickly through confession and to severing one's will, Nil then devotes about four hundred fifty words to self-support, to the avoidance of ill-gotten gains and haggling over prices or the wages of hired hands, and to the superiority of monastic 'charity of the soul'. A first false ending follows the next brief section on assigned departures from the scete, and a second false ending follows the subsequent extended sentence restricting the advising of 'brothers and outsiders' to the qualified. Next comes a solid 260 words or so devoted to preserving an unadorned church, before the *Predanie* trails off with curt strictures on food, avoidance of strong drinks, simplicity of cells, and the prohibition of women, female animals, and boys. The open-ended close allows for the type of addenda, which Nil himself, as well as Innokentii, made. It is found in several dozen copies from *c.*1500 onward, both with and without the *Ustav* of either type, as outlined in the next paragraph.

The *Ustav*, which is really not large for a *magnum opus* underlying a Church Father's fame,[7] is composed of twenty to twenty-six linked pieces—this number depending upon how one specifies the some one-hundred-fifty-word summary and sub-titled bridge at the end of *Slovo* 4, four sub-divisions of *Slovo* 5.1 on gluttony, and self-qualifying *peroratio* at the close of the work. Both varieties of the *Ustav* hearken back to the end of Nil's career. One, the PDP type, represented by, among others, the early sixteenth-century codex associated with Dionisii (Eparkh. 351), and another from the 1550s or earlier and linked to Innokentii (KB 25/1102), logically places the table of contents, which omits the *Foreword*, at its end. This recension was published (with KB 25/1102 as the base) by Borovkova-Maikova in 1912, translated by von Lilienfeld, and Grolimund, and adapted by the recent pseudo-translators. The other, IRI type, found in perhaps the earliest extant full copy hailing

---

could nicely read aloud Nil's *Predanie* in the twenty minutes normally allotted scholarly convention presentations.

7. It is about 25% longer than Hesychius's *On Watchfulness*, and three times the size of Philotheus's similar treatise or Evagrius's *Praktikos*, but just one fourth the size of the unglossed *Ladder*.

from Sora (KB 89/1166), as well as Nil Polev's early 1500s codex (Eparkh. 349), less logically places the *Foreword*-lacking Table of Contents at its start.[8] It was published first by Evgenii and Amvrosii in 1822 on the basis of a Novgorod-Sofiia codex and recently, on the basis of KB 89/1166, by the Prokhorov/Shevchenko team with his modern Russian translation. My own hunch is that the more logical PDP type, found in codices associated with Innokentii and Dionsii, who at the time of Nil's death were probably further removed from the master's literary activity, represents an earlier, author's version, but that Sorsky also approved the IRI type, associated with his final collaborator, Nil Polev. Either way—and so far as the content is concerned, it surely does not matter—the work divides neatly into three parts of roughly 8200–10,700 words, the first two of which Nil clearly envisioned as such.

The first part deals with the combined struggles for stillness and against the *logismoi*. The middle-sized *Foreword*, proclaiming hesychasm as the only correct path for monks, is a balanced elucidation of faithful and adapted statements from eight named and at least four unnamed Church Fathers. The likewise middle-sized *Slovo* 1 divides into five equal sections, one each for a stage of *logismic* war as devised by Climacus and honed by Philotheus. In the roughly forty-eight-thousand-word *Slovo* 2, the, longest of any of Nil's pieces, Climacus's struggle stage segues into expositions taken, or

---

8. We still await a detailed, satisfactory analysis of the manuscript convoy of Nil's major writings. For a description KB 24/1102, see Borovkova-Maikova, NSPU, xxv–xxxii, and for the re-dating, Prokhorov, 'Poslaniia', 135; for the others (but no description of KB 89/1166), KTsDRIVM, 364–366, and Prokhorov, PNSIK, 94–95. His unexplained dating of the Eparkh. 349 *Ustav* pages, 17–83v, 1520s–1530s, contradicts the KTsDRIVM watermark dating for the entire codex (1480s–1514), as well as Kloss's analysis of the paper and the handwriting, indicating copying in Kirillov, not Iosifov: 'Nil Sorskii i Nil Polev', 155–156, 161–167. The initial 154 leaves of KB 89/1116, all by one hand, constitute an extended, theoretical treatise, which omits the regulatory *Predanie*, but contains the IRI-type *Ustav* (11–130) and the three Epistles (131–154v). The *Ustav* is preceded by three pieces: two attributed to Anastasius of Sinai 'Whence the Human Soul?' (1–9), and 'Whence Are Set in Motion Blasphemous and Improper Urges and Words?' (9–9v), the latter often found in codices with the *Ustav*, and 'From the *Patericon* on Thoughts' (10–10v). Elena Shevchenko is preparing a publication of this manuscript.

adapted, first from the more analytical Gregory the Sinaite, and then from the more poetic Isaac and Symeon and a sprinkling of other Fathers. From the summit of their vision, Nil concludes with a chastising exhortation, and a menu of practical choices. The medium-small *Slovo* 3 (750 words), half from Isaac, less from Gregory, discusses strengthening oneself for these combats through humility. This first part concludes with another medium-small item, *Slovo* 4–a set of instructions for the controlled life, whereby the course of the day provides logical sequencing of subjects.

The second part of the *Ustav*—chiefly *Slovo* 5, with the brief, summary *Slovo* 6—is Nil's mini-treatise on Orthodoxy's classical eight *logismoi*. Dependent in content upon over a dozen Fathers, *Slovo* 5 is mid-way in size between their brief treatment by Evagrius/Pseudo-Neilos and the much longer Cassian. The longest subsections, on pride, despondency, lust, and gluttony, are middle-sized discourses in themselves (between nine hundred and thirteen hundred words), while the others, on anger, vainglory, sadness, and avarice, are like the smaller *Ustav* items (some three hundred to five hundred forty words). All eight commence with a Cassian or Cassian-like gnomic principle, present some perfunctory analysis, and then proceed to remedial attitudes and actions. The use of liturgical prayer at the end of the generalizing *Slovo* 6 provides an implicit bridge to the third part.

Four substantial discourses of roughly fourteen- and twenty-five hundred words comprise the bulk of this final third of the *Ustav*. The first two (*Slova* 7–8), whose order recalls *Steps* 6–7 of Climacus's *Ladder*, concern two central preconditions of spiritual success, memory of death and mourning (the Classical *penthos*). The first of these is a unique sermon. After a set of authoritative aphorisms establish the need for such remembrance, Nil expounds on the need to think concretely about the known deaths of others and abstractly about the process of dying itself and the Terrible Judgment. He then closes with actual prayers of repentance. Besides Nil's gleaning from at least seven named Fathers, the discourse contains his most extensive use of the New Testament in any writing, and prayers from two Lives and at least two of the great liturgists. The more didactic *Slovo* 8 has four sections: the need for tears, the necessity to pray for them, how to pray for tears, and how tears can be acquired and lead one to the spiritual summit. Climacus, Isaac, and Symeon predominate, supplemented by four other hymnographer-poets. *Slovo* 9 on guarding the gains of mourning follows as another brief breather, taken mainly from Evagrius/Pseudo–Neilos with a mite from Climacus. This subject elevates us to near the top of the latter's ladder, and Nil concludes with two more hefty items also located at least partially there. *Slovo* 10 on detachment and deadness to the world begins with a selection from Pseudo-Macarius, moves to glossing a bit of Climacus and Pseudo-Symeon, and ends with a lot of Isaac. The final *Slovo* 11 on proper timing and spacing of one's monastic development links together Climacus's lowest and upper rungs, that is, the beginning of one's monastic life and the ultimate goal. Fortified by Gregory, Isaac, and (Nikon's) Barsanuphius, it completes the circle by closing with a summary of the most basic principles for living outlined in the *Predanie*.

Centrality of Sources

> . . . putting my hope in God's grace, I have dared to utter a fraction of the words of these holy and spirit-bearing writings, so that we at least somewhat recognize by what wretchedness we are enveloped . . . .[9]

Nil's admitted reliance on sources has posed a challenge to the editors of modern publications, translations, and pseudo-translations. Professor Fairy von Lilienfeld performed the yeoman's labor of love in tracing down a large percentage of his sources in their original Greek for her German translation, issued in 1963. Monk Vasileios Grolimond followed by identifying another bunch and supplying Greek originals in his eighty-seven printed pages of endnotes to the authentic writings. Sr. Sophia Jacamon, Enzo Bianchi, and Father George Maloney added several more. Meanwhile, first Professor Ihor Ševčenko's procurement—for my translation of Iosif—in 1973 of a microfilm of the 1795 printed edition

---

9. *Ustav* 2.45.

of the *Pandekty* and the *Taktikon* of Nikon of the Black Mountain, then the microfilm collection at the Hilandar Research library, and finally a week with Saint Petersburg manuscripts at the Russian National Library have enabled me to make another leap forward by examining the underlying Slavic translations of most of Nil's sources and avoiding hypothetical ones (those ubiquitous *cf.*'s in the notes), which do not appear in the Slavic. At this point–and more work remains for another scholar or two to undertake–we can be sure that over ninety per cent of the *Predanie* and at least fifty percent of the *Ustav* together are exact, adapted, metaphrased, or paraphrased expressions of Nil's monastic authorities—more, if one were to include his pedagogic glossing of them.

Quantitatively, so far as I have been able to ascertain by measuring text, Nil's authoritative 'big five' sources are, in descending order, Isaac the Syrian (9.6% of the *Ustav*), Nikon (71% of the *Predanie*), Gregory the Sinaite (9.1% of the *Ustav*), John Climacus (7.8% of the *Ustav*), and, taken together, the body of liturgical prayer (6.9% of the *Ustav*). Next, but far below, is Symeon/Pseudo-Symeon the New Theologian (3.1% of the *Ustav*) and Pseudo-Macarius of Egypt (2.1% of the *Ustav*).

Tabulating the number of times a name is specifically mentioned yields a somewhat different impression; 'the Fathers' (39), Isaac and Climacus (25), Gregory the Sinaite (15), Symeon the New Theologian (13), 'the saints' (12), Basil of Caesarea (10), the psalmist David (7), Barsanuphius of Gaza (6), Neilos the Sinaite and 'the Divine/holy Writings' (5), Philotheus (4), and Ephrem the Syrian, Hesychius, Macarius of Egypt, Peter Damaskenos, and the Hymnographer(s)—implying John of Damascus (3). Twice Nil names Anthony the Great, Arsenius the Great (once in the *Testament*), Daniel of Scetis, Dorotheus of Gaza, Pope Gregory the Great, John Chrysostom, Maximus Confessor, Nicetas Stethatos, and Thomais the Martyr. Agathon (a desert Father), Andrew of Crete, Diodochus of Photice, Eugenia the Martyr, Patriarch German of Constantinople, Mark the Ascetic, Symeon the Studite, Pachomius the Great, and Theodore the Studite appear once. Altogether we arrive at a total of thirty-two named authorities. The differences among the more frequently used and/or explicitly cited are partly explained by the brevity or gnomic quality of all of the Basil and many of the Climacus and Pseudo-Symeon. The writers whom Nil does not or in some cases cannot identify comprise a rather significant seven in Church and monastic history and letters: Athanasius of Alexandria, Evagrius of Pontus, Gregory of Nyssa, John Cassian, Nicephorus Monachus, Nikon of the Black Mountain, and Symeon Metaphrastes.

The two patristic elephants in the scriptorium whom Nil declined to mention, though they could not have been a secret to the better read, are Nikon and John Cassian.[10] The encyclopedic *Pandects* and *Taktikon* of the eleventh-century Byzantine presumptive ex-soldier and ceonobiarch, Nikon of the Black Mountain (located outside of Antioch), served as a major source book for Russian ecclesiastics of Nil's time.[11] Because both works were printed by Uniate Basilians in 1795 in the fourteenth-century Rus Church Slavic version and were available to me as a graduate student on a tourist visa in 1969 in the GPB (now RNB) Rare Books Room, it seems strange that no Nil scholar to date has noted that Nikon provided the textual basis for almost the entire *Predanie,* including half of its citations from others. Nikon also served at the source for Nil's rearrangement of the Climacus-Philotheus matrix for presenting the stages of 'mental combat',[12] for two of Nil's four identified citations from Barsanuphius, and, partially, for the conclusion to both the *Ustav* and the *Forewords*

---

10. Iosif made no secret of his reliance on Nikon, but like Nil concealed the phrases taken or adapted directly from Cassian: Cf. MRIV 4^B.14–15 (not identified there as a source); Cassian, *Institutes* 7.29–30, 12.31/PSW 1:82, 93; HM SMS 468.3:232–232v, 8:242v. A review of the relevant parts of Sof. 1435, a 15th century copy of the *Taktikon* from Kirillov, confirms the reliability for our purposes of the 1795 printed version.

11. MRIV, 62–63.

12. Climacus presents his six stages of the attack of the *logismoi* and then determines what penances apply in this manner: 1,2,3,4,5,6,1a,2a,3a,4a,5a,6a. Nikon rearranges this sequence to read 1,1a,2,2a,3,3a,4,5,5a,6,6a. In *Slovo* 1, Nil, following Philotheus, extracts the '4' (struggle), only to use it to commence *Slovo* 2, also keeps Nikon's structure, and then expands on 1a, 2a, 3a, 5a, 6a, and finally Climacus's 4: *Ustav* 1–2.2. Further on this, see Goldfrank, 'Nil Sorskii and Nikon of the Black Mountain'.

to the collection of lives. In addition, the cumbersome Nikon may be the model for Nil's more compact corpus commencing with a rule and continuing with discourses and epistles.

The role played by John Cassian (c. 360–435), the Latin acolyte of the Desert Fathers, is more limited. Books 5–12 of his influential *Institutes*, which cover the eight *logismoi*, were translated into Slavic from an abridged Greek version later printed in the *Philokalia*.[13] Then the Slavic 'Kassian Rimlianin' (*the Roman/Italian*) became Nil's source for the structure of *Slovo* 5 and for four percent of its text, including half of the lead statements.[14] Nil also may have found in other source(s) two of Cassian's original passages that were bypassed in the abridgement.[15]

> If the writings . . . of Abba Isaac the Syrian alone survived, they would suffice to teach one from beginning to end concerning the life of stillness and prayer.[16]

Whether Nil would have agreed with this twentieth-century characterization we shall never know, but he did mark Isaac as 'writing most sublimely',[17] and utilized him more than any other authority. Purged of what might be seen as any possible Nestorian or Monophysite taints, Issac's first large set of ascetic homilies and letters of this seventh century mystic passed close to their 'original' order into Greek around 800. Relative to this Greek version, the re-ordering of the standard Slavic translation from the fourteenth century—maybe by a Bulgarian disciple of Gregory the Sinaite—

---

13. *Pace* Maloney's educated guess that Nil and Innokentii 'most likely became familiar with Cassian's works while on Mt. Athos' (RH, 185), 'Kassian Rimliamin' was available in Russia at least by the early fifteenth century, as in Eparkh. 369: KTsDRIVM, 378. On the creators of the *Philokalia*, see Constantine Cavernos, *St Macarios of Corinth*, and *St Nicodemos the Hagiorite*.

14. *Pace* Maloney again (RH, 184), Nil certainly did use a version of Cassian that included the fifth and sixth *logismoi*: *Ustav* 5.5.62, 65, 5.6.67.

15. See under *Ustav* 5.3.55, 5.8.89.

16. Elder Ieronymos of Aegina (1883–1966), cited in HTM, Dedication page.

17. *Ustav* 2.29.

seems from the outside like the single clumsy shuffling of a deck of seventy-nine, with two dropped cards randomly inserted, since the essential order is retained in two sequences, even as the older Greek division into chapters expanded by twelve.[18] It is by far the longest of the single-authored books on monasticism in Slavic, and Nil must have known the work inside out, as he used parts of at least twenty-four of the ninety-one homilies and epistles. Isaac figures especially in Nil's super-long *Slovo* 2 on hesychastic prayer (one sixth of it), the substantial *Slova* 8 on mourning (one eighth) and 10 on detachment (three sevenths), and the shorter *Slovo* 3 on strengthening in stillness and combat (a full one half).

> *And this blessed one, encompassing the writings of all the spirit-bearing Fathers,* . . .[19]

Such is Nil's summation of the *Ustav*'s most important authority for hesychastic prayer, the master-teacher Gregory the Sinaite (*c.* 1263–1346), though his complete original corpus is rather skimpy

---

18. See HTM, lxxvii–cvx, which misses, so far as I can conclude from the sources listed here and my own very limited work with the printed Greek and translated Syrian: i) that a Slavic translation (A) with an order closer to the 'Ancient Greek', surviving in a MS lacking five discourses, precedes the standard Slavic (B), as in the MSS used for this translation of Nil; and ii) that the re-ordering of (B) relative to the 'Ancient Greek' is a simpler explanation than a hypothetical re-ordering relative to (A), but the re-clustering of discourses by dividing or combining indicates an independent influence of either (A) or its direct Greek protograph on (B): cf. the HTM 'Table of Homily Equivalences', cxiii–cxv, and the chart in Fedotova, M.S. 'K voprosu o slavianskom perevode postnicheskikh slov Isaaka Sirina', 505 (each with a few mistakes); also Alfeyev, *The Spiritual World of Isaac the Syrian*, 29-31. The HTM 'Ancient Greek' order appears in the Slavic version (with the an ★ after the two discourses not within either sequence) as 1–4, 9, 16, 18, 22–23, 26–29, 33–34, 39–40, 49, 53–57, 59–79, 5–7, 19★, 25★, 8, 10–15, 17, 20–21, 24, 30–32, 35–38, 41–44, 46–48, 58.

The 1770 Leipzig printed Greek version, underlying several modern translations and the footnotes one finds in the four authentic translations of Nil, represents an attempt at a systematic re-ordering by Nikephoros Theotokis. Dana Miller's splendid HTM English Translation utilized the original Syriac as well as the Greek and created another new ordering. The modern Russian translations since Paisii Velichkovsky retain the Slavic (B) order.

19. *Ustav* 2.14.

for such an important figure. It is comprised of his slightly philosophical, systematic, wide-ranging 137 *Acrostic Chapters* (so named from the first letters of each, which taken in order spell the extended title), a few appended *Further Texts* or chapters, three discourses on stillness, and perhaps one on the Transfiguration. The last is not in the Slavic corpus, but two of three recently discovered supplementary chapters to *Signs of Grace and Delusion* are.[20] Nil borrowed heavily from the *Chapters* 115 and 117 on humility, but more so from Gregory's two instructive discourses on prayer. This copying and adapting from more than half of their chapters produced the critical mass of Nil's initial instruction on hesychastic prayer (making for two sevenths of the extra large *Slovo* 2).[21]

We are climbing Jacob's Ladder

The enslaved and toiling chanters of African-American spirituals were not the first 'soldiers of the cross' to employ this image. Rather, the all-inclusive, systematically constructed *Ladder* of John Climacus (c. 579-649) is one of the few nominally single-authored books to survive in tact through the ages, with the amount of appended *scholia* to each 'Step' providing variety, at least in the Slavic MSS.[22] Containing countless metaphors and aphorisms, it served as a

---

20. Balfour, *Saint Gregory the Sinaïte. Discourse on the Transfiguration*, 109–113; the HM SMS 456 and the Eparkh. 351 versions are not identical with Balfour's Greek or each other; see also Anthony-Emil N. Tachaios, 'Gregory Sinaites' Legacy to the Slavs'.

21. Unlike Eparkh. 351 from Iosifov, neither of the Hilandar MSS, which contain the Slavic Gregory, have the concluding section of the second of these discourses with a passage adapted by Nil: see *Ustav* 11.6. Nil also credited Gregory for a brief *Philokalia* Pseudo-John of Damascus tract, traditionally attributed as well to Athanasius of Alexandria and Ephrem the Syrian: see, below, *Ustav* 1.3, 16; also PSW 2: 333.

22. L.P. Saenko claims three translations: an 11th-century Bulgarian, represented by four extant Rus witnesses of the 12th–14th c.; a second Bulgarian one brought to Rus by Metropolitan Kiprian in 1387 and subsequently predominating there; and a Serbian one represented by a Iosifov collection codex from the 1360s–1370s: 'K istorii slavianskogo perevoda teksta Lestvitsy', 21–22. My own source searches in the Serbian HM SMS 184 (c. 1500), the Iosifov Russian Eparkh. 331 (1505), and the mid-16th c. VMCh versions did not reveal essential differences.

treasure house of spiritual wisdom for more than one later monastic Father. Selections from fourteen of the Steps and the separate *Treatise for the Pastor* appear. In fact, Nil's 'discerning'[23] Climacus is the mostly widely utilized authority and figures both in the *Predanie* and in the entire *Ustav*, except for two brief discourses (3, 6) and maybe four of the *logismoi*. Climacus is especially important for establishing authority in the *Predanie* (via Nikon), structuring the combat against the *logismoi* (*Slovo* 1), fighting lust (*Slovo* 5.2, one-fourth of it), promoting remembrance of death (*Slovo* 8, one-sixth), and arguing for proper timing (*Slovo* 11, two-fifths).

And he speaks beautifully

So wrote Nil ambiguously about the Psalmist David or the tenth-century Constantinopolitan mystic Symeon the New Theologian,[24] but the standard Slavic 'Symeon' still awaits its scholar. For our purposes we need only note that everything which Nil attributes to Symeon, as well as some unattributed extracts, can be located in a typical Russian 'Symeon'.[25] This collection normally contains a) from the *Catechisms*: 2–4, 5 (second half),[26] 6, 8, and maybe 26 (less than a sixth of all of them); b) from the *Hymns*: Preface, 3, 4, 6, 7, 13, 14, 28, 36, 37, 43, 46, 47, 56 (less than a fourth of all of them); c) an alphabetic guide for neophytes; d) a set of 'little chapters'; and e) two Pseudo-Symeonic 'Discourses on Prayer', connected with the crystallization of the breath-control method. One of these is cited by the thirteenth-century Nicephorus Monachus ('The devil . . . obtained entrance'),[27] the other ('Three

23. *To German* 7.
24. *Ustav* 8.6.
25. In one place, though, Nil seemingly takes a few words from a brief passage omitted in the Slavic: *Ustav* 2.12, note 27. Descriptions of Slavic 'Symeons' can be found in Gorsky and Nevostruev, *Opsanie . . . Sinodal'nogo* 1.2.164: 434–441, and *Opisanie . . . Solovetskogo . . .* 1.271(793): 422–426.
26. This is the '*O ezhe kako podobaet prevbyvati inokom*', utilized by Iosif (MRIV: 4ᴮ.12/6.3, 8ᴮ.28/6.34), and incorrectly described in the MRIV Bibligraphy as a combination of *Catechisms* 5 and 26.
27. Within his *Watchfulness and Guarding of the Heart*, followed by Nicephorus's own instructions, PSW *Philokalia* 3: 203–206; HM SMS 468: 79–81; PG 147: 959–961.

Forms of Prayer' or 'The Three Attentions'), is a briefer redaction of Pseudo-Symeon's 'Method of Prayer and Attention', brought to light in the 1920s by Irénée Hausherr SJ, and not quite the same as the *Philokalia* version.[28] The genuine Symeon figures mainly in two places, where his poetic vision can shine: the ecstatic depiction of successful prayer,[29] and the necessity of tears for genuine contrition.[30] Pseudo-Symeon's hand is subtler, as often as not un-attributed. Nil kicks off the *Ustav* with Pseudo-Symeon's leitmotif of stillness, and does the same for the stages of combat (*Slovo* 1) and for detachment (*Slovo* 10). He also figures strategically in the instruction on prayer (*Slovo* 2). As a complete corpus, the Slavic 'Symeon' may also have served as a model for Nil's using hymns didactically.

The beginning of purity of soul is stillness (ἡσυχία)

Perhaps, by the definition of its time referring to *anchoritism*, that is, solitude,[31] rather than stillness, the polymath Basil the Great of Caesarea (*c.* 330–79) penned this dictum to a certain 'Comrade Gregory'. All the same, both Isaac the Syrian and Peter Damaskenos recognized an authoritatively useful aphorism when they saw one and cited it well before Nil snatched it up.[32] So maybe Basil ought not appear as a surprise coenobiarch 'sleeper' among the 'starting five' among Nil's named authorities. From the painstaking researches of Jean Gribomont OSB, it is clear that the Slavic *Asceticon* (*Postnicheskie slova*) of Basil (chiefly Pseudo-Basil, some would say) is essentially of the Studite-Athonite type, but without the *Moralia*. It contains *De judiciae Dei, De fide*, the famous 'Ascetic Discourse', and 'Another Ascetic Discourse', the 'Longer Rules', 'Shorter Rules', 'Constitutions', and both sets of 'Penances'. Without

---

28. Cf. Hausherr, 'La méthode d'oraison hesychaste'; PSW 4: 64–75; HM SMS 456: 133–144v; HM SMS 468: 79–84v.
29. *Ustav* 2.35–39.
30. *Ustav* 8.6–8, 10.
31. Meyendorff, L'hésychasme: problèmes de sémantique', 543.
32. *Ustav* 10.3 and note.

Gribomont's concordance charts for the 'Longer Rule' and especially the 'Shorter Rules', one will be lost trying to move from the enumeration in the Patrologia Graeca series, or translations based on it, to the Slavic recension.[33] Basil/Pseudo-Basil's contribution to Nil's works includes precepts for observing poverty, labor, and obedience in the *Predanie*; practices for combating the *logismoi*, such as seeking an experienced therapist for depression (extreme despondency); and the principle of prudence that commences the concluding discourse on proper timing.[34] The 'Ascetic Discourse', by way of Gregory the Sinaite, is the ultimate source for Nil's sought after 'reliable teacher' in the *Ustav*, is repeated in all three of his major letters, and is specifically referenced the incipit of that work to the more 'academic' bibliographer German.[35]

Nil's seldom-used authorities sometimes play essential roles where they do appear. They may be found in large single-authored works or in shorter compositions contained in the pre-philokalic miscellanies. Among the latter stand the short summary texts of Climacus's murky Sinaite successors Hesychius (perhaps 7th–9th c., confused by tradition with the fifth-century Hesychius of Jerusalem) and Philotheus (maybe 9th–10th c.).[36] Philotheus is essential for the revision of Climacus's scheme for the stages of 'mental' combat (*Slovo* 1) and for the presentation of control over daily life and regular following of prayer with remembrance of death.[37] Hesychius is pivotal in the transition from the struggle against *logismoi* to the struggle for prayer, and then in Nil's concluding the all-important *Slovo* 2 with four equally valid types of 'watchfulness' or 'mental activity,' of which only one is pure prayer.[38] Neilos, a third, earlier, Sinaite and the 'cover' for Evagrius of Pontus, the heretically-suspect originator of the 'eight *logismoi*', dominates the

---

33. Gribomont, *Histoire du texte des Ascétiques de S. Basile*, 1–39, 89–90, 172–77.
34. *Predanie* 17, 21, 26, 27, 39, 40; *Ustav* 5.1.20, 25, 5.2.46, 5.6.81, 8, 19, 11.1; see below, under III. 'Technical Terms', text to note 177.
35. *Ustav*, Fwd 14–15, *To Gurii* 17, *To Vassian* 16, *To German* 10.
36. *Ustav*, Fwd. 11: see PSW 3:15; Chryssavgus, *John Climacus*, 235.
37. *Ustav* 4.2, 7.2.
38. *Ustav* 2.5, 58.

brief *Slovo* 9 on guarding (two fifths).³⁹ Some of the *Centuriae* (collections of a hundred brief chapters) of the great mystic Maximus the Confessor (ca. 580–662) could also be found in the miscellanies, and Nil especially liked the epistrophic combination of two of the Psalmist's verses, which Maximus recommended as an antidote to sexual passion.⁴⁰

Nil turned a bit to six others whose books were available in Slavic translation. The *Discourses* of Dorotheus of Gaza (sixth century), sometimes not identified, lurk in the *Ustav* comments on the individual *logismoi*, especially in the insistence that one do no evil to a fellow human and his attacks on pride of place or talent.⁴¹ The *Dialogues* or *Italian Patericon* attributed to Pope Gregory the Great (r. 590–604) supplied Nil with a larder of horrible deaths to be recalled and with the parabolic exegesis on the story of Achsah and Caleb.⁴² The *Memorial to His Soul* or *Treasury of Divine Knowledge* of the mysterious twelfth-century Peter Damaskenos (we have no idea who he was, much less if he actually hailed from Damascus)⁴³ treated all sorts of subjects in its own mode of classifications, lists, and progressions. It furnished Nil with another modulation of Climacus's stages of mental combat, including an ingenious tongue-twister, and some links to Basil and 'Neilos the Sinaite' regarding detachment and timing.⁴⁴ Nil employed the *Sayings* of the Desert Fathers rather sparingly, maybe only four times on his own and once from Nicephorus/Pseudo-Symeon. Had Nil not gone beyond the initial A section, he could have acquired all of his authenticated apothegms from Anthony, Arsenius, and Agathon, the most artful being: 'Even if a wrathful man resurrects the dead, his prayer is unacceptable'.⁴⁵ A likely Kirillov, Slavic recension of Theodore the Studite's *Little Catechisms* provided

---

39. *Ustav* 9.3.
40. See below, text to note 106, and *Ustav* 5.2.34.
41. *Ustav* 5.4.57–58, 5.5.63–63, 5.8.93–94.
42. *Ustav* 7.11, 8.13.
43. Jean Gouillard, remarks that despite Peter's approximate dates, he betrays no influence of Symeon the New Theologian: 'Un auteur spirituel byzantin de XIIe siècle'.
44. *Ustav* 1.9, 13. 18. 24. 26, 2.2–3, 11.1–2, 11.11.
45. *Ustav,* Fwd 3, 2.56, 5.4.57, 5.6.82; *Testament* 3; *To Vassian* 7.

Nil with an incantation from the Psalms to be used against all urges.[46] Finally, the gilded lips and pen of the prodigious and textually ubiquitous John Chrysostom (357–407)—filling no less than sixteen PG volumes—ought not be absent here, but Grolimund's thorough search yielded only the source for part of one of two attributed citations: the superiority of charity over adorning churches (actually adapted by Nil out of Nikon) and a clever poetic commentary on life being 'less than a road'.[47]

This mystery over Nikon's and Nil's 'Golden-mouth' take us to the puzzling problem of the semi-recluse Barsanuphius of Gaza (d. c. 540), and his erotapocritical (Q & A) correspondence with his disciple John. It is not, to my knowledge, found fully translated in the medieval Slavic corpus. Two of Nil's adaptations of authentic passages, including an extended one on proper timing, are located in Nikon, and a third as a Hilandar miscellany fragment.[48] Another, and a reference cited with Gregory the Sinaite, are enigmatic even in the original, and another still, probably from an unidentified Slavic translation, Nil combines with the Jesus Prayer.[49]

The divinely-inebriated Pseudo-Macarius (to metaphrase Father Maloney) makes for a problem of a different order.[50] A passage first

---

46. *Ustav* 6.3. The manuscript convoy of these brief and elegant homilies appears in dire need of a thorough study: in the Slavic alone, we have at least three different 16th c. types: Gurii Tushin's KB 85/210 with 33 homilies, Sol. 269/1134 with 46, and Tr-S 178/1941 with 103. The catalogue titles and incipits indicate that Theodore's *Little Catechism* 91, which Nil utilized, is only in the briefest, first named (67v–69v): cf. *Opisanie . . . Solovetskago* 1: 409–419; *Opisanie . . . Troitskoi* 1: 161-170; German Podol'nyi's earlier catalogue of Kirillov codices also included a *Fedorь Studitь*, which could have been the one Nil read: Nikol'skii, *Opisanie* A.8: 72.

47. *Predanie* 31; *Ustav* 7.13; Grolimund (NSA 366, note 23). In one of his *Prosvetitel'* sections, as we have seen, Nil copied Iosif's adaptation from Chrysostom's sermons found in the Slavic *Margarit*, but that is a different matter: see above, II. 'The Unexpected Bedfellow'.

48. *Predanie* 22, *Ustav*, Fwd. 5, 11.4–5.

49. *Ustav* 2.22, 5.1.8, 5.6.74.

50. Maloney, *Intoxicated with God*, 6–9. Unless I missed something, the statement that pseudo-Macarius influenced Iosif's 'hesychastic themes', is a stretch: Iosif's reliance on 'Macarius' stems from the Desert tradition and deals with the all-monastic motifs of non-possession and charitable labor: MRIV 5[B].2, 9; 6.39.

identified as from the genuine Pseudo-Macarius's *On the Guarding of the Heart*, but actually from the Slavic version of the initially identical *Homily* 19, is virtually reproduced in Nil's first major paragraph on detachment and is found separately in the Slavic.[51] On the otherhand, Nil takes from Symeon Metaphrastes's *Paraphrase of Macarius* ('Pseudo-Pseudo-Macarius'?), the metaphor of the 'eleventh rung' for the master of stillness who descends to teach, and for several notions regarding the battle against grief and despondency.[52]

Mention of Metaphrastes directs us to the problem of prayer in the *Ustav*. Prayer, after all, is *the* subject of Nil's treatise, and prayers of various sorts—as remedy for a specific ill, as penitential plea, or as homily—constitute about thirteen percent of the entire text. Nil produces adaptations from Metaphrastes' final penitential prayer from his Life of Eustratius the Martyr, Gregory of Nyssa's similar one for his (and Basil the Great's) sister Macrina, and from available canons by or attributed to Andrew of Crete, John of Damascus, and Patriarch Germanus of Constantinople.[53] Included as well here are two genuine supplicatory passages attributed to Ephrem the Syrian, one a Lenten prayer, the other from a recension of the Slavic *Paranesis*, a collection over a hundred identified sermons from the Greek 'Ephraim', not all of which have yet been found in Syrian originals.[54] Ephrem's alleged semi-tongue-twister, cropped from Gregeory the Sinaite, is another unauthenticated enigma.[55]

---

51. *Ustav* 10.2: KB 29/1106: 111–116 = PG 34.19: 641D–650B (*On the Guarding of the Heart* 13 = *Hom.* 19.1-2): cf. von Lilienfeld NSSS, 342, and Grolimund, NSA 426–427. The Slavic version of a brief citation from Pseudo-Macarius, 'On the Freedom of the Mind' remains unidentified: *Ustav* 5.6.79, and the Slavic 'Macarius' also awaits its monographer.

52. *Ustav* 2.41–43, 5.5.62, 5.6.70–71.

53. *Ustav* 7.14, 16–20, 26–28, 8.1516, 19, and, probably, others not yet identified; for example, Germanus's canon is found not only in Eparkh. 347, which I have seen, but also Tr-S 165/1720, 207v–208: Egorova, 'Russkie asketitechsekie sborniki', 194. Independent of the music, the texts of the pre-modern Slavic Orthodox hymns as well require a thorough study, and presently a good number of Russian scholars are undertaking this labor.

54. *Ustav* 5.8.96, 8.17; Bojkovsky and Aitzetmüller published two recensions of the Slavic Ephrem with Greek originals, a German translation, a concordance to the Assemani publication, and an index of Slavic words: *Altbulgarische Übersetzung*.

55. *Ustav* 2.16; see below, note 127.

Finally, besides reproducing the words of others without giving credit, Nil refers to 'the Fathers' or, less often, 'the saints' or 'an elder', over forty times. Those so far identified vary in origin: Agathon,[56] Cassian,[57] Climacus,[58] Dorotheus,[59] Isaac,[60] Maximus,[61] Nicetas Stethatos,[62] Peter Damaskenos,[63] Pseudo-Symeon,[64] and Matthew the Evangelist—perhaps mediated.[65] Yet perhaps one need not identify all such sources, as Nil uses 'the Fathers' or 'the saints' to introduce, conclude, and gloss various topics.[66] In this he is following, by citing, Barsanuphius, Climacus, Gregory the Sinaite, Isaac, and Pseudo-Symeon, who likewise used this device.[67]

This, in brief, is the status of our knowledge of Nil Sorsky's sources. Undoubtedly, a fresh look at all of this by someone more expert in Scripture and the Orthodox and Slavic patristic tradition and especially liturgy, would yield another batch of his sources and provide some needed correctives to what we, building upon our predecessors' work, have presented here.

The Acolyte as Adapter

> Insofar as the saints, having struggled sensibly and mentally, worked in the vineyard of their hearts, and having cleansed their intellect of passions, attained the Lord, and acquired spiritual knowledge, they directed us . . . to draw living water from the spring of the Divine

---

56. *Ustav*, Fwd. 4 (via Nicephorus/Pseudo Symeon NT), 5.4.57.
57. *Ustav* 5.2.33, 43; *To Gurii* 3.
58. *Ustav* 5.1.6, 5.8.95, 7.10, 8.1, 11.10; *To Gurii* 9.
59. *Ustav* 5.4.58, 5.8.95.
60. *To Vassian* 5.
61. *Ustav* 5.3.50; *To Gurii* 3.
62. *Ustav* 5.2.49.
63. *Ustav* 1.3, 8.11.
64. *To Vassian* 8.
65. *Ustav* 5.2.29 (Mt 5:28).
66. *Ustav*, Fwd. 10, 12, 1.15, 1.23, 1.27, 1.28, 2.5, 2.57, 5.1, 5.3, 5.1.6, 5.1.15, 5.2.30, 5.2.44, 5.6.82, 5.8.88, 5.8.92, 5.8.99, 7.1, 7.11, 7.24, 8.9, 8.10, *To Gurii* 9.
67. *Ustav*, Fwd. 15, 1.1, 1.5. 2.1, 2.3, 2.22, 2.26, 10.1, 11.4.

Writings, which are able to quench the passions that sear us and instruct us in all true knowledge.⁶⁸

The reader may have noticed that the lexeme 'adapt' continuously appears in the foregoing section. Indeed, Nil rarely copied, and his sources would have informed him by example that that was not necessary. For example, within a couple of printed pages, Gregory the Sinaite reproduces the same Gospel citation in three different ways.⁶⁹ So Nil would not have felt under any obligation to be precise in reproducing such words. In fact, more than once he had no compunction adapting a citation to produce a meaning different from the author's actual intent, but nothing objectionable for an Orthodox monk. Using Dorotheus's words that all ascetics must endure afflictions, Nil specifies this virtue for neophytes.⁷⁰ He may not have known about Heraclitus's adage about the impossibility of stepping in the same river twice, since 'everything flows', but he was quite comfortable in treating his sources as 'living water' to be mixed with other sacred verbal substances and cooked in his own way.

Moreover, as he explicitly pointed out regarding Symeon's manipulation of Climacus and the psalmist David,⁷¹ Nil liked to blend together different texts of one or more authors. One of his paragraphs on endurance, where he combines from Gregory the Sinaite's related *On Stillness and Two Modes of Prayer* (cap. 14), and *Sitting at Prayer* (cap. 1) is a fine illustration. If Greek letters represent the former, and Roman the latter, then Nil's order of Gregory's original word clusters runs as follow: a-b-ζ-η-e-d-c-β-α-γ/g-δ/h.⁷² A similar analysis solves a dilemma flagged by George Maloney, when, using English translations, he made a comparison of the Greek of one of Nil's sources and his purported 'Slavonic

---

68. *Ustav*, Fwd. 16.
69. *Stillness and Two Modes* 14, 15; *Sitting at Prayer* 1: PG 150: 1328A–1329A: cf. Mt 11:12, Mk 10:24; this, of course, is not so different from the Bible itself, as these two citations illustrate.
70. *Predanie* 24.
71. *Ustav* 8.8.
72. *Ustav* 2.16, and notes.

citation' in an attempt to show, by a rational process of elimination, 'that Nil used the Slavonic text rather than that of the Greek'.[73] Here, in fact, Nil uses not only two of Gregeory's texts, but commences with one Pseudo-Symeon expression and concludes with another—all, apparently, from the available Slavic.[74] In another instance, as if restoring the original Climacus, Nil modifies Gregory's adaptation of the former, adds from another of Gregory's text, and glosses it with Pseudo-Symeon, grammatically adapted.[75]

Nil's adaptive amalgamating extended to the realm of supplications. In recommending a penitential prayer, he played footloose and fancy free with the words, if not the emotions, of established chants. Anyone who knew the Slavic corpus of hymns—and it would have been impossible for a well-trained monk not to know them—could see how Nil created variations on previous composers themes (which is what these a capella songsters seem have done too).[76]

The total of Nil's some two dozen integrations of two or more texts—undoubtedly more remain to be identified—include, besides those mentioned so far, three or four of Isaac together,[77] similarly three of Symeon,[78] two or three of Climacus;[79] Climacus paired with Gregory the Sinaite,[80] with Isaac,[81] with Symeon (sort of),[82] with Peter Damaskenos,[83] and with Nicetas Stethatos;[84] Metaphrastes's Macarius paired with John Cassian[85] and possibly with Isaac;[86] Pseudo-Symeon paired with Hesychius;[87] Dorotheus

---

73. Maloney, RH, 178–179 (both translations faulty); Slavonic source found in Arkhangel'skii, *Nil Sorskii i Vassian Patrikeev*, 180, note 46.
74. *Ustav* 2.12, and notes.
75. *Ustav* 2.14, and notes.
76. *Ustav* 7:13–4, 16, 18–9, and notes.
77. *Ustav* 8.27, and notes.
78. *Ustav* 2.35–39, and notes.
79. *Ustav* 8.26, and notes.
80. *Ustav* 5.2.40, and notes.
81. *Ustav* 7.7, and notes.
82. *Ustav* 8.8, and notes.
83. *Ustav* 11.2, and notes.
84. *Ustav* 5.7.85–86, and notes.
85. *Ustav* 5.5.62, and notes.
86. *Ustav* 2.43, and notes.
87. *Ustav*, Fwd. 1, and notes.

paired with Cassian, and also with Anthony the Great via the *Apophthegmata*;[88] and Andrew of Crete triangulated with Metaphrastes's Eustratius and Gregory of Nyssa's Macrina.[89] Finally, in presenting the five stages of 'mental combat', Nil creates various combinations of Climacus, Philotheus, Nikon, Peter Damaskenos, Pseudo-John of Damascus/Pseudo-Gregory the Sinaite, and maybe Isaac.[90] Such was Nil's conscious, didactic, and artful pick and mix from the available ascetic salad bar.

Nil's sense of liberty extended to editing his sources as circumstances might dictate. To create an appropriate penitential prayer, he added Andrew of Crete's 'knowingly and unknowingly' to Macrina's (really Gregory of Nyssa's) confessed sins, and deleted 'for these physical torments are pleasure for your slaves' from Metaphrastes' Eustratius.[91] Elsewhere Nil converted Dorotheus's simple 'God, help my brother and me by his prayers' into the quasi-formulaic quasi-Jesus Prayer: 'Help Lord, my brother so-and-so (*imiarek*), *and by his prayers have mercy on me, a sinner*'.[92] And again, by tweaking Gregory the Sinaite's 'this order is excellent' into 'every measure is excellent', Nil underscored the paradox of Gregory's instruction that the uninitiated in stillness 'sing a lot and without measure'.[93] Finally, he either knew of the Greek original or could sniff a sloppy translation, when he replaced *smyslъ* (mind) with the hesychastic-technical term *umъ* (intellect) in Philotheus's dictum regarding nighttime prayer.[94]

Literary Devices

> For Climacus says, as though from the face of vainglory and pride: 'If you reproach yourself often before God, you have reduced us to cobweb'.[95]

---

88. *Ustav* 5.5.62–63, and notes.
89. *Ustav* 7.26–29, and notes.
90. *Ustav* 1.2–16 *passim*, and notes.
91. *Ustav* 7.28, and notes.
92. *Ustav* 5.4.58, and notes.
93. *Ustav* 2.25, and notes.
94. *Ustav* 2.51, and notes.
95. *Ustav* 5.8.97.

With these few words, Nil showed that he understood dramatic personification and indirect speech. Indeed, he is explicit or nearly so about more than a dozen other devices that didactic writers employ, such as the topic sentence and organization,[96] summary paragraphing,[97] categorization,[98] specification by differences[99] and types,[100] gnome,[101] simile-metaphor-metonymy (not strictly distinguished),[102] analogy,[103] parable (and hence allegory),[104] exegetical synecdoche,[105] repetition combining anaphora and epistrophe,[106] shift of address,[107] kerygma,[108] and recourse to authority.[109]

It goes without saying that Nil also knew such standard tricks of the homiletic trade as hyperbole, pathos, oraculum, commencing with a biting dictum, and the interweaving of the bad spell of damnation for unrepentant sinners with the Gospel of salvation for the faithful. The best example may be his sermon on the recollection of death (*Slovo* 7), which begins with principles, peaks with fearful graphic descriptions, and ends with supplications. As for devices, he likes polyptoton such as *umъ blagochestvivymъ razumomъ*[110] and *novoiavlenie . . . umu obъiavliaushchsia*,[111] and homoiophony—as in *obrashchaetsia . . . otvrashhaetsia*[112] and *privoditi . . . prěvoditi*.[113] He

---

96. *Ustav* 10.10.
97. *Ustav* 4.11.
98. *Ustav* 10.5.
99. *Ustav* 1, 5 (titles), and 5.1.18, 21 (sub-section headings).
100. *Ustav* 5.1.
101. *Ustav*, Fwd. 3.
102. *Ustav*, Fwd. 3, Fwd. 6, 2.32, 8.23.
103. *Ustav* 11.3.
104. *Ustav* 2.42, 8.13, 9.4.
105. I.e., the part stands for the whole, or the inverse: *Ustav* 10.7.
106. *Ustav* 11.2: *anaphora*—repetition at the beginning; *epistrophe*—at the end; also Maximus as in *Ustav* 5.2.34; cf above, text to note 38.
107. *Ustav* 5.2.36–38.
108. I.e., a Gospel-like proclamation: *Ustav* 7.7.
109. *Ustav* 8.8.
110. *Ustav* 1.23: *an intellect with pious intellection/knowledge.*
111. *Ustav* 1.2: *a new manifestation . . . manifesting itself to the intellect; polyptoton:* lexeme or root repetition.
112. *Ustav* 1.23: *is/is found . . . turn away.*
113. *Ustav* 5.2–3: *introduce . . . transduce/transform.*

occasionally uses ellipses;[114] employs ambiguously enigmatic hypallage—'it is the art/cunning of the Devil's evil';[115] and he talks about prayer with a polyptotonically prefaced common liturgical expression: . . . *vědiashche izvěstno iako vsegda s nami estь*.[116] This is just the tip of his stylistic iceberg.

Nil displays so much varied metaphrasis that one might suspect that he, formally or informally, studied or even taught it. He edits circularity out one of Climacus's definitions,[117] and creates internal rhyme in another.[118] He modifies and combines Gospel phrases and inserts *sъgrěsheniikhъ* (*of transgressions*) to provide an antimetabole for the parallel clauses of a fused version of the Saviour's celebrated pronouncements: *ashche ne ostavite bratu otъ serdetsь vashikhъ sъgrěsheniikhъ, i Otetsь nebestnyi ne ostavitь vamъ segrěshenii vashikhъ*.[119] Hardly original in this respect, Nil gives patristic models of some of these devices. For example, in repulsing lust, Maximus the Confessor combined two related Septuagint psalms displaying epistrophe and parallelism: *Izgoniashchii mia / nyne obydosha mia / radosti mia / izbavi mia / otъ obyshedshikhъ mia*.[120] Gregory the Sinaite twice used Climacus's 'Whip the warrior with Jesus' name, for there is no sturdier weapon than this on heaven or earth', once with a reversal, and then Nil combines these two with his own further reversal and minor changes.[121] Gregory also reversed himself in speaking of 'the two brutal and most burdensome passions, lust and despondency' to 'despondency, it is said, and lust', and Nil then reverses the imitated mode.[122]

---

114. *To Gurii* 13, 16.
115. *Ustav* 3.1, 5.6.80; *hypallage*: reversal of expected word relations.
116. *Ustav* 4.3.: . . . *knowing with certainty that he* (God) *always is with us*.
117. *Ustav* 1.24.
118. *Ustav* 2.55.
119. *Ustav* 5.4.56 and notes: *If you do not, from your hearts, forgive your brother of transgressions, neither will the heavenly Father forgive your transgressions:* cf. Mt 6:15, 18:35; *antimetabole:* reversed repetition.
120. *Ustav* 5.2.34 and notes: *Those pursuing me have now surrounded me, joy of mine: deliver me from those who have surrounded me.*
121. *Ustav* 2.40.
122. *Ustav* 5.6.76.

Such reversals of words or phrases constitute one of Nil's metaphrastic signatures, which he accomplishes in far too many ways to present here. They range from simple *b-a* and *c-b-a* switches[123] to a combination of stylistically kindred passages with word inversion,[124] to an *e-c-d* switch within a tongue-twister created by the Slavic translator of Peter Damaskenos.[125] Nil also knows how to breviloquate and improve alliterative parallelism[126] and to craft syllabically ascending polyptotonic alliteration.[127] Simply stated, Nil has a great ear: *slyshanie sъkrushaetъ slyshashchikhъ serdtsa*, he takes from the Slavic Isaac,[128] and writes to Vassian Patrikeev: *blagodateiu Bozheiu budeshi blagoderzostenъ*.[129]

Technical Terms

Insofar as many of the holy Fathers spoke of the 'action of the heart', 'mental preservation' and the 'guarding of the intellect' in different dialogues, just as each of them was instructed by God's grace, with the same knowledge, having first received the word from the Lord himself, who said: 'Out of the heart proceed evil thoughts and defile man'; . . . .[130]

Nil's very first words in the *Ustav*, adapted from Pseudo-Symeon and Hesychius, articulate the dilemma of terminological incon-

---

123. Many examples of the former, *Ustav* 1.6 for the latter.
124. *Ustav* 5.5.62.
125. *Ustav* 1.26: Peter Dam. (Serbian recension): *Ashte bo bi se bylo, ne byshe bezsvrъshennaago bestrastiia*, . . . ; Nil: *Ashte bo se bylo by, ne bysha bezsъvrshenago bestrastia*, ...
126. *Ustav* 2.55 and notes—Climacus: *Mnogoslovie oubo mnogazhdy vъ molitvě oumъ vъzmechstvi razlia; edinoslovie zhe mozhitseiu oumъ sъbira mozhetъ*; Nil: *Mnogoslovie bo mnozhitseiu umъ rastochii vъ molitvě; maloslovie mnozhitseiu sъbra*.
127. *Ustav* 2.16 and notes: Gregory Sin.: *Bolěznь boli bolězno*; Nil: *Boli bolěznь bolězneno*.
128. *Ustav* 10.14, and notes: *whose hearing crushes the heart of the hearers.*
129. *To Vassian* 10: *by the good grace of God you shall be goodly bold.* For further elaboration on Nil's style, see Goldfrank, 'Literary Nil Sorskii'.
130. *Ustav*, Fwd. 1; Gospel citation from Mt 15:19.

sistencies in our sources, not to say in their translation. Nil's word wizardry may have been a pedagogically useful form of what Nancy Partner called 'serious entertainment',[131] but the issue of combating demonic forces was too crucial to leave to verbal vagary. He not only preached ethics, for which every-day speech might suffice, but needed to rise above the quotidian to enlighten his educated followers. Following Gregory the Sinaite and other monastic Fathers, Nil operated within the Aristotelian conceptual world of Porphyry's *Eisagoge* and the *Dialectica* of John of Damascus, with their emphasis upon definitions, distinctions, linkages, and operational forces.[132] Nil used the word *measure* (μέτρον—also meaning degree of advancement and limit—no less than twenty-three times in the *Ustav*, and *sila* (δύναμις, that is, objective physical or spiritual *power* or *force*,[133] be it human, natural, or divine) at least thirty-five times. Moreover, as von Lilienfeld's numbered notes to her translation have already shown, Nil utilized quite effectively the ready-made Slavic equivalents of the Greek spiritual vocabulary.[134] Any interested reader might also consult the glossaries at the back of each of the four volumes of the PSW *Philokalia* for a dynamic analysis of the Greek originals of these and other essential words used by the theorists and practitioners of stillness.

---

131. Nancy Partner, *Serious Entertainments. The Writing of History in Twelfth-Century England* (Chicago: University of Chicago Press, 1977).

132. The issue of Nil's underlying epistemological premises goes well beyond this study. Suffice to say that the Sinaite tradition, starting with the Climacus, and well-expressed in Gregory's *Acrostic Chapters*, is permeated with classifications and ontological connections. Nil himself may have been original in applying the notion of 'differences' explicitly to foods and bodies in his discussion of gluttony (*Ustav* 5.1.18–26). For the modeling from Climacus, see *To German* 7. Robert Romanchuk is to be commended for raising this interesting problem. He states, regarding Nil's works, that he 'assimilated a sophisticated body of ascetic-philosophical thought' (email to H-EARLY SLAVIC@H-NET.MSU.EDU, 6 Aug. 2006).

133. The Old Slavic translators employed *krěpostь* for ἰσχύς = *strength, fortitude*, and *vlastь* for ἐξουσία = *authority*.

134. NSSSS: her lettered notes indicate sources.

Pomyslъ (λογισμός), a noun Nil employed in the *Ustav* maybe one hundred seventeen times,[135] a third more than any other, stands as the most difficult of all of these terms to translate. Occupying a privileged position in ascetic psychological analysis, some species of this thought-urge-intent-spirit-passion-image-temptation genus constantly attacks any believer from without or threatens to do so. With the crystallization of organized Christian monasticism arose the 'eight principle *logismoi*' of the East and then the analogous 'seven deadly sins' of the West.[136] But *logismoi* are not only evil. As Nil sees things, one should convert, contradict or replace a wicked *logismos*, such as despondency, with a good one, such as memory of death.[137]

Why classical Christian ascetics employed a *log-* lexeme and an equivalent of *reasoning* for this dynamic notion is an interesting question in itself, but the problem of what to do with the tentative Slavic *po-* prefix[138] and the *mysl-* = *thought/mind* root, which together carry the notion of an attempt, can torment the rigorous English translator seeking exact equivalents. Having consulted with scholars far more learned and able than I in these matters, I have decided to go with *urge,* which only once is used for the capacity to receive an urge from without or to generate one from within.[139] Otherwise *pomyslъ* is almost exclusively and unambiguously an urge. This frees up the more common translation, *thought* (*Gedanke, pensée, pensiero*), to be shared by two other *mysl-* derivatives, *pomyshlenie* and *myslъ*.

Hesychius, perhaps inspired by John Cassian, had already capitalized on the seeming proximity of the Gospel's διαλογισμός (*calculation, argument*), which exits the heart, to λογισμός, and the

---

135. In one identified place in Nil only, does a translator, here of Isaac, use *pomysly* (acc. pl.) instead for διαλογισμούς (here, *thoughts/urges 'of the soul'*): *Ustav* 2.32: for this Greek word, see below, text to note 140.
136. Hausherr, 'L'origine de la théorie orientale des huit pèches capitaux.'
137. *Ustav* 5.2–4, 5.6.69–70, 7.8.
138. In private conversations, my Russian Department colleague, Prof. Olga Meerson, insisted on the privileging of the prefix in Russian and especially Church Slavic.
139. *Ustav* 10.7.

Slavic translator(s) obliged by employing *pomyshlenie* for the former.[140] Among Nil's sources, translators also found *pomyshlenie* ideal for Hesychius's ἔννοια (*cogitation, act of thinking*), Hebrews' and Climacus's ἐνθύμημα (*reasoning, argument*), and Evagrius's νοήματα (in pl., *perceptions, ideas*).[141] *Thinking* might work as a common denominator in Old Russian, but as Nil himself utilized *pomyshlenie* eight other times,[142] four in the formula *word(s), deed(s), and thought(s)*, convention and consistency converge on *thought* as the best translation—but a thought that urges, no doubt.

Myslь, which in the Old Slavic translation of Isaac may be used for both διάνοια (*thought, mind, intention*) and ἔννοια, covers the act of thinking or even the organ of thought, besides generic *thought*.[143] The Slavic Peter Damaskenos treated the *pomyslъ* as something to be opposed by a type of *myslь*,[144] and the most frequent use of the latter in the *Ustav* comes precisely in the sections this Peter most influenced.[145] To complicate matters for us, though, Isaac's Slavic translator(s) also rendered διάνοια as *sъmyslъ* (*thought, mind, reason, intelligence* in Old Russian, *meaning* in the modern language) in four passages taken by Nil.[146] The translator of Patriarch Germanus's τῶν φρενῶν (gn. pl. of φρήν = *mind*) chose the same Slavic word, and Nil himself used it up to six times.[147] As *thought* always works for *myslь,*, and *mind* for *sъmyslъ*, we shall default to these two common English words.

---

140. *Ustav*, Fwd. 1. The Vulgate Mt 15:19 has *cogitationes* for διαλογισμοί, so Nil's sense of *pomysъ* may have been narrower than Cassian's of *cogitatio*.
141. *Ustav* 2.58, 7.3, 1.20, 9.3.
142. In the formula, *Ustav* 4.1, 7.24, 28, 29; elsewhere 5.2.28, 6.4, 8.22, 9.6.
143. *Ustav* 2.29-30, 33; 5.3.
144. HM SMS 454: 149-150, not always a precise equivalent of the Greek: *Treasury*, 207-208; φκ 3: 109.
145. *Ustav* 1.4, 8, 12, 16, 18, 19, 21; 2.3, 5.3. Nil also used *myslь* in *To Vassian* 3, *Sobornik, Postscr.* 1, and, from Climacus's ἔννοια (here, *thought* of death), in *Ustav* 5.8.85, where one early MS goes beyond Nil's normal use of *pomyslъ* and substitutes it for *myslь*.
146. *Ustav* 3.5 (twice), 5.8.98, 10.14, 10.15.
147. *Ustav* 2.6. 3.4 (twice), 4.6, 7.9, 8.7, 8.16 (from Patriarch Germanus); on φρήν, see below, note 162.

What about the *mysl-* adjective? Himself characterizing stillness as *myslenoe děanie* (or some lexical sibling) six times,[148] Nil freely employs *myslen-* as an adjective or adverb twenty-seven times. Only six of these stem identifiably from translated sources: once from Isaac's τῆς διανοίας[149] (*of the mind*), but the other times from νοῦς- adjectives which the PSW *Philokalia* translators would sometimes render simply as *noetic*.[150] The Slavic, however, requires that we use *mental*.

Now to *umъ*. As νοῦς in this literature specifically means *intellect*, the Slavic translators' choice of the *mysl-* root instead of *um-* for these adjectives indicates a degree of lexical flexibility with monastic phrenology. However, in the literature of stillness consulted by Nil, νοῦς—one of the two foci in the practice of stillness—is always *umъ*,. Nil used this word eighty-eight times in the *Ustav*, as well as once in the *Predanie*. At least fifty of these derived directly from twelve of his sources: Agathon, Pachomius in his Life, Pseudo-Macarius, Evagrius/Neilos, Climacus, Isaac, Philotheus, Hesychius, a Hymnographer, Symeon, Pseudo-Symeon/Nicephous, and Gregory the Sinaite—a spectacular, saintly baker's dozen if we include the Apostle Paul, who will 'pray in the spirit . . . and pray in the intellect'.[151]

Two more key words for Nil are inexorably entangled with *umъ*: one lexically—*razumъ*—and one functionally—*serdtsa*. In modern Russian *razumъ* (since the 1917–1918 orthography reforms written without the ъ) is a virtual synonym of *um* used as *intellect, mind*, but leaning also toward *reason*. It served different functions in the translated medieval literature, however, and pinning it down as Nil used it is difficult. Twice in the Slavic Isaac borrowed by Nil and also in a passage from Basil employed in all three Epistles, *razumъ* (γνῶσις), that is, *knowledge,* sometimes *deep and divine knowledge (gnosis)*.[152] In

---

148. *Ustav*, Fwd, Title, 3,5; 2.58 (twice), 4.11.
149. *Ustav* 8.3.
150. τοῦ νοὸς, τοῦ νοῦ, τοῦ νοος (*sic!*), νοητός, -ῶς: *Ustav*, Fwd. 1, 3, 6; 1.1, 1.6, 8.3.
151. *Ustav*, Fwd. 2, from 1 Cor 14:15, via Gregory the Sinaite.
152. *Ustav* 1.6, 3.2; *To Vassian* 16, *To Gurii* 16, *To German* 6.

another from Isaac, it is σύνεσις, meaning *wisdom, intelligence, science, knowledge*.[153] But in phrases from Climacus, Evagrius and Pseudo-Macarius, *razumъ* translates σκοπός, *aim, intention*.[154] Forced to be arbitrary here, I have decided to use *knowledge*, wherever possible. Where, however, *razumъ* is coupled with *umъ*, I may employ the lexical derivative *intellection*, and I also use *intent*, where it makes sense to do so. This frees *wisdom* for *mudrostь* (σοφία, φρόνησις) and allows *supreme wisdom* for *premudrostь*,[155] while their lexical cousin *mudrovanie* (φρόνησις in a Basil citation), gets *prudence*, except where the more neutral *reasoning* makes sense,[156] all of these finely fitting their specific frameworks.

Serdtsa (*heart*), found maybe seventy-three times in the *Ustav*, is simple to translate and fascinating to analyze, because the heart does not merely serve with the intellect as the other central focus of stillness. Just as the emotional side of normal people is much more basic to their character and life, and hence their prayer, than is the intellectual, so the interplay of the metaphorical and physiological in the turns of speech Nil borrows or creates concerning the heart is far more colorful than what relates to the intellect. The Psalms supplied the 'contrite and humble heart'; Proverbs, the 'lofty of heart; the Apostle Peter, the 'secret man of the heart';[157] *Hebrews*, 'thoughts of the heart'; and the Gospels, the heart that can physically become 'burdened' from gluttony, commit adultery, hold and release thoughts, and forgive.[158] From Isaac the heart is the 'guardian of urges', in which 'sweetness boils' and then can flow 'over the entire body'.[159] From Gregory the Sinaite, 'prayer of the heart'—or is it 'prayer working in the heart'—is 'the wellspring of all good', and 'pain of the heart born in piety suffices . . . for cheer'.[160] Ephrem prays for tears 'for the illumination of

---

153. *Ustav* 3.2.
154. *Ustav* 9.2–3, 10.2.
155. *Ustav,* 10.17, *To Gurii* 10.
156. *Ustav,* Fwd 14, 3.7, 9.6, 10.2 (thrice, from Basil), *To Vassian* 16.
157. *Ustav* 5.2.28, 5.8.89, 8.6; *To Gurii* 2.
158. *Ustav,* Fwd 1, 5.1.6, 5.2.29, 5.4.56, 7.3 (Hb 4:12); cf. Jr 31:33, 2 Cr 3:3.
159. *Ustav* 2.25, 2.33, 8.26.
160. *Ustav* 2.13, 2.21, 2.24.

his heart'.[161] Nil, maybe on his own, speaks of the heart's memory, recollections, and capacity to will; he compares the heart to a 'vineyard where one works; and he wishes that Gurii's heart be 'not a path or a stone or a thorn', but a 'blessed land' producing 'many a double crop for the salvation of the soul'.[162]

The *Ustav*'s first words, cited at the beginning of this section, pose the problem of different terms meaning the same thing—a problem, which Nil, following Hesychius, tried to solve by equating *dělanie mysleno (mental activity* or *praxis)* with *trezvěnie* (νῆψις)– also a requirement for all monastics. Hesychius posits four types of *trezvěnie*, from which the individual may select his or her focus: guarding against the assaults of urges, praying with the heart 'silent to urges', summoning Christ to one's aid, and keeping memory of death,[163] this last one presumably with concomitant mournful penitence. *Sobriety*, the classical definition of νῆψις, works perfectly well here, but we shall privilege *watchfulness*—the preferred rendition of the PSW *Philokalia*.

As a technical term, *praxis* may seem better than *activity* for the equivalent of a spiritual exercise, but as Nil's frequent use of *dělanie* equates with πρᾶξις (in this narrower sense),[164] ἐργασία (work, labor),[165] and κόπος (labor, toil),[166] most of this being spiritual, *activity* works best. Nil's use of the related *děistvo*, the ἐνέργεια of Climacus, Philotheus, Isaac, and Gregory,[167] is always *operation* and

---

161. *Ustav* 8.17.
162. *Ustav.* Fwd 16, 4.10, 7.9, 7.25; *To Gurii* 17; cf. Nil Polev's inscription, cited here opposite the title page. An anthropologist focusing on the Ancient Greek φρήν, which could mean the feeling/thinking/emotive heart as well as the mind (the essential Byzantine definition given by Sophocles, 1152), might balk at any attempt so to distinguish. As the sentence at the start of this section indicates, Nil, following his Pseudo-Symeonic source, analytically dismissed the heart-mind dichotomy.
163. *Ustav,* 2.58–59 and notes.
164. *Ustav,* Fwd. 7 (Philotheus), 14, 2.23 (Gregory); the related *děianie* also translates Isaac's πρᾶξις.
165. *Ustav*, Fwd 5 (Barsanuphius), 13, 2.15 (Hesychius, Nicephorus/ Pseudo-Symeon), 2.52 (Isaac), 11.6 (Gregory).
166. *Ustav*, Fwd. 3 (Agathon/Nicephorus), 6 (Isaac).
167. *Ustav,* Fwd. 7, 2.15, 32, 11.8, also 2.26 in verb form, and, independently, 4.11, 8.26.

always in relation to prayer. Replacing Isaac's *joys of the Spirit* with *operation of the Spirit*,[168] may even indicate some second-hand Palamite influence, but, Nil, even if he actually knew any of Gregory Palamas's writings on 'physics' and other matters, steered clear of them.[169]

Two more sets of terms demand our attention, as Nil consciously chose to use them in their order sanctified by tradition: the five stages of mental warfare and the eight urges.[170] The stages of battle, first articulated by John Climacus in his chapter ('step') on sexuality,[171] use the language of rape or seduction for the mental preliminaries which one must cut off, preferably from the start:

assault	*prilogъ*	προσβολή
coupling	*sъchetanie*	συνδυασμός
consent	*slozhenie*	συγκατάθεσις
captivation	*plĕnenie*	αἰχμαλωσία
passion	*strastь*	πάθος

Coupling, explained here as simple conversing, can just as easily be *copulating* or *intercourse,*[172] and *captivation*—just as readily *captivity.* One translator from the Greek even used *the state of seduction or captivity* for ἡ αἰχμαλωσία.[173] Since the issue here is mind warfare, I prefer the less carnal term where possible.

---

168. *Ustav* 8.26.
169. Palamas's strict distinction between God's 'energies' (i.e., operations), accessible to human participation, and God's inaccessible essence is an altogether different approach from Nil's adapted passage from the poetic Symeon the New Theologian's: . . . *my essence combines with your* [God's] *nature,* cited at the start of the next section, not to say Symeon's original: cf. Gregory Palamas, *Topics* 111, PSW *Philokalia* 4: 397; PG 150: 1197AB, and Symeon NT, *Hymns* 7: 28–29; SC 156: 211.
170. Cf. von Lilienfeld, NSSS 204, 221.
171. *Ladder* 15.74; PG 88: 896C–897A.
172. Izwolsky (p 96) chose *conjunction*; the PSW *Philokalia* translation of Peter Damaskenos (3: 207), and the Liubheid/Russel Climacus (p182) used *coupling*; the Lazarus Moore *Ladder* (p 157) employed *intercourse*; Maloney tried *intercourse of conversation* in RH (p 80) and then *dialoguing* in his 'translation' (pp 50–51).
173. Peter Damaskenos, *Treasury,* PSW 3: 207; φκ 3: 109. The others in the preceding noted chose *captivity,* except for Izwolsky's *enslavement.*

From among the urges, given here in genitive or adjectival form, the first four and last two are easy and self-explanatory:

gluttony	chrevoobьiastnyi	τῆς γαστριμαργίας
fornication	bludnyi	τῆς πορνείας
avarice	srebroliubnyi	τῆς φιλαργυρίας
wrath	gněvnyi	τῆς ὀργῆς
sadness	pechalьnyi	τῆς λύπης
despondency	unynia	τῆς ἀκηδίας
vainglory	tshcheslavnyi	τῆς κενοδοξίας
pride	gordostnyi	τῆς ὑπερηφανίας

The fifth is problematic, because 'beneficial grief over sins',[174] that is, πένθος (mourning),[175] is a spiritual requirement. Thus only pernicious, 'human' sadness, must be fought.[176] The sixth is even more problematic because ἀκηδία, originally *torpor, weariness*, came also to mean *anguish* and *low spirits*. Nil's use of *unynie*, depending upon the intensity involved, has the varying modern meanings: not only *dejection* and *despondency*, from which one can will one's recovery, but also *depression*. The latter may well require, as with Basil, a 'well-timed . . . structured discussion' with 'a man most experienced in life and most profitable in discourse', in other words, a therapist. But this is the extreme case.[177]

---

174. *Ustav* 5.5.65.
175. For a classical treatment of this central feature of Orthodox spirituality, see Hausherr, *Penthos*.
176. *Ustav* 5.5.62. Nil follows the Greco/Slavic John Cassian here; the PSW (1: 87–88) translator used *dejection* (an equivalent of the modern *unynie*), and Father Jerome Bertram tried *melancholy* (*Monastic Institutes*, 139–143), but they both defaulted to *sorrow* (and the latter to *sadness* as well) for that 'which is according to God' (2 Cor 7:10). Thus the choice of *sadness* by Izwolsky (pp 110, 116) and Maloney (RH, 94–95, also his 'translation') seems better.
177. *Ustav* 5.6.81: hence *despondency* seems more fitting than *listlessness* (PSW 1: 88–9) or *depression* (*Monastic Institutes*, 145–161). Izwolsky's *accidie* (pp 110, 116) and Maloney's synonymn *acedia* (RH, 95–97, also his 'translation'), if they are following the dictionary definition, privilege the early Greek meaning over the Russian and over how Nil used *unynie*.

A Bit on Nil's Hesychasm

> This, Master, shows me to be equal to the angels, and even renders me superior to them, for You are by essence invisible to them, and by nature unapproachable, but to me You are entirely wholly visible and my essence combines with Your nature.[178]

If there is one subject related to Nil on which the secular historian ought to cede wholeheartedly to others genuinely qualified to speak, hesychasm is that subject. For this I urge the interested reader to consult von Lilienfeld or Maloney,[179] with their commendable combination of scholarship, detail, religious insight, and didactic utility. They illuminate how all the pieces in Nil's teachings fit together and within Orthodox monastic traditions. They note, among other things, his thorough grounding in classical Palestinian-Sinaitic stillness, its antecedents, and its coupling of the struggles against passions and for pure prayer. They underscore his affinity for the high mysticism of Isaac and Symeon, but reluctance to write in this regard from personal experience. And they speak of his appropriation of the later medieval breath control techniques and the pedagogical program of Gregory the Sinaite, but avoidance of the Gregory Palamas's 'Taboric Light' theories. For my part, having probed some of Nil's key vocabulary, I shall limit my comments here to only a few observations concerning how Nil's grasp of these matters might appear to a friendly, modern outsider.

A puzzling problem concerns how, by Nil's teaching, the relationship of intellect and heart actually works? According to Nil's Isaac, the intellect not only receives data, analyzes, and conceptualizes, but also is the 'helmsman of the senses', which themselves can 'explain', and which itself senses, desires, engages in prayerful 'ecstasy'. And metaphorically, it 'commits adultery, if it withdraws from the memory of God'.[180] As for the relationship with the

---

178. *Ustav* 2.37 (from Symeon NT, with the capitals added here for clarity).
179. Von Lilienfeld, NSSSS, 133–154; Maloney, RH, 110–147.
180. *Ustav* 2.28, 30–33.

thinking-emotive-willful heart, it is from there, according to Philotheus, that images of attacking urges reach the intellect, where, according to Gregory the Sinaite, they can multiply.[181] Yet Gregory directs us, with the aid of controlled respiration, to 'confine the intellect within the heart' in order to 'protect' the latter.[182] Then, as Nil modifies Gregory in favor of the more poetic imagery of Isaac and Symeon, divine grace facilitates the prayer that frees the intellect from this captivity.[183]

Most if not all modern schools of psychiatry and psychology, while treating visions as a matter of personal religious experience, would dismiss this anatomy out of hand. However, in examining the place of the intellect here, one can see a form of the Freudian superego deployed to control the ego and id. The intellect of Nil's Isaac, as 'helmsman of the senses', fits this role, and has converted the heart, 'the guardian of urges', into an assistant, whereby mind/thought 'that swift of wing and shameless bird' is likewise stilled.[184] Regarding the relationship among mind, emotion, hope, and fear, stillness theory matches the operationally useful findings of psychologist and concentration camp survivor Bruno Bettelheim (1903–1990), author of *The Informed Heart*.[185]

At this point, however, the observer must remember that Nil is not simply a mystic, but a thoroughly Orthodox Christian mystic, who in his normal devotional life regularly took communion, and even supplied instructions for partaking of the body of the Lord with pre-consecrated bread in the absence of a priest.[186] Symeon's hymn, with the bold assertion in the citation at the head of this section, connects the mystical union of the Christian's liturgical communion with God with the personal communion of the successful, praying hesychast.[187]

---

181. *Ustav* 1.2, 2.10.
182. Of the classical theorists of stillness, none other than Gregory Palamas was aware of the metaphorical aspect of this notion: PSW 4: 193.
183. *Ustav* 2.8.13.
184. *Ustav* 2.29.
185. *The Informed Heart: Autonomy in a Mass Age* (Glencoe IL: Free Press, 1960).
186. See below, Appendix II. *Predanie Addenda* 45–47.
187. Symeon NT, *Hymns* 7:28–29; SC 156: 210–211.

Further on Nil's Non-Possession

And to have the title of the finest monastery in a place and a *multitude of brothers—this is the pride of the worldly,* the Fathers say—or, according to the prevailing custom now, from the acquisition of villages and accumulation of many properties, and from success in worldly things— what can we say about this?[188]

Nil's political non-involvement in any putative 1503 synodal debate over monastic land-holding is only one side of the story here. Besides the above-mentioned thirty percent of the *Predanie*,[189] about twice as much other text concerning prayer, avarice, pride, memory of death, and detachment deal with the practical, moral, and spiritual aspects of poverty.[190] Taken together they constitute a rather consistent theory of non-possession for all monks.

Relying on a combination of sources and rhetoric, Nil enunciates a number of key principles connecting monastic spirituality to avoidance of riches. From Isaac, the pure 'do not apply themselves to the beauties and pleasures of this world'.[191] From Climacus, any 'entanglements in the world' are 'irrational'.[192] From the Apostle Paul and perhaps Cassian, avarice is the 'root of all evil' and 'idolatry'.[193] Following Isaac and Barsanuphius, complete non-possession trumps any requirement that to give alms to the needy, in other words, a monk may not argue that he acquires in order to distribute charity, even though, as Basil teaches, if one has, one is required to give.[194] Rather, as from Dorotheus, 'charity of the soul', such as suffering 'offenses' from a brother, is higher than any material gifts.[195] From Chrysostom by way of Nikon, one is not

---

188. *Ustav* 2.8.95.
189. See above, under I, 'The Church at Large'.
190. *Predanie* 15, 17–20, 22–25, 31–34, 39–40; *Ustav* 2.43, 45–47, 5.3.49–55, 5.8. 91–92, 95–96, 7.18, 10.4–7; *To Vassian* 2–3.
191. *Ustav* 2.43.
192. *Ustav* 10.4.
193. *Ustav* 5.2.45.
194. *Predanie* 20, 22–23, 25 (from Nikon).
195. *Predanie* 24 (from Nikon).

guilty of 'not adorning a church', especially in favor of giving to the poor.[196] From the Life of Pachomius, 'it is unseemly to marvel at the work of human hands and exult in the beauty of buildings', lest the 'intellect' be 'deceived by artful phrases'.[197] From the martyr Eugenia, also via Nikon: 'it is not proper for monastics to have silver possessions'.[198] From his own analysis, pride over any accomplishment or former or present status is 'shameful', and 'true distancing from avarice and materialism, is not just not to have property, but not to desire to acquire it'—which 'directs us toward purity of soul'.[199]

Such principles, as well as general Christian ethics, dictate Nil's positive rules. Buildings and clothing shall be simple and unadorned. One must work to capacity to support oneself, never exploit the needy or even accept alms acquired from the exploitation of others, never haggle over prices or sue in court, and always seek needed goods 'everywhere obtainable and readily purchased'.[200]

It thus goes without saying, but Nil writes it twice, that seigneurial landholdings can be detrimental to the pursuit of monastic purity. It is in discussing pride that Nil adapts from Dorotheus the diatribe against the 'finest monastery, . . . multitude of brothers, acquisition of villages and accumulation of many properties', cited above. Nil then continues, as an accomplished homilist, to declaim other sources of such 'pride of the worldly':

> There are some who hold themselves high over nothing, that is, a *fine singing* voice or *fine enunciation* of tongue in singing, speaking or *reading*—what praise can man have from God for these, which are *not accomplished by his* volition, but are what the Fathers call *natural?* Others vaunt themselves for their mastery of craftsmanship—this is similar. There are also such who

---

196. *Predanie* 31 (from Nikon).
197. *Predanie* 34.
198. *Predanie* 32 (from Nikon).
199. *Ustav* 5.3.45, 5.8.95.
200. *Predanie* 15, 17–20, 25, 40; *Ustav* 5.3.54 (chiefly from Nikon and Basil).

even boast of this: if someone stemmed from parents of secular repute, or had kinsmen from among the eminent in secular glory, or himself enjoyed some rank or secular honor—these are madness: it indeed is proper to conceal them. If someone, from within the life of renunciation of one's own, *accept glory* and *honor from men*—this is shamefulness: it is proper to be embarrassed over these, ...[201]

Later, with regard to detachment, Nil adapts and glosses Climacus:

The work, he says, *of stillness is carefreeness from rational and irrational things, and prayer without sloth, and, thirdly, inviolable activity of the heart.* And among the rational things, he does not name *what we now hold as a custom* regarding the ownership of villages and control over many properties, and other entanglements in the world: for these are irrational.[202]

In the first case, the issue is clearly pride, in the second, carefreeness, really deadness to the world. Estates emblematize the most pernicious of 'entanglements in the world' or sources of collective pride for monks. If we agree with Ostrowski on the lack of a call for state-imposed secularization here,[203] we can also see why subsequent opponents of monastic land-holding considered Nil one of their own, and that defenders of it chose not to give his *Predanie* and *Ustav* the same official imprimatur afforded to his contemporary coenobites, Efrosin of Pskov and Iosif Volotsky.[204]

---

201. *Ustav* 5.8.95 (Dorotheus in italics).
202. *Ustav* 10.4–5 (Climacus in Italics).
203. See above under I. 'The Church at Large'.
204. See below under Epilogue: 'Love's Labors Lost?'

Nil's Nil in a Nutshell

This, Lord, do we opine: that a profitable rule for you is to nourish yourself in physical activities, gaging by power, but not above measure, and to meditate upon the Divine Writings, and to instruct yourself in handicrafts, and to love stillness.[205]

---

205. *Little Epistle.*

Epilogue
WIN SOME, LOSE SOME

Love's Labors Lost?

> In this, Iosif, you lie about me and my elder Nil, that we blaspheme the ancient and new wonder-workers. . . . Nil did not take any of their miracles out of their holy writings, but rather corrected from other correct copies.[1]

This belated and blatantly false charge, leveled by Pseudo-Vassian Patrikeev against Iosif in the 1550s, may also explain why Nil's *Sobornik* stayed put within a few great monastery libraries[2] had no impact on official Russian hagiography, and enjoyed a privileged status only in Kirillov, as *Guriev Sobornik*.[3] Due to the later controversy over monastic lands, Nil himself became a controversial figure, better kept within the cloister than out in the world. When the energetic hegumen Makarii assumed the long vacant archepiscopate of Novgorod (r. 1526–1542, as well as later as Metropolitan of Moscow, 1542–1563) and set about to compile new, expanded menologia (monthly readings) with Russian Lives and theological-didactic addenda, he not only omitted Nil's *Predanie* and *Ustav*— which did not prevent their continued copying and use by

---

1. Pseudo-Vassian Patrikeev, 'Debate with Iosif' 13, VPS, 280.
2. On its unique role in Kirillov, NSTRM, 97–98.
3. N. K. Nikol'skii, *Kirillo-Belozerskii monastyr'*, 285–293.

monks—but also bypassed the *Sobornik* and utilized the older, clumsier versions of those two dozen Lives.

A century and a half later, a Jesuit-influenced Ukrainian, Dmytro Tuptalo (1651–1709, as of 1702, Metropolitan of Rostov), provided the budding Russian Empire with new menologies. Heavily influenced by the revised hagiography of Makarii's much younger Flemish contemporary, the Carthusian Laurentius Surius (1522–1578), Tuptalo's twelve monthly volumes of classical and native hagiography are still in use among the Russian Orthodox, at home and abroad. The *Sobornik* has passed into the dustbin of antiquarian interest, of use only to scholars seeking to penetrate Nil's mind and the pedagogical-literary-religious culture of his time.

Making It

> And it is especially necessary now, I opine, O beloved ones, not to conceal this from you about the saintly elder Nil . . . even if he was in the last times, yet he was in no way inferior to those great men and ancient saintly God-bearing Fathers in courage, and spiritual struggles, and bravery against demons, and wisdom with words. The chapters of his treatise and that holy and pious cloister, in which this great elder lived industriously and pleasing to God, manifestly prove his genuine spiritual and verbal wisdom concerning the life of virtue.

So wrote Ivan Pleshkov in the 1660s in his *Tale of the Nil-Sorsky Scete* in a manner reminiscent of Nil Polev's colophon cited at the start of this book, and reminding us that courage in combat with Satan or his demons, as then understood, constituted a form of public service in the eyes of the devout.

The fate of the Sora scete or hermitage, which gradually and resolutely, if unofficially, developed the cult of its founder, requires only a few phrases. A beneficiary of court support and numerous entrance gifts, despite its accepting Patriarch Nikon's new service books only under duress[4] and despite its being a juridical satellite of Kirillov from 1641 through 1777, Sora flourished with a dozen or so brothers into the mid-eighteenth century[5]. But after languishing when 'Enlightenment' secularizing policies came into full swing in Russia, Sora revived as a coenobium in the 1830s. Subsequently it became such a materially prosperous local shrine, that the Kirillov archimandrite, in his capacity as the regional episcopal intendant, scolded the brethren and enjoined them (to no avail) to return to Nil's principles and self-support.[6]

As for Nil's original writings, not only did they remain prestigious among Russia's devotees of asceticism and stillness, but a set of pseudepigrapha turned up, blowing more than one modern scholar off course.[7] Then Paisii Velichkovsky (1722–1794), the Ukrainian-born strict coenobite, as well as reviver of Russian hesychasm and admitted admirer of Nil, partially recapitulated the master's career by going to Mt. Athos and learning Greek in order to improve and modernize Russian spiritual texts. First prompted by the inadequacy of the Slavic version of Isaac the Syrian, Paisii corrected it. He then turned to translating that mother of modern monastic miscellanies, the *Philokalia*—an Ottoman Greek product of his era.[8] Partially due to Paisii's influence, the Optina Hermitage (near Kozelsk, about a hundred-fifty miles southwest of Moscow) became the center of Russia's resurrected *starchestvo*—the intimate spiritual relation of elder and disciple.[9] Optina in turn inspired Filaret Drozdov, an outstanding conservative reformer as Metropolitan of Moscow, 1821–1867. The Imperial government recognized his moral authority and wordsmithing talents to the point of assigning him the delicate task, essential for the social peace, of

---

4. *Zhitie Korniliia Vygovskogo*, 433.
5. Romanenko, NDTRM, 159-179, 189-190, 195, 198-200.
6. P.N. Zyrianov, 'Russkie Monastyri i monashestvo v XIX - nachale XX veka', 320.
7. See von Lilienfeld, NSSS, 90-98; Ostrowski, 'Toward establishing the Canon', 41-42, and above, under III. 'Texts and Structures', note 3.
8. N.N. Lisovoi, 'Vosmnadtsatyi vek v istorii russkogo monashestva'; 208-217.
9. V.A. Kuchumov, 'Russkoe starchestvo', 232-237.

penning Russia's Emancipation Proclamation of 1861, which freed twenty million serfs from personal bondage.

Filaret's all-encompassing pastoral work included a very serious attempt simultaneously to rekindle coenobiticism and promote *starchestvo*. In 1852 he issued some rules and guidelines, with recommended reading for all monastics—male or female, coenobites, idiorrythmics, and scetites—during their obligatory cell time:

> ... first, Holy Scripture, second, the writings of the Holy Fathers and the Saints' Lives, and especially the ascetic writings of Saints Basil the Great, John Climacus, Abba Dorotheus, Ephrem the Syrian, Macarius of Egypt ... ; for several who are not beginners, also Isaac of Syria, Barsanuphius the Great, and the writings collected in the *Philokalia*, but not without the supervision and direction of experienced people, especially the latter, lest the lofty reading undertaken turn into a opportunity for the inexperienced for an incorrect application of insufficiently understood teaching and for reverie instead of genuine success in spiritual life.[10]

Only I think I left something out in the above citation. The initial set of Fathers actually reads:

> ... the ascetic writings of Saints Basil the Great, John Climacus, Abba Dorotheus, Ephrem the Syrian, Macarius of Egypt, Nil Sorsky; ....

Now if this doesn't represent 'making it' in the Orthodox sacred tradition, then what does? Nil's addition to the official Russian Church calendar as a saint in 1903[11] appears as an afterthought.

---

10. *Pravila blagoustroistva monastyrskoi zhizni*, 11.
11. Romanenko, NSTRM, 189.

PREFACE TO THE TRANSLATIONS

It took me so long to find out, I found out.

— John Lennon —

The aim of this translation is twofold. First I wish to let Nil speak for himself as best as he can in modern English, and this requires an attempt to reproduce some of his own turns and figures of speech and allow his ellipses to pass where others might fill in the missing word. Secondly, I hope to elucidate as much as possible what Nil is doing with his sources and where he is being original, something his sharper followers, who copied many of his sources into their own codices, certainly would have grasped. For both tasks, I need to be as literal as possible. In so doing I am aware of sound arguments for clarifying a little, with or without parentheses, and privileging the semantics of the receiving language. But I choose not to do so, except via footnotes.

A good example of the value of my method is a sentence from the *Ustav, Slovo* 3. The italics in my translation indicate where Nil has admittedly taken the words of Isaac the Syrian (but, in the paragraph, deceptively mixed with Gregory the Sinaite's). Here I am able to be strictly literal, as Nil's turns of speech, including both participles and his closing ellipsis (where he does not repeat the direct object *you*), are perfectly understandable. Nil's text and my English run as follows:[1]

---

1. NSSS, 37; PNSIK,128; *Ustav* 3.7.

> Ezhe bo *stoiati v dobrodětelekhъ ne tvoe estь, no blagodatь ta estь, nosiashchia tia na dlanekhъ ruku svoeiu,* sъbliudaiushte otъ vsekhъ sъprotivnykhъ.

> For *to stand* among *virtues is not of yourself, but is that same grace*², *carrying you on the palms of its hands,* protecting from all adversaries.

Compare this to the text of von Lilienfeld, who supplies two words (here underlined)—something Grolimund, whose modern Greek follows her German, does with parentheses. In both cases only a mite of Nil is lost:³

> In Tugenden bestehn, ist nicht dein <u>Werk</u>, sondern dies Gnade ist, die dich auf ihren Handflächen trägt <u>und dich</u> vor allen Feinden bewahrt.

> Διότι τὸ νὰ σταθῆς ἐν ἀρεταῖς δὲν ἔναι ἰδικόν σαυ. /κατόρθωμα/, ἀλλὰ ἡ χάρις εἶναι ἐκείη, ἡ ὁποία σὲ βαστάζει ἐπὶ τῆς παλάμης τῶν χειρῶν της /<u>καὶ σὲ</u>/ φυλάσσει ἀπὸ πάντα τὰ ἐναντία.

Prokhorov saw a need to clarify a bit more, and though he remained faithful to Nil's meaning, even more of the original Nil is lost. Prokhorov's additions of *ability* and *depends,* as opposed to *work,* have the effect of specifying glosses:⁴

> Ibo <u>sposobnostь</u> (*ability*) stoaitь v dobrodeteliakh ne ot tebia <u>zavisit</u> (*depends*), no estь <u>delo</u> (*work*) blagodati, nosiashchei tebia na ladoniakh ruk svoikh, sokhraniaia ot vsego soprotivnogo.

---

2. Literally, *that grace*; alt. transl., privileging the Greek original (ἡχάρις αὔτη): *grace itself.*

3. NSSS, 219; NSA, 168.

4. PNSIK, 129: *For the* <u>ability</u> *to stand among virtues does not* <u>depend on</u> *you, but is the* <u>work</u> *of Grace . . . .*

The less faithful translations and adaptations take liberties with meaning, at least with Nil's chosen metaphors. For example, in the case of Izwolsky, the 'hands' of 'grace' are now 'God's hands':[5]

> For it is not your <u>doing</u> that you stand in virtue, but <u>the effect</u> of grace, which holds you in <u>God's</u> hands and preserves <u>you</u> from <u>your</u> enemies.

Theologically, these are the same hands, but this is not as Nil expressed them.

Still, Izwolsky's tinkering is nothing compared to the change effected earlier by Archimandrite Iustin, who, among other things, glossed with his own simile in a way that substituted a word meaning *hands* or *arms* for Isaac's metaphor of the *palms of its* [grace's] *hands*:[6]

> Ibo <u>tverdo</u> stoatь vъ dobrodětelіakhъ samъ soboіu ne <u>mozheshь</u>: eto estь <u>dělo</u> blagodati, kotoraia nositъ tebia <u>kakъ matь svoe ditia</u>, na rukakhъ svoikhъ, sokhraniaia <u>tebia</u> otъ vsiakoi soprotivnosti.
>
> For you <u>cannot</u> stand/remain <u>firmly</u> among virtues on your own: this is <u>the work</u> of grace, which carries you, <u>as a mother her child</u>, in its hands/arms, preserving <u>you</u> from all adversity.

Iustin's text then became the basis of Jacamon's, for whom '*Indeed to* + *inf.* . . .' becomes '. . . *because you* + *ind.* . . . ,' and from her to Bianchi's team, which supplied *con le . . . forze* and a Biblical *cf.* footnote to Iustin's simile of *a mother her child.* In both of the 'translations', moreover, Iustin's *rukakhъ* (prp.) = *hands/arms* are now *arms* (*bras, bracchia*), purely and simply.[7]

---

5. Fedotov, *Treasury*, 109.
6. Iustin, 41.
7. Jacamon, 64; Bianchi, 66–67.

> . . . <u>car tu</u> ne <u>peut</u> rester par toi-même <u>ferme</u> dans les vertus: ceci est <u>l'oeuvre</u> de la grâce, qui te porte, <u>comme une mère son enfant</u>, dans ses <u>bras</u>, <u>te</u> gardant de toute adversité.
>
> . . . <u>perché</u> non <u>puoi</u> rimanere <u>saldo</u> nelle virtù solo <u>con le</u> tue <u>forze</u>: questo è <u>opera</u> della grazia che ti porta sulle sue <u>bracchia</u> <u>come una madre il suo bambino</u>[8] custodendo<u>ti</u> da ognio avversità.

Here we see one of dozens of examples of how Archimandrite Iustin's glossed adaptation become the foundation of a new redaction of Nil's *Ustav* in at least three languages.

Finally, in this learned, homiletic variant of 'telephone',[9] Father Maloney—building on Iustin's tradition, but re-creating or borrowing one of Izwolsky's additions (*God*), as well as another found in the Italian (*by your own power—con le tue forze*), and keeping Jacamon's *bras* (arms), constructed a new version of both Isaac's metaphor and Iustin's simile:

> For <u>you</u> <u>are</u> un<u>able</u> to stand <u>steadfast</u> in virtue by your own <u>power</u>. This is <u>the work</u> of grace which <u>upholds</u> you <u>as a mother</u> carries <u>a child</u> in her <u>arms</u>. <u>God's grace</u> protects <u>you</u> from all adversity.

The problem is not that Nil would have disagreed with the meaning of any of the altered sentences, or even, as pastor and pedagogue, have disapproved of the verbal liberties taken by his latter-day disciples; it is that he did not write their words on the basis of what he found in Isaac the Syrian. They are neither the words of Nil Sorsky nor are they replicative of the Russian hesychasm of his era.

---

8. Cf. Ps 131:2/130:2.
9. The game in which a line or circle of people pass along a message from one to another by whispering and then see how much has changed from the original to the ultimate formulation.

So let us enter Nil's classroom and, to the best of our ability, have him speak for himself, while we save our own commentary and analysis for introductory chapters, artificial paragraph divisions, and footnotes. This requires in some cases that we employ a technical term, such as *optic* as noun for *zritelnoe* (Philotheus's ὀπτικόν, *sight, organ of sight*), where the common word *eye* reads better, as Nil here chose not to substitute *oko* (for ὀφθαλμός).[10]

Time will tell whether this method and execution of translation are successful, or if I too tripped up in my days devoted to this endeavor.

---

10. *Ustav*, Fwd. 7.

PART II

NIL SORSKY'S ORIGINAL TEXTS

And everything that I have written, if it be pleasing to God and profitable for souls, let us so do. And if not, let there be something better, which is pleasing to God and profitable for souls.

— Nil Sorsky —

THE PREDANIE
(TRADITION)

On the Life of the Holy Fathers:[1]
This Is the Tradition[2] of the Elder Nil the Hermit
to His Disciples
and to All Who Ought to Have It.

[1] *With the omnificence[3] of our Lord, God, and Saviour Jesus Christ and His Most Pure Mother's assistance, I* have written this *soul-profiting[4]* writing for myself and *my genuine[5] lord brothers, who are of my ethos.[6]* I so call *you,* and *not disciples, for we all have but one Teacher—the Lord Jesus Christ, the Son of God, who has given us the Divine Writings.* And the holy Apostles and saintly *Fathers,* having instructed and instructing *humankind toward salvation,* insofar as *all of them first did good, and thus instructed* others—*yet I have done*

---

1. Cf. below, *To German* 8; *Sobornik,* Forew. 4.
2. *predanie.*
3. *vsedĕistviemъ* (instr.): alt. transl. (stretching the *dĕ*- lexeme): *omnipotence;* Greek original lost; if πανουργία, then the Slavic Nikon may be mistranslated, and should be *sagacity, wisdom.*
4. This paragraph up to here adapted from Nikon, *Taktikon,* Fwd., 1.
5. *prisnym* (dt. pl.): alt. transl.: *associate; eternal.*
6. *nrava* (gn. sg.), that is, *partake of my ways;* cf. below, *Testament* 1; MRIV 10.34.

113

nothing good[7] whatsoever, but only *speak the Divine Writings to those who accept them and would be saved*. And insofar as *Scripture says*, '*We are strangers here and sojourners*',[8] *but over there is eternal life and everlasting living after death, either in the peace or in the torment, which God will give unto each according to his deeds:*[9] this is why we should be concerned with living after death. *And I therefore* transmit this writing *to my* lords and *brothers, for my own salvation and all those who desire it, elevating conscience to the better and keeping it from negligence, bad living, offenses of evil- and fleshly-reasoning persons, and traditions of the wicked and the vain*,[10] which have come from our common Enemy and deceiver, and from our own sloth.[11]

[2]   *In the beginning, I have considered it proper to propound the faith.*[12] *I believe in one God, the Trinity,* glorified as *the Father, the Son and the Holy Spirit, of one essence*[13] *and inseparable.* Likewise in the incarnation of the Son of God I do believe, whom to be *perfect God and perfect man*[14] I do confess. All the rest of the entire confession of the Orthodox faith *I do accept* and confess *with all my soul.* Likewise *my Lady,* the holy, *most pure,* and real[15] *Mother of God,* with *abundant* faith and *love I* do confess, and extol, and glorify. And all the saints I do revere and accept and glorify. And I *unite* through

---

7. Cf. below, *Ustav,* Fwd 17, *To Gurii* 19, and *Sobornik, Forew.* 4, for *have done nothing good* (which is not in Nikon), also *Postscr.* 1; and *I have not done one good thing in life* in Symeon NT, *Hymns* 14: 47; Eparkh. 334.14: 85v; SC 156.14:268–269.

8. Ps 38:12/39:12; cf. Gn 23:4, 1 P 2:11.

9. Cf. Mt 6:27.

10. Nil omits Nikon's *urges* after *vain.*

11. [1] after note 5 adapted with some fidelity, alteration, and some word games, from Nikon, *Taktikon.* Fwd 7–7v.

12. Streamlined from Nikon, *Taktikon* Fwd 7v.

13. *edinosushchii* = ὁμοούσιος; literally, from the Slavic, *uniessential;* alt. (less accurate) transl.: *consubstantial.*

14. *perfect God and perfect Man*: not in Nikon, but cf. 'The Definition of Faith at Chalcedon', NPNF-2 14: 264; also Theodore Stud. *Testament,* BMFD 1:75–76; PG 99:1813C, but no Slavic copy identified; also the Sol. 270 (359/270) *Izmaragd,* 'Questions and Answers on the Holy Trinity', attributed to Cyrill of Alexandria: 163: 316v.

15. *sushchuiu* (fm. sg. acc. prs. act. prtcpl.): literally, *being* (used in the Slavic Nikon for a text extract, as opposed to a gloss).

the *grace of Christ*, and I *rush with all my soul*[16] to *the holy Synodal*[17] *Apostolic Church*. And all the teachings to be received from the Lord, and from the holy Apostles, *and the holy Fathers* of *the ecumenical and local councils,* and received from the other holy *Fathers* of the holy *Church*—having received, it passed down to us about the Orthodox faith and about *the practical* stipulations—all these *I do accept* and revere *with abundant faith* and love. And all *the falsely-named teachers* of *heretical* doctrines and traditions I and those living with me *anathematize*,[18] and may all heretics be *foreign*[19] to us.[20]

[3] *And insofar as* many reverent *brothers come to me* wishing *to dwell with us,* I often refuse,[21] for I am a *sinful and unknowledgeable*[22] man and *infirm*[23] *in soul* and body. But *the rejected ones do not leave me be, nor do they cease to harass me, and* therefore *troubles* occur for us.

[4] *And I observed this: that if also it be God's will for people to come to us,*[24] it is proper to hold to the traditions of the saints, and preserve God's commandments, *and effect the traditions of the holy Fathers,* and not make denunciations or contrive *excuses* for sins,[25] saying: '*Nowadays it is not possible to live according to the writings and follow the holy Fathers*'.[26] For even though we be infirm, it is proper

---

16. As above with *urge/pomysl'* (note 9), Nil omits *and breath,* as if avoiding two of the key issues which he handles in the spiritual treatise.

17. *sъbornyi*: alt. transl.: *Catholic,* but most surely, according to Orthodox thinking, not to be confused with *Roman Catholic.*

18. Adapted from 2 P 2:1.

19. On the problem of Nil, heresy, and modern scholarship, see above, I. 'The Church at Large', II. 'The Unexpected Bedfellow'.

20. Nikon, *Taktikon,* Fwd. 7v–8, but greatly rearranged, streamlined, juggled, and made coherent, as if Nil were editing Nikon; [2] also appears indirectly and maybe directly influenced by the credo of Theodore Stud., *Testament* BMFD 1.3:75–76; PG 99:1813B–1816A.

21. Alt. in several MSS: *have often refused.*

22. Cf. *Sobornik, Postscr,* Greek signature.

23. *nemoshchenъ*; alt. transl. (in almost every case this word is used): *weak, incapable.*

24. Nil omits here, among other things, *it is fit to live by all the coenobitic rules.*

25. *contrive excuses for sins*: Ps 140:4 (LXX).

26. '*Nowadays . . . Fathers*' not in Nikon, but possibly adapted indirectly from Symeon NT, *Discourses* 29.4: 312; SC 113:29, 178–179; cf. below, *Ustav* 2.44, *To German,* 12; Savva Chernyi, *Zhitie . . . Iosifa,* 468.

within one's power to follow the blessed Fathers *of everlasting memory—even if it be impossible for us to achieve parity with them.*

[5] And *if anyone has no wish for this,* let him cease to harass my wretchedness, *for I send such idlers away,* as I have said above. To such I do *not* come wishing[27] *to be in charge; rather those who come compel me to do this.*

[6] And *if those* living with us do not endeavor to preserve these and do not obey our words, which I speak to them according to the Divine Writings, *I* shall not answer for their self-regulation[28] and *am blameless.*

[7] But *if they wish so* to live, *freely and without cares, those we do accept,* telling to them *the word of God,* even if I myself do not perform, so that perchance *I, through the grace of Christ by the prayers of the beneficiaries, will be worthy of the word spoken in the Divine Ladder. These, who were an example of wallowing there in the slime, taught the passers-by, informing of their salvation, so that they, in turn, would not wallow in that slime; indeed on account of their salvation, the Lord delivered even these ones from the slime.*

[8] And again it says: *Do not desire to be a bitter judge of those who teach*[29] *by word, when you behold that they have been most lazily disposed in deeds, for many times verbal profit has made up for the want of deeds.*[30]

[9] And again, in another manner, *fearing the sin* of rejecting often, we are, as Saint Maximus said, *many who speak, but few who act,*[31] but no one should hide the word of God by his indifference, but should confess his infirmity and not conceal God's truth, lest we be guilty, along with transgressing the commandments, of misconstruing the words of God.

---

27. *fearing* in Nikon.
28. *samochinie* = ἰδιορρυθμία, as in Grolimund, NSA, 131: literally, *self-ordering*, alt. transl.: *individualism, arbitrariness*—clearly negative for Nil; cf. below, *Ustav* 11.6, *To German* 7, Innokentii, *Zavět* 15.
29. *a great deal* omitted.
30. Climacus 26.14:203, 15:225–226; HM SMS 184: 127v,144 v/VMCh-M: 909b, 919b; PG 88:1016BC; 1068C; cf. MRIV X.7.
31. Nikon freely adapts and glosses on Maximus Conf. *Centuria de charitate.* Prologue, 52; PG 90:960 / Фκ 2:3 (HM SMS 456:90).

[10] *And such are the words of the holy Fathers, and there are many, many others. On account of these, having searched the Divine Writings, we impart*[32] *to those who come to us and require them—moreover, it is not we, who are unworthy, but the blessed Fathers from the Divine Writings. Those who dwell with us are to endeavor to preserve them with care. This is what we desire and love.*[33]

[11] *If any brother, through sloth or negligence, falls away from his traditions*[34] *in some wise, he should confess this to the superior, and the latter, as is proper, shall correct the transgression.*

[12] And thus *if* the transgression occurs *in* a cell,[35] or anywhere *outside*, it should be *corrected through confession.*

[13] It is proper to have great *precision*, when one has gone anywhere outside his cell, especially to preserve the traditions.[36]

[14] *For many it is hateful*[37] *to cut off one's will for God, but every self-justification is greed.*[38] *Of these he said in the Divine Ladder: It is better expel than to abandon*[39] *to perform their own will. The expeller has often made the expelled more humble and further cut off his will. But the one who deems it philanthropy to make condescension to such men, will have made*[40] *him pitifully curse at the time of departure.*[41]

---

32. *predaemъ* (same root as *predanie* = *tradition*).

33. [3-11] are adapted, rearranged, or, as from [7] (*with the grace of Christ*) through the beginning of the[11] (*many, many others*), almost verbatim from Nikon, *Taktikon*, Fwd., 9–10; for the last phrase, cf. below, *Scete Typikon* 3.

34. Nil follows Nikon's personalized wording here: *otъ predannykhъ emu*, literally, from what has been given over to him—meaning *his rules.*

35. Nil substitutes *cell* for Nikon's *obitelь* = *dwelling/monastery/cloister.*

36. [11] is rearranged with two simple and one complex reverses, and [12–13] is adapted from *Taktikon*, Fwd. 10.

37. Here Nil combines Nikon's *ne nevidimo* (*not unseen*) and *ne liubimo* (*disliked*) to make *nenavidimo* (*hated/hateful*).

38. *likhoimstvo* = πλεονεξία; alt. transl.: *usury* (*growth acquisition*); Nikon's contextualization emphasizes the multiplying of illicit gains.

39. Ellipsis: Nil omits *poshlushnikomъ* (*postulants / underlings*).

40. I.e., *caused.*

41. With the first sentence of [14] greatly reduced, then almost exactly from the translated extract in Nikon, *Taktikon*, Fwd. 11, rather than the Slavic Climacus, *Liber* 14; PG 88:1200B; HM SMS 184:183; cf. MRIV 10.42.

[15] This has been *imparted* to us *precisely from the holy Fathers, that from the righteous toil* of one's manual labor, *the Lord, and his Most Pure Mother,* arranges for *daily food* and other *needed provisions.*[42] '*Whoever does not work*', said *the Apostle,* '*let him not eat*'.[43] Our life and our *provisioning shall be arranged by this.*[44]

[16] And it is proper that the work shall be done under a roof.[45] If, when *necessary, to drive a pair of oxen in a* clearing,[46] in order to plow, *and other toils of individual labor are commendable in a coenobium,* says *the Divine Writing, then for those living separately this is blameworthy.*[47]

[17] And if we cannot satisfy our needs through our own work *due to infirmity or some other* well-spoken[48] *cause*,[49] then we accept a few needed alms from devotees of Christ, but no excess.[50]

[18] *But to accept what has been forcefully acquired from others' labor is absolutely of no profit to us.*[51] For how then, having accepted these, can we keep the Lord's commandments: '*To the man wishing to sue thee in court and take away thy tunic, give up also thy cloak*',[52] *and such others*—our being *passionate and infirm.* Rather, we are to *flee and drive this away as a deadly poison.*[53]

---

42. Nikon, *Taktikon,* 1: 15v; cf. 18: 98, *Pandekty* 44: 341; also Nil's *Life of Athansius of Athos,* SNS 1.288/*Zhitie . . . Afanasiia Afon.,* 15–16; Efrosin Psk., *Izlozhenie* 6/NSSS 303.

43. 2 Thes 3:10. cf. Efrosin Psk., *Izlozhenie* 6/NSSS 303; MRIV 8ᴮ.2/6.2.

44. From *Whoever,* slightly altered from Nikon, *Taktikon* 1: 15; cf. below, *Ustav* 11.16.

45. I.e., inside.

46. Nikon has *in the monastery,* as if his fields were within the enclosure.

47. Slightly adapted from Nikon, *Taktikon* 18: 98.

48. *blagoslovnu* (acc. fm. sg.), technically, *benedictorily,* i.e, permissible with the superior's *benediction,* i.e., blessing.

49. *due to infirmity of body or . . . some other cause* not in Nikon, but, regarding the Superior's absence, Basil, *Longer Rules* 45:218; HM SMS 183.33: 73v; PG 31.45:1031C.

50. Cf., below, *Ustav* 11.17.

51. Nikon, *Taktikon* 1: 15v, 18: 98; as in Efrosin, *Izlozhenie* 7/NSSS 303.

52. Nikon, *Taktikon* 1: 16; cf. Mt 5:40.

53. Nikon, *Taktikon* 1: 15v; cf. below, *Ustav* 11.17.

[19] *In buying* provisions *and selling* handicrafts, it is proper not to *haggle* with a brother[54] but *rather to accept a loss* our*selves*.[55]

[20] Likewise for those working for us, if they happen to be laymen, it is improper to haggle over wages, but give with a blessing and dismiss in peace.[56]

[21] It is improper for us to have excess goods. *That one is 'to give to him that asks and him that would borrow turn not away'*[57]—*this has been commanded to the wicked*, says *Basil the Great*.[58]

[22] *For he who has no excess needed*[59] *provisions need not make such gifts. And if he says: 'I have nothing', he is not lying*, says *Barsanuphius the Great*.[60]

[23] That *is an obvious monk, who need not give alms; for he can say with a unveiled face, 'Lo, we have forsaken all and followed in your footsteps'*,[61] Saint Isaac writes: *Non-posse*ssion *is superior to such giving*.[62] The monk's alms *are to aid a brother with a word at a time of need* and to console the afflicted with *spiritual* discretion.[63] But even this is for those who are able.

---

54. Cf. Nil's *Life of Athansius of Athos*, SNS 1.288; but not in the early Greek *Zhitie . . . Afanasiia Afonsk.*, 15–16.

55. Nikon, *Pandekty* 46: 361; maybe from Evagrius *On Asceticism and Stillness*, 35; φκ 1:41–42.

56. Cf. Efrosin Psk., *Izlozhenie* (23): 54–55/NSSS 311.

57. Citation from Mt 5:42.

58. Adapted, including Mt 5:42, from Basil, *Shorter Rules* 101: 268; HM SMS 183.114: 107v; PG 31:1152D; also Nikon *Pandekty* 20: 147.

59. . . . *ought but* in the original.

60. Nikon, *Pandekty* 20: 149; from Barsanuphius and John 620: 165; SC 468.620: 44–45, directed to laymen in the original.

61. Mt 19:27; a little shortened from Isaac Syr. 21: 109–110; HM SMS 179.14: 74v–75; Gk 79: 300; also in Nikon, *Pandekty* 20: 150; cf. MR IV III.24, for Iosif's first, strictest 'order' of ascetics.

62. This phrase is in an HTM variant (21: 110, line 5), but not in the the printed Greek (79) or HM SMS 179 (14); cf. HM SMS 179.56: 275; Gk 23: 100; HTM 4:37–38: *For your rank* (stepenъ = βαθμίς) *is higher than the rank of alms.*

63. Abstracted from Isaac Syr. 21:110–111/HM SMS 179.14:75, 77–77v, Gk 79:300, 302.

[24] For neophytes to *endure* afflictions, *offenses* and insults *from a brother*—'*and this is charity of the soul and is as superior to the physical as the soul is superior to the body*', says Saint Dorotheus.[64]

[25] And if any *stranger*[65] comes to us, *comfort* him as much as in our power, *and afterwards*, if he needs it, *give him the blessing of bread and dismiss him*.[66]

[26] Departures from our dwellings[67] are *not* to be made *simply and spontaneously*,[68] but only authorized and necessary ones. For untimely and unblessed exits from our cells are improper, as Basil the Great says: '*The superior*[69] *shall assign work to the brotherhood in good order*. Likewise he shall *command to each his suitable* and appropriate *departure*'.[70]

[27] *He who is sent* shall not renounce his obedience in the Lord—that is, he shall *not* treat his service as grounds for *indifference*, but shall be steadfast *with fear of God* and much watchfulness, so that *profit* accrue to himself and *those with him*.[71]

[28] *Everything that I have written*[72] *in this writing*, I wish *to be done* both while I live and after my death.

[29] And in our cells it is proper that only those, whom we ascertain to possess the artistic power to listen and speak profitably

---

64. Adapted from Dorotheus, *Discourses* 14.7:210; Eparkh. 347.16:164v; PG 88:1785A–1788A, addressing all monks, who *cannot even help . . . by words,* [so they] *bestow mercy* upon a brother's soul by not rendering evil for evil. Cf. Isaac Syr. 48: 234; Eparkh. 324.85: 480/HM SMS 179.85:385v-386; Gk 73:290: *As by nature the soul is better than the body, so the work of the soul is better than of the body.*

65. Nikon's *stranger* (near Antioch) is, specifically, a pilgrim en route to or from the Holy Land.

66. From Nikon, *Taktikon* 2:19v; *blessing bread* or *blessing of breads* (*khlebъ*) in the printed *Taktikon*; cf. Efrosin Psk., *Izlozhenie* (23): 54–55/NSSS 311.

67. *obitelei* (gn. pl.); alt. transl.: *cloisters*.

68. From Nikon, *Taktikon* 1: 16v, applied to receiving gifts.

69. *post of superior* in the original.

70. From Ps-Basil, *Const.* 43: 217; HM SMS 32: 72; PG 31: 1029AB.

71. Adapted from Ps-Basil, *Const.* 44: 217; HM SMS 32: 72; PG 31:1029B–1032A.

72. Cf., below [30] and *Sobornik, Forew.* 2.

and so make discourse effecting the edification and rectification of souls, advise brothers and outsiders.[73]

[30] And everything that I have written, if it be pleasing to God and profitable for souls, let us so do. And if not, let there be something better, which is pleasing to God[74] and profitable for souls.[75]

[31] As for *adorning of churches*, Saint John *Chrysostom* writes: 'If someone recommends[76] donating *sacred vessels or some other adornment to the church, direct him to distribute to the poor,*[77] *for no one'*, he said, *'has ever been* condemned[78] *for not adorning a church'*.[79] And other saints say the same thing.

[32] The *saintly* martyr *Eugenia did not accept* the sacred *vessels of silver* brought *to her, saying: 'It is not proper for monastics to have silver possessions'*.[80]

[33] Therefore it is not proper for us to possess even the sacred vessels in gold and silver, and likewise other extraneous adornments, but to offer only what is necessary for the church.

[34] Pachomius the Great did not desire the very building of the church to be adorned. For he built a church in his cloister at Mochos and *erected columns of most seemly brick inside. He then thought that it is unseemly to marvel at the work of human hands and exult in the beauty of buildings. So he took a cable, bound the columns*

---

73. Cf. MRIV 23.27, where neither neophytes nor young monks, as opposed to officials and council elders, are permitted independently to enforce Iosif's coenobitic rule.

74. Adapted from Nikon, *Taktikon*, 2:19–19v; cf. below, *Ustav* 11.19, *To Gurii* 1; *Sobornik, Forew.* 2.

75. For [30], cf. also below, *Sobornik, Forew.* 2, *To German* 4.

76. *sъvetuet*: Nikon has *vъproshaetъ (asks)*.

77. For Nikon's original of what Nil adapted here, John Chrysostom, *In Matthew* 80.2; PG 58: 726.

78. *osuzhdenъ*: Nikon has *povinenъ (guilty)*.

79. [31] from Nikon, *Pandekty* 21: 160v; for the original adapted by Nikon: John Chrysostom, *In Matthew* 50.5; PG 58.40.4: 508-509.

80. Almost verbatim from Nikon, *Pandekty* 34: 254v; abstracted and altered from *Vita sancti Eugeniae*, PL 73.9:612B = PL 21:1113C: '*We abound and superabound in all good things. I urge you, dearest Mother Melanthia, rather to divide them among the suffering indigent and needy*'.

and commanded the brothers to pull with all their might until the columns tilted and were unseemly. And he said: 'Let not the intellect, disinformed by artful praises,[81] *become the devil's catch, for many are his artifices'.*[82] And if this great and holy man so spoke and acted, how much more is it fitting that we guard against such things: for we are infirm and passionate and disinformed by the intellect.

[35] Regarding food and drink, let each prepare *nourishment according to the power*[83] of his body and soul, fleeing surfeit and hedonism.

[36] To drink to drunkenness any drink is completely improper for us.[84]

[37] The *healthy* and the young shall *wear down their bodies by fasting*, thirst, and *labor* as much as possible.[85]

[38] The old and *infirm* shall take a little comfort.[86]

[39] It is *improper* for oneself *to have* in our cells any valuable and adorned *vessels* or other such objects.[87]

[40] Likewise, it is proper to have cell buildings and our other habitats all be inexpensive and unadorned, as Basil the Great says: *'everywhere obtainable and readily purchased'*.[88]

---

81. *za khitrostnye khvaly*: alt. transl. and possibly with the double entendre: *praises of artistry/cunning*; cf. below, *Ustav* 3.1.

82. Almost as in Nil's edition of *Vita Pachomii*, SNS 3:518; Gk: *Sancti Pachomii Vita Altera* 46:215.

83. Cf. below, *Ustav* 4.8, 5.1.9, *Little Epistle*.

84. The formula is closest to Innokentii, *Zavět* 7; cf. also 'Ustav Pavla Vologskogo', 245; Pakhomii Serb, *Life of Kirill*, 24/DRIU 36; MRIV 9ᴮ.5 /7.5; Kornilii Komel'skii, *Ustav ili pravila* 3:175; *Stoglav* 52:174-177.

85. *as much as possible* here: cf. below, *Little Epistle*.

86. For [37-38], cf. *Ustav* 4.8.

87. Basil/Ps-Basil, *Longer Rules* 20.184; HM SMS 183.15: 53; PG 31: 969D-972A. Cf. Isaac Syr. HTM 4:38; HM SMS 179.56: 275v; Gk 23:100: *Sweep your cell clean of foods and superfluous articles*.

88. From Basil/Ps-Basil, *Longer Rules* 20.186; PG 31:973C, but not as in HM SMS 183.15: 54, which abbreviates; cf. *Longer Rules* 22.187; HM SMS 183.17: 55; PG 31:977A.

[41] *It is not proper for women to enter into our* scete[89], nor to *keep any female beasts of any kind for service or any other* purpose; this is forbidden to us.[90]

[42] Likewise *it is not fitting to retain boys* in our service, *and we should guard against* all types of smooth, *effeminate faces.*[91]

---

89. *cloister (obitel')* in Nikon.
90. Adapted from Nikon, *Taktikon* 1: 16v; for female animals, cf. Theodore Stud., *Testament* 5:10/BMFD 1.3.5: 77; PG 5:1820A; BMFD *Regulations* 86: 410; almost identical text to Nil in Innokentii, *Zavět*, 14; cf. Efrosin Psk., *Izlozhenie* 10/NSSS 305-306.
91. Cf. below, *Ustav* 5.2.43; Appendix III, Innokentii, *Zavět*, 14; also John Tzimiskes, *Typikon* (for the Athos Laura) 16, 25, BMFD 12:238, 240, and derivative Athonite regulations referenced, 243, 244. Nil adapts Nikon's same words here to prohibit boys and young men.
  In Nil Polev's and Nil Sorsky's Eparkh. 349, first the supplementary articles on the church and communion follow as translated here in Appendix II, and then comes the IRI type of *Ustav*: see above, III. 'Texts and Writings', text to note 8, and below, note 1 to *Ustav*, Fwd.

THE USTAV
('ON MENTAL ACTIVITY')

[*][1] The knowledge[2] within these writings[3] encompasses the following: what activity is proper for a monk to have, who wishes in truth to be saved in these times—that it is proper to act both mentally and sensibly, according to the Divine Writings and according to the lives of holy Fathers, as much as possible.

---

1. = PDP [19]. So that readers more easily grasp the dual tradition of the structure of the Introduction to the *Ustav,* the order of the text here follows the earliest Kirillov and Iosifov MSS, KB 89/1166 and Eparkh. 349 (published by Prokhkorov and Shevchenko), while the enumeration of paragraphs follows the authoritative PDP-type MSS such as Eparkh. 351 and KB 25/1102 (published by Borovkova-M and the basis of von Lilienfeld's, Grolimund's, and the adapted translations). See above, III, 'Texts and Structures,' note 8 and its text paragraph.

2. *razumъ,* probably as σύνεσις (here as a branch of knowledge) as below, *Ustav* 2.32; alt. transl.: *science, meaning:* see above under III. 'Technical Terms', text to notes 152–156.

3. *razumъ pisanii*; perhaps lexically adapted from the Preface to Barsanuphius, *Glavy* in Eparkh. 351: 205: *razumei pisanaa k tebě,* (which MS contains Dionisii Zvenigorodskii's copy of Nil's *Ustav*); cf. AfED 365 (Iosif, *Prosvetitel'*, Sl. 5), . . . *razum v pisaniikh.*

[4]Exposition of the Chapters

1. On the Differences of the Mental Battle Against Us, of Victory and Defeat, and that Passions Are Earnestly to Be Resisted.
2. On Our Combat Against Them, and How to Defeat Them, with Remembrance of God and the Guarding of the Heart, That Is, with Prayer and Stillness of the Intellect, and How to Effect This; Herein Also on Gifts.
3. On How and by What Means to Fortify Onself during the War of Mental Struggle.
4. On the Control of All Activity in Our Life.
5. On the Differences of Our Combat and Victory over the Eight Principal Passionate and Other Urges.
6. In General, Against All Urges.
7. On Remembrance of Death and of the Terrible Judgment: How to Learn about Them, So That We Possess These Urges in Our Hearts.
8. On Tears and How it Is Proper for Those Who Would Acquire Them to Act.
9. On the Guarding of These Things.
10. On Detachment and True Carefreeness, Which Is Deadness to Everything.
11. On How it Is Proper to Effect this Activity Not Ahead of Time and in Appropriate Measures, and on Prayer for These, and Other Needs.[5]

---

4. = PDP [20].
5. *and on Prayer for These, and Other Needs* not in the title at the start of the text of *Ustav* 11.

From the Writings of the Holy Fathers on Mental Activity. Why This Is Necessary and How It Is Proper to Strive toward It.
Foreword.

[1]   Insofar as many of the *holy Fathers*[6] spoke of the *activity of the heart, mental preservation* and the *guarding of the intellect* in different dialogues, just as each of them was instructed by God's grace, with the same knowledge,[7] having first received the word from *the Lord* himself, who *said: 'Out of the heart proceed evil thoughts and defile man'*;[8] *and who taught to clean the insides of the vessel*,[9] and said: *'In spirit and truth it is proper to worship the Father'*.[10]

[2]   And to this he[11] adds, with the *Apostle* speaking, *'If I pray with my tongue'*, that is, my mouth, *'my spirit prays'*, that is, my voice, *'yet my intellect is barren; I shall now pray in the spirit, I shall also pray in the intellect'*.[12] *And* this, *the Apostle* having testated concerning prayer of

---

6. Ps-Symeon NT, but not in the Slavic texts which I have seen, mentions Mark the Ascetic, John Climacus, Hesychius, Philotheus, Isaiah the Solitary, Barsanuphius, and one of the collections of Desert *apophthegmata*: from among these, Nil failed explicitly to utilize only Isaiah.

7. Iosif also uses this expression, *edin razum (the same knowledge / understanding / aim)*, in the same sense concerning all Scripture and patristics, as well as the opposite sense, to characterize forced conformity under ancient, pagan tyrants, as well as the alleged, present heretics: *Prosvetitel'* 4: 167, 5:207, AfED, 507.

8. From Mt 15:19-20 and adapted from Hesychius, *On Watchfulness* 178: 194; HM SMS 456.76: 182v; Eparkh. 344.175: 467v; PG 93.2.76: 1537AB/Фк 1:178:169; cf. Cassian, *Institutes* 6.2: 95/*Eight Vices* 2 75; HMS 468.2:225; cf. below, *Ustav* 7.3.

9. Cf. Mt 23:26. Down to here, the entire paragraph, except, explicitly, for *God's grace* and *the same knowledge*, (instead: *all fed divine manna*) is seemingly adapted and recast from a combination of Nicephorus / Ps-Symeon NT, *Watchfulness*, 204, and Ps-Symeon NT, *Three Methods* 71; HM SMS 468:79, 83; PG 147: 961B, Hausherr, *Méthode* 160-162/ Фк 5: 85-86, texts which sometimes appear almost as one in the Slavic MSS. Cf. Cassian, *Institutes* 6.2: 95 / *Eight Vices* 2: 75; HMS 468.2:225.

10. Adapted from Jn 4:23–24.

11. I.e., the Lord.

12. Adapted from 1 Cor 14:14–15 (NT citation in quotation marks).

the intellect and especially *affirmed*, speaking thusly: '*I prefer to say five words with my intellect rather than a myriad of words by the tongue*'.[13]

[3]   Saint *Agathon* said: *Bodily activity is a mere leaf, while the inner, that is, the mental, is the fruit*. And to this the saint adds a *terrible dictum*: '*Every tree*', he said, '*which does not bear good fruit*', that is, *the guarding of the intellect*, '*shall be cut down and cast into the fire*'.[14]

[4]   And again the Fathers said: He who only prays with his mouth, but neglects the intellect, prays to the air, for God attends to the intellect.[15]

[5]   Saint Barsanuphius the Great says: *If interior activity with God does not help a man, he toils in vain over externals.*[16]

[6]   And Saint Isaac named *bodily activity without the mental*[17] '*a barren womb*'[18] *and* '*dry breasts*', *for it cannot*, he said, *approach divine knowledge.*[19]

[7]   And many other holy Fathers so spoke, and all agree with this. Thus the Blessed Philotheus the Sinaite, speaking of *monks, who have activity only, and in their simplicity do not know* of mental *contests, victories and defeats, and for that reason are negligent of their intellect*, directs *to pray for them and instruct them, so that during the operation of evil beings, they refrain and* especially *cleanse* their intellect, which is *the optic*[20] *of the soul.*[21]

---

13. 1 Cor 14:19, the original and Nil omit *in the church*, but the original adds *and so forth*. This paragraph adapted from Gregory Sin., *Stillness and Two Ways* 6: 267; HM SMS 640: 109–109v; PG 150:1320B.

14. Adapted from Nicephorus's interpreted rearrangement from Agathon 9, *Sayings* 21; PG 65:112AB, citing Mt 3:10 (within ''): *Watchfulness*, 198–199; PG 147:953AB; Slavic original not within the consulted Ps-Symeon NT mss.

15. Source not identified.

16. Barsanuphius, Fragment, HM SMS 468: 72v; Barsanuphius and John 119: 87; SC 427: 452–453; cf. Arsenius 9; *Sayings*, 9; PG 65:89BC.

17. Nil omits *purity* (i.e., alters from . . . *without mental purity* . . .).

18. *neplodna* (literally, *fruitless*); *beschadna* = ἄτεκνος (*childless*) in the original.

19. Adapted, by converting a metaphor into a metonymy, from Isaac 6:53–54; HM SMS 179.58:293v /Eparkh. 324.58: 363v; Gk 56:222.

20. *zritelnoe* = ὀπτικόν, a substantivized adjective = *organ of sight, instrument*, metaphorically, *eye*; see above, 'Preface to the Translations', text to note 10.

21. Orig.: *cleanse the optic of the soul*, with Nil repeating *their intellect* as a reversed gloss; abstracted and adapted from Philotheus, *Watchfulness* 37: 30; Eparkh. 344.31:356–356v; Фк 2:286.

[8] And insofar as the earlier holy Fathers, not only anchorites[22] and those who lived in interior hermitages in solitude, preserved their intellect from everything, acquired grace, and attained impassivity and purity of the soul, so also those who lived in monasteries—and not only those who remained far from the world, but even those who were in cities, like Symeon *the New Theologian*,[23] and his elder Symeon the Studite[24] in the middle of the Imperial City,[25] in the great cloister of Stoudion—in such a populous city—shone like heavenly lights with spiritual gifts, and similarly were Nicetas *Stethatos*[26] and many others.[27]

[9] Thus Blessed Gregory the Sinaite not only taught anchorites and solitaries watchfulness and stillness, that is, the guarding of the intellect, but also directed those living in coenobia to attend and take care for this, knowing that all the saints acquired the grace of the spirit through the performing of the commandments, first sensibly and then mentally.[28]

[10] Otherwise, the holy Fathers said, this wondrous and great gift is not acquired.[29]

[11] The Blessed Hesychius of Jerusalem speaks thus: *As it is impossible to live this life without eating and drinking, so it is impossible, without guarding of the intellect,[30] which is called watchfulness, for the soul*

---

22. *otьshьlnikь*: may also mean *wanderer*.
23. For Symeon's disciplinary rule, *Discourses* 26: 274–283; SC 113.26: 68–97; Eparkh. 333: 251v–275.
24. See Symeon the Studite, *Discourse ascétique* 20:90–94.
25. *tsarstvuiushchii grad* (usually in Slavic, *Tsargrad*): Constantinople.
26. Nil cites Nicetas Steth. below, *Ustav* 5.7.86–87.
27. Cf. Gregory's list of recommended readings, which includes *the New Theologian and his disciple Stethatos: Stillness and Two Ways* 11:273; HM SMS 640:113; PG 150:1321D.
28. *myslěně*; *umně* (intellectively) on the margin of KB 89/1166; other texts have *umně* instead of *myslěně* in the text. Fwd. 9, abstracted from Kallistos, *Zhitie . . . Grigoriia Sin.*, Eparkh. 348:298v; Gk: 19:42.
29. Source not yet identified.
30. Nil omits: *and purity of the heart*.

*to reach anything spiritual,³¹ even if someone compels himself out of fear of torments not to sin.*³²

[12] For the true doer of God's commandments, the Fathers said, is not only to preserve them in deeds, but also to protect with the intellect against transgressing what has been commanded.³³

[13] *And this great and exquisite* and *light-generating activity,* said Symeon the New Theologian, *accrues for many through instruction, but the rare ones, without instruction, have received this from God by the vigor of the activity and the heat of faith.*³⁴

[14] So speaks Gregory the Sinaite and other saints: *It is no small feat,* they said, *to find a reliable*³⁵ *mentor in* this wondrous *activity; and they called him 'reliable', whose activity and prudence are witnessed in the Divine Writings, and who has* acquired *spiritual discretion.*³⁶

[15] And as the saints said that even then a reliable teacher for such things was hardly to be found,³⁷ now with extreme scarcity it is proper to search industriously. *And if a one cannot be found, the* holy *Fathers directed us to* meditate on *the Divine Writings,*³⁸ having heard the Lord himself saying: '*Study the Scriptures, and in them* you shall

---

31. Nil omits: *pleasing to God or free oneself from a committed sin* in the Slavic Hesychius; . . . *from sins of thinking* (κατὰ διάνοιαν) in the original.
32. Abbrev. from Hesychius, *On Watchfulness* 109:181; HM SMS 456.2.6: 170/ Eparkh. 344.2.6:451; PG 93.2.7:1513B/Φκ 1.181: 170.
33. Source not identified; perhaps adapted from Hesychius, *On Watchfulness,* 80–81, 85:176; HM SMS 456.76–77, 82: 166–166v; PG 93.80–81, 84:1505A, CD/Φκ 1.85:154.
34. Combined from Hesychius, *On Watchfulness* 90.177; HM SMS 456.87:167v; PG 93.1.88:1508BC / Φκ 1.90: 154, and Nicephorus (Ps-Symeon NT), *Watchfulness,* 205; PG 147:962B / Φκ 4: 26; HM SMS 468:79v, following a citation allegedly from Symeon, but rejecting Heyschius's greater optimism concerning experience.
35. *neprelestna* (acc. sg.), literally, *undeceiving, guileless;* alt. transl. of the original and its source, but not their Slavic transl.: *unerring:* cf. Basil/Ps-Basil, *Ascetic Discourse* 63/19; HM SMS 183:180v; PG 31:632B.
36. Adapted from *Sitting at Prayer* 7: 284; HM SMS 456:73v–74; PG 147:1341B, the characteristics of the reliable teacher themselves adapted from Basil/Ps-Basil, *Ascetic Discourse* 63; PG 31:632B; cf. HM SMS 183:180v; cf., below, *To Vassian* 16; *To Gurii* 17, *To German* 6.
37. Cf. Isaac 23:117; HM SMS 179.16: 81–81v; Gk: 32:135; Gregory Sin., *Sitting at Prayer* 7:284; Eparkh. 351:95; PG 150:1341B.
38. Adapted from Nikon, *Taktikon* 5:41v–42v.

find *eternal life*'.[39] '*For whatsoever was written afore time* in the Holy *Scriptures, was written for our instruction*',[40] says the holy Apostle.

[16] Insofar as the saints, having struggled sensibly and mentally, worked in the vineyard of their hearts, and having cleansed their intellect of passions, attained the Lord, and acquired spiritual knowledge, they directed us, who are fired by the flames of passions, to draw *living water*[41] from the spring of the Divine Writings, which are able to quench the passions that sear us and instruct us in all true knowledge.

[17] And therefore I, most *sinful and unknowledgeable*,[42] having collected from the Divine Writings what the spirit-bearing Fathers said about these things, have written as a reminder for myself,[43] not as a doer of these—for I, *indifferent and lazy*,[44] *have never done anything good*,[45] but have been devoid of all virtue, spiritual and corporeal.

[18] And I have been like some slave, purchased by the unseemly passions and completely subject to them,[46] because I am not among those in cheerful health with calmness toward passions. Being instead under the yoke of the disease of passion, I have rather spoken these not from myself, but from the Divine Writings.[47] *I have gathered* a little from a lot, *as a dog from the crumbs falling from the table*[48] of words of his lords, the blessed Fathers, so that soon afterward we shall be their imitators.[49]

---

39. Adapted from Jn 5:39 (here as proof of Jesus's divine filiality).
40. Rom 15:4; cf. 1 Cor 10:11.
41. Cf. below, *To Vassian* 16.
42. Cf. below, *Ustav* 11.19; *To Vassian* 1, *Sobornik, Postscr.* Signature.
43. Cf. below, *Ustav* 11.19.
44. Cf. Mt. 25:26, MRIV 1ᴮ.9/1.9.
45. Cf. above, *Predanie* 1, and below, *To* Vassian 1, To *Gurii* 19; *Sobornik, Forew.* 4.
46. Cf. Rom 7:14.
47. Cf. below, *Ustav* 11.18.
48. Climacus 25.3: 191; HM SMS 184:118v; PG 88:988D; cf. Mt 15:27.
49. Other sources not identified.

Sections * [PDP 19] and ** [PDP 20—the Table of Contents] follow in many many MSS before *Slovo* 1: see above, note 1.

On the Differences[1] of the Mental Campaign Against Us, of Victory and Defeat, and that Passions are Zealously to be Resisted.[2] Discourse 1.

[1]   The campaign *against us, of mental battle,*[3] *victory, and defeat, the Fathers said, is differentiated: first is assault, then coupling, afterwards consent, then captivation and afterwards passion.*[4]

[2]   *The assault,* said *the* holy Fathers John Climacus and Philotheus the Sinaite and others,*[5] is a simple urge*[6] *or image of something encountered newly manifested, conveyed*[7] *into*[8] *the heart and manifesting itself to the intellect.*[9]

[3]   Gregory the Sinaite says: *The assault is a recollection*[10] *arising from the Enemy, saying, 'Do this or that', as at the time of Christ, our God: 'Speak, that these stones become bread'.*[11]

---

1. *razlichii* (prp. pl.), *differences* as the technical transl. (from 'academic' grammar); alt. transl.: *types, kinds.*
2. KB 25/1102 adds: *By the same elder Nil the Hermit.*
3. Adapted from Philotheus 16; Eparkh. 344.1:343v; Фк 2.1:274.
4. From *battle,* adapted from Philotheus 35: 29; Eparkh. 344.30:355: Фк 2.34:285 / Hausherr, *Méthode,* 140: cf. Climacus, *Ladder* 15.75; HM SMS, 184:93v; PG 88:896C; Nikon, *Pandekty* 12: 84v, and III. 'Centrality of Sources', under note 12.
5. Climacus and Nikon: *the blessed ones define* . . . .
6. As in Philotheus: not *word* (λόγος = *slovo*), as in Climacus and Nikon.
7. As in Climacus/Nikon: not *having been born,* as in Philotheus.
8. The Slavic translation of Climacus retains the Greek directional dative, which may not have been so understood by Nil's Russians; *borne within* may be better.
9. Only in Philotheus 35:29; Eparkh. 344.30:355v; Фк 2.35:285.
10. From *Acrostic Chapters* 60: 222; HMS.640:72; PG 150:1256C.
11. Ps-John Dam., *Virtues and Vices,* 338; HM SMS 468: 261v; PG 28:1400A/ Фк 2:235; cf.; Mt 4:3; Lk 4:30.

[4]   And this simply means any random thought[12] that may be brought into a man's intellect.

[5]   And *they* say that it is *without sin*,[13] and *bears neither praise nor reproach*,[14] *for it*[15] *is not within us.*[16]

[6]   For it is impossible that no assault against us of an urge from the Enemy occur,[17] as Symeon the New Theologian says for this: *The devil with his demons, ever since he caused man to be driven from Paradise and God for disobedience, obtained an entrance mentally to unsettle everyone's reason.*[18]

[7]   It pertains to the most successful and the perfect[19] not to be unsettled, but it happens even to them *at times*, as Saint Isaac says.[20]

[8]   *Coupling, they say, is to converse with what has appeared, in passion or dispassionately,*[21] that is, *the welcoming to the urge coming from the Enemy*—in other words, *a meditation or conversation with it of our own free choice.*[22] It means to contemplate any thought whatsoever conveyed to the intellect.

[9]   This, they said, *is not always without sin,*[23] but it *bears praise* when one arrays in a *God-pleasing manner.*[24]

---

12. *myslь*.

13. Climacus 15.74–75; HM SMS, 184:94; PG 90:897AB; cf. Nikon, *Pandekty* 12: 84v; Philotheus 35:29.

14. Adapted from Peter Dam. *Treasury* 207; HM SMS 454:149v; Фк 3:109.

15. Omitted: *whether the eight urges will disturb or not disturb.*

16. Ps-John Dam., *Virtues and Vices*, 337; HM SMS 468:261v; Фк 2:235.

17. Ps-John Dam., *Virtues and Vice*, 338; HM SMS 468:261; PG 28:1400A; Symeon NT, *Discourses* 3.5: 64; Sol. 193.5: 53; SC 96:294–295; cf. Evagarios, *Praktikos* 6 / PG 40:1224AB.

18. *slovesnoe* = τὸ λογιστικὸν; omitted: *night and day*; from Ps-Symeon NT, *On Prayer*, as in Nicephorus, *Watchfulness* 203; HL,SMS 468.79 / Eparkh, 334: 112; PG 147:959–960.

19. *those in the rank of purity* in the original.

20. From Isaac Syr. 69:335–336; Eparkh. 324.46:232–232v; HM SMS 179.46:188–188v; Gk 49:199–200, referencing the Syriac Macarian tradition.

21. As in Climacus 15.74; HM SMS, 184:93v; PG 88:896D; Nikon, *Pandekty* 12.84v.

22. Ps-John Dam., *On the Virtues*, 338; HM SMS 468:261v;.PG 28:1400A.

23. Nil reverses word order as he adapts from Climacus/Nikon or Philotheus: *Ladder* 15: 74, PG 88:897A; Nikon, Philotheus 35:29.

24. Adapted from Peter Dam., *Treasury* 207; HM SMS 454:149; Фк 3:109.

[10] We array then in this manner: if someone does not *cut off the assault of a wicked urge*,[25] but converses with it a little, and the Enemy imposes on him to contemplate with passion, he shall strive to transpose it into something good.

[11] And how we transpose thoughts[26] into good things—if God grants the word, we shall speak later.[27]

[12] *Consent*, they said, *is the voluptuous nod*[28] *of the soul to* the urge or image *that has appeared to it*;[29] that is, when someone, welcoming the *urges* presented *by the Enemy* and conversing with them mentally, for a little while consents in his thought to what the Enemy's urge says.[30]

[13] This, they say, is *relative to the state of the ascetic*,[31] and here is the state of each type of ascetic. If someone is progressing and has received aid from God to drive off urges, if he grows slothful and in his negligence does not strive to turn away the wicked urges, he is not *without sin*.[32]

[14] If, being a neophyte and still too infirm to drive off the assaults of the wicked one, even if he concurs a while with the wicked urge, but immediately confesses to the Lord, repenting and reproaching himself, and he calls upon him for help—as it is written,

---

25. As in Climacus 15.74; HM SMS, 184: 93v; PG 88:896D; Nikon, *Pandekty* 12:84v; cf. Philotheus, 36:30; Eparkh. 344.31: 355v; Фк 2.36:285.

26. *mysli*: alt. transl. here: *urges*.

27. Cf. below, *Ustav* 5.3–4, 5.7.79, 8.25; *To Gurii* 8.

28. Alt. transl.: *bow* (nod in Clmacus's original, translation, and Nikon).

29. As in Philotheus 35:29:, Eparkh. 344.30:355v, (Hausherr, *Méthode*, 140), not Climacus 15:74, HM SMS, 184:93v; PG 88:896D.

30. Possibly inspired by Isaac Syr. *Ascetic Homilies* 54:269; HM SMS 179.30:140; Gk: 33:144–145: *Do you think to lecture those* (demons) *who are six thousand years old* (i.e., as old as creation)?

31. Climacus 15: 74, HM SMS, 184:93v; PG 88:897A; Philotheus 35:29; Eparkh. 344.30:355v; Nikon, *Pandekty* 12:84v.

32. Cf. Peter Dam., *Treasury* 1:207; HM SM 454:149; Фк 3:109.

'*Confess to the Lord and call upon his name*',[33] —God *in his mercy*[34] will forgive him on account of his infirmity.[35]

[15] This is also said by the Fathers regarding mental consent, when someone is unwillingly defeated in this struggle by an urge, for the root of his intellect is firmly resolved not to sin and not to commit any lawlessness in deed.

[16] And Gregory the Sinaite says: 'Next *the passions*, and after *combat, consent*. And what *consent* means here, said this saint, *is*: anyone who *willingly* accepts *the urges of the Enemy*, conversing and interacting with them, is defeated by them, and no longer wages war against passion, but firmly agrees within himself to commit the sin; or if he has sought to *effect in deed*[36] what he has already agreed to in his thought, but has been thwarted by the time or place or any other cause. And this is most grave and is classed as penitential.[37]

[17] *Captivation is either the violent and involuntary abduction of the heart, or the permanent coupling to what is encountered and is destructive of our best state.*[38]

[18] 'Violent and involuntary abduction of the *heart*' occurs when the intellect is taken captive by urges, that is, *forcibly abducted* to wicked thoughts, *being unwilling*[39] —but with God immediately helping, you return to yourself.

[19] When, as if carried by a storm and waves, it is led out of a good state to wicked thoughts, unable to come to a quiet and peaceful state—it mostly occurs from clamor and frequent and

---

33. Lxx Ps 104:1; cf. Acts 22:16; the Hebrew /King James Ps 105:1: *give thanks*.

34. Cf. Ps 106:1/107:1.

35. Cf. on repentance here, Peter Dam., *Treasury* 1:207; HM SM 454:150; Фк 3:109.

36. Possibly rearranged from Ps-John Dam., *Virtues and Vices*, 338; HM SMS 468:261v (contrast Gregory Sin., *Acrostic Chapters* 70, 73, *Further Texts* 4, SM HMS 640:73v, 74v, 104-104v [here No. 141]); PG 150:1257C, 1250B, 1301A.

37. *vъ zapreshcheniikhъ*: (literally) among those [offenses] subject to penance/ among the forbidden; Nil's other probable source(s), not identified.

38. *ustroenia* (gn.) = καταστάσεως (gn.): metaphrased from Climacus 15.74; HM SMS 184:93v; PG 88:896D, rather than Philotheus 35:29.

39. Adapted from Peter Dam., *Treasury*, 207, HM SMS 454:149v; Фк 3:109.

idle conversations—this is 'permanent coupling to what is encountered' and 'destructive' of 'good state'.

[20] *This is judged one way at the time of prayer and otherwise not at that time, and one way when from neutral[40] and otherwise from wicked thoughts.*[41]

[21] If at the time of prayer one be captured by wicked urges, it is most grave, for at the time of prayer to God one is to concentrate one's intellect and attend to prayer, turning away from all thoughts.

[22] If it be not at the time of the prayer and in connection with the necessities of life, such occurrences are without sin, for even the saints handled the necessities of this life with a blessing.[42]

[23] When, said the Fathers, the intellect is with pious intellection[43] in any urge, it is with God; but from wicked urges, it is always proper to turn away.[44]

[24] *And passion, they truly say, is what over a long period of time has been nesting*[45] *in one's soul, and is henceforth brought there to it by habit,*[46] *as if into its ethos, and is henceforth voluntarily in him, most familiarly coming,*[47] *over amid the tempest of passionate urges* imposed by the Enemy, bolstered by frequent *conjunction*[48] and conversation, and becoming a habit from much meditation and imagining.

---

40. Literally, *concerning 'middle'* (o srednikhъ = ἐπὶ μέσοις), another technical term from grammar.
41. Climacus 15: 74; PG 88:897AB; cf. Nikon, *Pandekty* 12:84v: *pomyshlenie* as ἐνθύμημα.
42. *blagoslovne* = benedictorily (with, or as if with, explicit permission).
43. *umъ blagochestivymъ razumomъ*: alt. transl.: . . . knowledge, gnosis, understanding.
44. Alt. (more literal) transl.: *to avoid, be removed.*
45. Nil omits Climacus's *passionately* (strastne = ἐμπαθῶς).
46. *obychai:* alt. transl.: *custom* (in the sense of legal custom). Source for [23] not identified.
47. As, but with a reversal, from Climacus 15:74; Eparkh. 331.15: 203/ HM SMS 184: 93v; PG 88:897A.
48. Adapted from Peter Dam. *Treasury,* 3: 207, but not fully in HM SMS 454:149v or Фк 3:109.

[25] This occurs when the Enemy frequently presents any passionate thing to a man and inflames him to love it above all else, and he, *volens nolens,* is mentally defeated by it. This especially occurs from carelessness, from frequently having coupled and conversed, that is, voluntarily having thought about that thing unseemingly.

[26] *In all cases this is liable either to a measured*[49] *penance or to a future torment,*[50] which means to repent and *to pray for deliverance from* such *a passion*[51] *as one is liable to future torment for non-repentance, not for the battle. 'For if it were so, that there were no imperfect dispassion, few could receive remission',*[52] as Peter Damaskenos says.

[27] And it is proper for anyone attacked by any passion whatsoever zealously to oppose it, the Fathers say.

[28] As we say regarding sexual passion: if someone be assailed by passion for someone's face, he should stay away from him: from conversing, cohabiting, robe-touching, and sniffing.[53] In all of these, if someone does not protect himself, the Fathers said, he effects the passion and fornicates in his heart via the urges; he ignites the furnace for *passions,* leading in wicked urges like *beasts.*[54]

---

49. *měrilnomu* (dt. sg.; *ravnoměrnoe* [acc. sg.] in the original): alt. transl.: *corresponding*—added by Peter Damaskenos to the Climacus citation.

50. Combined from Climacus 15.74: 158; PG 90:898B. (= HM SMS 184:94/ VMCh-M: 890a) / Nikon, *Pandekty* 12:84v, and Peter Dam., *Treasury,* 207; HM SMS 454:149v; Фк 3:109.

51. Combined from Climacus 26.79: 213; PG 90:1029B (=VMCh-M: 913c) / Nikon, *Pandekty* 12:84v, and Peter Dam., *Treasury,* 207; HM SMS 454:150; Фк 3:109.

52. With a reversal (or two in the published KB 25/1102[!]), from Peter Dam., *Treasury,* 207; HM SMS 454:150; Фк 3:109; cf. Climacus, *Ladder* 26.82: *It is not possible that all be dispassionate, but it is not impossible that all be saved . . . . ,* also cited by Peter Damaskenos here; see also above, under III. 'Literary Devices', note 125 and text thereto.

53. Cf. Climacus 15.76:159; PG 88:898C, and Basil/Ps-Basil, *Ascetic Discourse* 66/24; HM SMS 183:183; PG 32:637AB.

54. Cf. Symeon NT, *Discourses* 5:118; Sol. 193:18-18v; SC 96:378–381.

On the Combat against These, and How to Defeat Them with Remembrance of GOD and the Guarding of the Heart, that is, with Prayer and Stillness of the Intellect; and How to Effect This—Herein also on Gifts. 2.

[1]   *The combat* against these the Fathers *establish*[1] *as an equipotent force against the combatant,*[2] *who willingly is either defeating or accepting defeat*[3] intellectively—what is, simply stated, that we are to resist wicked urges with whatever force we have.

[2]   *This results either in a crown or a torture:*[4] *a crown for the victors, torments* for transgressors, *who have not repented* in this life. And it is a transgression, which *results in torments,* says Peter Damaskenos, when it comes into effect, while the brightest *crowns* are woven for those who fight harder and do not weaken in the face of the Enemy's great onslaught.[5]

[3]   An intelligent and excellent fight, *the Fathers* say, is *cutting off* the *beginning of the urge* that has come—what is called the assault—and praying unceasingly. For, they said, '*he who* resists *the first,* that is, the assault of an urge, *cuts off all the last ones*[6] at once,

---

1. *ustavliaiutъ* (3rd pl. prs.) = ὁρίζονται, *(decree),* thus carrying both definitional and categorical consequences, as is evident in the following sentence: see below, *To German* 5.
2. I.e. a force equivalent to the force that assails the ascetic-combatant.
3. Adapted from a combination of Nikon, *Pandekty* 12:84v and Climacus 15.74:158; HM SMS 184:93v/VMCh-M: 889d–890a; PG 88:896D–897A.
4. Climacus 15.74: 158; HM SMS 184:94 / VMCh-M: 890a; PG 88:897A; cf. Peter Dam, *Treasury,* 207; HM SMS 454:150; Φκ 3:109.
5. Perhaps adapted from Peter Dam., *Treasury,* 206; HM SMS 454:149v; Φκ 3:109.
6. Climacus 15.74:158; HM SMS 184:94; PG 88:897B.

because *the one who intelligently* combats *the mother of evils, that is, the wicked assault, repulses with thought.*[7]

[4] And it is proper to *struggle to render the intellect deaf and mute at the time of prayer,*[8] as Neilos the Sinaite said.

[5] And *hold the heart in stillness away from every urge, even if it nonetheless appear good,*[9] as Hesychius of Jerusalem says, because, he said, *upon dispassionate urges the passionate follow, as is known from experience, and the admittance of the first becomes a cause of the second.*[10]

[6] And insofar, it is said, as following good urges, wicked ones enter into us, for this reason it is proper to try to be silent in thought, *even regarding urges considered right*, and always *gaze into the depths of our hearts,*[11] *saying: 'Lord Jesus Christ, Son of God, have mercy on me';* all of it, and sometimes *only a part: 'Lord Jesus Christ, have mercy on me'*, and then alternating to *'Son of God, have mercy on me'*, as this is simpler for neophytes, said Gregory the Sinaite. It *is improper*, he said, *to alternate often*, but in due time.[12]

[7] Nowadays, *the Fathers* add a word: after they *say 'Lord Jesus Christ, Son of God, have mercy on me'*, they forthwith say: 'a sinner'.[13] This is also appropriate, especially befitting us, the sinful.

---

7. *myslemъ* (instr.): with a play on the earlier *pomyslь* (urge), added by the Slavic translator (or lost in the printed Фк); from *the one who . . .* adapted from Peter Dam., *Treasury* 207; HM SMS454:150; 3:109.

8. Evagrius (Ps-Neilos Sin.), *Chapters on Prayer* 11:27 (PSW 11:58) HM SMS 468:11: 99; Eparkh. 344.11:330v (attrib. to *Nil Postnik* = *Neilos the Ascetic*); PG 79:1169C / Фк 1.11:178.

9. Hesychius, *On Watchfulness,* 1.15, 20:164, 165; HM SMS 456 1.16, 20:157, 157v / Eparkh. 344. 16, 20:432v, 433; PG 93:1485B, D / Фк 1:15, 20:143, 144.

10. Adapted from Hesychius, *On Watchfulness,*163:191; HM SMS 2.60:179v; PG 93:2.61:1532B / Фк 1.163:166.

11. From *gaze . . .* from Ps-Symeon NT, *Three Methods* 71; HM SMS 468:83; Hausherr, *Méthode*, 158–159.

12. [6] Created by Nil in part from words and phrases of Gregory Sin., *Stillness and Two Ways* 2:264, and *Sitting at Prayer* 2:275–276; HM SMS 640:106–106v, 117–117v; PG 150:1316AB, 1329B.

13. Cf. 'Poslanie Arkhim. Pechersk. Dosifeia', 234 (early 15th c.), though Gregory the Sinaite does not add *a sinner*: on antecedents in Luke, Agathon, and Symeon NT, see Maloney, *Russian Hesychasm*, 135, note 137.

[8] And so speak *diligently,* be you standing, *sitting,* or lying down, and *confine your intellect within your heart and hold your respiration as much as you can, so that you do not breathe often,* as says Symeon the New Theologian and Gregory the Sinaite: *Call upon the Lord Jesus* with longing, endurance, and patience, *turning away* from all *urges.*[14]

[9] And what these saints said—*hold respiration, that is, not to breathe often*—experience quickly teaches that it greatly helps the concentration of the intellect.

[10] And *if* you cannot pray *in stillness of the heart,*[15] without *urges,* but see them multiplying *in your intellect, do not be fainthearted*[16] over this, but still persevere in *praying.*[17]

[11] And the blessed Gregory the Sinaite, knowing full well that it is impossible for us, the passionate, to defeat wicked urges, said this: *No neophyte restrains*[18] *his intellect and drives off urges, if God does not restrain him and drive away the urges. It is for the powerful to* restrain the intellect and *drive away urges, and even they do not by themselves drive them off, but with God they struggle against their attack, clad in*[19] *his grace and panoply.*[20]

[12] *And you, if*[21] *you see,* he said, *the uncleanness of wicked spirits, that is to say, urges, stirred up*[22] *in your intellect, do not be horrified or*

---

14. Both adapted from and closer to Gregory Sin., *Stillness and Two Ways* 2:264, HM SMS 640:106, PG 150:1316B, than his apparent source, Ps-Symeon NT, *Three Methods,* 72–73; HM SMS 468:84, 80; Hausherr, *Méthode,* 164–165, 160 / Фк 5:86–87.

15. For this formulation, Gregory Sin.. *Acrostic Chapters* 99:233, HM SMS 640:82v, PG 150:1271C; also in Ps-Symeon NT, *Three Methods* 71; HM SMS 468:83v; Hausherr, *Méthode,* 161.

16. *startled* in the original.

17. [9–10] adapted from Gregory Sin., *Stillness and Two Ways* 2:264; HM SMS 640:106–106v; PG 150:1316AB.

18. *uderzhavaetъ*: alt. transl.: *maintains.*

19. *obolcheni* (nm. pl. pst. pssv. prtcpl.): alt. mod. transl.: *invested with.*

20. Expanded from Gregory Sin., *Sitting at Prayer* 4:276, 277, by adapting the title of the previous chapter: HM SMS 456:60, 61; PG 150:1332A, CD; *grace* is in neither PG 1332CD nor Фк 4:81, but is in the Slavic and, differently (*clothed in the armor of His grace*) in the PSW transl.; cf. Eph. 6:11.

21. Formula from Ps-Symeon NT near a citation below, *Ustav* 2.14: *Three Methods* 70; HM SMS 468: 82v /Sol. 193: 25: 158; Hausherr, *Méthode,* 158 / Фк 5:84; *if* commences the citation from Gregory.

22. Nil omits: *or metamorphized.*

amazed; even if some good conceptualizations[23] *of certain matters appear to you, pay no heed, but restrain your respiration as much as possible and confining your intellect within your heart.*[24] *And, instead of armament, summon the Lord Jesus often and assiduously, and they shall flee, as if* invisibly *seared by the fire of* the divine *name.*[25] If the urges greatly harass you, *rise and pray against them*, and then hold more firmly to your original activity.[26] And how *to pray* against urges, this, *with God's help,* we *shall recount*[27] next.

[13]   If, even after you have prayed against them, they still parade about and multiply, so that you cannot protect your heart with your intellect, orally recite a prayer at length, with firmness and patiently. And if torpor and exhaustion envelop you, summon God for help, and compel yourself to the limits of your power, not desisting from prayer, and at that moment all of these will completely fall away from you, driven off with God's help. And when your intellect is calmed down from urges, *attend once more* to your heart and prayer of the soul or the intellect. For *there are many virtuous deeds, but they are particular; prayer of the heart is the wellspring of all good,*[28] *and it waters the soul*[29] *like orchards,*[30] said Gregory the Sinaite.

---

23. *razuměnia* = νοήματα (nm./acc. pl.).

24. Slightly adapted from Gregory Sin., *Stillness and Two Ways* 2: 264; HM SMS 456 48v-49; PG 150:1316B.

25. Slightly adapted from Gregory Sin., *Sitting at Prayer* 4:277, HM SMS 456: 61; PG 150:1332D, probably from Climacus in Gregory's next sentence: *Beat/ Flog your enemies with Jesus's name* (*Ladder* 21.7; PG 88:945C).

26. Abstracted and adapted from Gregory Sin., *Sitting at Prayer* 4: 277; HM SMS 456:61v; PG 150:1332D.

27. Seemingly adapted from Ps-Symeon NT, *Three Methods* 72; Φκ 5:86; but Hausherr, *Méthode,* 163, is different here, and HM SMS 468:84, Sol 193.25:160v, and Eparkh. 334 omit part of the PSW 4:72 text (lines 6 from *by reading* through line 20), including this passage.

28. From *there are,* adapted from Gregory Sin., *Stillness and Two Ways* 6:267; HM SMS 640:109v; PG 150:1320BC.

29. *wellspring of virtues . . . food for the soul* in Climacus's original, whom Gregory is citing in both related passages: 28.1:250; PG 88: 1129A; cf. below, *Ustav* 2.25.

30. From *is the wellspring,* adapted from Gregory Sin., *Sitting at Prayer* 5:279; SM.HMS 640:120; PG 150:1333D.

[14] And this blessed one, encompassing the writings of all the spirit-bearing Fathers, following the others, enjoins assiduously to take care of prayer, abstaining within it from all urges, if it is possible, not only the evil, but also the seemingly good. *For stillness,* he said, *is the deponing of speculations,*[31] *lest you, by attending to them as good, destroy the greater;*[32] and to *seek the Lord within the heart,*[33] which means *with the intellect to protect the heart in prayer and always be fixed within it,*[34] as Symeon the New Theologian said.

[15] This activity, he said, *to protect the intellect within the heart, devoid of any urges,*[35] is most *agonizing* for the unaccustomed, *not only for neophytes,* but even for experienced practitioners, *who have not yet,* by the operation of *grace, received* and *maintained the sweetness* of prayer *within* their hearts. And it is known from *experience,* that for the infirm, this *activity* is considered to be very *brutal and arduous.* When, though, one acquires grace, one prays *effortlessly* and with *love,* comforted by that grace.[36] For when *the operation of prayer* comes, it *truly* holds *the intellect* to itself,[37] and *gladdens* and frees from *captivity,*[38] said the Sinaite.

[16] Therefore it is proper to endure in prayer, turning away as much as possible from all urges, and not rise to chant too early. *In endurance,* he said, *may your sitting be, on account of him who said,*

---

31. *domyshleniemъ* (dt. pl.): *razuměnii* = νοημάτων (gn. pl.) in the original; cf. Climacus 27.51:245; HM SMS 184: 157v; PG 88:1112A: *stillness is the deponing of conceptualizations,* cited and augmented elsewhere by Gregory with *of the sensible and the intellective*: HM SMS 640: 119v; PG 150:1333B. Nil omits: *which are not divinized by the Spirit,* but restores the dt. pl. of the Slavic Climacus's *razuměniemъ*.

32. Gregory Sin., *Stillness and Two Ways* 9: 270; HM SMS 640: 112; PG 150:1324A.

33. Gregory Sin., *Sitting at Prayer* 1:259; HM SMS 640:117; PG 150:1329A.

34. Ps-Symeon NT, *Three Methods* 70-71; HM SMS 468:83 (grammatically adapted); Hausherr, *Méthode,* 159 / Φκ 5:85.

35. *devoid of any urges* from Gregory Sin., *Stillness and Two Ways* 9; HM SMS 640:111; PG 150:1321B.

36. [15] adapted from Ps-Symeon NT; *Three Methods,* 71; HM SMS 468:83-83v; Hausherr, *Méthode,* 159–161.

37. *warms the intellect* in the original.

38. Adapted from Gregory Sin., *Stillness and Prayer* 3, 1:259, 258; PG 150:1308BC, 1305; Gregory mentions only *captivity* in *Cap.* 1, not *freeing.*

'*enduring in prayer*',[39] *and do not rise quickly due to painful exhaustion*[40] *or an intellective cry of the intellect.*[41] And he cites the word of *the Prophet*: ill-afflicted like those '*in pain and about to give birth*',[42] and *what Saint Ephrem said: Pine over pains painfully, and thereby bypass the pains of vain pains.*[43]

[17] And he directs *to bow with shoulders and head in pain and endure oft times with desire, summoning the Lord Jesus for help, bending downward*, and *gathering the intellect within the heart, if indeed it is open,*[44] he said. And he cites the *word of the Lord himself: 'Violent'*, he said, *'is the kingdom of heaven, and the violent ravage it'.*[45] *'Violence'*,[46] *the Lord showed to be zeal and pain over these,*[47] he *says.*[48]

[18] *When*, he said, *the suffering, clamoring intellect is exhausted and the body*[49] *and the heart aches from intense and constant calling upon the Lord Jesus,*[50] *then permit it some chanting as a little relief, giving it*

---

39. Acts 1:14 (referring to Mary and the disciples at Jesus's tomb); cf. Col 4:2 (here for prophetic enlightenment).

40. In the original: *due to exhaustion from painful labor.*

41. *radi . . . umu razumnago vъpitia*, as in the Slavic transl. of διὰ . . . τὴν τοῦ νοός νοηρὰν βοὴν; Nil omits *and perpetual strife.*

42. " from Mc 4: 9; from *In endurance . . .* adapted from Gregory Sin. *Sitting at Prayer* 1:275; HM SMS 456: 59–59v; PG 150:1329A.

43. Segment from Gregory Sin., *Stillness and Two Ways* 14:273; HM SMS 456:58; PG 150:1328BC; the Slavic retains the root repetition of the original; no Ephrem original identified. See above, under III. 'Literary Devices', note 127.

44. Segment from *Sitting at Prayer* 1: 275; HM SMS 456:59; PG 150:1329A.

45. Mt 11:12; cf. Mk 10:24.

46. Segment from *Stillness and Two Ways* 14: 273; HM SMS 456:57v; PG 150:1328A.

47. Segment from *Sitting at Prayer* 1:275; HM SMS 456:59v; PG 150:1329A.

48. Word adapted from *Stillness and Two Ways* 14:273; HM SMS 456:57v; PG 150:1328A.

49. Nil's rearrangement allows *the body* to be the second subject of either *is exhausted* or *aches.*

50. Using as the basic text up to here *Stillness and Two Ways* 9: 269, Nil intersperses words and phrases from *Cap.* 1: 263 and 7: 268: HM SMS 640:105v; 110, 111; PG 150:1313A, 1320D, 1321BC.

some rest.[51] *This, he said, is the finest system*[52] *and the teaching of the very wise;*[53] and he directs that we do it, *either in solitude or with a disciple. If,* he said, *you have a faithful disciple, let him recite the psalms, and you attend to your heart, admitting no*[54] *image of a dream or picture of a vision,*[55] lest you be *deceived.*

[19] Mental daydreams occur even when *the intellect stays within the heart* and effects prayer, he said, and these submit to *no one, except the perfect* in the *Holy Spirit,* who have succeeded in Christ Jesus in not daydreaming.[56]

[20] And thus this saintly man says, himself *having diagnosed*[57] *from experience,* to make every effort over prayer, a *few*[58] psalms due to the *onset of despondency, and troparia of repentance*[59] *without singing:* according to the words of *Climacus, 'these* people *do not sing'.*[60]

51. Segment paraphrased with some of the lexemes of *Stillness and Two Ways* 7:268; HM SMS 640; PG 150:1320D.
52. *chin* = τάξις = *procedure* (general or specific), arrangement, protocol, rank, order.
53. Segment almost as in *Stillness and Two Ways* 7:268; HM SMS 640:110; PG150:1320D; see below, [25].
54. Segment from two distinct parts of *Stillness and Two Ways* 9:269–270; HM SMS 640:111, 111v–112; PG 150:1321C, D.
55. *image* in Gregory, but *image of a dream and picture of a vision,* presented in a stylistic chiasmus (*mechtani zhe zraka i obraza videni*), adapted from Isaac Syr.'s different construction, but same sense of these words, and replaces Gregory's *urges, either sensible or intellectual, not from the Holy Spirit*: Isaac 23:116; HM SMS 179.15:79v; Gk: 31:134.
56. From *image of a dream . . . ,* adapted and combined from Gregory Sin., *Sitting at Prayer* 4:278; HM SMS 456:61v; PG 150:1333A, as well as Isaac. Cf. *Acrostic Chapters* 118:240, *Stillness and Two Ways* 10:270–271, *Sitting at Prayer* 7:282–283; HM SMS 640:90v–91, 112v; PG 150:1281D–1284A, 1324BC, 1340CD.
57. *razumĕvь* (pst. act. prtcpl.) = ἐγνωκώς.
58. *two or three* in the original.
59. As in the Slavic and PSW *Phiokalia* versions: PG has *nocturnal troparia,* many of which exist in both the liturgies and the recommended prayers before one goes to sleep.
60. Climacus 7.52:121; HM SMS 184:68/VMCh–M:875a; PG 88:813A, arguing, in reference to mourners, that vigorous singing *destroys compunction.*

[21]   For 'pain of the heart born in piety'[61] suffices for their cheer, as Saint Mark said, and spiritual warmth is granted for their joy and comfort.[62]

[22]   And he directs to recite the *Trisagion*[63] with *every* chant[64] and *Alleluia* always by the *system of the* ancient *Fathers: Barsanuphius and Diadochus*[65] *and others.*[66]

[23]   And that elsewhere he said, the *typikon*[67] *for activities* stipulates *to pray* for an *hour, read* for an hour, *sing* for an hour, *and thus pass the day;*[68] this is good, he said, according to the time, *measure, and power* of each of the athletes.[69] And he has set these according to one's volition: either to keep to this, or to preserve constant control, that is, be at all times *engaged in God's work.*[70]

[24]   And *when*, with the grace of God, prayer becomes sweet and operates in the heart, he directs one to commit even more to it. For if, he said, *you observe prayer operating in your heart and not*

---

61. Gregory (or one of his sources) altered the sense of this definition of the remembrance of God: Mark the Ascetic, *On Those Who Think They Are Made Righteous by Works*, 131:136; PG 65.122:947C / Φκ 1.131:118.

62. For *warmth of the soul* engendered by the Holy Spirit, among Gregory's sources, Diodochus of Photice, *On Spiritual Knowledge* 74:278; SC 5:132. Φκ 1.74:257.

63. Literally, *Thrice Holy*, referring to the liturgical hymn commencing: *Holy God, Holy Pantokrator, Holy Immortal, have mercy on us*; cf. below, *Scete Typikon* 9.

64. *pěnie* (= *hymn, chanted prayer*): *psalm* in the original.

65. For one of Gregory's sources of such eucho-therapeutic psalmody, Diodochus of Photice, *On Spiritual Knowledge* 73:278; Eparkh. 344:306–306v; SC 5:132 / Φκ 1.73:257; for spiritualizing liturgies, including, specifically, the *Trisagion*, Barsanuphius and John 241:107–108; SC 451:186–191; No. 74 and 181 (SC 427:350–355, 582–585, as in Grolimund, NSA, 380, note 22, do not work here).

66. [20–22] copied or adapted from Gregory Sin., *Stillness and Two Ways* 9:269–270; HM SMS 640:111v–112v, PG 150:1321BD.

67. *ustavъ*: νόμος/*zakonъ* used in a metaphor of Mosaic Law in the original.

68. Cf. Gregory Sin., *Acrostic Chapters* 99:233; HM SMS 640:82v; PG 150:1272C. The entire *Cap.* 99 is a typikon abstract or fragment, entitled *On Stillness*, in HM SMS 456:26 and 640:82, with each hour's activity listed.

69. *podvizaiushchikhъ* (gn. pl.): *ascetic/struggler* in its original sense of *wrestler/athlete*.

70. Abstracted from Gregory Sin., *Sitting at Prayer* 5:278-279; HM SMS 640:119v–121; PG 150:1333B–1336B.

ceasing to move, do not ever leave it and rise to sing, unless it leave you by design.[71] *For you have left God within, calling*[72] *from without, inclining from the heights into the depths. Moreover, you make noise unto it, and thus agitate the intellect away from its tranquility. Indeed stillness is called by its name, that it be had in peace*[73] *and tranquility, for God is peace above*[74] *all noise and clamor.*

[25] *For those who do not know the prayer which is 'the wellspring of virtues',*[75] *according to* the words of *Climacus, watering them as if*[76] *orchards of the soul, it is proper to sing a lot, and without measure, and always be engaged in a diversity of many things. For the action of stillness is one thing, and that of the coenobium is another.*[77] *And every measure*[78] *is excellent according to the very wise.*[79]

[26] *Therefore it is necessary to sing in measure, as the Fathers said, devoting oneself more*[80] *to prayer, though when sluggish, to sing or read the deed-filled lives of the Fathers.*[81] *For a ship needs no oar when the wind swells the sail and* carries it across *the passionate sea,*[82] *but when at a standstill, is pulled across by oars or a galley.*

[27] To those who *contentiously cite the holy Fathers or certain ones here who stand at all night vigils and do ceaseless singing,* he directs

---

71. *po smotrĕniiu* = οἰκονομικῶς, so, it seems, God's design, not the monk's; contrast von Lilienfeld: *wiel es dich gegen deine Absicht verlässt* (NSSS, 212).

72. *prizyvae*, as in the Slav. transl. for προσλαλῶν (conversing).

73. *smirenie* = εἰρήνη: alt. (sole modern) transl.: *humility*.

74. *beyond* in the original.

75. Climacus 28.1:250; HM SMS 184:162 / VMCh-M: 930a PG 88:1129B; see above, [13].

76. The PG Gregory has *watering the orchards—the powers of the soul.*

77. Cf. Climacus 28.20:252; PG 88:1132D-1133A: *The joy of prayer for those living in a community is one thing, and another thing for those praying in stillness/solitude*; also 27 *Scholia* 4, PG 88:1117C; [24–25] to here from Gregory Sin., *Sitting at Prayer* 5:278–279; HM SMS 640:120; PG 150:1333B-D. Contrast above, *Ustav,* Fwd. 9.

78. *this order* (*syi chinь* = αὕτη ἡ τάξις) in the original.

79. Bridge here, seemingly adapted from *Stillness and Two Ways* 7:268 HM SMS 640:110; PG150:1320D; see above, [18].

80. *mnozhae*: τὸ πλεῖστον = *mostly* in the original.

81. *dĕiatelьnaa zhitiia otchьskaa*, as in the Slavic Gregory Sin.; *deeds* (τὰ πρακτικὰ) *of the Fathers* in the original.

82. Original and Slavic transl., literally: *sea of passions*.

us to *respond from Scripture: 'Not all are perfect in all things, due to want of zeal and exhaustion of their power';*[83] *yet the small among the great are not in all ways small, and the great among the small are not in all ways perfect.*[84] *And never did all the ascetics, now or of old, tread the same path or keep to it to the end.*[85]

[28] Regarding *those who have advanced* and have *attained to enlightenment,* he said: *They do not need to recite psalms, but silence and abundant prayer and vision, as they are coupled with God, and they have no need to tear their intellect away from him and place it into confusion. The intellect of such people commits adultery, if*[86] *it withdraws from the memory of God, and clings lovingly to the most worthless things.*[87]

[29] And Saint Isaac, writing most sublimely about them, relates as follows: *When* that *ineffable joy befalls them, and cuts prayer from their lips,* and then, he said, *are stilled the lips and the tongue, and the heart—the guardian of urges, the intellect—the helmsman of the senses, and thought*[88] *—that swift of wing and shameless bird.*[89]

[30] *And thought*[90] *no longer has anything to do with prayer, motion, or self-determination,*[91] *but is instructed with an instruction by another power,*[92] *but does not instruct, and by captivity is contained at that hour and abides among incomprehensible things, and does not know where.*[93] And he calls this *the awe and vision of prayer, and not prayer,*

---

83. Also in Nikon, *Pandekty* 29:202; cf. *Prosevetitel'* 4:160; MR IV III.29, XIII.3; Macarius/Ps-Macarius, *Homiliae* 29.1–5:168–169, 32.1–3:178–179, 36:187; PG 34:716B–720A, 733B–736B, 749AC; no Biblical citation identified.
84. From Climacus 26.92; PG 88:1033B, not identified by Gregory.
85. [26–27] almost exactly as in Gregory Sin., *Sitting at Prayer* 5:279; HM SMS 640:120v; cf. PG 150:1330D–1336B.
86. *When* in the original.
87. From Gregory Sin., *Stillness and Two Ways* 8:268, HM SMS 456:52v; PG 150:1320D–1321A.
88. *myslъ* = διάνοια: alt. transl.: *the mind.*
89. Segment from Isaac Syr. 23:116; Eparkh. 324.15:87v–88; Gk: 31:134.
90. Here, following Isaac, Nil combines the predication of both *umъ* = νοῦς and *mysl* = διάνοια.
91. *samovlastie,* literally, *autocracy;* αὐτεξούσιον = *authority over oneself* in the Greek Isaac.
92. *siloiu innoiu* = ἑτέρᾳ δυνάμει; alt. transl.: *by another force.*
93. Segment from Isaac Syr. 23:119; HM SMS 179 16:83v; Gk: 32:137.

for the intellect does not pray with prayer, but is above prayer[94] —*for in the discovery of something better, prayer is abandoned—and is in ecstasy.*[95] *And it has no desire for anything, and, according to the word of the Apostle, 'whether in the body, or out of the body, knows not'.*[96]

[31] For prayer he named *the seed*, and this *the gathering of the harvest, where the reaper marvels at the ineffable sight of how from the poor and bare seeds, which he sows, the ripened ears of grain have suddenly sprouted before him.*[97]

[32] *And the Fathers name it prayer, because it has its cause in prayer, and at the time of prayer this ineffable gift is granted to the saints.*[98] *However they wish, they make of its appearance in order to firm up the urges*[99] *of the soul, but no one knows precisely its name. For when by the Spirit's operation the soul moves toward those Divine things and is made God-like by incomprehensible union, it is illuminated in its movements by the ray of the higher light. And when the intellect becomes worthy of sensing the future bliss, it forgets itself and all the things existing here, and makes no further movement whatsoever.*[100]

[33] And elsewhere he says, that *at the time of the prayer the intellect is rapt beyond desires into thoughts*[101] *about incorporeal things, where senses are not permitted to explain them.*[102] *Suddenly joy fires inside you, which silences the tongue within its incomparable food.*[103] *And from the heart constantly boils a kind of sweetness that imperceptibly attracts*

---

94. Segment adapted from Isaac Syr. 23:116; *Eparkh.* 324.15 (end); HM SMS 179 15:79v is defective; Gk: 31:134.

95. Segment adapted from Isaac Syr. 23:121; HM SMS179 16:87; Gk: 32:140; *above prayer* is also in the previous segment.

96. 2 Cor 12:2-3. Segment from Isaac Syr. 23:119; HM SMS 179 16:84/ *Eparkh.* 324.16:92; Gk: 32:140.

97. From Isaac Syr. 23:117; HM SMS 179.16:81/*Eparkh.* 324.16.92v; Gk: 32:135.

98. Adapted from Isaac Syr. 23:119-119v; HM SMS 179.16:87; Gk: 32:138.

99. Here *pomysly* = διαλογισμούς (acc.pl.) in the Greek Isaac.

100. From Isaac Syr. 23:118-119; HM SMS 179.16:82v-83/*Eparkh.* 324.16. 89v-90; Gk: 32:136–137.

101. *vъ mysli* (used as prp. pl.) = εἰς τὰς ἐννοίας.

102. Punctuation here, consistent with the Greek original, from both Slavic Isaac's, Eparkh. 349:31, and Prokhorov, PNSIK, 118, but not Borovkova-M, 28.

103. *pishcha* = delectable (very tasty dish).

the entire man entirely time and time again. *A certain food and joy descend into the entire body, such that a tongue of flesh cannot describe it, until all earthly things appear as ashes and dung in its recollection. And when*, he said, *this food comes upon a man, raging within his entire body, in that hour this man assumes that the kingdom of heaven be nothing else, only this.*[104]

[34]   And still in another place he says: *He who has found the joy of God not only does not gaze at passions, but does not pay heed to his own life, God's love being sweeter then life, and knowledge according to God*[105] *sweeter then honey and the honeycomb, from whom love is begotten.*[106]

[35]   But these are *inexpressible* and *indescribable*,[107] as Symeon the New Theologian says: *What tongue can express? What intellect can explain? What discourse*[108] *can describe? For it is awesome, truly awesome, beyond discourse. I behold light not of this world while sitting in the middle of the*[109] *cell on the bed?*[110] *Inside myself I behold the creator of the world, and I converse, and I love, and I eat, well nourished on the vision of God alone, and, uniting with him, I rise above heaven. And this I do know for certain and in truth, but where my body is then, I know not.*

[36]   And conversing about the Lord, he said: *He loves me, and takes me into himself and envelops me in his embraces. Being in heaven, he is also within my heart, here and there for me to behold.*[111]

---

104. from Isaac Syr. 68:333; HM SMS 179.45:185v–186v/Eparkh. 324.45: 228–228v; Gk: 8:38–39, where HTM sees a series of rhetorical questions in the original.

105. *izhe po Božě razumъ* = ἡ κατὰ Θεὸν σύνεσις (= *science*): alt. free transl.: *theology.*

106. Adapted from Isaac Syr. 62:298; HM SMS 179:38:158v–159 / Eparkh. 324.38:191v; Gk: 38:163–164.

107. Alt., freer transl. (Pelikan 2:258): *beyond speech and beyond words.*

108. *slovo* = λόγος: alt. transl.: *word.*

109. *my* in the PG Latin; *the* in the original Greek; no article in Slavic.

110. *odrъ* (nm.-acc) = κλίνης (here as gn.); also *couch* (including for reading).

111. [35–36] adapted from Symeon NT, *Hymns* 13:45–46; Eparkh. 118.13:126–126v; SC 156:260–263; (Latin: PG 120:526B-D).

[37] And directly to the face of the Lord he says: This, *Master, shows me to be equal to the angels, and even renders me superior to them, for you are by essence invisible to them, and by nature unapproachable, but to me you are* entirely wholly visible and my *essence combines with* your *nature.*[112]

[38] And writing of these, he relates: *The eye has not seen, and the ear has not heard, nor has it entered into a heart of flesh.*[113]

[39] And being among these, not only *does he not wish* to leave his *cell,* but *in a pit dug in the earth* wishes to *be concealed, so that there,* he said, drawn in, *outside of the entire world, I shall see my immortal master* and *creator.*[114]

[40] And agreeing with him further, Saint Isaac said: *When, for a man, the veil of passions is taken away from the eyes of reason and he gazes upon that glory, his reason immediately rises in awe. And if God did not set a limit to such things in this life, regarding how much it be proper to remain among them,*[115] *and, moreover, if it were allowed for the span of man's life, he would not exit* from there, *from his wondrous vision of them.*[116]

[41] But in his mercy God has caused *grace* to diminish from the saints for a while, so that they may accomplish *the provisioning and the care of the brothers with a discourse of ministry,* that is, instruction in piety, as Saint Macarius says of those who have attained perfection: *They are entirely sacrificed to the* love and *sweetness of those wondrous visions.*[117] *And if,* he said, *someone always possessed* grace[118]

---

112. Symeon NT, *Hymns* 7:28; Sol. 271/793.11:90–90v; SC 156:211.

113. Symeon NT, *Hymns* 13:46; Eparkh. 118.13:126-127; SC 156:262-265, adapting from 1 Cor 2:9 (. . . *heart of man* in 1 Cor.).

114. Symeon NT, *Hymns* 28:147–148; Sol.14:99–99v; SC 174:298–299.

115. Borovkova-M and PNSIK treat this clause as a question following the previous one, which the Greek original could allow, though the printed Greek indicates otherwise.

116. Almost as in Isaac Syr. 43:214–215; HM SMS 179.79:462–462v; Gk: 17:62–63.

117. Adapted from Symeon Metaphrastes, *Paraphrase of Macarius* 92:326; HM SMS 468.92:52; Фк 3:209: a rewrite of Ps-Macarius, *Liber de Charitate* 9, PG 34:916C.

118. *it* (standing for *grace*) in the original.

such as this, he would not be able to undertake the construction and labor of discourse, or hear or speak of things here, or have the slightest care for this.[119]

[42]   And with a parable, he expounded on those made *perfect* by grace: that *one is ascended to the twelfth rung, but grace,* he said, *weakens, and, having descended one step, he stands on the eleventh, as it is said.*[120] *And therefore the perfect measure is not sustained for them, so that they will have time to devote to the brothers and to provide with a discourse of ministry.*[121]

[43]   But what can we say of those, who in this yet mortal body have *tasted* immortal foods and already in this transitory world have been worthy of a fraction of that *joy* which is stored the *heavenly* fatherland? They do not apply themselves to the beauties and pleasures *of this world*, nor do they fear afflictive and vicious things, *for they have the boldness to say with* the Apostle:[122] '*Nothing shall separate us from the love of God*',[123] and so forth.[124]

[44]   *Yet these things pertain,* according to the words of Saint Isaac, *to those who were beholders and ministers of these things, or who were instructed by such Fathers, taught the truth from their lips, and all who spent their lives making such inquiries.*[125]

[45]   We, though, are useless, guilty of many sins and filled with passions, and therefore it is unworthy for us to hear such discourses. But, putting my hope in God's grace, I have dared to utter a frac-

---

119. Adapted from Symeon Metaphr., *Paraphrase of Macarius* 93:326; HM SMS 468.94:52-52v; Фк 3:209; cf. PG 34:916D–917A.

120. Symeon Metaphr., *Paraphrase of Macarius* 93:324; HM SMS 468.93:52; Фк 3:209; cf. PG 34:916D.

121. Symeon Metaphr., *Paraphrase of Macarius* 93:326; HM SMS 468.94:52v; Фк 3:209: cf. *Liber de Charitate* 10, PG 34:916D–917A.

122. *Paul* in the original.

123. Abbrev. from Rom 8:38-39: cf. Chariton courting martyrdom in SNS 2:46; *Acta* SS 7:574F; *Cercare Dio*, 52.

124. [43] adapted from Isaac Syr. 68:333; Eparkh. 324.16 89; Gk: 8:38–39; perhaps influenced by Symeon Metaphr., *Paraphrase of Macarius* 80, 85, 89, 106: 320, 322, 324, 331; HM SMS 468:47v, 49, 50v, 56; Фк 3:203–204, 205, 207–208, 214.

125. Isaac Syr. 23:117; *Eparkh.* 324.38:163–164; Gk: 32:135.

tion of the spirit-bearing words of these holy Writings, so that we at least somewhat recognize by what wretchedness we are enveloped and to what mindlessness we surrender ourselves, striving for participation and success in this world, acquiring perishable objects, and on their account marching into clamor and fights, and effecting a loss for our souls. And this, we reckon to be beneficent, and we count ourselves praiseworthy.

[46] But *woe to us, for we are not coming to know our souls, nor* understand *into which life we have been called*, as Saint Isaac says. *And we reckon that the life of this world*, either *afflictions* or *comfort, amounts to something*;[126] and from our sloth, love of the world and negligence, we say that this was appropriate for the *ancient* saints, but is neither necessary nor possible for us.[127]

[47] But it is not so, it is not! Indeed it is impossible for those, who willingly throw themselves into passions and do not wish sincerely to repent and endeavor in God's work, and who love the futile cares of this world. But the Lord will pity and benefit and glorify all who fervently repent, who seek him[128] with great love and with fear, who gaze only on him, and who execute his commandments. All Divine Writing says so.

[48] Many ancient Fathers were practitioners and teachers of this, and they edified and fortified one other. But in these days, such having become scarce, if someone endeavors in God's work, grace especially enlightens[129] and helps, henceforth and forever.[130]

[49] And it[131] calls those who do not desire to struggle, who lead others into indifference, and despair, and say that now the *ancient* granting of gifts from God does not occur, 'the *deceived* and

---

126. Adapted from Isaac Syr. 43:215; HM SMS 179.80:372v–373/Eparkh. 324.80:462v–463; Gk: 17:63.
127. Cf. above, *Predanie* 4; below, *To German* 12.
128. Alt. transl.: *it*.
129. *vrazumliaet*: alt. trans: *instills knowledge, understanding*; cf. below, 4.11, 11.13.
130. Cf. Gregory Sin., *Acrostic Chapters* 95:232; HM SMS 468:81v; PG 150:1269BC.
131. That is, *all Divine Writing* of [47].

the deceivers of others'.[132] Some of them do not wish to hear, if there is *grace* in present times. They are *darkened by great insensitivity, incomprehension,* and *little faith,* said Gregory the Sinate.[133]

[50]   Having learned[134] all of this from the holy Writings, and if we desire to have true diligence in God's work, we first remove ourselves, as far as possible, from the vanity of this world, and endeavor to diminish the passions, that is, to preserve the heart from wicked urges, and thereby fulfilling the commands, and with the guarding of the heart, we always have prayer. *This is the first stage of monastic growth, and otherwise it is impossible to diminish the passions,*[135] says Symeon the New Theologian.

[51]   And at night it is indeed especially proper to endeavor in this activity, said the Fathers. For the blessed Philotheus the Sinaite said that *at night, especially, the intellect*[136] *is* to be purified.[137]

[52]   And Saint Isaac says: *Let every prayer that you offer at night be, in your eyes, worthier than all the acts of the day. For the sweetness, which is bestowed upon ascetics during the day, flows out from the light of nocturnal action.*[138]

[53]   And the other saints concur with this. Thus Climacus said: *At night give more to prayer, less to song.*[139]

[54]   And elsewhere he says: *Fatigued,* the worker,[140] *having risen, prays.*[141] And so it is proper for us to do, when the intellect is fa-

---

132. Cf. Gregory Sin., *Acrostic Chapters* 135:250–251; HM SMS 456.44v–45; PG 150:1297CD; cf. below, *Predanie* 4.

133. Adapted from Gregory Sin., *On the Signs of Grace and Delusion* 1:257–258; HM SMS 456:65–65v; PG 150 1305BC.

134. *uvěděvshe:* var.: *uviděvshe* = *having seen.*

135. Cleverly adapted from Ps-Symeon NT, *Three Methods,* 73, 74; HM SMS 468:84v, 85; Hausherr, *Méthode,* 167, 168.

136. *umъ* = νοῦς, as in the original, though *smyslъ* = *mind* in the Slavic Philotheus.

137. Adapted from Philotheus 27.27; Eparkh. 344.5:345v; Φκ 2.27:283.

138. Metaphr. from Isaac Syr. 64:308; HM SMS 40:165v; Gk: 34:147.

139. Edited from Climacus 27.77; Eparkh. 331 27:356v / VMCh-M:929c; PG 88:1116C.

140. *watchman* in the original and Slavic translation.

141. Climacus 27:23; Eparkh. 331.27:331v / VMCh-M:925ab; PG 88:1100B.

tigued in prayer: permit it a little singing, whatever canon[142] one has—psalms, some *troparia*, or something else.

[55]   *For verbosity oft times has scattered the intellect in prayer, while* brevity[143] *oft times has concentrated,*[144] said that same John Climacus.

[56]   During the wandering of urges, attend especially to reading—as Saint Isaac said: *At the time when your intellect is scattered, attend more to reading than prayer*[145] —or to manual work, as *the angel* imparted to Anthony the Great.[146]

[57]   And for neophytes, upon the onslaught[147] of urges, manual work with prayer, or any service,[148] is most beneficial, said the Fathers, and, especially at a time of afflictions and urges of despondency, is fitting.[149]

[58]   The Blessed Hesychius of Jerusalem proposes four *forms* of this mental activity *to guard against assaults*; or *to hold one's heart most deeply, silent to any urge, and to pray*; or *to call upon the Lord Jesus Christ for aid*; or *to have remembrance of death. All these*, he said, prevent[150] *evil thoughts,*[151] and to whichever one turns, these constitute *watchfulness,*[152] that is, *mental activity*.

[59]   Having examined all these, let each of us struggle by the proper system for himself.

---

142. *pravilo* = (here) a piece of liturgical music; alt. transl.: *cell rule*.

143. *maloslovie* (literally, *few words*, opposed to *mnogoslovie* = *verbosity*); the original has *edinoslovie* = μονολογία: *repetition of a single word or phrase* (as in mystical prayer).

144. Metaphr. and slightly altered from Climacus 28.10; *Eparkh*. 331.28:368v / VMCh-M:930d; PG 88 1132B; cf. Nikon, *Pandekty* 29:204, which is faithful to Climacus.

145. From Isaac Syr. 64:307; HM SMS 179.40:65; Gk: 34:146.

146. Cf. Nikon, *Pandekty* 44:346v; MRIV 8^B.9. In the original, and also Nikon and Iosif, the angel commands manual labor as a counter to *despondency and mental gloom*. Anthony 1, *Sayings* 1; PG 65:76AB.

147. *nashestvie*: a little word play with *razshestvie* = *wandering* of [56].

148. *sluzhenie*: can mean *labor, liturgical service*, or *ministering* to another's needs.

149. Cf. below, *Ustav* 5.6.77, *To Vassian* 7.

150. *vъzbraniaiutъ* (also means forbid, *reproach*): *shut the door to* in the original.

151. *pomyshleniia* (nm./acc. pl.), translating ἐννοίας.

152. Metaphr. and adapted from Hesychius 1.13-18:164-165; HM SMS 456.14-19:157; Eparkh. 344:432v; PG 93:1485/Φκ 1.13-18:143.

On How and by What Means to Fortify Oneself at the Onset of a War of Mental Struggle. 3.

[1] This fortifying in the *combat* of our struggle is stated in all the writings, so that we neither wax pusillanimous *nor turn despondent*, when we are attacked by wicked *urges* most fiercely, nor halt *our course* along the path, which is in the arena. For it is the *art*[1] of the devil's evil,[2] regarding our defeats by filthy urges, to make us ashamed to *gaze upon God* with repentance and pray against them. Through continual repentance and ceaseless prayer we defeat them, and do not turn our backs to our enemies, even if we receive a thousand wounds per day from them. And we resolve absolutely not to withdraw from this life-bearing activity even until death.

[2] For with these *secretly* occurs for us a *visitation* of *divine mercy*. And not only to us, the passionate and infirm,[3] but even to those standing *on a high rank*[4] *of purity, and remaining* within a life of *stillness*, worthy of praise, *under the arm of the knowledge*[5] of the Lord, *occur* mental *falls,* and after these *peace and comfort,* as well as *chaste and gentle urges,* says Saint Isaac.[6]

[3] How often does it occur to an inferior man, who copiously from his lack of training is struck and cast down, ever in a state of powerlessness, that when he grabs the standard from the

---

1. *khitrostъ* = τέχνη; alt. transl.: *craft*; also used negatively for *cunning*.
2. Nil's seeming hypallage (syntactic reversal) for *the devil's evil art*, but the notion is abstracted from Isaac Syr. 39:189; HM SMS 179.60:307–307v; Gk: 51:209; cf. below, Ustav 5.6.80.
3. See below, Ustav 7.8.
4. Again *chin*.
5. *razumъ* = γνῶσις.
6. [1–2] freely adapted from one of the themes of Isaac Syr. 69:336–339; Eparkh. 324.46:231v–238v; Gk: 49:200–205.

hands of the warriors, *the sons of giants,*[7] his name is elevated and praised more than the athletes renowned for victories, and he receives the crown and the gifts of honor above all of his companions![8]

[4] This *the saints*[9] prove to us and remove doubt from our mind, lest during mental combat we weaken in mind and, at the *time of disturbance* from of the *attack of filthy urges*, turn *to despair.*[10]

[5] Also, when a visitation of *grace* occurs, do not become carefree, *nor be elated, but confess*[11] *to God,* and *thank him, and prostrate on the memory of your transgressions, which occurred at the time of loosing*[12] *against you: where you descended then, and how you acquired a beastly intellect. And recall the wretchedness of your nature.*[13] And *take unto yourself*[14] *the unclean urges and the unseemly idols, which in feverish times were implanted within your mind,*[15] *and the hour of confusion and disorder of urges, which just recently rose against you in the blindness of darkening: how swiftly you inclined to passions and conversed with them in the darkening of your mind.*[16] And, remembering all this, repent and *reproach yourself.*[17] But *understand that Divine Providence brings all of these upon us, that we be humbled.*[18]

---

7. Maybe from Isaac Syr. 6:61; HM SMS 179.58:303; Gk: 56:230; adapted from Nm 13.33.

8. Source not identified, but something cobbled from Isaac is possible; also some inspiration from Climacus 4.113:95; HM SMS 184:47v; PG 88:724C.

9. Isaac is citing the Syriac Macarius.

10. Freely adapted from Isaac Syr. 69:336–337; HM SMS 179.46:189–190/ Eparkh. 324:46:236–236v; Gk: 49:201.

11. *ispovězhsia* (imprv.) = ἐξομολόγησον = *confess, acknowledge with praise.*

12. *popushchenie*: God's releasing or allowing evil forces to operate.

13. [5] to here metaphrased from Isaac Syr. 69:338; HM SMS 179.46:191-192; Gk: 49:203.

14. Alt. transl.: *take as genuine; ruminate over.*

15. *smyslъ* = διάνοια here and later in this citation.

16. This segment almost exactly as Isaac Syr. 69:337; HM SMS 179.46: 190v; Gk: 49:202.

17. From Gregory Sin., *Acrostic Chapters* 117:239; HM SMS 640:89v; PG 150:1281A.

18. Metaphr. from Isaac Syr. 69:337-338; HM SMS 169.46:191; Gk: 49:202, bridging to the next citation from the same text of Gregory the Sinaite.

[6]   For the Blessed Gregory the Sinaite says: *Unless a man be forsaken, defeated and subjugated,*[19] *enthralled by every passion, by*[20] *urge and spirit defeated, and not finding help from his deeds, or from God, or from anything else at all, so that he soon will come into despair, violated*[21] *in every way, he cannot be contrite and regard himself below everyone, even the last of slaves, worse than the demons themselves, as one completely violated and defeated. And this is Providence's dispensational*[22] *and chastising humility, by which a second and superior thing is given by God, namely, divine power, operating and accomplishing all things—on account of which one always sees oneself as his vessel, and on this account working God's miracles.*[23]

[7]   Attend with fear: *if you* do not humble your reasoning,[24] *grace will abandon you, and you will completely fall*[25] *among things, in which by urges alone you will be tempted.* For *to stand* among *virtues is not of yourself, but is that same grace,*[26] *carrying you on the palms of its hands,*[27] protecting from all adversaries.[28]

[8]   To attend to this with precision is proper for us, so that from us there be no cause at all for wicked urges to wax stronger against us, and then for us not to walk right along God's path, but dissolutely and unguardedly.[29] Indeed to conduct one's life with great earnestness and zeal, controlled according to all the Divine Writings, as much as possible doing everything in pious humility,

---

19. *poobladanъ*: alt. transl.: *possessed*.
20. Alt. transl. of the instr. case: *in*.
21. As in the Slavic translation; *humiliated/humbled* in the original.
22. *smotritel'noe* (nt. sg,) = οἰκονομική (fm. sg.), that is, *according to the 'divine economy'*.
23. Exactly as Gregory Sin., *Acrostic Chapters* 117:240; HM SMS 640:90–90v; PG 150:1281C-D; cf. below, *Ustav* 5.8.91, 93.
24. *if you take pride in her* [*Grace's*] *gifts* in the original.
25. Var. (as in Borovkova-M, 35): *podaeshi* = *give* (2nd sg. prs.); Nil's original *padaeshi* = πίπτεις = fall, as in PNSIK, 128, Eparkh. 349:37.
26. Alt. transl., privileging the Greek original (ἡ χάρις αὕτη): *grace itself*.
27. Metaphr., with just *grace*, not also *divine providence* acting on the monk's behalf, from Isaac Syr. 69:337–338; HM SMS 179.46:191; Gk: 49:202–203.
28. For overall translation/adaptation commentary on this sentence, see above, 'Preface to the Translations'.
29. Cf. below, *To Gurii* 17–18.

is for him who wishes to apply himself to God's love and truly be saved, and without slackening and without carelessness always to do the Lord's work.

On Control over Every Activity in Our Life. 4.

[1] To have this under control in our life is always to abide as much as one can in God's work, and in all aspects in every undertaking, with soul and body, word and deed, and thoughts.

[2] *As we, while[1] first living in the world, in its vanity,[2] and with all our intellect and senses we slaved for sinful deceit,* says the Blessed Philotheus, *so it is especially proper for us, having crossed over to the life in God, to slave with all our intellect and senses for the living and true God and for God's righteousness[3] and volition,[4]* and to execute his holy commandments and to remove ourselves completely from all things displeasing to God, according to Scripture, which says: '*I have directed myself toward all your commandments, and I have hated all paths of unrighteousness*'.[5]

[3] And, rising from sleep, one should first glorify God and confess before him, and then these activities: prayer, chanting, reading, manual work, or any other task. But at all times hold the intellect suspended in great reverence and trust in God, and do all things for his well pleasing and not for vainglory or pleasing of men, knowing with certainty that he always *is with us,*[6] who is *everywhere and fills all things.*[7] *Having implanted the ear, he hears all,* and *having created the eye, he looks everywhere.*[8]

---

1. Nil omits: *in our ignorance.*
2. Nil omits: *of our intellect.*
3. *pravda:* alt. transl.: *justice.*
4. To here from Philotheus, 29; Eparkh. 344.29:355; Фк 2.33:285.
5. *nepravdy* (gn. sg): alt. transl.: *injustice*; from LXX Ps 118:128.
6. *God is with us* (*S nami Bog*): the choir's refrain of a standard hymn by that name of Great Compline: cf. Ps 45:8, 12/46:7, 11.
7. From the standard Orthodox evening prayer to the Holy Spirit: *O Heavenly King, the Comforter, the Spirit of Truth, Who art everywhere and fillest all things* . . . .
8. Adapted from Ps 93:9/94:9; cf. Prv 20:12.

[4] And if a conversation occurs, it should be in accordance with God, guarding against complaining, condemnation, idle chatter, and contention.

[5] Likewise with eating and drinking, and this is to be with fear of God.

[6] And especially during sleep one should be reverent inwardly in mind and outwardly in all his members tidy.[9] For *sleep is a brief image of eternal sleep, that is, death,*[10] and *lying on the bed should be considered laying in the grave.*[11]

[7] And in all these one should always see God before one's eyes, according to what was said by David: *I have always gazed upon the Lord before me, because he is at my right hand, lest I budge.*[12] He who does this always is in prayer.

[8] And if someone has a *healthy body*, it is proper to *wear* it down through *fasting,* vigils and *laborious* activity; if prostrations or manual work, it is proper to do them with labor, so that it[13] be enslaved to the soul and redeemed[14] from passions by Christ's grace.[15] But if the body is *infirm*, nourish it according to its power.[16]

[9] But neither the healthy nor the infirm are ever to be indifferent toward prayer, but even when engaged in a necessary task, the intellect shall secretly meditate.[17] And it is proper to do this with fear. The physical activity of the physically hale and hearty will be called to account according to each one's power. As for the mental, which is to maintain the intellect in piety and trust in God and commit to his love, this is incumbent for all, even in grave illness.

---

9. *blagosъpriatannĕ*—here a clever play with words, since the verb *sъpriatati* means *to clean/prepare*, when the direct object is a body for burial.
10. Cf. Climacus 19.1; HM SMS 184:10v/VMCh-M:894b; PG 88:937A.
11. Adapted from Climacus 7.18; HM SMS 184:63v; PG 88:805A.
12. Ps 15:8/16:8, reproducing LXX.
13. *the body.*
14. Alt. transl.: *he* (rather than just his body) *be redeemed.*
15. Nil's run-on sentence here.
16. For [8], cf. below, *Predanie* 37-38; *Ustav* 5.1.9; *Little Epistle*.
17. *skrovno da pouchaetsia*: alt. transl.: *meditate on the mysteries.*

[10] Likewise we must have *love for our neighbors* in accordance with the Lord's *commandment*.[18] And if they chance to be near us, we are to manifest this in words and deed, if we are able to keep also God's.[19] And if they be far from us, we are to unite with them in our intellect with love,[20] and drive away from our hearts any evil recollection of them. And we are with humility to submit our soul to them and with good will gratify them. And if God gazes upon us as such, he will forgive our transgressions[21] and accept our prayers like a good gift, and grant us his mercy in abundance.

A SUMMARY OF THE PRECEDING AND EXPLANATION OF WHAT FOLLOWS

[11] By the grace of God we have spoken, from the holy Writings, a little about mental activity and about what is in it[22] of the differentiation of Enemy combat against us, and of our combat with these, and that the best mode of combat is to have one's heart in prayer without urges. And having spoken about their operation, we have dared to indicate for everything[23] a fraction of the holy Writings[24] concerning what grace those practitioners of these things are worthy to attain—my being unworthy to touch these things. And we have also spoken of the means by which those laboring in these things are to fortify themselves and what kind of controlled life those who exert themselves in this most superior and premier combat for great victories, that is to say, stillness of

---

18. Cf. *Sobornik, Forew.* 4; cf. Lv 19:18, Mt 19:19, 22:39; Mk 12:31, Lk 10:27, Rom 13:9; Gal 5:14, Jas 2:8.

19. Some MSS add *love* or *commandment* here, but not Eparkh. 349:39, Eparkh. 351:26v, or KB 89/1166 (PNSIK, 130).

20. Cf. below, *To German* 5.

21. Cf. below, *Testament* 3.

22. Nil's switch to sg.

23. *vsikhъ*; alt. reading: *v sikhъ*: in/for these.

24. Literally: *in (for) these/of everything a fraction we have dared to indicate the holy Writings*—whether Nil is playing a word game here is not clear, but his sense is.

intellect and true prayer, should traverse. Henceforth, with God enlightening,[25] we shall speak of the other types[26] of different combats and victory.[27]

25. *vzrazumliaushchu* (dt. abs.): alt. transl.: *instilling knowledge, instilling understanding*; cf. above, Ustav 2.48, below, 11.13.
26. *obrazy* (pl.); alt. techn. transl.: *species* (= εἶδος).
27. Var. *for victory.*

5. On the Differences of Our Combat and Victory over the Eight Principal Passionate and Other Urges.

[1]   The Fathers speak of different types[1] of combat by which we are to establish[2] victory over wicked urges according to the measure of each of the atheletes: to pray against urges, to contradict them, and to scorn and drive them off.[3]

[2]   To scorn and drive off pertains to the perfect, and to speak out in opposition, to the most experienced, but for neophytes and the infirm, to pray against them and introduce good urges against the wicked, because Saint Isaac directs to *defraud the passions* by means of *virtues*.[4]

[3]   And Peter Damaskenos says: *Let us keep, as prepared work, the good assault with thought*.[5] And other Fathers so speak. So when we are violated by urges, unable to pray in humbleness and inner calmness, then it is proper to pray against them and transduce[6] into useful ones.[7]

[4]   And as to how we pray and transduce into useful ones, we shall present the holy Writings concerning this.[8] For the Fathers

---

1. See above, *Ustav* 4.11, note 26.
2. *postavliati*: var.: *vъstavliati* = raise.
3. Romanchuk argues that this represents an explicit reference to the three stages of Neoplatonic pedagogy ('ethics', to acquire correct comportment; 'physics', to grasp the nature of things; and 'epoptics', to become an initiate or adept)—something which scholarship has yet to recognize in the development of Eastern Christianity (private communication).
4. Adapted from Isaac Syr. 6:58; HM SMS 179.58:299; Gk: 56:227: *It is better with a recollection of the virtues to defraud passions than to resist one.*
5. Alt. transl.: *the mind*; culled and adapted from the Slavic Peter Dam., HM SMS 454:150; the published and translated Greek does not have an equivalent of *myslemъ* in this passage: *Treasury*, 207-208; Фк 3:109.
6. *prevoditi* = transfer/transpose/change: the English cannot fully capture Nil's word play here, paralleling *privoditi* = introduce, above, [2].
7. See above, *Ustav* 1.9-10, and below, *Ustav* 5.6.79, 8.24; *To Gurii* 8.
8. See also, below, *Ustav* 8.24.

speak of eight all-embracing urges from which many other passionate urges are born: 1 of gluttony, 2 of fornication, 3 of avarice, 4 of wrath, 5 of sadness, 6 of despondency, 7 of vainglory, 8 of pride.

[5]   And as they propounded gluttony as the primary of all,[9] we shall speak first of it, so that we, the unknowledgeable, not alter the system[10] *of the very wise,*[11] but, following the words of the holy Fathers, shall so act.

[12]On Gluttony. 1.

[6]   If the urge of gluttony vexes, recalling various and most delicious, classy dishes, which are eaten beyond need, and at the wrong time, and without measure, it is proper then first of all to recall the words spoken by the Lord: '*Do not burden your hearts with overeating and drunkenness*',[13] and, having prayed to the Lord himself and summoned aid, to contemplate the Fathers' dictum, that this passion in monks is the root of all evil, especially *fornication*.[14]

[7]   From the beginning of life, the transgression of our progenitor, the first man *Adam,* was by this sin.[15] For having touched the forbidden food, he fell away *from Paradise* and brought *death* upon the entire race,[16] as it is written: '*Beautiful for the gaze and fine*

---

9. Cf. Climacus 14.30; HM SMS 184:83v/VMCh-M:884; PG 88:868D: *the prince of passions*.
10. *chin*: alt. transl.: *order*.
11. See below, [18]: *judgment/discretion of the thoughtful*.
12. Var.: Some MSS precede with: *The First Gluttonous Urge*.
13. Lk 21:34 (Slavic); cf. MRIV 9^B.1/7.1.
14. Cf. Climacus 14.5, 12, 17, 21, 27, 29, 36; also Cassian, *Institutes* 5.11:75 / *Eight Vices,* 74; HM SMS 468.1:224v; Фк 1:62; also Gregory Sin., *Sitting at Prayer* 281; HM SM.456:64v (PG 150.6:1337CD).
15. Isidore the Priest made this link: *Sayings* 1:106; PG 65 1:1233D-1236A, as did Basil/Ps-Basil, *Ascetic Discourse,* 67; HM SMS 183:184; PG 31:630A, and Gregory Sin., *Sitting at Prayer* 280; HM SMS 456:63-63v; PG 150.6:1336D.
16. Cf. Rom 5:12.

for food was the fruit that killed me'.[17] And from then even to this day, many, having submitted to the stomach, have fallen with a great fall, as the holy Writings recount.

[8] Know then,[18] that the savor and fragrance of food soon turn into stench and manure[19] and have nothing of profit, says Barsanuphius the Great.[20] And having understood this, reproach yourself for desiring these, which quickly change from savor and fragrance into such stench. And thus, partaking of food in measure and at proper times, defeat the passion.

On the Measure of Food

[9] This is the measure of food, *the Fathers have said*: if someone sets for himself how much to receive per day, and if he concludes that it is a lot and it burdens him, he immediately subtracts from it. And if he perceives that he is eating little and cannot thereby maintain his body, he immediately adds a little. And having thus experimented well, he sets how much can sustain the power of his body, not for savor, but according to need.

[10] And he thus receives, *thanking God*, and he also should condemn himself, as being unworthy even of this small comfort.

[11] To *encompass all* of nature *with a single rule is impossible*,[21] because *bodies have a great difference in strength*,[22] as copper and iron from wax.

---

17. Cf. Gn 3:6, cited in this context by Symeon NT, *Discourses* 26.8:280; Sol. 193.22:125; SC 113:86–87; Prokhorov notes an analagous *sticheron* from the Matins of the first Friday of the Great Fast: PNSIK, 135.

18. Alt. transl.: *You know* . . . .

19. *gnoi* (prp. sg.); alt. transl.: *pus*, or an impolite synonym for *manure*.

20. No source identified: von Lilienfeld (NSSS, 222) and Prokhorov (PNSIK, 135) claim 'No 30' of the *Dobrotoliubie russkoe* (*Russian Philokalia*); Bianchi's (p 88) 'Ep. 16.2' is cryptic, and, if SC 426.16:190–193, falls short, as does Grolimund's Q86 (NSA, 394).

21. Basil, *Longer Rules* 19:183; HM SMS 183.14:51v; PG 31:968A.

22. *Ibid.;* here and also the ital. 5.1.5, 9–10 from Gregory Sin., *Sitting at Prayer* 6:280 HM SMS 456:63v; PG 150.6:1336D–1337B; for [11], Cassian, *Institutes* 5.5:71 / *Eight Vices,* 73; HM SMS 468.1:223; Фк 1:63.

[12]   A general measure for neophytes is to end a little hungry.[23]

[13]   If some one takes enough for sufficient satiety, it is without sin.

[14]   If he over-sates a little, *he should reproach himself*, and thus on account of a fall, raise *a victory*.[24]

On the Time for Food

[15]   As for the time for touching food, the Fathers said to fast until the ninth hour. If someone desires to allow more, it is by his volition.

[16]   They have generally established this as the day declines— that during the spring and summer equinoxes the ninth hour strikes[25] when the sun has passed the second hour after midday.[26] In summer and winter in the northern lands the hours of day and night increase and decrease greatly, unlike in the Mediterranean, in Palestine or in Constantinople. For that reason it is proper for us to act in accordance with the time, as it is fit.

[17]   On the non-fasting days, it is proper to advance the hour for food, and, if necessary, eat a little at suppertime.[27]

On the Differences of Food

[18]   [28]As for the differences of foods, *we should partake a little of the savor of all dishes present. This is the discretion of the thoughtful,*[29]

---

23. Cf. SNS 2:54; Acta SS 27:577C; *Cercare Dio*, 58: Chariton Confessor's instructions to his disciples; cf. Cassian, *Institutes,* 5.8.73/*Eight Vices,* 74; HM SMS 468.1:224; Фк 1:62, but for all monks.

24. Adapted from Gregory Sin., *Sitting at Prayer* 6:281; HM SMS 456:64; PG 150.6:1337BC.

25. Literally: *occurs.*

26. This 9:00 logically should be 3:00 p.m. (15:00) at the equinoxes, but Nil's "ninth hour" seems to start at 2:00 (14:00) and end at 3:00 (15:00).

27. Cf. Appendix I: *Scete Typikon* 8.

28. The '1' printed at the start of the paragraph in Borovkova-M, 42, is not found in KB 89/1166 (PNSIK 28), Eparkh. 349:43, or Eparkh. 351:31.

29. Cf. above, [5].

said Gregory the Sinaite: not to select this and reject that, so that *God be thanked* and *modesty* of soul be rectified. Thus we shall *avoid conceit and not loathe God's good creations.*

[19]   *As for those infirm in faith or soul, abstinence from delectables is useful, for they do not believe,* he said, *that they will be preserved by God. And the Apostle instructed them to eat herbs.*[30]

[20]   And if one *is harmed* by a certain dish or from some *infirmity* or from nature, he should not force himself to take it, but shall take something more useful than that, says Basil the Great, as it is not proper *to attack the body* with the *same foods by which we sustain* it.[31]

[21]   On the Differences of Bodies.[32] If someone has a healthy and strong body, he should weaken as much as possible, so that he deliver himself from passions and subjugate his soul to Christ's grace.

[22]   If it is infirm or ill, he should give it a little rest, lest it decline terminally.

[23]   It is proper that *the athlete be in want, without satiating himself,*[33] but give the body just *its needs, both foods and drink.*[34]

[24]   At the time of the enemy's battle against the body, it is especially proper to abstain. For many, who did not control their stomach, have fallen into the disgraces of passions[35] and the unspeakable pit of filth.[36]

---

30. [18–19] from Gregory Sin., *Sitting at Prayer* 281; HM SMS 456:63v–64; PG 150 6:1337AB; cf. Rom. 14:2.

31. Adapted from Basil/Ps-Basil, *Longer Rules* 19:184; HM SMS 183:14:52v; PG 31:969A.

32. No text, which I have seen, has the logical, separate heading here.

33. From Gregory Sin., *Sitting at Prayer* 281; HM SMS 456:63v; PG 150 6:1337A.

34. Adapted from Basil/Ps-Basil, *Longer Rules* 19:183; HM SMS 183.14:52; PG 31:968C: *either dry or liquid food* in the original.

35. Alt. gram. transl.: *passions of disgrace/dishonor.*

36. Cf. MRIV 9[B].4/7.4, Trad. 7.3, 9.1: (chiefly) *pit of fornication* (arising from drunkenness).

[25] When the stomach is within the good order of abstinence, it becomes a gateway for all virtues together.[37] *If you control your stomach, you will enter Paradise,* says Basil the Great: *If you do not, you have become the waste of death.*[38]

[26] If someone, on account of the *labor of a journey or a most burdensome task,* condescends to[39] his body a little and adds a little to the normal requisite, this is not blameworthy as regards to food, drink, and all forms of rest, because he has done it with discretion in accordance with his power.[40]

Of Fornication: The Second Urge

[27] *Great is* our *struggle against the spirit of fornication, and very fierce, having double combat in soul and body.*[41] Therefore it is always proper resolutely to strive, vigilantly and soberly, to preserve our heart free from this urge, especially at holy gatherings, when we shall partake of the sacraments. For at that time the enemy strives by all means to defile our conscience.

[28] And when these urges vex, it is then proper to have fear of God and to remind ourselves that nothing can be concealed from God, down to the tiniest thoughts of the heart, and for all of these God is judge and inquisitor; and also to recall our vow, which we confessed before angels and men, to remain in chastity and purity. And chastity and purity means not only *the outer* life,

---

37. Contrast Climacus 14.34:144; HM SMS 184:84; PG 88:14:969B: gluttony as *the door of passions.*
38. Basil/Ps-Basil, *Ascetic Discourse* 68; HM SMS183:184-185v; PG 31:641B; cf. MRIV 2ᴮ.3/2.24; Nil's and Iosif's Slavic texts are identical, but not the same as HM SMS 183, indicating, perhaps, a common indirect source, or, possibly, one borrowing from the other; see above, III. 'Centrality of Sources', texts to notes 34-35.
39. I.e., *indulges.*
40. Maybe adapted from Basil/Ps-Basil, *Longer Rulers* 19:183; HM SMS 183.14:51v-52 (Nil either metaphrased the Slavic in italics or used another translation.); cf. below, 11.1.
41. Shortened from Cassian, *Institutes* 6.1:95 / *Eight Vices,* 75; HM SMS 468.1:224v; Фк 1:63; cf. *To Gurii* 7 (used for blasphemy).

but also *the secret man of the heart*.⁴² When he is clean from filthy urges, this is very honorable and beloved before God.

[29] He who copulates with the urge of fornication, willfully and greatly⁴³ defiling himself, *commits adultery in his heart*,⁴⁴ the Fathers said.

[30] And sometimes it happens to come in deed, and if it comes in deed, we understand what a calamity it is after the completion of the affair, that about no other transgression do the Fathers speak, as about this. They call it 'the fall', because it renders the fallen devoid of confidence and drives him to despair.

[31] It is useful, I reckon, at the time of the war of fornication, for us to think through for ourselves, in what image⁴⁵ and order we are, that we tread in the image of angels, and how we can trample our conscience and outrage this holy rank with this abomination.

[32] It is also fitting to recall the shame and disgrace, which are from men, in order that we be able to repel this improper urge. For if we are found in this filth before gazing men, do we not prefer to die, rather than be found in this shame? Thus, by every means possible, we must zealously cut off this urge.

[33] To have this great and terrible victory over them always, one should *diligently pray*⁴⁶ to God, as the holy Fathers teach.

[34] For Maximus the Confessor has directed us in this manner to pray against the urges of fornication, taking the words spoken by David: '*Those pursuing me have now surrounded me*,⁴⁷ *joy of mine: deliver me from those who have surrounded me*'.⁴⁸

---

42. From 1 P 3:4: cf. the Epistle's chastity theme; also *To Gurii* 2.
43. *o mnoze*: alt. transl.: *frequently*.
44. From Mt 5:28.
45. *obraz*: alt. transl.: *icon, model, form, rank*: cf. *Prosvetitel'*, Sl. 11.
46. Adapted from Cassian, *Institutes* 6.1:95 / *Eight Vices*, 75; HM SMS 468:224v; Фк 1:63; cf. *To Gurii* 8.
47. Ps 16:11 LXX: (combining here *me* of Ps 7:1, 17:9 and the sentence using *us* of Ps 17:11 from the Hebrew/KJ.).
48. Ps 31:7 LXX (from the Hebrew/KJ, combining aspects of Ps 17:13, 31:7, 43:4, from the Hebrew/KJ); from Maximus Conf., *Centuries on Love* 2.18:68; HM SMS 456:102 (this Serbian version omits the second *me*); PG 90:989B. On

[35] John Climacus says about this: *the one, who said 'God, attend to my aid'*[49] *and other similar words, presents a witness for praying against urges.*[50]

[36] It is also requisite to summon for aid those who have struggled for chastity and purity, just as Daniel of Scetis commanded a brother embattled by fornication to pray and summon to his aid the martyress Thomais, who was slain for her chastity, and to speak thus: 'God, by the prayers of the martyress Thomais, help me!' And immediately he was delivered from the passion of fornication, after having prayed at her tomb.[51] Having such witnesses, we too so pray and summon for aid those whom we find in the holy Writings to have struggled for chastity and purity.

[37] When *combat fiercely* sets in, *immediately rise and extend hands and eyes toward heaven to pray*, as Gregory the Sinaite directed, *and God*, he said, *drives them away.*[52]

[38] And pray this way, as Saint Isaac says: '*You are the mighty one, Lord,*[53] *and yours is the struggle. Do attack and prevail in this, Lord, on our behalf.*[54]

[39] And as John Climacus taught, saying: *Cry to the One, able to save, not with artful words, but humble*[55] *utterances:*[56] 'Have mercy on

---

the poetics, see above III. 'Centrality of Sources', text to note 40, and 'Literary Devices', text to note 106.

49. Ps 69:2/70:1.

50. Rearranged from Climacus 26.79; HM SMS184:135/ VMCh-M 913d; PG 88:1029B.

51. Adapted from Clugnet, 'Vie et récits de Daniel le Scétiote', 66–67.

52. Gregory Sin., *Sitting at Prayer* 4:277; HM SMS 456:61–61v; PG 150:1332D.

53. From. Ps 88:9/89:9: alt. transl.: (as the Slavic lacks the definite article): *You are mighty.*

54. Isaac Syr. 39:195; HM SMS 179 60: 315; Gk: 54:216; no direct Biblical source identified, despite the Biblical quality.

55. HM SMS 184:95v is defective, cutting *expressions/words, but humble* from the original, which Nil's version follows.

56. Nil omits from Climacus: *in front of everyone.*

me, Oh Lord, for I am infirm'.[57] *And then will you come to* know[58] *the power of the Most High, and you will drive off the invisible invisibly.*[59]

[40]   And always *with Jesus's name whip the warriors:*[60] *for something sturdier,* he said, *than this weapon you will find neither in heaven nor on earth.*[61]

[41]   *The demon observes the times with us. When we are unable physically to pray against him,* the same Climacus says, *then he especially attacks us.*[62]

[42]   Indeed attend precisely, oh monk, and do not wax *lazy* at the time of great combat with filthy[63] *urges* always to *pray* just as we have previously sketched. *Raise the eye, in body or in soul,* in accord with the time and the measure of your power. And if you become a practitioner of this, you will come to know *from experience that with the invisible aid of the power of the Most High,* they are decisively defeated by our *volition.*[64] If you wax *lazy,* later you will be shamed for possessing a soiled conscience, your having been defeated by them.[65]

[43]   It is proper to understand as well this evil subterfuge of the devil, said the Fathers, that if ever be brought from him *to our*

---

57. Ps 6:3/6:2; cf. *To Gurii* 3.
58. *experience* in the original and SMS 184:95.
59. Climacus 15.81; HM SMS 184:95v–96/VMCh-M: 891a; PG 88:900CD; Nil drops from the original: *with invisible help.*
60. That is, the *enemy.*
61. Adapting Climacus 21.7; HM SMS 184:104v–105/VMCh-M: 896a; PG 88:945C, probably inspired by its use in Gregory Sin., *Stillness and Two Ways* 2:264; HM SMS 456:49; PG 150:1316BC; cf. *Sitting at Prayer* 4:277; HM SMS 456:61; PG 150:1332D; cf. *To Vassian* 6; *To Gurii* 5.
62. Adapted and condensed from Climacus 15.80; HM SMS 184:95v /VMCh-M:890d; PG 88:900B; In Climacus, the specific demon is *arrogance.*
63. *evil* in the original.
64. *they* refers back to the *filthy urges;* cf. *To Gurii* 4; *by our volition* not in KB 66/1189 (PNSIK, 142) or some other early texts.
65. No full source for [42] identified, but appears adapted from Climacus 5.81:160 / VMCh-M: 891a; HM SMS 184:95v–96; PG 88:900C, together with Isaac Syr. 39:195; HM SMS 179.60:315v–316; Gk: 54:217.

urge a recollection of female or youthful, fine-looking faces,[66] even if pious ones, even if it be deemed not passionate, quickly sever them. For if we linger on these, immediately the evil seducer will convert and cast down the *urge* into abominable *and filthy* lusts.[67]

[44] And there are also times, when we ourselves are distraught at urges of fornication, and, pondering them, we censure ourselves for desiring these obscenities, fitting only for dumb beasts,[68] said the Fathers.[69] If these, moreover, are unnatural ones, they are alien even to cattle, and we indeed are attacked by them.

[45] But it is especially proper that neophytes preserve themselves, lest they in any way linger among them: for even if we reckon we are struggling with them, we shall find ourselves engaged in passion. Therefore it is best completely to cut off *the assaults, which is the start of the urge*.[70] Indeed to engage and regulate these urges in a well-pleasing manner is only for the strong.[71]

[46] *Keep yourself* from conversations with women and from gazing upon them, and flee from the company of youths and from the sight of those *effeminate and smooth faces*:[72] for this is the net of the devil for monks, as one of the Fathers said.[73]

[47] And, if it is possible, let us *not* be *alone* with them, as Basil the Great says, not even over *a necessity*.[74] For nothing, he said, is more necessary than the soul, on account of which Christ died and resurrected.[75]

---

66. Cf. above, *Predanie* 42, and below, Appendix III, Innokentii, *Zavět* 14.

67. Possibly some adaptation from Cassian, *Institutes* 5.12:101 / *Eight Vices*, 76; HM SMS 468.2:226-226v; Фк 2:64.

68. *bezslovesnymъ* (dt. pl); alt. transl: *for madmen*.

69. Source for [44] not identified; perhaps some inspiration from Isaac Syr. 39:193–194; HM SMS 179.60:312v–314; Gk.: 54:214–215.

70. Possibly some adaptation from Cassian, *Institutes* 5.12:101 / *Eight Vices*, 76; HM SMS 468.2:226v; Фк 2:64.

71. Alt. trans, from the Borovkova-M punctuation and continuing into [46]: . . . strong, *keeping yourself . . . and fleeing from . . . .*

72. Cf., above, *Predanie* 42, and below, *To Gurii* 6.

73. Other sources for [46] not identified.

74. Cf. Basil/Ps-Basil, *Longer Rules* 33:199; HM SMS 183 26:61–61v; PG 31:997BD.

75. Specific source not identified, though implicit throughout the Basilian corpus, including the Liturgy attributed to him.

[48] And *do not wish to hear* from anyone *improper conversations*, which incite *passions*.[76]

The Third Urge of Avarice.

[49] The *disease* of *avarice, outside of nature, arises from little faith* and *lack of* intelligence,[77] said the Fathers: thus the *struggle* with it is not great for those who *attend* to themselves with the fear of God and who desire truly to be saved. But when it waxes firm in us, it becomes the most evil of all. And if we submit to it, it leads to such destruction, that *the Apostle* was to call it not only the '*root of all evil*',[78] anger, affliction, and so forth,[79] but even to name it '*idolatry*'.[80] Many indeed on account of avarice not only fell away from pious life, but sinned against faith and suffered in soul and body, as it is recounted in the holy Writings.[81]

[50] It is said by the Fathers, that one who amasses gold and silver and puts his *hopes* in this, does not have belief that there is *God, who cares* for him.[82]

[51] And also the holy Writings say the following: if someone is controlled by pride or by avarice, or by any one passion derived from them, the demon does not assail him further with another passion, for this single one is enough for his destruction.

[52] Therefore it is proper for us to preserve ourselves from this destructive and soul-decaying passion and pray the Lord God, that he drive away from us the spirit of avarice.

---

76. Cf. Basil/Ps-Basil, *Ascetic Discourse* 69; HM SMS 183:184v; PG 31:641C; Nikon, *Pandekty* 12:86v (attributed to Basil); *To Gurii* 6.
77. Just *lack of faith* in the original: cf. Nicetas Steth. 55:122; HM SMS 468.55:Фк 3.2.55:311.
78. 1 Tm 6:10.
79. Cf. Climacus, 17.14; HM SMS 184:90/VMCh-M: 892d–893a; PG 88: 829A.
80. Col 3:5, Eph 5:5, 3; [49] partially adapted from John Cassian, *Institutes* 7.1–2, 6:107, 109; *Eight Vices*, 77–79; HM SMS 468:227v–229; Фк 1:65–67; cf. *O sreboliubi i liuboimĕnii*, Eparkh. 344:94v.
81. Cf. Acts 5:1–11.
82. Cf. Maximus Conf., *Centuries on Love* 3.18:85; HM SMS 456:114–114v; PG 90:1021AB/ Фк 2.3.18:29.

[53] And it is proper for us to abstain from the possession of not only gold and silver, but also all things, except for the bare necessities in clothing, in footwear, in the construction of cells, in vessels and in all utensils.[83]

[54] And it is proper for us that all these be *inexpensive, unadorned, easy to acquire*,[84] and unremarkable, so that on account of them we do not fall into worldly entanglements.

[55] True distancing from avarice and materialism,[85] though, is *not just not to have property, but not to desire to acquire it*.[86] This directs us toward purity of soul.

The Fourth Urge of Wrath.

[56] If the spirit of wrath torments, compelling to *maintain an evil memory*[87] and urging in *fury* to render evil to him who has offended, then one should remember the word spoken by the Lord: '*If you do not, from your hearts, forgive your brother* of transgressions, *neither will the heavenly Father forgive your transgressions*'.[88] Indeed everyone, who wishes to obtain a pardon for his transgressions, is indebted[89] first from his heart to pardon his brother. So indeed is it commanded from God to beg forgiveness of *debts, just as we forgive*.[90] And if we ourselves do not forgive, it is apparent that we shall not be forgiven.[91]

---

83. Cf. above, *Predanie* 31–33, 39–40.

84. Cf. above, *Predanie* 40; Basil/Ps-Basil, *Longer Rules* 20.186/HM SMS 183.15:54; PG 31:973C.

85. Literally, *silver-love and thing-love*.

86. Cf. Cassian, *Institutes* 7.21:119 (not in the *Philokalia* or Slavic 'Eight Vices', such as HM SMS 468.3:227v–232v or Eparkh. 369.3:159v–167; cf. MRIV 4ᴮ.14/3.14.

87. *zlopominanie* = μνησικακῶν, i.e., *vindictiveness, rancor, animosity*; the linkage of fury/rage (here *iarostь*) to maintaining vindictiveness is found in Maximus Conf. *Centuries on Love* 2.49:64, HM SMS 459 98v–99; PG 90.2.49:1000D–1001A/Фκ 2.2.49:20.

88. Mt 6:15, with *from your hearts* adapted from Mt 18:35.

89. *dolzhenъ*: alt. transl.: *must*.

90. Mt 6:12, Lk 11:4 (from the Lord's Prayer).

91. Cf. Peter Dam., *Treasury*, 95; HM SMS 454:24v–25; Фκ 3:22.

[57]   And if it is proper to understand, even if we reckon that we are doing something good, but we do not abstain from wrath, it is unacceptable, because, it is said by the Fathers: *Even if a wrathful man resurrects the dead, his prayer is unacceptable.*[92] This is said by the Fathers, not that a wrathful man can resurrect the dead, but showing the abomination of his prayer.

[58]   Therefore it is improper for us in any way to be wrathful and to do *evil unto a brother, not only by deed* or *word, but also by appearance,* for one can *offend his brother by a single look,*[93] as is said by the Fathers: *and cast wrathful urges from the heart.*[94] *This is* forgiveness of the heart and this is the great victory over wrathful urges: to pray for an offending brother,[95] as Abba Dorotheus directs, and so speak: '*Help* Lord, *my brother* so-and-so, *and by his prayers have mercy on me, a sinner*'.[96] And this is love and charity: to pray for a brother. And to summon his prayers for help—this is humility: also to do good unto him to the best of our ability.

[59]   And thus are fulfilled the commandments of the Lord, who *says:* '*Love your enemies; bless them that curse you; do good to them that hate you; pray for them who commit offence against you*'.[97] Such great recompense has the Lord promised for this, above the others! For not only the kingdom of heaven, he said, not some other comfort or gift, as for the others,[98] but adoption. . . . '*indeed you will be,* he said, *the sons of your Father who is in heaven*'.[99]

[60]   And the Lord himself, our God Jesus Christ, who laid down this commandment and promised this great recompense in

---

92. Agathon 19, *Sayings* 23; PG 65:113C; (not located in the KB 8/1246 Slavic *Alphabetic Patericon*); Nil omits *to God*.

93. Abbrev. from Dorotheus, *Discourses* 8(8.5):152; Eparkh. 347.10:101; PG 88:1712CD; cf. Isaiah 8, *Sayings* 70; PG 65:181CD.

94. Source not identified.

95. literally: *a brother who has offended*.

96. Adapted and combined from a) Dorotheus, *Discourses* 8(8.5):154; Eparkh. 347.10:103; PG 88:1713BC; b) the Jesus Prayer; c) the formulaic *so-and-so (imiarek = name stated)* found in ritual ordinaries and epistle models.

97. Lk 6:27-28 (as in the Slavic Gospel); cf. Maximus Conf., *Centuries on Love* 2.49:74; HM SMS 456.2.49:106v–107; Фк 2.2.49:20.

98. I.e., *other good deeds*.

99. Mt 5:45 (Gk:-Slav: literally: *in the heavens*).

order to teach, did this, thereby giving us a model, so that we become imitators of it to the best of our ability. Indeed, how much evil did he endure from the Judaeans[100] for the sake of us sinners! And not only did he not become wrathful towards them, but he even prayed for them to the Father, saying: '*Father, pardon them* this sin'.[101]

[61] And all the saints, having tread this path, acquired grace, that[102] they not only did not render evil to those who had offended, but did good unto them, prayed for them, covered their shortcomings, and, rejoicing in their rectification when they came to sense their evils, taught them with love and charity.

The Fifth Urge of Sadness

[62] *Not small is our struggle*[103] *against the spirit of grief,*[104] because it throws *the soul into ruination and despair.*[105] And if the grief be human, from humans,[106] it is proper cheerfully to endure and to pray for those who have caused grief,[107] and just as it was already said, *knowing surely,* that *not without Divine Providence do all things happen to us,* and that God sends all things to us for our *benefit* and for the salvation *of our souls,* even if at the present time we do not consider it *beneficial* – but later we shall *be assured* that it is beneficial just as God arranges, and not as we desire.

---

100. *Iudei* (Gk: Ἰουδαῖοι), as opposed to *zhidovin/zhidove* for the rabbinical Jews of Nil's time.
101. From Lk 23:34.
102. *ezhe* here is ambiguous in this ideal world where the practice of virtues and the operation of grace have a dynamic interrelationship: what follows *ezhe* can be cause or result.
103. Through *our struggle:* cf. Symeon Metaphr., *Macarian Chapters* 48:305; HM SMS 468:36v; Фк 3.48:189, used for the general struggle against Satan.
104. *skorbnyi: skorb* can also mean *distress, affliction, anguish,* or just *sadness.*
105. Starting from *is our struggle:* cf. Cassian, *Institutes* 9.1, 9:139, 142/ PSW 1:87, 88; HM SMS 468.5:236, 237; Фк 1:74, 75-76: only the Slavic text has *ruination* as well as *despair.*
106. *from humans* is in the margin Nil Polev's Eparkh. 349:38v.
107. Alt. transl.: *offended, insulted.*

[63]   For this reason it is not proper to be seduced by human urges, but whole-*heartedly* to believe, that the all-seeing eye *of God* gazes upon everything, and without his will nothing can befall us, and on account of *his mercy* he sends all these to us, so that we, having been tried in them and suffered, shall be crowned by him, because no one has ever been crowned without *trials*.

[64]   Therefore we are to send up our *thanksgiving* for all these to the Lord as our *Benefactor*[108] and Saviour. The lips that are *ever grateful will receive God's* benediction,[109] and into the grateful *heart* falls grace, says Saint Isaac. So, preserve yourselves from complaining against those who have caused grief, for he also says: *God bears all the infirmities of man, but He does not tolerate the eternal complainer, if*[110] *He does not punish*[111] *him*.[112]

[65]   It is proper for us *to have* the beneficial *grief, which is over sins, with good hope* towards God *through repentance*, knowing surely that there is no sin which defeats God's love for man, but he forgives everything to those who repent and pray. *Thus, this grief becomes intermixed with joy, and renders man earnest towards every good and endurant of any pain*. 'For *grief in God*', said *the Apostle*, 'works repentance to salvation irrevocably'.[113]

---

108. From [62], *knowing surely* . . . , composed in part with words and ideas from Dorotheus, *Discourses* 13 (13.1-3):192–93; Eparkh. 347.15:144v–147; PG 88:1761B–1764C, influenced by, among others, Anthony 5: *Sayings*, 2; PG 65:77A: *Noone untested will be able to enter the Kingdom of God*.

109. blagoslovie: the third of five *blago-* words in these two sentences, the other four being *blago-da-* words: blagodarenie (*thanksgiving*), blagodariashche (twice: *giving thanks*—prs. prtcpl.), blagodatь (*grace*).

110. Alt. transl.: *even if.*

111. *pokazhetь* (3rd sg. prs.) = *nakazhetь* in the original transl. = παιδεύσῃ (3rd sg. aor. subj.): alt. transl.: *teach*.

112. From Isaac Syr. 48:229; HM SMS 179.85:379–379v; Gk: 73:284. The HTM translation (based on the Syriac original), unlike the Greek and Slavic, treats the punishment as inevitable.

113. The Biblical citation of the last sentence is combined and adapted from 2 Cor 7:9-10. The original Greek ἀμεταμέλητον (adv.) means both *not regretted* (*unregrettedly*) as in the SMS 468 Slavic (Middle Serbian) Cassian and Slavic biblical. (= *neraskaanno*: Sof. 34:144v), and *irrevocably*, as in Nil (*neotlozhno*). [65] is adapted from Cassian, *Institutes* 5.10–11:142 / *Eight Vices*, 88; HM SMS 468 5:237v; Фк 1:75, and, perhaps, some other source.

[66]   But *the opposite grief*, which is conveyed to us by demons—it *is proper for us* zealously *to cast* from the heart, *just like the other* evil *passions*, and *by prayer*, reading, and *communication* and conversations *with* spiritual *people* to *eliminate it*, because it is the cause of all evil. For if it lingers in us, it immediately puts on the cloak of *despair* and renders the soul empty and downcast, infirm, *impatient,* and *lax* in *prayer* and reading.[114]

The Sixth Urge of Despondency

[67]   When despondency becomes most firmly established against *us*, our soul ascends to a great *struggle. Fierce and most grave is* this spirit, *joined and cooperating with the spirit of grief.*[115] This war forcefully assaults those who are in stillness.

[68]   When those cruel waves rise against the soul, a man does not reckon at that hour that he will ever obtain deliverance from them. Rather, the Enemy so attacks him with urges, that today seems so evil,[116] and then in the next days it will be worse, and suggests to him, that he is forsaken by God, and He has no care for him, or this is occurring beyond Divine Providence, and these happen only to him, and have not happened and do not happen to others.

[69]   But it is not so, it is not!! Not only upon us, sinners, but even upon his saints, who have pleased him throughout the ages, God, as a tenderly child-loving Father to his children, applies the spiritual rod out of love and for advancement in virtues. Soon a transformation invariably happens to them, and God's visitation, mercy, and succor after them.[117]

---

114. Adapted from Cassian, *Institutes* 5.12–13:143 / *Eight Vices* 88; HM SMS 468 5:237v–238; Фк 1:75–76.

115. Cassian, *Eight Vices* 6:88; HM SMS 468 5:238; Фк 1:76 (different from the opening of the full *Institutes* 10:145).

116. . . . . *no sitse pomysly nalagaetъ emu vragъ, iako dnesь tako zlo,* . . . . : alt. transl.: . . . *so attacks him with the thoughts that today is so evil,* . . . .

117. If Nil is consistent, then both uses of *them* (first in the dt. *simъ* and then in the prp. *sikhъ*) refer to the *cruel waves* of *despondency,* not *his saints*.

[70] Just as in that gruesome hour the man does not reckon that he can persevere in the struggle for the good life, rather, the Enemy is manifesting all good things to him as abominable, so again after the transformation of them, all the good things appear to him as pleasing, and all of his past grief as naught. And he is painstaking within the good, wonders at the superiority of the transformation,[118] desires never to stray from the path of virtue, and understands that God, in His mercy, arranges these for him for his own benefit, and out of love, as chastisement, applies such measures. And he is kindled with the love of God, knowing with certainty, that *the Lord is faithful and will not* ever *allow upon us trials beyond our power.*[119]

[71] And the Enemy can do nothing at all to us, except by God's allowance: *for it is not so much that his*[120] *desire* saddens the soul, but rather that it is allowed *by God.*[121] And having understood this from experience, he grows wise from previously occurring transformations and endures courageously the attack of these savages, as he knows that through this the monk manifests his love for God, if he courageously endures it and from this advances successfully.

[72] *Indeed nothing so mediates for a crown for a monk, as does despondency, if he forces himself*[122] *without weakening onto the divine activity,*[123] said John Climacus.

[73] And when this terrible *attack* occurs, it is proper then firmly to arm against the spirit of ingratitude and also to fear blasphemy. For at that time the Enemy wages war by means of all

---

118. Alt. gramm. correct transl.: *transformations for the better/best.*
119. 1 Cor 10:13, as in Symeon Metaphr., *Paraphrase of Macarius* 39:301; HM SMS 468:33v; Фк 3.38:185.
120. I.e. *the Enemy's.*
121. Seemingly adapted from Symeon Metaphr., *Paraphrase of Macarius* 39:301; HM SMS 468:33v; Фк 3.39:185.
122. Almost as in the Slavic Climacus 13.12:139; HM SMS 184:80/ VMCh-M: 882b–c; PG 88:860C, reversing the clause order of the original, which follows: *At the time of despondency the forceful/violent appear.* cf. above, Ustav 2.17, and Mt 11:12.
123. Cf. MRIV 1ᴮ.17, 1.12.

these, and then the man is filled with doubt and fear. And the Enemy impresses upon him that it is impossible for him to be pitied by God, and receive forgiveness for sins, and be delivered from eternal torments and saved. And the invasion of other evil urges occurs, which are impossible to commit to writing. And even if one reads, if one serves,[124] they do not leave him.

[74]   *At that time* it is proper firmly to display the following: as much as possible, not to stand in despair and not to be indifferent toward prayer. And if one can fall on one's face in prayer, this is most fitting, that he pray thus, as Barsanuphius the Great says: '*Lord, see my grief and have mercy on me. God, help me, a sinner*'.[125]

[75]   And as Saint Symeon the New Theologian directs: *Do not allow upon me, Master, beyond my power, trials,*[126] *or grief or sickness, but grant me release and strength, in which to endure this with gratitude.*[127]

[76]   And sometimes, *raising our eyes to heaven and our hands up high, pray,*[128] as the blessed Gregory the Sinaite directed us to pray against this passion. For these *two passions* he called *brutal: fornication, as it is said, and despondency.*[129]

[77]   And struggling thus, apply yourself as much as possible to *reading*, and force yourself upon *manual labor*, for these are the great helpers in times of that need.[130]

---

124. I.e., takes part in a church service; alt. implicit transl.: *or if one serves.*

125. Adapted from the Christian adaptation of Ps 142:9/143:9 by Barsanuphius and John 543; SC 451:686–687, combining with the Jesus Prayer: Slavic transl. of Barsanuphius not identified.

126. Cf. 1 Cor 10:13, and above, *Ustav* 5.6.70.

127. Adapted from Symeon NT, *Hymns* 36:195; Eparkh. 334.16:9; SC 174.36:454–457; cf. the Latin PG *Divinorum Amorum Liber* 23, PG 120:560C.

128. Gregory Sin., *Sitting at Prayer* 4:277; HM SMS 456 4:61v; PG 150:1332D–1333A.

129. Gregory Sin., combining *Ibid.* and *Acrostic Chapters* 110:238; HM SMS 456 110:30; PG 150:1277A.

130. Insofar as this is supposed to be Gregory Sin., cf. *Stillness and Two Ways* 9:269; HM SMS 456:535-53v; PG 150:1321BC (but here not anti-despondency); cf. Climacus 13.16: HM SMS 184:60v / VMCh-M: 882d:861A: *psalmody and manual labor are my* [despondency's] *enemies.* Cf. above, *Ustav* 3.7, and below, *To Vassian* 7.

[78]   At times when these things[131] do not cease to approach, then there is also a great need[132] and requirement of much fortitude,[133] and with all power to strive to pray against the spirit of ingratitude and blasphemy, and to say thus: '*Be gone from me, Satan*; I *worship the Lord* my *God, and* I *serve only him*',[134] and, 'I accept with gratitude all illnesses and distress, as they are sent from him for the curing of my transgressions, as *it is written*:[135] '*The wrath of the Lord shall I bear, for I have sinned unto* him.[136] As for you, may ingratitude and blasphemy return to your head[137] and the Lord writes this for you: "*Depart from me*"[138] and may God, who *created* me *in his image and likeness*, destroy you'.[139]

[79]   And if even after this, it[140] still vexes, transpose the urges onto some other thing, divine or human:[141] let *the soul, desirous of pleasing God*, be *possessed first of all of patience and trust*, as Holy Macarius writes.[142]

[80]   Indeed it is the art of the enemy's evil[143] to set despondency within us, so that the soul withdraw from trust in God. For God never abandons a soul, that trusts in Him, to be overcome by temptations, since He knows all our infirmities. And if it is not

---

131. I.e., *the attack of despondency.*

132. *nuzhda*—the same root as the *violent* Kingdom of God and the violent, who force themselves on it in Mt 11:12; cf. Climacus 13.12, and above, *Ustav* 2.17, 5.6.72.

133. PNSIK (p. 153) breaks the long paragraph here and converts the following infinitive into an imperative.

134. From Mt 4:10: Jesus's reply is transferred from a restatement of the 2nd sg. imprv. OT Law to a 1st sg. affrm.; cf. Dt 10:20.

135. Likely also Mt 4:10, maybe as well Mt 4:4, 4:7, or Lk 4:4.

136. Mc 7:9.

137. *na verkhъ tvoi*: literally, *peak, cupola*; cf. an analogous expression attributed to Kirill of Turov in Sreznevskii 1:466; cf. here and for the text to note 133, the analogous and related, brief 'On the Urge of Blasphemy', Sof. 1468:168v.

138. Cf. Ps 6:8/6:9, and *Ustav* 6.6.

139. Cf. Gn 1:26, Wsd (LXX) 2:23-24.

140. *despondency.*

141. From [78], *say thus*: almost as in *To Gurii* 8; cf. above and below, *Ustav* 1.10–11, 5.3–4, 8.24.

142. Macarius/Ps-Macarius, *Liber de libertate mentis* 13, PG 34:945BC; Slavic version not identified.

143. Cf. above, *Ustav* 3.1.

unknown to men how much a mule, how much an ass, how much a camel can bear a load,[144] and they burden them with the possible, likewise it is known to the potter for how much time to fire his *vessels,* lest if for too much, they crack, or if they be taken out before sufficient firing, they will be useless.[145] And if so much knowledge be among humans, does not God's much greater, indeed, immeasurably greater knowledge comprehend how much trial is proper to inflict upon each soul, so that it is tested and fit for the heavenly kingdom, and not only future glory, but also here to attain the consolation of the good Spirit.[146] Comprehending this, one must endure courageously in stillness within the gates.

[81] At times it requires a man most *experienced in life* and *most profitable in discourse,* as Basil the Great says: *For often,* he said, *a well-timed*[147] *and unblemished going out* to such men and *a conversation in measure*[148] can *smash the despondency that is in the soul, and after one has recovered and breathed a little, makes one most seriously engage the struggle for piety.*[149]

[82] But to endure then in stillness without going out is better, the Fathers say, themselves having understood from experience.[150]

---

144. Var. some texts: *vremia* (время = time) for *bremia* (бремя = burden).

145. The potter analogy seemingly adapted from Symeon Metaphr., *Macarian Chapters* 39:301; HM SMS 468:33v; Фк 3.39:185.

146. Alt. transl.: *of good spirit* (less likely, in the light of *consolation* here).

147. *blagovremenně*—adapted from the Slavic Basil's *blagodrъznovenno* = *well spoken, freely speaking.*

148. i.e., *structured discussion.*

149. Ps-Basil *Const.* 7; HM SMS 183 6:152; PG 31:1365D–1366A.

150. Nil here changes the thrust of Basil, that it is inane simply out of pride not to leave one's cell, even when such action is rational, in favor of the more stringent principle of the Desert Fathers: Arsenius 11, Ammonas 4, Macarius 27, 41, Moses 6, Paphnutius 5, *et al.*: *Sayings,* 9, 22, 112, 116, 118, 171; PG 65:89C, 120BC, 273B, 281B, 285B, 3809CD; *Paterik azbuchhny* 7–7v; cf. Bianchi 89, n. 60.

The Seventh Urge of Vainglory

[83] Much watchfulness is required of us *against the spirit of vainglory*, because it very secretly by every *artifice* steals our *initiative*,[151] makes a monk devoid of achievement, and strives to slander our work, so it be not according to God, but for the sake of vainglory and pleasing men.[152] Therefore it is at every moment proper for us carefully to inquire of ourselves, sensibly and mentally, so that our work be by God and for the soul's profit, and totally flee all human things, *always having before our eyes that, spoken by Holy David: God has scattered the bones of those who please men*;[153] and always to *discard the urges* of those who *praise* this and compel the *doing* of something for the sake of pleasing *men*. And let us wholeheartedly affirm the urge that we do everything *according to God*.[154]

[84] For when someone truly makes an initiative toward God, and due to infirmity is unwillingly defeated by an urge, but confesses, praying to the Lord, and translates these urges away from vainglory, he will be immediately forgiven and praised by the One, who sees our initiative and heart.

[85] *Let us do this*,[155] whenever we begin to *devise any things for vainglory: let us recall our private prayers of mourning*[156] *and of the terrible*

---

151. *predlozhenie* = *propositio* (of Latin transl.): alt. transl.: *proposition, statement of purpose, purpose*; cf. *Life of Theodore Synkeotes*, SNS 3:390; *Vita S. Theodori Siciotae* 35D.

152. *chelověkugodie* = ἀνθρωπαρέσκεια.

153. Literally, *please men*: exactly as in Cassian, *Institutes* 11.19:170–171/ *Eight Vices* 92; HM SMS 468 7: 241; Фк 1:79; citation from Ps 52:6 (LXX).

154. Exactly with *always having . . . who seek popularity*, otherwise freely constructed with some of the words of Cassian, *Institutes* 11.19:171 / *Eight Vices*, 91-92; HM SMS 468 7:24; Фк 1:78–79.

155. Adapted from Nicetas Steth., *On the Practice of Virtues*, in the Slavic text: HM SMS 468.72:190v/Eparkh. 344:385; PG 120:889A.

156. *plachia/placha* (gn. sg.): alt. transl., as in NSSS and PNSIK, treating this as a gerund, but further removed from Climacus's original: *Mourning, let us also remember our special prayers of the terrible appearance . . . .*

appearance,[157] *if we* have them. *If not, then let us conjure up the thought*[158] *of our departure*[159] *and totally repel shameless* vainglory. *If not in this manner, then let us* at least attend[160] *to the shame, which follows upon vainglory. For the self-exalting one will be totally humbled*[161] *even here, before the future*[162]—this is what John Climacus says.

[86] And *whenever* someone *praises us,*[163] or the *assault* of the urge of *vainglory* is *conveyed* by unseen enemies to our intellect, *making* us more worthy *than others* present of the honor of majesty and the *height of thrones,*[164] *let us* immediately, quickly *recall in our intellect the multitude* and gravity *of our* transgressions,[165] or any of the most evil ones, and *maintaining* it *in the intellect* say: *'If the doers of such things are worthy* of these praises, . . .'.[166] Then *we will* immediately *perceive ourselves unworthy*[167] of those human praises, and the demonic urges will *flee, and no* longer *confound us with power,* said Nicetas Stethatos. *If,* he said, *evil deeds are not within you, then* think a bit about[168] *the commandments of perfection and you will find*

---

157. *predstoianiia* (gn. sg.): literally, *(our) standing before* (that is, before the tribunal of the Last/Terrible Judgment), hence *(court) appearance.*
158. *myslъ* = ἔννοια, and in the Slavic; alt. (Eparkh. 349, KB 25/1102) *pomyslъ*: here = *thought, imagining,* not *urge.*
159. I.e., *death.*
160. *fear* in the original.
161. Cf. Mt 23:12/Lk 14:11; here the Gospel text altered by Climacus.
162. *future age* in the original: adapted and textually simplified from Climacus, 22.41:178; HM SMS 184:109v / VMCh-M: 898cd; PG 88: 956BC.
163. Adapted from Climacus, 22.42:179; HM SMS 184:109v / VMCh-M: 898d; PG 88:956C.
164. Adapted from Nicetas Steth., *On the Practice of Virtues* 81:100; HM SMS 468.72:190/Eparkh. 344:385; PG 120:889A/Фк 3.81:292: alt. transl. for *of thrones* = *prestolъ* (gn. pl.) = προεδρίας (gn. sg.): *of the foremost seats.*
165. *illegalities* in the Greek and Slavic originals; adapted from Climacus 22.41:178; HM SMS 184:109v; PG 88:956C.
166. Nil employs here an *anacolouthon* (break in grammatical sequence), which Prokhorov (PNSIK, pp 156–157) treats as a rhetorical question.
167. Adapted from Climacus 22.42:179; HM SMS 184:109v / VMCh-M: 898d; PG 88:956C.
168. *pomysli* (2nd pers. imprv.), perhaps a word play on *pomysli*: *compare* [yourself] *to* in the original; verb missing in the HM SMS 468 Slavic.

yourself insufficient, like a small *pool* relative to the greatness of *the sea.*[169]

[87]   And so always striving, let us by all means preserve ourselves from *vainglory.* For if we be not sober, we shall become seriously involved with vainglorious urges, *which,* immediately upon *solidifying, will give birth to* arrogance and *pride* that are *the beginning and end of all evils.*[170]

The Eighth Urge of Pride

[88]   Concerning arrogance and pride, what is one to say? For while the names differ, haughtiness and loftiness-of-heart and puffiness and the others that are named by the Fathers, they converge toward one meaning.

[89]   And all these are *most wretched,*[171] as it is said in Scripture: *The Lord opposes the proud;*[172] and *every one who is lofty of heart is* an *abomination to the Lord,* and is called *impure.*[173] How can he who has God as an opponent, is abominable to Him and stands impure before Him, ever, in any way, or anywhere expect to obtain any good thing? *And by whom will he be pitied?*[174] *And who will purify him?*[175] Even to speak of these is woeful. For he who is defeated by these is himself the demon and the attacker and always has destruction readied within himself.

---

169. Adapted from the Slavic Nicetas Steth., *On the Practice of Virtues* 81:101; HM SMS 468.72:190v/Eparkh. 344:385v; PG 120:889B / Фк 3.81:292.

170. Adapted from Climacus 22.45:179; HM SMS 184:110 / VMCh-M: 698d; PG 88:956D.

171. Gregory Sin., *Acrostic Chapters* 115:238; HM SMS 456 115:31; PG 150:1279C (applied as self-deprecation in combating pride in source of [91].

172. Prv 3:4 (LXX)/Jas 4:6/1 P 5:5.

173. Adapted from Prv 16:5 mixed with Lk 16:15 (whence *abomination*).

174. Adapted from Climacus's sequel to the extract from Prv 3:34/Jas 4:6/1 P 5:5. cf. the two abbreviated in succession, almost as in Nil, in Cassian, *Institutes* 12.6:176, but not in the brief redaction represented by HM SMS 468 8:241-242v, Eparkh. 369.8:182-184, Фк 1:79-80, and PSW 8:79-80.

175. Adapted from Climacus's sequel to his adapted extract from Pr 16.5; [89] adapted and expanded from Climacus 23.9; HM SMS 184.23:110v/VMCh-M: 899b; PG 88:965D-968A.

[90] For that reason it is proper for us always to fear with trembling the passions of pride and to flee them, contemplating this inside ourselves, that nothing good can be accomplished without the aid of God.[176] But if we are abandoned by God, then, *like a leaf fluttering* or dust *swept up by the wind*, we shall be confused by the devil, mockery for *the Enemy*, and mourning for men.[177]

[91] And understanding this, let us in every way conduct our life in humility. *And this is the beginning* of it: *to hold oneself beneath all others, to reckon oneself the most sinful* and worthless of all men, and, *as being beyond nature, the filthiest of all creations*, and *worse than the demons*, as one violated and defeated[178] *by them.*[179]

[92] And it is proper to act thus: always select the *last seat* among the brothers, both *during meals and at assemblies*;[180] and *wear the meanest clothing*; and *love degrading tasks*;[181] and, upon meeting a brother, be first with a low and prompt bow; and love silence; and do not put on airs in conversations; and do not be contentious in discourse; and be neither shameless nor ostentatious; and do not wish to compose your own sermon,[182] even if it be deemed good, because, the Fathers said, among neophytes, the inside of a man conforms to his outside.[183] Basil the Great said: Do not trust one

---

176. Cf. Cassian, *Institutes* 12.12:179, but not in the brief HM SMS 468.8:241–242v / Фк 1:79–80 redaction.

177. Maybe inspired by Isaac Syr. 37:184; HM SMS 179.21:113; Gk: 85:349.

178. *dominated/ruled by them* in the original, cited fully in 5.8.93.

179. Section somewhat adapted from Gregory Sin., *Acrostic Chapters* 115:238–239; HM SMS 456:115:31–31v; PG 150:1279BC; cf. above, *Ustav* 3.6, and below, *Ustav* 5.8.93.

180. Adapted obversely from Mt 23:6 and Basil/Ps-Basil, *Ascetic Discourse* 69; HM SMS 183:85; PG 31:644B: *They love to have the places of honor at banquets and the best seats in the synagogues.*

181. From *last seat* partially reversed from Isaac Syr. 71:345; HM SMS 48:198; Gk: 81:307.

182. *slovo* (= word, sermon, discourse) *svoe sъstaviti*: alt. transl.: *say / interject your own word.*

183. Source not identified.

who is unguarded on the outside to be in a good state on the inside.[184]

[93] Vainglory and pride are defeated, while humility increases, by reproaching oneself *and so speaking*, as Gregory the Sinaite has written: *Whence could I know precisely of human sins, their quantity and quality, whether they surpass or rival my own lawlessness? And through ignorance, O Soul, we are beneath all men, as earth and dust under their feet. How can I not take myself to be the filthiest of all natural creation due to my immeasurable lawlessness beyond nature. In truth even animals and cattle are cleaner than I, the sinner. And therefore I am beneath all others, as if I lie, carried down into Hell before death. Who does not know that the sinner in his senses is worse than the demons, as their slave and subject, and thus locked up away with them in the darkness of the abyss? In truth he is worse than the demons,*[185] *who is ruled by them, and therefore thou hast inherited the abyss, wretched* Soul!*[186] Inhabiting earth, hell, and the abyss before death, how you deceive yourself in your intellect, calling your sinful and defiled self righteous, after having made yourself as a demon with evil deeds. Fie on your tempting and deceit, you demonical dog, corrupt and most stinking, for on their account you are dispatched to the fire and darkness'*.[187]

[94] This too is told of *monkish pride*, a man, who with regard to the many labors and struggles he has stored and to the malice he has endured over virtues—the urge of pride assaults him with regard to the pious life.

[95] And to have the title of the *finest monastery* in a place and a multitude of brothers—this is *the pride of the worldly*,[188] the Fathers said—or, according to the prevailing custom now, from the acquisi-

---

184. Source not identified: cf. Basil/Ps-Basil, *Longer Rules* 22:189; HM SMS 183.17:56; PG 31:980CD, regarding modest dress, referencing 1Tm 2:9, 3:2.
185. Cf., above, *Ustav* 3.6, 5.8.91.
186. If the PG publication is accurate, the Slavic translation added *soul* here.
187. The words of the speech, if not the adapted introduction, precisely (with two trivial exceptions) as in Gregory Sin., *Acrostic Chapters* 115:238–239; HM SMS 456.115:31–31v; PG 150:1280CD.
188. Adapted from Dorotheus *Discourses* 2:97; PG 88.2.5:1645A; Eparkh. 347.4:41.

tion of villages[189] and accumulation of many properties, and from success in worldly reputation—what can we say about this? There are some who hold themselves high over nothing, that is, a *fine singing* voice or *fine enunciation* of tongue in singing, speaking or reading—what praise can man have from God[190] for these, which are *not accomplished by his* volition, but are what the Fathers call *natural*?[191] Others vaunt themselves for their skill in craftsmanship—this is similar. There are also such who even boast of this: if someone stemmed from parents of worldly repute, or had kinsmen from among the eminent in worldly glory, or himself enjoyed some rank or worldly honor—these are madness: it indeed is proper to conceal them. If someone, from within the life of renunciation of one's own, *accept glory* and honor *from* men[192] —this is shamefulness: it is proper to be embarrassed over these, rather than hold oneself high. For those who glory in these—*their glory* is *shame*.[193]

[96] And if it is due to the virtuous life, as it is said, the urge of vainglory and pride is shameless in making assaults; against such there is no victory like praying to God and saying: '*Lord, Master, my God, drive the spirit* of vainglory and pride *from me*, but *the spirit of humility grant to me, your slave*'.[194]

---

189. *selo* = *village;* also *field*.
190. If one substitutes *praise* . . . *from God* to *glory* . . . *from God*, then we have a part of Jn 5:44 used in the penultimate sentence of [95].
191. Adapted from Climacus 22.31:177; HM SMS 184:99 / VMCh-M: 897d; PG 88:953B, combined with Dorotheus, *Discourses* 2:97; Eparkh. 347.4:41–41v; PG 88:1645AB.
192. Adapted from Jn 5:44 (*from each other* in Jn).
193. Cf. Phil 3:19, applied to the gluttonous (as is MRIV 9ᴮ.3/7.3).
194. Adapted from the (Monday-to-Friday) Lenten Prayer attributed to Ephrem the Syrian; cf. also Dorotheus, *Discourses* 2.102; PG 88:1652C. *Lord and Master of my life! Take from me the spirit of sloth, faint-heartedness, lust of power, and idle talk. But give rather the spirit of chastity, humility, patience, and love to your servant. Yes, O Lord and King! Grant me to see my own errors and not to judge my brother; For you are blessed unto ages of ages. Amen.*

[97]   And *reproach yourself,* as has been written above.[195] For Climacus says, *as though from the face*[196] of *vainglory* and *pride: If you reproach yourself often*[197] *before God, you have reduced us to cobweb.*[198]

[98]   *Pride,* says Saint Isaac, *is neither when this urge comes to our mind, nor if one is overcome by it temporarily.*[199] For he said: *God will not punish nor condemn a man from a single involuntary movement of the urge, not even if at a given time we agree with it, but if that time we goad*[200] *the passion. The Lord does not set down a stipulation or call us to account for such laxity,*[201] *but truly for welcoming the notion as meet and profitable, and not reckoning it to be a terrible harm*[202] *for him. Especially if someone has exemplified this passion in word and deed, he will be condemned.*

[99]   And the Fathers also say this about vainglory and every passion.

---

195. [93].
196. *litsa* (gn. sg.); alt. transl.: *mask,* i.e., *voice.*
197. *openly/sincerely* in the original.
198. Literally, *you are considering us as cobweb*: qualifying phrase adapted, but the imagined speech of pride and vainglory almost *verbatim*: Climacus, 23.37:183; HM SMS 184:113 / VMCh-M: 900c; PG 88:969D.
199. Isaac Syr. 57:283; HM SMS 179.34:150v; Gk: 37:162.
200. *pobodemъ* (1ˢᵗ pl. prs.): literally *butt.*; orig. κεντήσωμεν (1ˢᵗ pl. aor. subj.) = *goad, spur on, prick*; not understood here in the sense of *butting against* in order to repel.
201. *neraděnie*: alt. transl.: *indifference.*
202. Abbrev. and slightly adapted from Isaac Syr. 64:309; HM SMS 179.40:167; Gk: 34:148; applied in the original to fornication, not pride.

6. In General, on All Urges.

[1]   Against all evil *urges* it is proper to summon God for aid, insofar as *we do not* always *have the power* to oppose wicked *urges* as Saint Isaac said: But *there is no other* such *aid as God*.[1]

[2]   For this reason, pray to the Lord Christ assiduously with sighs and tears in this manner, said Neilos the Sinaite:'Have mercy on me, Lord, and do not let me perish! Have mercy on me, Lord, for I am infirm! Shame, Lord of my trust, the demon[2] who combats me! Shine above my head in the day of the demons' attack. *Fight* the enemy *who fights me*,[3] Lord! Calm with your tranquility the urges raging about me, Word of God'.[4]

[3]   Theodore the Studite, having taken from David, directed so to pray against unclean urges:'*Judge those who injure me and impede*[5] *those who fight me*',[6] and the rest of the psalm.

[4]   And as the Hymnographers wrote:'*Concentrate my scattered intellect, Lord. Purify my withered*[7] *heart. As unto Peter, grant me repentance; as unto the publican, sighing; as unto the harlot, tears, so that I call unto you. Help me.*[8] Deliver me from filthy urges, because, *like the*

---

1. From Isaac Syr. 54:269; SMS 179.30:140v; Gk: 33:144–145.
2. Alt. transl.: *Shame, Lord, the hopes of the demon* . . . .
3. Cf. Ps 34:1/35:1, and [3], below.
4. Precise source not identified: von Lilienfeld (NSSS, 255, note f) and Grolimund (NSA, 406–407, note 2) identify possible models in Neilos Sin.: PG 79, among them: 260BC, 393BD, 509D–512A,—all from his letters, which Nil Sorsky almost assuredly would not have directly known.
5. *vъzbrani* (imperv . . , for πολέμησον): alt. transl.: *battle, fight off.*
6. Slightly altered from Ps 34:1/35:1 as in KB 85/210:68 = Theodore the Studite, *Small Catechesis* 91:311/PG 99.91:627B; *Petites Catéchèses* 91.198-199, recommending Ps 35:1-3/34:1-3, but not the entire psalm, as Nil implies; cf. below, *To Gurii* 3; also Nil's redaction, *Life of Martinian*, SNS 3:351. Nil's . . . *boriushtimъ mia* adapts the Slavic Theodore's and Psalter's . *boriushtimsia so mnoi.*: cf. Tr-S 313:25v.
7. *oliadĕvshee:* alt. transl.: *uncultivated, weedy, barren.*
8. http://www.st-sergius.org/services/SlavOK/Tone3-2.pdf: for Monday: *na stikhovněskikhiry umilitel'ny, glasъ* 3 (p 23).

waves of the sea, my iniquities[9] *rise up against me, and, like a ship in the deep, I am drowning in my own thoughts.*[10] *Rather, Lord, direct me by repentance into the calm harbor and save me.*[11] I grieve intensely over the impotence of my intellect, how without so wishing, I truly suffer an inexorable turn. On this account I sing unto you, Holy, Deo-Princely[12] Trinity, help me: station me within the good'.[13]

[5] Thus and similarly speaking from the holy Writings what is necessary against each urge and required at each time, we summon God to our aid for all them, and he will suppress them.

[6] And if ever something like this befalls us, the infirm, when wicked urges are harassing us, we are to prohibit, speak against, and drive them away. And this is not to be simple and happenstance, but similarly with the name of God, from the words of the Divine Writings, and in the likeness of the holy Fathers, we say this to each urge: '*May the Lord rebuke you*';[14] and again: '*Depart from me, all workers of iniquity*';[15] turn away from me, workers of wickedness,[16] that I may *meditate in the* commandments of my God.[17]

[7] And from the example of that elder, who said: 'Begone, wretched one, come, beloved one': A brother, who overheard this and reckoned that he was conversing with some people, asked him, saying: 'With whom were you conversing, Father'? He replied: 'I drove off evil urges, and I summoned the good'.[18]

[8] And if this is necessary for us too, let us say this and similar things.

---

9. bezzakoniia: lit. *lawlessnesses*.
10. *pomyshlenii* (instr. pl.): *sogrěshenьmi* (instr. pl.) = *transgressions* in the original.
11. http://www.st-sergius.org/services/SlavOK/Tone2-2.pdf, *Ponedělьnikъ Utra. Po a-mъ stikhiolovii sědalьny umilitelьny, glasъ 2* (p 10).
12. *bogonachalnaa* (nm. sg.) = θεαρχική, where one might expect the formulaic *zhivotvoriashtaa* = *life-creating*.
13. Source not identified.
14. Jude 9.
15. Ps 6:8/6:9; cf. above, *Ustav* 5.6.78.
16. Possibly another version of Ps 6:9.
17. Cf. Ps 1:2
18. Source not identified.

On Remembrance of Death and the Terrible Judgment: How to Learn about Them, So That We Possess These Urges in Our Hearts 7.

[1]   The Fathers say, that in our activity it is really necessary and useful to have remembrance of death and of the terrible judgment.[1]

[2]   And Philotheus the Sinaite *establishes a protocol[2] of sorts* for effecting this. *From morning to mealtime,* he *said, be engaged in remembrance of God, that is, in prayer,*[3] *and in the guarding of the heart, and afterwards, having thanked God, it is proper* to be heedful *of death and of the judgment.*[4]

[3]   And as we are endeavoring in this, it is proper for us above all else to have within ourselves the Lord's spoken words: *'In this night* the angels *will require your soul from you'*;[5] and 'to *answer about the idle word on the Judgment Day',*[6] he said; and *'for the thoughts of the heart to defile man',*[7] and to remember the utterance of the holy Apostles, 'that *the end is drawing near',*[8] and *'the day of the Lord will come as a thief in the night',*[9] and *'it is incumbent upon us all to stand*

---

1. Cf. below, [10], an oft-expressed principle, but no source identified.
2. *chin.*
3. *the Jesus Prayer* in the original.
4. Abbrev., rearranged, and adapted from Philotheus, 2:16; HM SMS 456.2-3:222v–223/Eparkh. 344.2:345; Фк 2:274; Nil adds *and of the judgment.*
5. From Lk. 12:20; cf. MRIV 4ᴮ.15/3.17.
6. Mt 12:36: cf. MRIV 2.14.
7. Adapted from Mt 15:18; cf. above, Ustav, Fwd, 1.
8. From 1 P 4:7.
9. Almost as in 2 P 3:10; cf. 1 Th 5:2.

before Christ's tribunal,[10] and *'the Word of God* will *judge* not only deeds and words, but also *thoughts of the heart'*.[11]

[4]   The premier[12] of the Fathers, Anthony the Great says: *Thus it is proper for us always to hold within ourselves, that we shall not remain in this life this entire day.*[13]

[5]   And John Climacus: *Remember*[14] *your end,*[15] *and you will for ever not sin;*[16] and elsewhere he says: Let *remembrance of death always be with you,* he said.[17]

[6]   And Isaac the Syrian: *Always*[18] *fix in your heart, O man, that one is to depart.*[19]

[7]   And not only did all the Saints keep this activity but the seculars proclaimed the *rule of philosophy*[20] to be remembrance[21] *of death.*[22]

[8]   So what shall we, the passionate and the infirm,[23] do? How shall we learn this activity, so that in a short while we hoist *this*

---

10. 2 Cor 5:10.
11. Adapted from Heb 4:12: see above, III. 'Technical Terms', text to note 158.
12. *nachalьnikъ* = *first in rank, first in time.*
13. Freely adapted from Athanasius Alex., *Life of Anthony* 19; SNS 3:170; PG 26:872A.
14. Var.: *remembering.*
15. *poslednaia* (pl.), replicating τὰ ἔσχατα (of Si 7:36).
16. Climacus 6 (postscript); HM SMS 184:61v / VMCh-M:872d; PG 88:800A, as in Si 7:36 (Vulg. 7:40).
17. Adapted from Climacus 6.11; HM SMS 184:60 / VMCh-M: 870c; PG 88:796A.
18. Word added from the following sentence in the original.
19. Isaac 64:315; Eparkh. 324.41:207; Gk: 34:151. (HM SMS 179.41 is defective/incomplete here.)
20. *vněshnii* (nm. sg.) *ustav*: alt., possible 'academic' transl.: *the profane/secular definition*; cf. John, Patriarch of Jerusalem, *Life of John of Damascus*, SNS 2:329, *vněshnie liubomudretsi (philosophers)*; the equivalent is not in PG 94:441B, but *vněshnia mudrosti* (gn. sg.) = τῆς ἔξωθεν σοφίας in Nil's *Life of Anthony*: SNS 3:233; PG 26:973B.
21. *meditation* in the original Climacus.
22. Adapted and combined from Climacus (speaking of 'Hellenes') 6.24:113; HM SMS 184: 61v; PG 88:797C; and Isaac Syr. 56:278; HM SMS 179:91: 405v; Gk: 25:107, the latter dealing with silence up to martyrdom.
23. See above, *Ustav* 3.2 (also within an adapted citation from Isaac).

urge in our hearts? For *to possess* this *remembrance perfectly* within oneself is a *gift of God*[24] and *wondrous grace*,[25] as Saint Isaac said.

[9] But flight of the mind and darkened oblivion do not give us leave to remain and meditate within these things. Often ruminating about them and conversing amongst each other about death, we are unable to implant and affirm these words in our hearts. However, on this account we shall not be pusillanimous nor abandon this activity, because with God's help, labor and time, we shall enter into it.

[10] And if one wills, let him act in this way and remember first[26] the written words, understanding, how *necessary and useful this activity is:*[27] *As among all foods, bread is the most necessary, so is the memory of death among other* virtues;[28] and *it is impossible for a hungry man not to remember bread, so for one who desires salvation not to remember death,*[29] said the holy Fathers.[30]

[11] And he shall also concentrate his intellect on what the Saints, such as the blessed Gregory the Dialogist and many others said in the writings about various terrible deaths.[31]

[12] And I also reckon it beneficial for us to recall to memory the various deaths, seen or heard of, which took place in our times. For many, not only laymen, but also monks, who lived in prosperity and loved the life of this age, having hopes of longevity and having not yet reached old age, were suddenly harvested by death. And

---

24. *gift of God*: adapted from Climacus 6:20; HM SMS 184:61 / VMCh-M: 871b; PG 88:797B.
25. Otherwise freely adapted from Isaac Syr. 49:238-39; HM SMS 179.86: 388-388v; Gk: 39:167-68.
26. *prezhde*: alt. transl.: *above, that is, . . . the above written words . . . .*
27. Cf. above, [1].
28. Altered from Climacus 6.4; HM SMS 184: 59v/VMC-M: 870ab; PG 88:793C: *activities* in the original.
29. Slightly altered from Climacus 26-*Summary.*43:234; HM SMS 184: 150/ VMCh-M: 922c; PG 88:1088D.
30. Cf. above, [1].
31. Gregory/Ps-Gregory the Great, *Dialogues* 4.22-25:215-217; Eparkh. 317.4.22-25:336v-340/*Paterik rimskii* 4.22-25:407-411; PL 77:4.21-24 (Gk: 22-25):353A-356D.

among them some could not make any response in that hour of death, but were snatched straightaway as they were, sitting or standing; and some expired while eating and drinking; others suddenly died en route; and yet others lying in their beds, having intended to rest their bodies by this brief and temporary sleep, and thus fell into eternal sleep. And for several of them, there were torturous inquests, awful terror, and horrible fears in that last hour, as we know, of which a few recollections can frighten us not a little.

[13] And bringing all of these to our memory, let us ponder: *where are* our friends and acquaintances, and what has any of them gained by it, if he was honored and famous and *authoritative* in this world, or possessed riches or abundant *bodily nourishment? Have not all of these come to* corruption, stench, and *dust?*[32]

[14] And let us recall what the Hymnographers said about these. *What food of life does not become a partaker of sadness? Or what glory survives immutable in this world? But all are weaker than a shadow, all more deceptive than a dream, and in one hour death lays hold of all of this.*[33] *In truth everything is vanity,*[34] *which is of this life, as it will not abide with us. The wealth of this life will not precede us there, nor will the glory of this age accompany us, but when death comes, it will corrupt*[35] *all this.*[36] And *understanding* thus the vanity of this age, why *are we disquieted in vain,*[37] busying ourselves in *matters of life?* This *road indeed is short, by which we run. This life is smoke, steam, dust, ash, that appears for a moment and suddenly perishes.*[38]

---

32. Possibly from *By the Holy, Humble Monk, John the Damascene*, Eparkh. 355:207v-209.

33. Alt. transl.: *all of this obtains death*. From *Order of the Service of the Dead*, John of Damascus's Hymn, Tone 1; cf. Noli, *Prayer Book*, 180.

34. Eccl. 1:2, 12:28.

35. *pogubitъ*: alt. transl.: *destroy*.

36. From *Service of the Dead*, John of Damascus's Hymn, Tone 3.

37. *disquieted in vain*: Ps 38:7, 13/39:6, 12. cf. below, *Ustav* 7.17.

38. Adapted from *By the Same Monk Damaskon*, Eparkh. 355:210-210v; cf. *Service of the Dead*, John of Damascus's Hymn, Tone 4.

[15] And it is less than a road, as Chrysostom says.[39] For a road, when the traveler is traveling,[40] if he wishes to go to some country, he goes; and whither he wishes not, he goes not. And when he lodges at an inn, he knows when he arrived and when he will leave. If he arrived in the evening, he will leave in the morning, and he also has the authority if he wishes to stay longer at the inn. We, though, *volens nolens* depart this life, but know not when. Nor have we have any power, if we still wish to remain here. But all of a sudden comes upon us the truly terrible mystery of death, and the soul is violently wrenched from the body—severed from the elements[41] and the coupling of a natural union by God's will.

[16] And what shall we then do, if before that time we have not been concerned, have not schooled ourselves in this, and are found unready? And in that bitter hour we shall understand *how great a struggle a soul has, when it is separating from the body*.[42] Alas, how much it then suffers, *and there is no one who takes pity on it. It raises the eyes to the angels and prays to no avail. It extends the hands toward men and has no one helping it*, only the good deeds with God. Thus understanding our *brief life*,[43] let us be concerned about that hour of death, not giving ourselves over to the tumult of this world and in its useless concerns.

[17] '*For each earthborn is disquieted in vain*',[44] as indeed Scripture said. Indeed, even if we acquire the whole world, yet we shall settle in *the grave*, having *taken nothing* of this world: not *beauty* nor *glory*, nor *authority*, nor *honor*, nor any other delight of life.[45]

---

39. Source not identified; Chrysostom's Commentary on Ps 118:5 (KJ 119:5), as in Grolimund (NSA, 410–411, note 16), is a stretch.
40. Alt. transl.: *a traveling traveler* . . . .
41. *sъstavъ* (gn. pl.): alt. transl.: *substances, nature*.
42. *By the Same Monk Damaskon,* Eparkh. 355:210v; cf. *Service of the Dead,* John of Damascus's Hymn, Tone 2.
43. From *Service of the Dead,* John of Damascus's Hymn, Tone 2; cf. Noli, *Prayer Book,* 180.
44. Combining LXX Ps 48:3 and Ps 38:7,12/39:6, 13.
45. Theme adapted from Ps 39:6, 49:6, 16-17/38:7, 48:7, 17-18; cf. above, *Ustav* 7.14.

[18] Indeed, let us *gaze*[46] *into graves and behold* our created beauty disfigured and despicable, shorn of seemliness; and upon seeing the *bare bones, we say, to ourselves:* '*Who is king or pauper, who is glorified or inglorious*'?[47] Where are the beauty and delights of this world? Is not everything obscenity and stench? And lo, the most honorable and craved things of this world have become useless and have fallen away like a withered flower. And *as a shadow passes*[48] *by*, so has everything human come to ruin.[49]

[19] And let us marvel over these, saying to ourselves: 'Oh *wonder, what is this mystery concerning us? Whence are we given over to corruption? Whence are we attached to death? In truth, it is by the command of God*,[50] as it is written. "*Due to the transgression of the command*,[51] *the tasting of the tree long ago in Eden, when the serpent spouted its venom, disease befell Adam. For this reason death for all generations entered, devouring man. But* by the depth of his ineffable wisdom, the decisions bestowing life upon us and programming death, *the Lord came, dethroned the serpent, granted us* resurrection,[52] and is resettling his slaves into another life."'[53]

[20] And thus let us take within our intellect the second coming of the Lord and our resurrection and the terrible judgment, ourselves expounding the words of the Lord from the Gospel, as the divinely voiced Matthew wrote: '*And after the grief*, he said, *of*

---

46. *I gazed* in the original.

47. [17–18]: adapted from *By the Same Damaskon*, Eparkh. 355:211–211v; cf. *Service of the Dead*, John of Damascus's Hymn, Tone 5; cf. Noli, *Prayer Book*, 180.

48. Wsd 2:5.

49. Thematically related to *Service of the Dead*, John of Damascus' Hymn, Tones 3–4; cf. Noli, *Prayer Book*, 180.

50. From the *Service for the Dead*, John of Damascus's Hymn, Tone 7; cf., according to Grolimund, 411, n 20, a special Tone 4 hymn ('Ἰδιόμελον), from the *Euchologion*.

51. *transgression of the command*, adapted from *Service for the Dead*, John of Damascus's Hymn, Tone 7; cf. Noli, *Prayer Book*, 181; also Grolimund, NSA, 411, note 20, references to special prayers for the dead from a Greek *Euchoglion*.

52. *repose* in the original.

53. John of Damascus, Tone 2 conclusion to the Saturday Matins preceding Lent, as extracted by Grolimund, NSA, 412, n 21.

those days, the sun shall darken, and the moon shall not give her light, and the stars shall fall from heaven, and the heavenly powers shall stir. And then shall appear the sign of the Son of Man,[54] *and then shall all the earthly tribes wail. And they shall behold the Son of Man coming on the clouds of heaven with power and great glory, and he shall send his angels with a great sound of a trumpet, and they shall gather together his elect from the four winds, from the ends of the heavens to the other ends'.*[55]

[21] John, the beloved disciple of the Lord, thusly records His words: '*The hour is coming, in which all the dead who are in graves shall hear*[56] *the voice of the Son of God, and those who have heard shall come to life, and they who done good shall come forth, unto the resurrection of life, and they that have done evil, unto the resurrection* for *judgment'.*[57]

[22] And again Matthew: '*When the Son of Man shall come in his glory, and all the holy angels with him, then shall he sit upon the throne of his glory, and before him shall gather all nations, and he shall separate them one from another, as a shepherd separates sheep from the goats, and he shall set the sheep on his right hand, but the goats on the left. Then shall the King say to those on his right hand: "Come, blessed ones of my father, inherit the kingdom prepared for you from the foundation of the world."*[58] *To those on his left hand he shall say: "Depart from me, cursed ones, into the everlasting fire, prepared for the devil and his angels."* [59] *And these shall go into everlasting torment,*[60] *but the righteous ones into life eternal"'.*[61]

[23] And what, brothers, is more bitter and gruesome than that terrible and dread accounting[62] and the spectacle of seeing all

---

54. Omits: *in heaven.*
55. Mt 24:29-31, literally (as in the Greek NT): alt., KJ transl.: *from one end of heaven to the other* (avoiding the multiple heavens of Antiquity).
56. *uslyshat*: alt., possible transl.: *having heard* (as gerund).
57. Adapted from Jn 5.28-29; *of judgment* (κρίσεως—negative in this case) in the original Greek; KJ: *of damnation*.
58. Mt 25:31-34.
59. Mt 25:41.
60. *muku* (fm. acc. sg.), as in the Slavonic Matthew: Tr-S 108:216.
61. Mt. 25:46; for [22], maybe inspired from Ephrem/Ps-Ephrem, *Slovo o pokaian'i*, Eparkh. 357:107v-109 (where Mt 25:46 directly follows Mt 25:41) in an otherwise more extended exposition from Mt 25).
62. *otvětъ*: alt. transl.: *answer, response.*

those who sinned and did not repent being sent to eternal torment by the righteous judgment of God, and savagely trembling and crying out and weeping to no avail? How can we not wail and cry, when we take within our intellect those terrible and gruesome torments, which, Scripture calls *'eternal fire'*,[63] *'the outer darkness'*,[64] *'the deep chasm'*,[65] *'the gruesome sleepless worm'*,[66] *'the gnashing of teeth'*[67] and all other sufferings, awaiting those who have sinned greatly and evilly have angered the most gracious God with their wicked ways,[68] *among whom I, the wretched one, am foremost*?[69]

[24] What fear, brothers, will be upon us, when *the thrones* will *be set*,[70] *and the books opened*,[71] and God then will sit at judgment with glory and with the angels themselves standing, trembling before him? And what shall we do then, who are men guilty of many sins, when we hear him summon the blessed of the Father into the kingdom of the Lord, and sending the sinners off to torment, and separating from the elect? And how shall we answer or respond then, when all of our deeds will stand in indictment against us, when all of our secrets will be manifest, by which we transgressed by day and by night, in word, deed, and thought?[72] And what shame will then envelop us, because then nobody will be able to reject sins? With true unmasking, with immense fear seizing the sinful,[73] the righteous shall enter the heavenly palace with joy and merriment, receiving the reward for their good deeds.

63. Mt 18:8, 25:41.
64. Mt 8:12, 22:13, 25:30.
65. Lk 16:26 (as in Ostr.: KJ: *great gulf*; also *Interpeted Luke*: Tr-S 113:71).
66. Maybe adapted from Is 66:24 or Lk 9:44, 46: *where their worm does not die*.
67. Mt 8:12, 22:13, 25:30.
68. *nravy*; alt. transl., as in *Predanie* 1, *ethos*.
69. Maybe from Romanos Melodos, *The Terrible Judgment* 5.22: 264-65.
70. From Dn 7:9 (Ostr. word-order reversed).
71. Rv 20:12.
72. Cf. Grand Compline Tuesday-Thursday *Troparion*: *How fearful is your judgment, Lord, when the Angels stand round, mortals are brought in, the books are opened, deeds are examined, thoughts are tried*: http://www.anastasis.org.uk/great_compline.htm; also the 'Prayer for One Defiled in a Dream' (*Molitva oskvrьnьshemusia vь sьně*) in Prokhorov, *Entsiklopediia*, 197.
73. Alt. (gram. correct but logically inconsistent) transl: *With immense fear seizing those truly unmasking the sinful*, ...

And who can recount, brothers, that fear and dread of the second coming of the Lord and of that terrible and irrevocable judgment? As one of the Fathers was to say: were it possible to die then, the entire world would die of that fear.[74]

[25] Therefore, let us fear and be horrified and take this within our intellect, even if the heart is unwilling. Let us compel it to contemplate this, and let us speak to our soul.

[26] 'Alas, darkened *soul*,[75] the departure from the body *draws nigh*.[76] Until when will you not *turn from evil ones*? Until when will you languish *in despondency*?[77] Why do you not contemplate the terrible hour of death? *Why do you not quail*[78] before the terrible *judge*ment of the *Saviour*?[79] What will you answer, how will you respond? For here stand your deeds, indicting you and accusing you. Hence, *soul*, while you have time, draw away from shameful *deeds*, take up the *good* life, hurry, anticipate, and *cry* out with faith:

[27] '"Lord, *I have sinned* vilely *before you*;[80] but I know *your clemency, Lover of Man*:[81] therefore *I fall and pray to your* goodness,[82] *that your mercy come upon me, Master, as my soul is troubled and* pained[83] *over its departure out of my* wretched *body, lest the counsel of the wicked*

---

74. Precise source(s) not identified from among the available storehouse of Last Judgment homiletics.

75. Andrew Cr., 1ˢᵗ Mon. Ode 2; PG 97:1336C. The notes for the *Great Canon* in [26–28] indicate clusters of words.

76. Andrew Cr., 1ˢᵗ Mon. Ode 4; PG 97:1347B; also 1ˢᵗ Thur. *Kontakion. the end draws nigh* in the originals.

77. Andrew Cr., 1ˢᵗ Mon. Ode 9; PG 97:1381A.

78. Andrew Cr., 1ˢᵗ Thur. Ode 2; PG 97:1340C.

79. Andrew Cr., 1ˢᵗ Wed. Ode 8; PG 97:1376D.

80. Andrew Cr., 1ˢᵗ Mon. Ode 6; PG 97:1357C.

81. Andrew Cr., 1ˢᵗ Tue. Ode 1; PG 97: 1333A. Here, states the marginal note to KB 25/1102, commences a prayer, attributed to the Great Martyr Eustratius and to Macarius, hence a confusion with Macrina; the same mistake is found in cinnabar on p. 30 in the (unidentified) *Slovo* 7 in the XVI c. KB 29/1106: 25-33, in the text after *Lover of Man*; it is also, on the margins of p. 227 of the XV–XVI c. Sof. 1444, and elsewhere, but Eparkh. 349: 66v has the possibly correct прⁿпб. макр.).

82. *mercy* in the original: Andrew Cr.: 1ˢᵗ Thur. Ode 1; PG 97:1333C; the basic text switches now to Metaphrastes's Eustratius.

83. *weakens* in the original.

Adversary shake it and confine it in the darkness for my past sins, known and *unknown, in this life.*[84] *Be merciful to me, Master, so that my soul not behold the dark gaze of wicked demons, but that your radiant angels take it.*

[28] "'*Having the authority to forgive sin, forgive mine, so that I repose;*[85] and *so that my sin, which I have committed through the infirmity of our nature, by word, deed and thought,*[86] *knowingly and unknowingly,*[87] *not be before you; so that I be found before you, upon the dismantling of my body, not having any filth in the image of my soul,*[88] and *so that the dark hand of the prince of this world, who would pluck*[89] *me down into the depth of hell, not take me, a sinner. Rather stand before me and be my Saviour and intercessor.*[90] *Have mercy, Lord, on my soul, defiled by the passions of this life; but accept it,*[91] cleansed by penitence and confession, and lead me with your authority up to your divine judgment.

[29] "'And when you come, God, onto earth in glory and sit, Merciful One, on your throne to judge your righteous justice, and all of us, naked as the condemned, stand before your irrevocable judgment, then you will make an investigation of our transgression, that we *transgressed in word, deed, and thoughts.* Then, Most Gracious One, do not indict my secrets and do not shame me before angels

---

84. *for my ignorance in this sinful life* in the original.

85. *forgive mine so that I repose,* perhaps adapted from Ps 38:14/39:13.

86. Re-worded from Symeon Metaphr., *Martyrium S. Eustratii/Muchenie . . . Eustratiia* 32, PG 116:505B;VMCh Dec.13:976; the prayer is found separately in Sof. 1444:461–462 (a 1520s miscellany containing the IRI type *Ustav*, preceded by Anastasius the Sinaite on blasphemous urges and followed by the Nil's three Epistles (pp 166–267).

87. *knowingly and unknowingly,* for committed sins, maybe from Andrew Cr., 1ˢᵗ Wed. Ode 5; PG 97:1356C.

88. from [28], also adapted from Gregory of Nyssa, *Life of St Macrina,* 180; PG 46:984D–985A; Slavic original not identified, but should be available in an January menaion.

89. storgnuti (var. *vъstorgnuti* - both prs. inf.)—literally, *uproot*; Greek original: κατασπᾶσαί (aor. inf.) = *pull down, demolish, pluck (fruit), lower.*

90. Nil omits: *for these physical torments are pleasure for your slaves,* specific to Eustratius's ongoing martyrdom.

91. Slighty adapted from Symeon Metaphr., *Martyrium S. Eustratii/ Muchenie . . . Eustratiia* 32, PG 116:505C;VMCh Dec. 13:976–977.

and men, but spare me, God, and have mercy on me. For I am contemplating your terrible tribunal, Most Gracious One, and, indicted by my conscience, I quail and fear judgment day, and am in great sorrow for my wicked deeds, and I am perplexed over how shall I answer you, Immortal King, having so bitterly angered you. With what boldness can I, filthy and prodigal, gaze upon you, the Terrible Judge? But, Lord of glory, clement Father, and Son only-begotten, and Holy Spirit, have mercy upon me and deliver then from the unquenchable fire and make me worthy to stand to the right of you, Righteous Judge.'"[92]

---

92. Themes can be found in Romanos Melodos, *Terrible Judgement*, 5, 24:234-267. Also, the entire [20-29] is suggestive of a juggling and re-scrambling of words, themes, and rhetorical devices of Ephrem Syr., *Slovo . . . o vtoromь prishestvьi Khristovĕ, Paranesis* 95-95 (Old. Bulg.), 232-253; Gk:. Thwaites, 93A-104D; Assem 3:119C–134A. This section also has the earmarks of a sermon delivered in front of a Last Judgment icon: cf. MRIV, 111–112, and Goldfrank, 'Who Put the Snake on the Icon'.

On Tears
and How It is Proper for Those
Who Would Acquire Them to Act. 8.

[1]   Speaking and contemplating thus, or in a similar manner, if, by the grace of God, we acquire tears in them, it is proper to mourn[1] *with all* our power and *strength*.[2] For, the Fathers said, by mourning one is delivered from *the eternal fire and other*[3] future torments.

[2]   *And* even *if* we can*not* mourn[4] much, let us *compel* our*selves*[5] *with pain to produce* at least *a few small drops. For these are judged by* our *good judge,* Climacus says: *as in all things, so also in tears there is*[6] *natural power. For I have seen,* he said, *small drops shed as if blood, with pain, and I have seen wellsprings flow painlessly. And I have judged those who toil more by the pain, not the tears—and, I reckon, God as well.*[7]

[3]   If we are unable to acquire even a small tear, due to our weakness or negligence or any other reasons, let us not fall away, nor be pusillanimous, but let us grieve and sigh and suffer and sadden over the pursuit of this with good hope. *For grief of the mind completes the* measure[8] *for all physical deeds,*[9] says Saint Isaac.

---

1. Alt. transl.: for *mourn* and its cognates: *weep*.
2. Climacus 7.5; HM SMS 184:62/VMCh-M: 871d; PG 88:804A.
3. Maybe referencing Climacus 7.21; HM SMS 184: 63/VMCh-M: 872d; PG 88:805B.
4. Climacus 7.22; HM SMS 184: 63v/VMCh-M: 872d; PG 88:805C.
5. Climacus 7.17; HM SMS 184: 63/VMCh-M: 872c; PG 88:805A; Nil omits the criticism of those who force *tears without thinking*.
6. Nil omits the unnecessary *estb* from the Slavic Climacus.
7. Somewhat altered from Climacus 7.23; HM SMS 184: 64/VMCh-M: 872d; PG 88:805C.
8. *měra*: i.e., *makes up for the shortfall: completes/fills/takes the place* (*město*) in the original; Izwolsky (p 126) and, following her, Maloney (exactly in *Russian Hesychasm,* p 131, mixed with the Iustin adaptation in *Nil Sorsky,* p 98), misrepresent Isaac and Nil as having said, . . . *is superior to bodily actions/exceed any amount of bodily deeds.*
9. Recast from Isaac Syr., 51:243; HM SMS 179.89: 392v; Gk: 58:234.

[4] And again Climacus said: *Those, who in pursuit of tears, call themselves wretched and condemn themselves with sighs, moroseness, and sadness of soul, and profound suffering and perplexity, even if these are considered nothing,*[10] *are able safely to fill the place of the tears.*[11]

[5] And sometime, due to an infirmity, a want of tears happens, as Saint Isaac says, not only to those who search of them, but even to those who have *acquired and received the gift of tears: they cease and fervency cools* due to *bodily infirmity.*[12]

[6] And Symeon the New Theologian, speaking of tears and directing *always to mourn:*[13] *Even if* by some *ineffable* design or a hindrance due to some cause, *a dearth befalls someone, . . .*[14] he said. And again, having taken from Scripture, he so spoke: *David said:'A contrite spirit is an offering to God; God will not destroy a contrite and humble heart'.*[15] *And he speaks beautifully.*[16]

[7] Therefore, with a contrite and humble spirit and heart, we are to grieve in the mind, be sad, and seek tears. For *to seek*, if we truly so wish, is proper, as Holy Scripture directs.[17]

[8] Especially Symeon the New Theologian writes of these things in detail, and *recalls the words of David*, and, adding the writing of *Climacus* in their midst, said: *And he who wishes to know full well shall delve into the book itself.*[18]

---

10. *profitable* omitted from the original.
11. Recast (by placing the *even if* clause at the end) from Climacus 7.47; HM SMS 184:66/VMCh-M: 874b; PG 88 809D.
12. Adapted from Isaac Syr. 6:60; HM SMS 179.58: 302v; Gk: 56:229.
13. Cf. Symeon NT, *Discourses* 4.12-13:80-86; Sol. 193.5: 61; SC 96.4: 318-319: alt., free transl. of the gerunds: . . . *speaks* . . . *directs.*
14. Symeon NT, *Discourses* 4.12:85; Eparkh. 118.5:73; SC 96:360-61.
15. Symeon NT, *Discourses* 4.14:87; Sol. 193.5:81v; SC 96:366-367; cf. Ps 50:19/51:17.
16. The ambiguously directed *And his speaks beautifully* adapted from Symeon NT, *Discourses* 4.12:85; Eparkh. 118.5:72; SC 96:360, referencing his own mentor Symeon the Studite; cf. *Discourses* 4.14:87.
17. Cf. Mt. 7:7-8, Lk.11:9-10; Symeon NT, *Discourses* 4.15:87; Eparkh. 118.5:74v; SC 96:368-369.
18. *khotiai navyknuti vъ samuiu knigu da vъniknet:* adapted from Symeon NT, *Discourses* 4.12:84; Eparkh.118.5: 71; SC 96:358-359 (with six extracts from the Psalms and one from Climacus 6.13)—the alliterative gnome here, in Professor Romanchuk's opinion, affirming the monk's hermeneutic reading (private communication).

[9] But only if one's bodily nature is not exhausted, for then it is not profitable to war against nature.[19] Indeed the *body* is *infirm*, and *when you compel* it *to work beyond its power, you inflict darkness upon darkness on the soul and place even more confusion upon it*,[20] says Saint Isaac, and the other Fathers concur with this.

[10] This is what the Fathers said about true infirmity, and not contrived, which is infirmity of the urge. In other cases, it is good to compel oneself,[21] said Saint Symeon. For having written more about this, he said: *If our soul be in such a disposition*, it will never cross over[22] *without tears*.[23]

[11] But we, if unable to elevate ourselves to such a degree, let us strive to reach at least a small fraction of these things and entreat the Lord God for them with an aching of the heart, insofar as the holy Fathers say that the *grace of tears* is a *gift* of God, one of the greatest,[24] and direct to entreat the Lord for it.

[12] Indeed the Blessed Neilos the Sinaite says: *Before all else*,[25] *pray for the receiving of tears*.[26]

[13] Blessed Gregory, the most holy Pope of Rome, writes: If one is persevering in good works and has become worthy of other gifts, but has not received tears, it is proper to entreat, *either out of the fear of the judgment or out of love of the heavenly kingdom: first they bewail the evil they have done, and thus next, greatly burning*

---

19. Slightly abridged from Isaac Syr. 20:103; HMS 179.70:341v; Gk: 29:125.
20. Slightly juggled from Isaac Syr. 48:235; HM SMS 179.85:387; Gk:73:291.
21. More implicit than explicit in this part of Symeon NT.
22. *preidetъ*: alt. trans: *finish*, i.e., *make it*.
23. Adapted from Symeon NT, *Discourses* 4:85; Eparkh. 118.4:72v-73; SC 96.4:362-363.
24. See below, *Ustav* 8.20; Peter Damaskenos's 'Third Stage of Contemplation' sees tears along with, grief, radiant urges, gifts of grace, and gifts of tears: *Treasury*, 121; HM SMS 454: 54-54v; Фκ 3:43.
25. *first* in the original.
26. Evagrius/Ps-Neilos Sin., *On Prayer* 5.56; (PSW 1:58); HM SMS 468 5:98v/ Eparkh. 344.5:329; PG 79:1168D/Фκ 1.5:177.

*with love, they enter.*²⁷ And he cited a parable from Holy Scripture: *'Achsah,*²⁸ *the daughter of Caleb, who was sitting on a donkey, after sighing*²⁹ *entreated her father for watered land, saying: "As you have given me some arid, add for me some with water." And the father gave her some with water on the hill and some with water in the valley'.*³⁰ And he *interprets Achsah to be a soul, sitting on a donkey, that is, on the irrational*³¹ *movements of the flesh, and that after sighing she entreated her father for watered land—this reveals that with great sighing we are to entreat our Maker for the gift of tears.*³² And other saints concur with this.

[14] So how do we entreat and pray for these and from where shall we commence? Only from the Divine Writings, *for we are insufficient to conceive something on our own. But our sufficiency is*³³ the Divinely-inspired Writings,³⁴ as the saints wrote.

[15] Andrew of Crete: '*Whence shall I begin to mourn*³⁵ *the deeds of my passion-ridden life? What beginning shall I make for the present lamentation? But, as a merciful one,* Lord,³⁶ *grant me tears of compunction,*³⁷ *that mourning to you, the Creator of all and Maker, our God, I confess to you how much I have sinned before you with my wretched soul and my filthy flesh, and, fortified with your help, abandon my former irrationality and offer you tears of repentance'.*³⁸

---

27. I.e. enter the heavenly kingdom (as used in Antiochus's *Pandekty*: Sreznevskii 1:389).
28. In Slavic, *Askhas.*
29. Not in Jos., but in Gregory.
30. From Jos 15:17-19.
31. *beslovesnyi* = ἄλογος.
32. Adapted and rearranged from Gregory/Ps-Gregory the Great, *Dialogues* 3.34:173-175; Eparkh. 317:276-279 / VMCh-M:(11):161a-161d/321-322/*Paterik Rimskii*, 3.34:330-335; PL 77.3.34:299B-302A.
33. Adapted from 2 Cor 3:5.
34. *from God* in 2 Cor 3:5.
35. *Otkudu nachnu plakati*: alt. standard gramm. transl., losing Nil's repetition of the *nach-* lexeme in the next sentence: *Whence shall I mourn.*
36. *Christ* in the original.
37. *umilenie*: alt. and modern transl., *tenderness.*
38. Adapted, re-ordered from Andrew Cr., 1ˢᵗ Mon, Ode 1; Eparkh. 370:142-143; PG 97:1332AC.

[16]   Germanus of Constantinople: '*My God, the Creator of the whole world, my Maker, who of old sprang the springs of waters from uncut rock*[39], *who* sweetened *the bitter* waters,[40] *grant springs of tears for the pupils of my eyes,* fill *my head with purifying waters, and make of my brows ever-pouring clouds. For delusion of mind*[41] *and filth of soul requires the hyssop*[42] *of your love of man, Master, water of the heart of the eye, constant rains or lakes for tears, or soul-cleansing springs*'.[43]

[17]   Ephrem: '*Grant, Master, tears to me, the unworthy one,* for the illumination of my heart *at all times, so that, having illuminated my heart, I spring* springs *of tears with sweetness in pure prayer, and so that the great writ of my sins be dissolved in small tears, and by this small lamentation, quench the yonder*[44] *fiery flame*'.[45]

[18]   From Symeon the New Theologian:[46] '*Lord, Maker of all, give to me yourself a helping hand, and purify my filthy soul, and grant me tears of repentance, tears* of love, *tears of salvation, tears purifying the darkness of my intellect, making me luminous from above, so that I will behold you, the light of the world,*[47] *the enlightenment of my wretched eyes*'.[48]

[19]   The Hymnographer:[49] 'Oh *Christ, King* of all, *grant me* warm *tears, so that I mourn with my soul, which I have vilely destroyed.* Give me, Christ, *a cloud of tears of divine compunction,*

---

39. Cf. Ex 17:5-6.
40. Cf. Ex 15:23-25.
41. *smysla* (gn. sg.) = τῶν φρενῶν (gn. pl.).
42. A traditional purgative, once called 'the grace of God', cf. Ps 50:9/51:7; *You shall sprinkle me with hyssop and I shall be clean* comes at the end of a standard Orthodox funeral service (though not Noli, *Orthodox Prayer Book*): http://www.goarch.org/en/ourfaith/articles/article9218.asp.
43. Partially arranged and adapted from 'Germanus', *Stikhi,* Eparkh. 347:303-303v; Gk: Grolimund, NSA, 419, n 14.
44. *tamo*: i.e. in the other world: maybe here from Ephrem Syr., *Parenesis* . . . *Altbulgarische* 95:248, used in this sense.
45. Slightly adapted from Ephrem Syr., *Parenesis* . . . *Altbulgarische* 77:252-253; cf. 'On Compunction', ed. Thwaites, 107; ed. Assemani 1:154F.
46. Alt. reading in several MSS, including Borovkova-M's KB 25/1102: *From the New Theologian.*
47. *light of world*: Jn 8:12.
48. Abbrev. and slightly adapted from Symeon NT, *Hymns* 4:23-24; Eparkh. 118.8:78-78v; SC 156:194-197.
49. Var. *The Hymnographers* (omitted in KB 89/1166).

for you are generous,[50] so that I mourn and *wash away the filth* that is of lasciviousness, and I stand *purified* before you. *Give me tears, God, as of old to the woman-sinner*.[51]

[20] And further verses and others similar to these, which are from the holy Writings, are proper diligently to recite from the depth of the heart in *an entreaty* for *tears, and let us often pray to the Lord*, as Saint Isaac says, *that he grant us this gift of tears, superior and transcending other gifts; for if we acquire it, by it we shall enter into purity of soul*, and we shall receive all good spiritual things.[52]

[21] There are some, who have not yet acquired the gift of *tears* in its perfection, who gain it by one or another means: this one from the mysteries of[53] the designs of the Lord's love of man; that one *from* reading the stories of the lives and struggles and teachings of the saints; this one by the simply-worded Jesus prayer; still another comes to compunction by some prayers created by the saints; yet another becomes remorseful *from* certain canons or troparia;[54] a different one by recalling his sins; and another *from memory of death* and the judgment; and still another *from* the longing for future delights; *and from* various *other* methods.[55]

[22] Now if one acquires *tears* in any such manner, it is proper to continue this and *maintain* the mourning *until it passes*,[56] insofar, said the Fathers, as he who wishes to free himself of sins, frees himself from them by mourning, and he who wishes to avoid

---

50. Literally: *as generous*.
51. From the Great Compline liturgy, including the Tuesday and Thursday *Troparion*; cf. Lk 7:37-38.
52. Juggled from Isaac Syr. 37:178; HM SMS 179.21:110v; Gk: 85:342.
53. Var.: *and*.
54. I.e. liturgical chants, such as the ones that Nil had adapted here; see below, Appendix I. *Scete Typikon*.
55. Structurally and slightly textually adapted from Climacus, 7.32; HM SMS 184:65/VMCh-M: 873b; PG 88:808BC. Climacus's more dynamically complex list is: . . . *from nature, from God, from adverse afflictions, from the praiseworthy, from vainglory, from fornication, from love, from memory of death, and many other things*.
56. *goes away* in the original: freely adapted from Climacus, 7.25; HM SMS 184:64/VMCh-M: 873a; PG 88:808A.

acquiring them, avoids acquiring them by mourning.[57] For this is the path of repentance and its fruit. And regarding any disaster that befalls us and all the enemy's thoughts, it is proper to weep before God's goodness, so that He aid him. And he will rest soon, if he prays with knowledge.

[23]   Symeon the New Theologian terms *all the virtues an army, and the king and general, compunction and weeping.* For the latter, he said, *arms and reinforces and teaches how to wage war with the enemy in all initiatives, and protects against the opponent's troops.*[58]

[24]   Now if ever our intellect be amongst un*praiseworthy* urges, or adverse ones, or any things heard or seen by us, or *love of the natural*, or a worthless *affliction*, and if we acquire tears thorough any of these, it is proper to transpose[59] onto profitable objects— onto the divine Doxology,[60] or onto confession, or onto *death*, and the judgment, and torments, and *other things*[61]—and so mourn. For Climacus says: *to transplant*[62] *tears from the adversary's or natural objects onto spiritual ones is praiseworthy.*[63]

[25]   Yet when, by the grace of God, *of its own accord* and *without our deliberation and striving, our soul* becomes *compunctious and tearful, this is a visitation of the Lord*[64] and *tears of piety*, and *it is proper to preserve them like the pupil of the eye, until they depart*; for these bear *great strength* for destroying sins and passions, more than tears *caused by our own striving and skill.*[65]

---

57. Source and its possible continuation not identified.
58. Adapted from Symeon NT, *Discourses* 4.11:82-83; Eparkh. 118.5:69-69v; SC 96:352-355 (PG 120:488C-489A).
59. I.e., redirect the intellect; cf. above, *Ustav* 1.10-11, 5.3-4, 5.6.79; *To Gurii* 8.
60. *slavoslovie* (technically, the divine liturgy): alt. transl.: *glorification of God* (in the more general sense).
61. Categories or words for categories abstracted from Climacus, 7.32; HM SMS 184:65; VMCh-M: 872bc; PG 88:808BC.
62. *izhe ... presaditi*: should be *ezhe . . . presaditi*, as in the original, or *izhe . . . presaditъ = he who transplants . . . .*
63. Almost as in Climacus 7.34; HM SMS 184:65; VMCh-M: 873c; PG 88:808C.
64. *the Lord has come uninvited* in the original.
65. Somewhat adapted from Climacus 7.25; HM SMS 184:64/VMCh-M: 873a; PG 88:805D-808; cf. Peter. Dam., *Treasury* 3:107; HM SMS 454:38v-39; Фк 3:31.

[26] And when, though attentiveness, that is, the guarding of the heart, by divine *grace* an operation *of the Spirit*[66] appears in prayer, implanting *heat* that warms the *heart* and *comforts* the soul, and kindling *ineffably* love toward God and men, and cheering the intellect, and granting *sweetness* and *rejoicing* from the inner reaches, then *tears*[67] pour forth of their own accord[68] and flow forth freely from oneself, comforting the aching soul, *which is like an infant, at once weeping to oneself and smiling brightly*,[69] as Climacus says. May the Lord make us worthy of these tears, because for us, still *beginners*[70] and inexperienced, *there is no other solace greater than this*.[71]

[27] And when, *by God's grace, this*[72] gift is increased in us, then occurs the *easing of wars and calmness*[73] *of urges*, for the *intellect*[74] is satisfied and delighted by the ample nourishment of prayer, *by some unrecountable sweetness flowing out from the heart, and falling over the entire body*,[75] and transposing the pain of all limbs into sweetness. This is *the solace born of mourning*,[76] says Saint Isaac in the words of the Lord, to each by the *grace granted*[77] him. At such times, a man is in joy *not to be obtained* in this age,[78] and *no one knows of this, but only those who have given of their entire soul to this work*.[79]

---

66. *děistvo dukhovnoe*: alt. transl.: *spiritual operation*; orig. *radosti dukhovnye* = *joys of the Spirit/spiritual joys*.
67. Possibly freely inspired by Isaac Syr. 68:331; HM SMS 179.45:184v; Gk: 8:36.
68. *samoskhodně*: literally, *automatically*.
69. As in Climacus 7.55; HM SMS 184:68/VMCh-M:875a PG 88:813B.
70. Maybe from Climacus 7.32; HM SMS 184:64v/Eparkh. 331:139/VMCh-M:873b; PG 88:808B.
71. From Climacus 7.51; HM SMS 184:67v; PG 88:813A; the original speaks of consolation at time of death.
72. Maybe from Isaac Syr. 68:331; HM SMS 179.45:1 84v; Gk:8:36.
73. *utishenie*; var. reading: *utěshenie* = *solace/consolation/comfort*.
74. [74] up to here: Isaac Syr 18:96; HM SMS 179.59:305v–306; Gk: 9:42.
75. From Isaac Syr. 35:158; HM SMS 179.73:350/Gk: 24:104.
76. Adapted from Isaac Syr. 37.178; HM SMS 179.21:110; Gk: 85:342; a bit later Isaac cites Mt 5:4: *Blessed are they that mourn, for they shall be comforted*.
77. Rom 12:3, 6.
78. *a monk encounters solace not to be found here* in the original.
79. Adapted from Isaac Syr. 37:178; HM SMS 179.21 :110; Gk: 85:342-343.

On the Guarding of These Things. 9.

[1] When the Lord, by his grace, makes us worthy to acquire tears and to mourn or to pray in purity, then it is proper by all means to guard oneself against the spirit of anger and other improper urges, for it is by either the inner urges that the Enemy then strives to confuse us, or schemes to bring rebellion and war from without, striving to despoil our work.

[2] As Climacus said: *Whenever you pray watchfully, you will soon be at war against anger, for this is the enemies' intent.*[1] For that reason, he said, *we must always effect every virtue, especially prayer, with abundant feeling.*[2] Likewise, after prayer one is to strive to be above wrath and anger and other soul-harming things, because, he said, *freedom from anger among beginners, as if by reins,*[3] *is tied down by tears,*[4] and if we release the reins and do not steer well, it will immediately run amuck.[5]

[3] So also speaks Neilos the Ascetic: *The demon highly envies the praying man and strives with every contrivance*[6] *to impede*[7] *his intent. For he does not stop the moving of thoughts of things through the memory and inciting all passions by means of the flesh, so that he enable the entangling of the man's good course and his departure to God. When the most wicked demon, having done a great deal, is still unable to hinder the zealot's prayer,* then *he weakens a little, but afterward seeks revenge upon*

---

1. *razumъ* = σκοπός, as below in [3] (in acc.); alt., less fitting, transl.: *understanding*; see above, III. 'Technical Terms', text to note 154.

2. *chiuvstvo*: alt. transl.: *feeling, sensation, sensibility, senstivity*: Climacus 28.38-39; HM SMS 184:165v-166/Eparkh. 333:276v /VMCh-M:932bc; PG 88:1136CD.

3. *brozdoiu* (instr.) = χαλινῷ (dt.); alt., but inferior transl.: *bridles*.

4. Adapted from Climacus 8.26; HM SMS184: 7v/VMCh-M: 878cd; PG 88:833B.

5. Literally, *act disorderly*.

6. *koznь* = (here) μηχανή also μελῳδία (as deceit), τέχνη (as artifice).

7. *vъzbraniti* = κωλύειν (*impede, reproach, forbid*); also, as in the original, λυμήνασθαι (*outrage, dishonor, destroy*): PG 79.46:1176D/Φκ 1.47:180.

the man who prayed. Either he will, after kindling that man's anger, destroy the good[8] *inner disposition created by the prayer, or, having stirred the man to irrational*[9] *lust, defile*[10] *his intellect. For that reason, he said, having prayed properly, expect the improper and stand courageously defending your fruit.*[11] *From the start it was established 'to work and to guard',*[12] *so that in working you do not leave the product unguarded. If not, you will gain no profit by praying.*[13]

[4] And this saint cites from the ancients,[14] that one is '*to work and to guard*'. For Scripture says that '*God* created Adam[15] and placed *him* in *Paradise to work and to guard Paradise*'.[16] And here he calls the work of Paradise prayer and guarding—safeguarding from unbecoming urges after prayer.[17]

[5] And when the Lord visits us during this, let us in every way keep ourselves from improper urges, let alone words and deeds, and watch over our senses vigilantly then, lest a war be aroused against us by them.

[6] And if perforce the soul falls into thoughts,[18] let us immediately flee to the Creator with an entreaty, and he will destroy them all, for no activity is better and more free from concern. And so, if God grants the power, let us guard our souls in fear of him, not allowing the intellect to dissipate from infirmity of urges, nor idle merriment to rob its acquisition of compunction, and to

---

8. As in the Slavic; *best* in the original Greek.
9. *besslovesnyi* – also as *dumb*, may imply *animal* here.
10. *pokhuliaetb* = ὑβρίζει; alt. trans of the Slavic: *insult, ridicule*.
11. I.e., *gains*, as in the Greek original.
12. *to work* (or *till*) *and to guard* (or *keep*): Gn 2:15.
13. *Verbatim* from Evagrius/Ps-Neilos Sin., *Chapters on Prayer* 46-48:62; *Eparkh.* 344.47-49:332v; PG 79.46-48:1176D-1177A/Φκ 1.47-49:180-181.
14. That is, the books of the Old Testament.
15. *the man* (nm.= *Adam* {אדם} in the original Hebrew) in LXX and the Slavic Gn 2:7, but *Adama* (acc.) here maybe from LXX Gn 2:16.
16. Adapted from Gn 2:7, 15-16 (as in KB 3/8:13-13v).
17. Perhaps, if available, directly or indirectly, from Neilos Sin., *Ascetic Discourse*, 214-215; PG 79:748B, but perhaps just Nil's didactic gloss; cf. MRIV 8ᴮ.16/6.13, where the profit from safeguarding work is ambiguously material, as well as spiritual.
18. *pomyshlenia* (pl.): here maybe as a synonym for *pomyslb*.

destroy the soul on account of the infirm tenuousness of an urge.[19] Rather, after tears and prayers, let us preserve ourselves within this prudence.

---

19. *radi neutverzhenia slabago pomysla:* alt., less likely transl.: *from the tenuousness of an infirm urge.*

On Detachment and True Carefreeness, Which Is Deadness to Everything. 10.

[1] *These wonderful activities*, of which we spoke, *require thorough detachment and carefreeness*,[1] *which is deadness to everything*, with all effort and attention devoted solely to the work of God, *as have said the great Fathers*, who came to know with their grasp of *supreme wisdom*.[2]

[2] Indeed the great Macarius says: *He, who wishes to approach God, to be worthy of life everlasting, to be a dwelling of* Christ,[3] *and to be filled with*[4] *the Holy Spirit, so that he can effect the fruits of the Spirit according to all of the Lord's commandments in purity and without blemish, must commence with the following: firstly, believe in God with certainty and surrender his entire self to the words of his commandments; and totally renounce the world, so that the intellect not be busied with a single visible thing,*[5] *but just have the one Lord and his commandments before the eyes, and strive to be pleasing to Him alone, and always to remain in prayer, expecting God's visitation and help, ever keeping his intellect's intent*[6] *in this; and always compelling himself toward all good deeds and toward the Lord's commandments, as much as possible; and, despite the heart's unwillingness caused by the sin it contains,*[7] *believing that the Lord, having come, shall settle in him, and shall perfect*[8] *and strengthen him in all the*[9]

---

1. *bezpopechenie*; var. reading: *popechenie* = *care*
2. *premudrostь* = σοφία, the highest form of wisdom, used with *Divine*; text likely culled from Isaac Syr. 37:163-64; HM SMS 179.21:100-01; Gk: 85:327, and Ps-Symeon NT, *Three Methods* 70-72; HM SMS 468:82v-84; Hausherr, *Méthode*, 158-164. Фк 5:84-86. See below, [10].
3. *God* in the original.
4. *worthy of* in the original.
5. Break here in Macarius/Ps-Macarius adapted citation.
6. *razumъ* = σκοπός; see above, III. 'Technical Terms', text to note 54; *intellection* also works, retaining the polyptoton (root repetition) of *razumъ uma*.
7. Break here in Macarius/Ps-Macarius adapted citation.
8. *disciplines* in the original.
9. *his* in the original.

commandments, and the Lord himself *shall be the dwelling of the soul;*[10] *and at all times remember the Lord, expecting him in much love.*[11] *Then the Lord, beholding such a purpose*[12] *in him and good zeal, will effect his mercy with him and deliver him from his enemies and from the indwelling sin within him, filling him with the Holy Spirit. And thus, without compulsion and without toil, he will do all of the Lord's commandments*[13] *in truth;*[14] *and, even more, the Lord in him.*[15] *And he will then offer the fruits of the Spirit in purity.*[16]

[3] And Basil the Great *says that the beginning of purity of soul is stillness.*[17]

[4] And John Climacus: *The work,* he said, *of stillness is carefreeness from rational*[18] *and irrational*[19] *things, and prayer without sloth,*[20] *and, thirdly, inviolable*[21] *activity of the heart.*[22]

10. *the soul shall become the dwelling of Jesus Christ* in the original; break here in Macarius/Ps-Macarius adapted citation.
11. *goodness and love* in the original.
12. Literally, *volition (proizvolenie)*, but *purpose* in the original.
13. *commandments* omitted in several early MSS; cf. below, *To German* 6; *Sobornik, Forew.* 4.
14. Literally, in the original, *out of truth.*
15. Ellipsis here of the original's full predicate: ποιεῖ ἐν αὐτῷ τὰς ἰδίας ἐντολὰς = *will do* (i.e., cause to be done) *His very own commandants in him.*
16. [2] Abbrev. and somewhat adapted from Macarius/Ps-Macarius, *Hom.* 19.1-2:128; KB 29/1106:111v-113; PG 34:641D-644D; cf. *On the Guarding of the Heart* 13, PG 34:836B-837B; and see above under III.'Centrality of Sources', note 52 and text thereto.
17. Basil the Great, *Epistolae* 2 (*To Gregory*), PG 32:228A; reversed from Isaac Syr. 37:173; Eparkh. 324.21:119 (HM SMS 179.21:107v-108 defective); Gk: 85:336; also cited in Peter Dam., *Treasury,* PSW 3:106; Φκ 3:321; but HM SMS 454:38 is defective, and Eparkh. 118:177 has *mlъchanie* (silence), not *bezmolvie* for ἡσυχία; Ps-Basil, *Const.* 7.1-2, PG 31:1363BC, as in Grolimund (NSA, 427-428, note 2), is a stretch.
18. *blagoslovn-*: also = *benedict-* = *blessed/approved* (by an authority).
19. *be(z)slovesn-* alt. transl.: *dumb* (as in animals lacking speech).
20. So in the Slavic Climacus; *without hesitation* (ἄοκνος), i.e., *resolute* in the original.
21. *nekradomo* = ἄσυλος, i.e., *cannot be seized/stolen,* that is, diverted: cf. Moore transl., note 1.
22. Abbrev. from Climacus 27.46; HM SMS 179:157v/Eparkh. 331:349-349v/ VMCh-M: 927c; PG 88:1109B.

[5] And among the rational things, he does not name *what we now hold as a custom* regarding the ownership[23] of villages[24] and control over many properties,[25] and other entanglements in the world: for these are irrational.

[6] But as for *conversations which occur in good form*[26] and are intended for the salvation of the soul, it is proper to hold them at an appropriate time and in measure with spiritual and pious fathers and brothers.[27] But if we do these unguardedly, we shall, against our will, *fall into the second*; And we have called the rational *the first*, while the *second* are: contentiousness and contrariness, and also murmuring and censuring, and denigrating and insulting, and other evils, into which we *fall* due to *the previous rational*.[28]

[7] *It is naturally*[29] *impossible*, he[30] said, *for him who has not learned his letters, to meditate on books; and it is more impossible for him who has not acquired the first, to pass through both with reason*.[31] And this, in common, simple discourse, is to say: it is impossible for him who has not studied letters,[32] to speak according to books or to read or lead a service,[33] and it is more impossible for him, who has not acquired the first, that is, *being without care for rational and irrational*

---

23. *pritiazhanie*: alt. transl.: acquisition.
24. *selo*: alt. transl.: *arable field*.
25. *iměnie*: includes movables, as well as real estate.
26. Ital. in [5-6] partially from Isaac Syr. 4:35; HM SMS 179.56: 272v; Gk: 23:98.
27. Cf. above, *Predanie* 29.
28. i.e., *due to non-carefreeness from previous rational things*: freely adapted from Climacus 27.46; HM SMS 179:157v/Eparkh. 331:349-349v/ VMCh-M: 927c; PG 88:1109B: the first part reads in the original: *The work of stillness is carefreeness from all previous* (omitted by Nil, above in [4]) *rational and irrational things. Opening to the first, one falls into the second.*
29. *estestvennĕ* = φυσικῶς: in modern parlance, *scientifically*.
30. That is, Climacus.
31. *slovomъ* (instr.) = λόγῳ (dt.), literally, *by the word*, and continuing Climacus's root repetition of *rational* and *irrational*, as in Climacus 27.46; HM SMS 179:157v/ Eparkh. 331:349-349v/ VMCh-M:927c; PG 88:1109B.
32. *gramota* (also = γράμματα), here as *the ABCs* or *reading and writing*: the original and even Nil may also refer to formal 'academic' grammar, as the discipline of reading texts.
33. *konarkhati* = κανοναρχεῖν: to perform the *canonarch*'s duties or, simply, to chant.

things, i. e., deadness to everything,[34] to make chants with knowledge without sloth and pray with attentiveness, that is the activity of the heart. For here chanting means standing for the chant without sloth, and the activity of the heart—the throne of[35] prayer and the watch over the intellect.

[8]   And elsewhere: *A small hair disturbs the eye, and a small care makes stillness traceless.*[36]

[9]   And again: *He, who had tasted prayer, often soiled his intellect from the utterance of a single word, and, having stood at prayer, did not find his habitual, beloved thing.*[37]

[10]   And also Symeon, the New Theologian: *Let your life*, he said, *be still and carefree, deadened to all.*[38] And first having sketched this, afterwards he instructs in prayer and attentiveness.[39]

[11]   And Isaac says to those who *wish truly to practice stillness* and *purify the intellect in prayer: Withdraw far from the visions of the world, and sever conversations, and do not wish habitually to host friends in your cell, not even in good form, except for some, who are like-minded, harmonious, and fellow-initiates. And fear disturbances from coupling*[40] *of*

---

34. Slightly adapted from Ps-Symeon, *Three Methods* 72; HM SMS 468:84; Hausherr, *Méthode*, 163-64/Фк 5:86.

35. I.e., *sitting at*.

36. *bezъvěsti* (literally, *unknown*) *tvoritъ bezmolvie:* Climacus 27.51; HM SMS 184:158/Eparkh. 331:350v-351/VMCh-M: 927d; PG 88:1109D.

37. That is, *his habitual, beloved prayer.* Climacus 28.50; HM SMS184: 166v/ Eparkh. 331:369/VMCh-M: 932d; PG 88:1137B.

38. Cf., above, in *Ustav* 10.7; *peaceful with all*, in Nicephorus, *deadened . . .* in Ps-Symeon: combined and adapted from Nicephorus (in the Slavic as Symeon NT), *Watchfulness* (as in the Latin version, not *Philokalia*); HM SMS 468:80; PG 147:963D, and Ps-Symeon NT, *Three Methods*, 71; HM SMS,468:84; Hausherr, *Méthode*, 163-164/Фк 5:86; cf. above, [1].

39. See III. 'Centrality of Sources', text to note 24, on the Slavic version of Ps-Symeon NT's *Three Methods of Prayer.* Here Nil seems to refer specifically to the instruction which follows in the next paragraph of his source: *Three Methods*, 71-73; HM SMS 448:84-84v; Hausherr, *Méthode*, 164-65/Фк 5:87.

40. *sъvъkuplenia* (gn. sg.): here used to translate ὁμιλίας = *conversation*.

the soul, which habitually moves involuntarily, even when severing and renouncing[41] *external coupling.*[42]

[12] And he says this, which we know from experience: Indeed, when we put an end to *such conversations, even if they are reckoned to be good,*[43] immediately after ending the conversations we face *turmoil of the soul;*[44] *even when we do not desire them, they move involuntarily within us and continue coupling with us for no short a time, insofar as superfluous and untimely words even to our near and beloved ones create turmoil* and utterly corrupt the *guarding of the intellect*[45] and mystical meditation.

[13] Elsewhere he speaks most harshly against these in the following manner: *What evil is seeing and conversation for those who truly abide in stillness, O brothers, even more than those released from stillness! As a blast of ice suddenly falling upon the buds in the orchard withers them, so human conversations, even if they are extremely brief and intended to be conducted for a good purpose, wither the flowers of virtue, which bloom again from the admixture of stillness and surround with softness and youth the orchard of the soul, planted by the outflowing of waters*[46] *of repentance. And as a blast of hoarfrost seizing new shoots, consumes them, so also human conversation to the root of the intellect, which has begun to sprout a blade of virtues.*

[14] *And if the conversation of those abstaining from something, but having a small deficiency of something, usually harms the soul, how much more so is the spectacle and babble*[47] *of commoners and fools,*[48] *not to say laymen! For just as a noble and honorable man, when he is intoxicated, forgets his nobility and dishonors his rank, and his honor is ridiculed by the alien urges, which have entered him from the power of wine, so the chastity*

---

41. Alt., but inferior transl. in this context: *Sever/Cut off and renounce external intercourse/conversation.*
42. From *Withdraw*, exactly as in Isaac Syr. 4:35; HM SMS 179.56:272v-273; Gk: 23:97-98 (up to *Withdraw*, adapted).
43. Cf. below, *To Gurii* 13.
44. *intellect* in the original.
45. Adapted from Isaac Syr. 19:98; HM SMS 179.69:336-336v; Gk: 13:50.
46. *outflowing* (Heb. streams) *of waters*: Ps 1:3.
47. Nil's reversal: *the babble and spectacle/sight* in the original.
48. *prostetsь* (gn. pl. = ἰδιωτῶν:) *i iurodivykhъ* (gn. pl.= μωρῶν—also the Slavic for *holy fools*) alt. transl., privileging the Greek lexemes, *idiots and morons.*

of the soul is muddied by the sight and conversations of men, and it forgets the form[49] of its guarding. Its watch over its desire is expunged from its mind, and its entire foundation of a praiseworthy state eradicated.

[15]   And *if conversation and expansiveness of volatility, befalling him who abides in stillness, or proximity to these, that is, to see and to hear, suffice, due to frequent viewing and hearing the visitor, to chill and muddy his mind to divine things, and if in a brief time they effect such vanity, what should we say of constant meetings and long involvements in such things?*[50]

[16]   And elsewhere he also says: *He who loves the discourse of the world is stripped of his life, and I have nothing to say of him, but with a wail to lament a lamentation inconsolable, whose hearing crushes the hearers' hearts.*[51]

[17]   And again he said elsewhere that *the* single *sight of the laity can give strength to the passions to weaken the ascetic and alter his wisdom and dedication.* Therefore *it does not befit a monk to associate with those who embattle him, but to withdraw far from the proximity of all by whom his freedom*[52] *is tempted. When a man comes unto God to make a covenant with God, he is not only to refrain from all such, but not see any* class[53] *of laymen, nor hear their words, nor anything about them.*[54]

[18]   And this saint writes many more such things,[55] and other saints too: so it is to be believed as absolute truth.

---

49. *obrazъ* = τρόπος: alt. transl. here: *manner, method.*
50. From [13], almost exactly as in Isaac Syr. 19:99; HM SMS 179.69: 337-338; Gk: 13:51-52.
51. The Slavic translation creates onomatopoea that betters the original Greek Isaac Syr. 15:86; HM SMS 8:60v; Gk: 43:179; see above, under III. 'Literary Devices', text to note 128.
52. Freedom from sin, that is—a monastic extension of the Christian notion of redemption, framed partially in the language of the Mosaic deliverance of the Hebrews from Egyptian bondage into voluntary servitude to God.
53. *chin*: alt. transl., *rank.*
54. Adapted and rearranged from Isaac Syr. 37:169-70; HM SMS 179.21:104v-105; Gk: 85:332.
55. Grolimund, NSA, 431, note 13, cites applicable passages in at least five other discourses or letters of Isaac.

On How It Is Proper to Effect This Activity Not Ahead of Time and in Appropriate Measures 11.[1]

[1]   And these most fine and God-pleasing activities are proper to effect with discretion, in good time, and in fitting measure, as Basil the Great says: *Anticipate all doings with prudence: for without prudence, even the good becomes evil, due to lack of timing and lack of measure. And when prudence establishes a good time and measure, a marvelous profit is acquired.*[2]

[2]   And Climacus, taking from Scripture,[3] says:[4] '*a time for everything under heaven*',[5] *for all things of our holy life—a time for each*,[6] he said; and a little further with a repetition:[7] *a time for stillness and a time for calm clamor; a time for ceaseless prayer and a time for sincere*[8] *service.*[9] *So let us not, being deceived by haughty ardor, seek the time before the time and at the time receive not*,[10] insofar as *a time to sow labors and a time to harvest ineffable graces.*[11]

---

1. Cf. above the more accurate title in the Table of Contents.
2. *occurs* in the original. Slightly adapted from Ps-Basil, *Const.* 14; HM SMS 183.7:153v; PG 31:1377B; the connection of Basil to proper timing for practitioners of stillness is also made in Peter Dam. *Treasury,*138; HM SMS 454:74v; Фк 3:56.
3. *as Ecclesiastes says* in the original.
4. Nil omits *If.*
5. Eccl. 3:1.
6. Climacus 26.87:214; HM SMS 184.126/Eparkh. 331:296v/VMCh-M: 914b; PG 88:1032B.
7. *porechemъ* (here seen as instr. sg. of a var. of *porechenie* = a rhetorical anaphora); alt. transl. as 1ˢᵗ pl. prs./fut. verb: *we say*; cf. von Lilienfeld, NSSS, 251, Grolimund, NSA, 220 (*sagt er,* ἔπε = *he says*); Prokhorov, PNSIK, 195 (*prodolzhim* = *we continue*).
8. Literally, *unhypocritical.*
9. *sluzhby* (gn. sg.), retaining the ambiguity of church service/office and personal service/office, the latter also being a duty: cf., *inter alia*, Basil/Ps-Basil, *Ascetic Discourse* 70; PG 31:645BC; MRIV 8ᴮ.25-26/6.42.
10. I.e., *seek* [our] *time* [for stillness] *before the* [right] *time and* [then] *at the* [assigned] *time, we do not receive* [the gifts of grace]. creating a more effective *epistrophe* than in the original; the idea and some of the wording is also found in Peter Dam., *Treasury,* 138; HM SMS 454:74v; Фк 3:56.
11. From Climacus 26.87:214; HM SMS 184:126-126v/Eparkh. 331:297v; PG 88:1032C, rearranged and put into *breviloquentia.*

[3]   And elsewhere he proposed by an analogy:[12] *As it is not without hazard for one untested against many fighters to detach himself*[13] *for single combat, so it is not without harm*[14] *for a monk, before much testing and schooling from the passions of the soul to commence stillness: for*[15] *the one receives much harm*[16] *to the body, the other to his soul.*[17] *For there are but few who pass*[18] *into true*[19] *stillness, and only those, who have received God's solace,*[20] *for encouragement*[21] *in toils, and assistance in battle.*[22]

[4]   And *the great Barsanuphius, to a brother, who read in the Patericon, that one, truly to be saved, must first bear the vexations, abuses,*[23] *degradations,*[24] *and* such from *men in the likeness of the Lord and thus come to perfect stillness, which is the elevation onto the cross, that is, mortification of* all things:[25] *the elder replied, saying:'The Fathers have spoken well, and it is not otherwise'.*[26]

[5]   To *another one he said: Before a man gains*[27] *himself, a cause proper to stillness* effects[28] *arrogance:* for *gaining oneself means*[29] to exist

---

12. *pritcheiu* (instr.): can be any of the comparative figures of speech and devices, including *parable*, as well as *proverb*.
13. I.e., from his unit.
14. Alt. transl., closer to the original Greek, *peril*.
15. *it happens that (estъ bo* = πέφυκε . . . γάρ) omitted.
16. Alt. transl., closer to the original Greek: *many perils*.
17. Climacus, 4.73; HM SMS 184:41 / VMCh-M: 859b; PG 88:712A.
18. *so to say* omitted.
19. Alt. transl., as in the original: *truly into.*
20. *utěshenie* = παράκλσιν (acc. sg.), with the implied visitation of the Holy Spirit.
21. *uvětъ* = παραμυθίαν (acc. sg.): alt. transl.: *soothing, consolation, aid*.
22. Climacus, 4.119; HM SMS 184:48v/VMCh-M:864a; PG 88:725C.
23. *ponesheniia* (nm./acc. pl.) = ὀνειδισμούς (acc. pl.) in Nil's possible second source (see note 26, below): *unichizheniia* = ἐξουδενώσεις = *humiliations, scornings* in the Slavic Nikon, Nil's apparent chief original; Nil also changes the thrust from accepting deserved reproaches and punishments for specific transgressions.
24. *beschestia* (nm./acc. pl) = ἀτιμίας (acc. pl.): also a Muscovite legal term for actionable offenses against someone's honor.
25. *of the flesh* in the original.
26. Recast and abridged from Barsanuphius (and John) 185, as cited in Nikon, *Pandekty* 29:201; cf. SC 427:590-593; and possibly combined with No. 345, to which Grolimund compared: NSA, 432-433, SC 450:358-361.
27. *priobriashaetъ* (3rd sg. prs.): cf. Mt 18:15 (KJ): thou hast *gained* thy brother.
28. Literally, *a cause of stillness brings* (Nikon/Barsanuphius: *leads to*).
29. Literally, *is*.

in humility[30] *without blemish.* And he also said: *If you dare to go beyond your measure, then understand that what you have, you shall destroy,* so retain *the middle,* attending to *God's will.*[31] *For if one wishes to be free from cares ahead of time,* the common[32] *Enemy will prepare more confusion than rest and lead him to say that it would have been better for me not to have been born.*[33]

[6]   The saint so states because multiple deception follows this, as Gregory the Sinaite tells: *Many inexperienced in stillness have been deceived in ancient times and now; and, after many toils, much shame and laughter befalls neophytes and self-regulators,*[34] *who mindlessly say they represent the practitioners of stillness. For the memory of God, in other words, prayer of the intellect, is superior to all activities and the premier of virtues, as it is God's love; and those who shamelessly and boldly wish to come to God and converse often with him, compelling themselves to possess him within themselves, are easily rendered dead*[35] *by demons, if they are let loose. He who is bold and contemptuous beyond his rank and station, making his quest with haughtiness, drives his objective away ahead of time. It is for the mighty and the perfected to battle demons in single combat, and draw against them the sword,*[36] *that is the word of God;*[37] *but the infirm and neophytes, as if fleeing into a stronghold of piety and fear, renouncing battle, and not daring ahead of time to wage war, avoid death.*[38]

30. *in humility* taken from Barsanuphius (and John) 316, as in note 33.
31. Adapted from Barsanuphius (and John) 314:119, as cited in Nikon, *Pandekty* 29:201-201v; cf. SC 450:308-309.
32. *our* in Nikon/Barsanuphius.
33. *not . . . born*: Mt 26:24; adapted from Barsanuphius (and John) 316, as cited in Nikon, *Pandekty* 29:201v; cf. SC 450:312-313, in Nikon attached directly to (the non-numbered) 315.
34. Cf. above, *Predanie* 6, and below, *To German* 7; Appendix III, Innokentii, *Zavĕt* 15
35. *umershchvaetsia,* the same verb used for the monastic virtue of *deadness/ mortification* of fleshly desires, earthly concerns, and, virtually, if not literally, of the flesh itself.
36. *of the spirit* (strangely, it seems to this translator) omitted.
37. *the sword . . . word of God*: Eph 6:17; cf. in Nil's redaction, Chariton Confessor's instruction to 'cut off' *logismoi* 'with fasting and the sword of prayer': SNS 2:55.
38. abridged and somewhat recast from Gregory Sin., *Sitting at Prayer* 7:282-283; PG 150:1337D-1340C; Eparkh. 351.7:92-93v (not in HM SMS 456 or 640); cf. MRIV 10.35.

[7] It is proper for us, who hear this, to protect ourselves from venturing into the heights ahead of time, so that no one, having damaged himself, destroy his soul, but only to proceed in the appropriate time and in a middle measure, as is seen to be more convenient—Scripture testifying that *'the middle path is free from pitfalls'*.[39] And an appropriate time means first to undergo schooling with people.[40]

[8] And the middle path is living with a single, or at most two brothers, as John Climacus said. He directed *those who most genuinely desire to serve Christ* to *select for themselves appropriate places, forms, and residences.*[41] And *in three orders,*[42] he said, lies *valiant the entirety*[43] of *monastic life:*[44] *either solitary retirement,*[45] *or to practice stillness with some one or at most two; or the coenobium*. And he cited from Scripture:[46] *'Do not incline to the right or to the left, but tread the royal road'*.[47] *Indeed the middle of the above-mentioned has been the most suitable for many, that is, stillness with one or two*. *'Woe to him who is alone'*, he said: *'if he falls into despondency or sleep or sluggishness, or despair: there is none*[48] *among men to raise him up'*.[49] And he cited the word of *the Lord* himself, who *said:'Where two or three are gathered together in my name, there am I among them'*.[50] And elsewhere: *'Two are good'*, Scripture

---

39. Literally, *not for stumbling*: slightly altered from Barsanuphius as in Nikon, *Pandekty* 29:201v: cf. Dt 5:32/5:29, plus many OT images of paths with stumbling blocks.
40. I.e., coenobitic training.
41. sĕdalishcha (nm pl.), literally, *seat/throne*, understood generically as a type.
42. *ustroenykhъ* (prp. adj.) for καταστάσεσι (dt. pl. noun): Nil omits *of residence*.
43. *doblestveno sъderzhanie:* alt. transl.: *the valiant content*: perhaps a Slavic transl. confusion of γενναι– = *valiant/noble* for γενικ– = *generic*.
44. *zhitel'stvo* = πολιτεία; alt. transl. (here): *citizenry, society, rules of conduct*.
45. *uedinenoe oshel'stvo* = ἐν . . . ἀναχωρήσει; Nil omits *stradalichьstvĕmъ* (instr.) = ἀθλητικῇ (dt.) = *ascetic's/contestant's*.
46. Nil here, knowingly or unknowingly, corrects the original, which credits *Sobornikъ* = *Ecclesiastes* for all of these biblical gnomes.
47. Combined from Prv 4:7 and Nm 20:17 (cf. KJ: *king's highway*).
48. *no other/second* in Eccl.
49. *Woe . . . up* (in quotes): from Eccl 4:10.
50. Mt 18:20, shortened and recast from Climacus 1.25-26; HM SMS 184:17/ VMCh-M:845a; PG 88:641C-644A (not as in Nikon, *Pandekty* 4.36v, though Nikon's citation also ends here).

said, 'rather than one',[51] that is, it is good for a father with a son[52] by the operation of the Spirit of God to struggle in their undertaking.[53] And a bit later: *He who without help endeavors to battle spirits is killed by them.*[54]

[9]   After recounting the good usages of a few individuals,[55] he said: *Human cohabitation is completely opposed to them, their being able with a mentor[56] to ascend from stillness,[57] as from a harbor, to heaven, not needing to cohabit with coenobitic clamor and scandals, and not tempted.*[58]

[10]   But *those who are* overcome *by passion of the soul are not to touch stillness,*[59] let alone solitude, the Fathers directed.[60] And the passions of the soul are *vainglory, presumption,*[61] *wickedness,*[62] and others deriving from them. *He who is sick with these and embarks on stillness, is like someone leaping off a ship, imagining that he will reach land safely on a single plank,*[63] said Climacus. *Whosoever battle with slime,* that is, with bodily passions—this is not to be simply and haphazardly, but *timely,* and not in solitude, and only if *they have a mentor, for solitude requires angelic strength.*[64] And recollecting several

---

51. Eccl 4:9.
52. Nil reverses Climacus: . . . *good for a son with a father* . . . .
53. Alt. transl.: *for the anticipated.*
54. Condensed and slightly altered from Climacus 4.73; HM SMS 184:41/ VMCh-M:859b; PG 88:712AB.
55. *rare . . . souls . . . separated from malice, hypocrisy and mischief.*
56. *nastavliaiushchimъ* = ὁδηγοῦντος; alt. transl.; *mentoring.*
57. *and* omitted from the original.
58. *neiskusnymъ* (dt. abs.) = ἀπείρατοι (nm.pl.): alt. transl. (closer to the common usage, but less logical here, given the earlier life of such adepts): *inexperienced*; Climacus 26.179; HM SMS 184:147/VMCh-M:921a; PG 88 1073B.
59. Adapted from Climacus, *Ladder* 27.13 (1097D).
60. Perhaps adapted from Climacus 27.13; HM SMS 184:153; PG 88:1097D.
61. *mněnie* = οἴησις = *opinion*; alt. transl. of the Greek: *conceit*; cf. *To German* 7.
62. These three apparently culled from Climacus 26.179 and 27.36; HM SMS 184:147, 156; PG 88 1073B, 1108A.
63. Climacus 27.13; HM SMS 184:153; PG 88:1097CD; also in Nikon, *Pandekty* 29:202v.
64. Expanded and slightly recast with a reverse from Climacus 27.14:238; HM SMS 184:153/Eparkh. 331:332; PG 88:1097D.

more passions of the soul,[65] he says: *He who is troubled by these dares not see[66] a trace of stillness, lest he suffer[67] some kind of trance.*[68]

[11] And we find many other wondrous and great Fathers in the holy Writings, who so taught and acted. Indeed Saint Isaac extolled *stillness above all*[69] and called *Arsenius the Great perfect at stillness*;[70] and he had servants and disciples.[71] And similarly Neilos the Sinaite[72] and Daniel of Scetis,[73] who had disciples, as the Writings recount of them, and many others.

[12] And everywhere throughout the holy Writings, stillness with one or with two is praised, just as we[74] were eye-witnesses at the Holy Mountain of Athos. And in the regions of Constantinople[75] and in other places are many such habitations. If a spiritual elder is found anywhere having a disciple or two, and if there be a need sometimes, three; and if any nearby are engaged in stillness, by coming at the proper time, they are enlightened by spiritual conversations.[76]

[13] But we, as unknowledgeable neophytes, enlighten[77] and firm up each other, as it is written: '*a brother aided*[78] *by a brother is*

---

65. *wrath, . . . , hypocrisy, and vengefulness/memory-of-evil* in Climacus.

66. *viděti* – the Slavic Climacus retaining the Greek idiom here.

67. *postrazhetъ*, changed by Nil from *priobriashtetъ* = κερδήσῃ = *obtain*, which might have appeared to imply a positive result.

68. *istuplěnie* (nm./acc.) = ἔκστασιν (acc.): alt. transl. here: *madness, hysteria*: Climacus 27.36; HM SMS 184:156/Eparkh. 331:346-346v; PG 88:1108A.

69. From, *inter alia*, Isaac Syr. 4:38; HM SMS 179.56:275; Gk: 23:100.

70. Literally in Nil, *the perfect hesychast*: perhaps from Isaac Syr. 76:377; HM SMS 179.55:238; Gk: Epistle 4:373.

71. Nil's redaction, *Life of Arsenius the Great*; SNS 3:452-453; cf. *Zhitie . . . Arseniia*. 13.

72. Peter Dam., *Treasury* 253; Фκ 3:146 has Neilos saying that even among crowds of people, the dispassionate man prays as if alone (but this is not in the Slavic Peter).

73. Clugnet, 'Vie et récits de l'abbé Daniel le Scétiote,' 60-67.

74. Perhaps Nil and his disciple Innokentii Okhliabinin, rather than a generic, collective *we*: see above, II. 'The Compatible Companion'.

75. *stranakhъ* (prp.) *Tsarigrada* (gn.): a rather vague formulation: alt. location of this phrase at the end of the previous sentence.

76. Cf., below, Appendix I, *Scete Typikon* 8, 10.

77. *vъrazumliaemsia*: with a repetition of the *razum*-lexeme *nerazumii* (nm. pl.) = *unknowledgeable, unintelligent*: cf. above, *Ustav* 2.48, 4.11.

78. *pomogaemъ* (LXX: *zastupaemъ*).

like a fortified city'.⁷⁹ And we have a *reliable teacher*:⁸⁰ the divinely-inspired Writings. Therefore this seems suitable for us: habitation with one or two faithful brothers, like-minded in the work of God, and learning the will of God from the holy Writings. And if God bestow upon someone greater understanding, let brother edify brother and friend succor friend, when we are warred upon by demons and harassed by passions, as Saint Ephrem says: and we shall thus, by God's grace, direct ourselves to good deeds.⁸¹

[14] But first of all, it is proper for us to *predispose ourselves by prayer*, when we *shall erect* an abode⁸² *of stillness*, so God may grant us *the means*⁸³ *for completion*, as Climacus said, which is *patient*⁸⁴ *sitting, lest we be, upon the laying of the foundation, the laughingstock of enemies and an impediment to other workers*.⁸⁵ But let us be preserved in good deeds by the grace of our Lord God Jesus Christ, by the prayers of our most pure Mistress, the Mother of God, and all the saints that have shone through their virtuous deeds.

[15] And this we *understand: that it is not due to the effecting of excessive rules* that we do this—select *a residence of stillness*, as Saint Isaac said. *For it is known that communion with very many renders an extra hand in this*,⁸⁶ but that we depart from unprofitable unrest and clamor and other things displeasing to God.

[16] And let us abide in his commandments, obtaining our necessities from our own labors.⁸⁷ If we cannot, then accepting a

---

79. Prv 18:19 (LXX).
80. Cf. Basil/Ps-Basil, *Ascetic Discourse,* 63; HM SMS 183: 180v; PG 632B; and above, *Ustav,* Fwd. 15.
81. No source identified. A textual break without a sub-heading follows in Dionisii Zvenigorodskii's Eparkh. 351.74v.
82. *tower and cell* in the original Climacus (just *tower* in Lk), *pillar and cell/shed* in the Slavic original.
83. *svoistva* = ἰδιώματα, literally, *the specifics*; alt. transl.: *qualities.*
84. *patience,* added here, is the subject of a nearby paragraph in the original: Climacus 27.70; HM SMS 184:160/VMCh-M: 928d-929a; PG 88:1113CD.
85. Rearranged and adapted from Climacus 27.75; HM SMS 184 160v / VMCh-M: 929bc; PG 88:1116BC; cf. its inspiration, Lk. 14.28-29.
86. Shortened from Isaac Syr. 64:316; HM SMS 41:171; Gk: 34:152.
87. Cf. above, *Predanie* 15.

few alms from wherever his goodness provides,[88] but let us by all means withdraw from excess.[89]

[17] So as from a deadly poison, we flee[90] fights and suits[91] and quarrels over material gains,[92] doing those activities, which are pleasing to God—chanting, prayer, reading, meditation on the spiritual, manual work, and any service of labor partaking of God, according to the inner power of the man.

[18] And thus we send glory in good works up to the Father and the Son and the Holy Spirit, to one God in the Trinity, now and always and unto ages of ages. Amen.

[19] Indeed we, the *unknowledgeable*,[93] within the *meager limits*[94] of our *knowledge, have written these things*[95] as a reminder to myself and to those similar to me, who are in the *rank of disciples*,[96] *if they so desire*.[97] For not from myself, as I said in the beginning of these writings, *but from the Divinely*-inspired *Writings of the holy Fathers*,[98] enlightened by knowledge. So all that is here is not without the witness of the Divine Writings. *And if anything be found in these* that is *displeasing to God and not profitable for the soul on account of our lack of knowledge*,[99] *let it not so*[100] *be, but let God's perfect*

---

88. *usmotritъ*—literally, *look over*, but here connected to *smotrěnie*, used for the Divine Economy, an equivalent of *Providence*.
89. Cf. above, *Predanie* 17.
90. Cf. above, *Predanie* 18.
91. *tiazha/tiazh*; variant reading: *miatezh* = *unrest/tumult*.
92. *likhoimstvъ* (gn. pl.): alt. transl.: *usury*.
93. *nerazumii* (nm. pl.): alt. transl.: *unintelligent, stupid*; see above, *Ustav*, Fwd. 17, and below, *To Vassian* 1, *To Gurii* 1.
94. Literally, *by the poverty of the measure*.
95. From Nikon, *Taktikon* 2:19v.
96. *v chinu uchimykhъ* (gn. pl. prs. pssv. prtcpl.); cf. Iosif, 'To Arkhimandrit Vassian', PIV 140; MRIV 10.34; and below, *To Vassian* 1.
97. From *Predanie* 1.
98. Seemingly adapted from above, Ustav, Fwd. 18.
99. *nerazumia* (gn. sg.): alt. trans: *incomprehension; stupidity*.
100. From/in Nil's *Sobornik, Forew.* 2; from Nikon, *Taktikon*, Fwd., 7.

and welcome[101] *will be done,*[102] *and I beg forgiveness.*[103] *If,* concerning *these things, someone knows*[104] *something more and more profitably*[105] *let him so act, and we rejoice over it. And if anyone obtains profit in these, let him pray for me,* a sinner, *so that I* may obtain *mercy* before *the Lord.*[106]

101. *blagopriiatna,* literally, *well-received; blagougodno = well-pleasing* in the *Sobornik, Forew.* 3.
102. Adapted from Nikon *Taktikon* 2:19v; cf. Lk 11:2 (The Lord's Prayer).
103. From/in Nil's *Sobornik, Forew.* 3; cf. below, *Testament* 3, but also the colophon of the Bulgarian (or Bulgaria-located) translator of Athanasius the Great's *Life of Anthony:* SNS 3:235.
104. *razuměvaet:* the fifth use of the *razum-* lexeme in [19]: alt.transl.: *understands.*
105. From Nikon, *Taktikon* 2:19v.
106. Last clause freely adapted from/to *Sobornik, Forew.* 3; cf. also *Predanie* 30.

THE THREE EPISTLES*

*Unlike Nil's other three authentic Epistles, usually found together in the order presented here, the *Little Epistle*, also so presented, follows in only one codex.

An Epistle of the Elder[1] Nil to a Brother[2], Who Queried Him over Urges. 1ˢᵗ Epistle.

[1] You have promoted[3] a laudable desire, O beloved, to seek to hear the word of God for your confirmation, for preservation from evil things, and meditation[4] toward the good. But, it was fitting for you to learn this from those with good knowledge. You, though, *demand this from me, the unknowledgeable and sinner.*[5] For I am of no use, and *in the rank of disciples,*[6] and therefore have refused and postponed a great deal—not as if not wishing to render service to your good volition, but on account of my lack of knowledge and sins. For what shall I say, *my having never done any good thing?*[7] What is knowledge to a sinner? Only sins. But because you have often forced me onto this, that I compose for you a sermon for the edification of virtue, *so I have dared to write* this *to you, which is above my measure,*[8] my *not* being able *to scorn your request, lest you be* further *grieved.*[9]

[2] Your question concerning assailing urges of yore, from the worldly life. This you yourself know from experience: how much grief and perversion this transient world has, how much evil savagery it inflicts on those who love it, and how it jeers at those who slaved

---

1. Var.: *Great Elder.*
2. Vassian Patrikeev: see above, II. 'Once a Boyar . . . .'.
3. *podvignuti*, with the double entendre of having *podvig* = *struggle, feat,* as well as *po-dvig-*, where *dvig-* = *move* as the basic verb form.
4. *pouchenie*: alt. trans, *instruction.*
5. Cf. above, *Ustav,* Fwd. 17, 11.19, and below, *To Gurii* 1, *Sobornik, Postcr.,* signature.
6. See, above, *Ustav* 11.19.
7. Cf. above, *Ustav,* Fwd. 17, and below, *To Gurii* 19, *Sobornik, Forew.* 1.
8. Cf. below, *To Gurii* 1.
9. Cf. below, *To German* 9-10.

for it, as it is departing, seeming sweet to them when it caresses with things, afterwards it becomes bitter. Indeed however much they reckon its good things to be multiplying, when they sustain them, that much grief grows for them. For what are reckoned its good things are visibly good, but inside filled with much evil. On this account, to those possessing genuine knowledge the apparently good thing shows its real self, so that it not be beloved by them.

[3]   What happens after the passing of out of this life? Place your thought firmly within what is said: How has the world profited those who cling to it?[10] If they had any *glory and honor and riches*,[11] hasn't all of this become nothing, and *passed like a shadow*,[12] and *disappeared like smoke*?[13] And *many* of them, *who* inter-communed[14] within the things of *this world* and *loved* its course, were, at the time of youth and *prosperity, harvested by death*,[15] *like the flowers* of the fields, having bloomed, *fallen off*,[16] and involuntarily were taken from here. And when they sojourned in this world, they did not know its foul *stench*, but strove for *beauty*[17] and physical comfort, finding knowledge applicable for the profits of this world, and they passed through the teachings that crown the body in this passing age. And if they received all of this, but did not care about infinite bliss, what can one think of them? The world has nothing more insane than them, as a certain wise saint said.[18] And some of them were most pious and focused their intellect on thoughts about the desire for salvation of the soul, and had battle with passions and effected the models of virtue insofar as was possible, wishing to free themselves and depart from this world, but were unable to tear away from its snares or avoid its subterfuge.

---

10. Cf. Mt 16:26.
11. Cf. above, *Ustav* 7.14, 17.
12. Cf. above, *Ustav* 7.18: Wsd 2:5 (LXX).
13. Cf. above, *Ustav* 7.14; cf. Ps 101:12, 4/102:11, 3.
14. *soobrashchaetsia:* maybe a neologism, combining the sounds of *soobshchat'sia* and *obrashchat'sia* (*commune with* + *turn towards*).
15. Cf. above, *Ustav* 7.12.
16. Cf. above, *Ustav* 7.18; Ps 102:15/103:15.
17. Cf. above, *Ustav* 7.18.
18. Source not identified.

[4] God, having loved you, and taking you from this world, has by his mercy and plan[19] placed you in the ranks of his service.[20] Therefore you must most abundantly thank his mercy[21] and do everything in your power towards his gratification and the salvation of your soul, *forgetting* the worldly *past* as useless, and reaching *to the* virtuous *future*[22] as intermediary for eternal life. Rejoice, step onto the honor of the calling of the Most High, granted in the heavenly fatherland to former ascetics.

[5] And what you have said to me concerning *unclean*[23] *urges, conveyed by the enemy* of our souls.[24] Do not be absorbed so much by grief, *nor be horrified*, because *harassment*[25] from this *befalls not only us, the infirm and the passionate*, say the Fathers, *but those* who are succeeding, and *remaining in the praiseworthy life*,[26] and having become partially worthy of spiritual grace. And an attack by such urges often befalls them, and they are engaged in a great struggle on account of these, and they barely repel these with the grace of God, while always striving for the severance of these.

[6] And you, taking consolation from this, assiduously sever wicked urges. Maintain[27] against them a *continuous* victory, the prayer, summoning the Lord Jesus. Indeed, driven off by this summons, they go away in flight. As John Climacus said, *with Jesus's name beat the warriors: for something sturdier than this weapon*[28] *does not exist*.[29] If

---

19. *stroenie*—another equivalent of the *Divine Economy*.
20. A reference to the fall of the Patrikeevs; see above under II. 'Once a Boyar . . . .'
21. Var: *goodness*.
22. Literally, *past worldly* (pl.) . . . *future virtuous* (pl. — *things* understood): cf. Phil 3:13.
23. Cf. *Ustav* 2.12.
24. Cf. *Ustav* 1.1, 5.86: *to the intellect* in the *Ustav*.
25. Cf. *Ustav* 2.12.
26. Seemingly adapted from *Ustav* 3.2, but without the reference to Isaac; cf. above, *Predanie* 16, 32, *Ustav* 2.11, 7.8.
27. Alt. transl., attaching to the previous sentence: *maintaining/having*.
28. As in *Ustav* 5.2.40, from Climacus; cf. below, *To Gurii* 5.
29. Here closer to Climacus's *you will not find*: Climacus 21.7; HM SMS 184:104v–105/VMCh-M:896a; PG 88:945C.

those *attacking*[30] you wax *greatly* in might, then, *rising and extending hands and eyes toward heaven*,[31] fervently say with compunction:'*Have mercy on me, Lord, for I am infirm*.[32] *You, Lord, are the mighty one*,[33] *and yours is the struggle. You should fight and prevail on our behalf, Lord*'.[34] *If you do this tirelessly*,[35] *you will learn* completely *from experience that they are defeated by the power of the Most High*.[36]

[7]   And do some kind of *manual work*, for with this the *wicked urges*[37] are driven off. And this is the tradition[38] of an angel to one of the great saints.[39]

[8]   And memorize some Scripture,[40] placing the intellect therein, and this impedes the *entrance of the demons'* [41] offensive against us. And that is the discovery of the holy Fathers.

[9]   Guard yourself *from improper conversations, hearing, and viewing, which incite*[42] and *strengthen* unclean *urges*,[43] and God will aid you.

[10]   Concerning *the terrors* of which you speak, *this is child's stuff*, not of a manly soul, and this is uncharacteristic of you. And when such befall you, *struggle lest they control you*, and brace your heart to hope *in the* Lord and say to this yourself:'I have the Lord protecting me, and without his will no one can harm me in any

---

30. Adapted from *Ustav* 5.2.42, citing Climacus.
31. Almost as *Ustav* 5.2.37, citing Gregory Sin.
32. As in *Ustav* 5.2.39, citing Climacus 15.8, citing Ps 6:3/6:2.
33. *You . . . mighty one*: Ps.88:9/89:9.
34. Almost as *Ustav* 5.2.38, from Isaac Syr.
35. *nelěnostno*: literally, non-lazily.
36. Adapted from *Ustav* 5.2.42.
37. Maybe from Climacus 15.82:160; HM SMS 184:96/VMCh-M:891ab; PG 88:901A.
38. *predanie* as *rule* or *instruction*.
39. For [7], cf. *Sayings*, Anthony 1:1; *Paterik azbuchnyi*, 3v; PG 65:76AB; Nikon, *Pandekty* 44:346v; MRIV 8ᴮ.9; and above, *Ustav* 2.56-57, 5.6.77; also *Little Epistle*.
40. Cf. *Life of Theodore Sinkeotes*, SNS 3:397; *Vita S. Theodori* Siceotae, 36D; *Life of Anthony* 3:21; SNS 3:151; PG 26:845A.
41. Seemingly inspired by Ps-Symeon NT, as *Ustav* 1.6.
42. Possibly combining *Ustav* 5.2.47, 10.15, from Basil, Nikon, and Isaac Syr.
43. Cf. above, *Ustav* 3.8.

way. If he allows anything against me, to cause me to suffer, I do not react viciously, and I do not desire to annul his desire[44], because the Lord knows better than I and desires useful things for me. And for all these I graciously thank his goodness'. And thus with the *good grace of God* you shall be *goodly bold*.[45]

[11] Always *arm yourself with prayer* against this. And when this happens to you in certain *places*, then especially strive to arrive there extending your *hands in the image of the cross,* and, *summon the Lord Jesus*.[46] And, with the aid of the Most High, *you will not fear the terror of the night, and from the arrow that flies by day*.[47]

And thus about this.

[12] All the other[48] things which are praiseworthy and clean[49] and virtuous—contemplate and do them, being prudent in goodness and hating all evil.

[13] Have obedience to the *mentor* and the other fathers in the Lord *in every good deed*.[50]

[14] As for the *service*[51] with which you are now *entrusted*, or if you shift to another, serve with a bright presence[52] and *graceful* zeal, *as if for Christ* himself,[53] holding *all the brothers as saints*.[54] *If* a word, question or answer for someone *occurs to you*,[55] converse

---

44. I.e., *I do not wish to upset his plan* (for me).
45. Isocolic double alliteration here: *blagodatъiu Bozheiu blagoderzostenъ budeshi*: cf. below, *To Gurii* 16; see above under III. 'Literary Devices', text to note 127.
46. [10-11] partially combined from Climacus 15.81-82:160 and 21.1-2,7; HM SMS 184.95v, 104-104v/VMCh-M: 890d-891a, 89d-896a; PG 88:900, 945BC, 900C-901A. Cf. above, *Ustav* 2.12.
47. Ps. 90.5/91.5: *and* added by Nil.
48. Alt. transl.: *Furthermore*, starting the sentence.
49. *chsta = chista* (nt. pl. nm./acc.); var.: *chestna = honorable*.
50. Cf. Basil/Ps-Basil, *Ascetic Discourse* 63; HM SMS 183:181; PG 31:632BC, among others.
51. Alt. transl.: *office*.
52. *prědlozhenie*—alt. transl: *start; offering*.
53. Basil/Ps-Basil, *Ascetic Discourse* 70; PG 31:645B; HM SMS 183:185v.
54. Alt. transl.: attach *holding all the brothers as saints* to the next sentence: Symeon NT, *Discourses* 26.5:278; SC 113:80-81; cf. *Capita practica et theologica* 123, PG 120:669D—but not located in a Slavic MS.
55. Nil's formal way of saying *if you have something to say to somebody*, indicates its rarity and seriousness.

eloquently and sweetly with *spiritual* love and true humility, not lazily and not offending the brother. Cleave unto *the reverential fathers,* even that *timely and in measure.* Stay away from those who are not such, and *be on guard,*[56] and endeavor *not to reproach or condemn anyone*[57] over anything, even if something appears not good to you. Rather consider yourself totally sinful and unfit in everything.

[15] If something be needful to you from the superior or the other *exemplary*[58] fathers for it, pray first and consider for yourself if it is useful, and then ask. And if it is not arranged for you as you desire, do not be embittered or enraged that they did not act according to your desire, even if what you deem what you desire to be good, but proceed with patience, and do everything with calmness and with forbearance. And if you be *pleasing to God and* directed to the salvation *of your soul,*[59] God will inform someone to fulfill your need and to give you both time and a helping hand.

[16] Be fervent[60] in heeding *the Divine Writings,* and with their words, as if with *living water,* give drink to your soul and endeavor, as much as possible, to act according to them. And thus strive to submit to those *having the knowledge of the Divine Writings* and *spiritual prudence* and a lifestyle *witnessed* in *virtues,*[61] and to be an imitator of their life.

[17] Have patience in afflictions and *pray for those who afflict* you and hold them as *benefactors.*[62] And know that what I tell you is the knowledge of the Divine Writings, reciting the wishes of

---

56. *sъkhraniai zhe sia,* with an ambiguous place in the sentence: either an independent injunction or attached to *from those who are not such.*

57. For [14], cf. above, *Ustav* 4.4, 10.5, from Isaac Syr., Basil.

58. *vъobrazhenykhъ* (gn. pl.); cf. Kornilii Komel'sky, *Ustav,* DRIU, 174.

59. Cf. below, *To Gurii* 1.

60. *userdenъ* alt. trams: *painstaking;* var. *potrebenъ* = *thorough.*

61. Adapted from *Ustav,* Fwd. 14, from Gregory Sin. and ultimately Basil/Ps-Basil, but with a revisiting of the latter's *having the knowledge of the Divine Writings:* Basil/Ps-Basil, *Ascetic Discourse* 63; PG 632B; cf. HM SMS 183:181; cf. below, *To Vassian* 16, *To Gurii* 17, *To German* 6.

62. Cf. above, *Ustav* 5.5.62; Mt 5:44; maybe directed to Vassian's experience, but culled from generic treatment.

divine beneficence, that from the ages the saints, *who effected righteousness and received the promise* walking in the paths of the virtues, not only endured misfortunes and afflictions, but their path was tread by both the cross and death. And this is the sign of *divine love*, that afflictions are inflicted on someone over an activity of righteousness. And this is called a *'gift of God'*,[63] the Apostle having written: '*This was given to us by God, not only to believe in Christ, but also to suffer for him*'.[64] For it makes a man a participant in Christ's passion[65] and like unto the saints, who endured afflictions for his name. And otherwise God does not benefit those who love him, he only sends a trial of afflictions. And God's beloved differ from the others in this, that they live in afflictions, while those who love this world make merry with foods and rest. And this is the path of righteousness, to endure trials of afflictions over piety. And placing on this path,[66] God leads his sufferers into eternal life.

[18] Therefore it is joyfully proper for us to walk without blemish onto the path, walking in the Lord's commandments, wholeheartedly thanking him, that he, loving us, has sent us this grace, incessantly praying to his his goodness, remembering the end of our afflictive life and the unending bliss of the future age.

[19] And *may the God of all* joy and *comfort, comfort your heart*[67] and preserve you in his fear, with the prayers of the most pure Mother of God and all the saints.

[20] In your prayers, for the sake of the Lord, do not forget me,[68] a sinner, who speaks the good to you, yet does not do, so that the Lord lead me out of a deluge of passions and a swamp[69] of sins.

---

63. *divine love, gift of God*: may be from Jas 1:12, 17.
64. Cf. Phil 1:29.
65. *strastb*: cf. 2 Cor 1:5, where the cognate *stradanie* is used in the same way.
66. An apparently conscious ellipsis.
67. Cf. 2 Cor 1:3-4 (in ital.), and, with a reverse, *To German* 9.
68. literally, *make me unforgotten*.
69. *timĕnie*, suggestive also of *tma/tьma* = myriad.

The Same One's Epistle to Another[1] Concerning Profit.

[1] That your holiness conversed mouth to mouth[2] with me, most honorable father, and so also you have sent me writings about the same thing. You request from my meagerness to send you a profitable written word, which is *for the pleasing of God and the profit of the soul.*[3] *I* indeed am *a sinful and unintelligent man*[4] and defeated by all the passions; I feared to commence such a thing. Therefore I refused and set aside. But because your spiritual love has edified me to dare above my measure[5] to write fitting things to you, I therefore have persuaded myself in this.

Your first question concerning urges of fornication: how to resist them.

[2] The striving and struggle over this is not only for you but for all who are struggling together with God, because, the Fathers say, *this contest is great, having a double war, in soul and body,*[6] and nature contains nothing more compelling than this. *Therefore it is by every means proper resolutely to strive, vigilantly and soberly, to preserve our heart from these urges, having the fear of God* before ones eyes, to recall our vow, which we confessed to remain in chastity and purity. And chastity and purity means not only the outer life, but also the secret man

---

1. Gurii Tushin: see above, II. 'The Best of the Bookmen'.
2. I.e., *face to face.*
3. Cf. above, *To Vassian* 15, *Predanie* 30, *Sobornik, Forew.* 2, Nikon, *Taktikon* 2:19–19v.
4. Cf. above, *Ustav*, Fwd 17, 11.19, *To Vassian* 1, and below, *Sobornik, Postscr.* Signature.
5. Cf. above, *To Vassian* 1.
6. Cf. above, *Ustav* 5.2.27, from (without attribution) Cassian.

of the heart,[7] *when he cleanses*[8] *of filthy urges.*[9] Accordingly, *by every means possible, zealously cut off this urge.*[10]

[3]   *To* establish *this great victory over them, one should diligently pray*[11] *to God, as the holy Fathers* passed down,[12] in *different* forms, but all *with the same knowledge.*[13] *For* one said, *taking words spoken by David:'Those pursuing me have now surrounded me,*[14] *joy of mine: deliver me from those who have surrounded me'.*[15] And another so *spoke about these:'God, hearken to my aid'*[16] *and other similar words.*[17] And again another said from them:[18] *'Judge those who injure me and hinder those who fight me'*, and the rest of the psalm.[19] Summon for aid with what you hear in the writings of those who struggled over chastity and purity. When *combat fiercely* sets in, *immediately rising and extending hands and eyes toward heaven to pray,*[20] *'You are the mighty one, Lord, and yours is the struggle; you should fight and prevail in this, Lord, on our behalf'*,[21] *and cry to the* Omnipotent One *for aid, able to save, with humble utterances: 'Have mercy on me, Oh Lord, for I am infirm'.*[22] This is the tradition of the saints.[23]

[4]   And *if you* pass through these struggles, *you will come to know from experience* that with the grace of God *they are utterly defeated* with these.[24]

---

7. *secret man of the heart* from 1 P 3:3-4.
8. An ellipsis, lacking the reflexive *himself.*
9. From *Therefore*, almost as in *Ustav* 5.2.27-28.
10. As in *Ustav* 5.2.32.
11. *diligently pray*, adapted from Cassian, as in *Ustav* 5.2.33.
12. Almost as *Ustav* 5.2.32.
13. Cf. above, *Ustav*, Fwd 1.
14. From *Those*, Ps 16:11 (LXX), as in *Ustav*. 5.2.34, from Maximus Conf.
15. Ps 31.7 LXX, as in *Ustav* 5.2.34, from Maximus Conf.
16. From *God*: Ps 69:2/70:1. as in *Ustav* 5.2.35/Climacus.
17. From *spoke about*: abbrev. from *Ustav* 5.2.35 or Climacus.
18. The 'words', that is, the Psalms of David.
19. Ps 34:1/35:1: attributed to Theodore Stud., *Ustav* 6.3.
20. As in *Ustav* 5.2.37, from Gregory Sin.
21. As in *Ustav* 5.2.38, from Isaac Syr.
22. Abbrev. and adapted from *Ustav* 5.2.39, from Climacus; citation from *Have mercy*, Ps 6:3/6:2.
23. Cf. above, *Ustav* 5.2.33-42.
24. Adapted from *Ustav* 5.2.42.

[5] *Always with Jesus's name* as a *weapon whip the warriors: for something sturdier than this* victory does not exist.²⁵

[6] *Keep yourself* from the *seeing of faces* and the hearing of *conversations* of those, who *incite passions*²⁶ and raise up unclean urges, and God will preserve you

Thus about these.

Your second question on the urge of blasphemy.

[7] And *this urge* is outrageous and *very fierce.*²⁷ It *vexes*²⁸ resolutely and unceasingly. And not only now, but in of old it befell the great Fathers and holy Martyrs, even at the very time when tyrants wished to inflict wounds upon their bodies and bitter deaths for confessing of faith in our Lord God Jesus Christ.²⁹

[8] *And one has victory over this urge thusly,*³⁰ in that *not one's soul, but an unclean demon is responsible.*³¹ *Say this against the spirit of blasphemy:* 'Be gone from me, Satan; I worship the Lord my God, and I serve only him.*³² As for you, may ingratitude and blasphemy return to your height, and the Lord writes this for you: Depart from me³³ May God, who created me in his image and likeness,*³⁴ destroy you'. And if after this, it still rages acting outrageously,³⁵ *transpose the urges onto some other thing, divine or human,*³⁶ so long as it be not beyond propriety.

---

25. Adapted from *Ustav* 5.2.40, from Climacus via Gregory the Sinaite, or triangulated also with *To Vassian* 6.
26. Adapted from *Ustav* 5.2.45, 47, partially inspired by Basil; cf. above, *To Vassian* 9.
27. Adapted from *Ustav* 5.2.27 (against fornication), from Cassian.
28. Adapted, maybe, from *Ustav* 5.2.28 (against fornication).
29. Nil's copying (and maybe editing) connected tyrants, blasphemy, and martyrs differently: see above, Part II, 'The Unexpected Bedfellow,' text to note 84.
30. Adapted from *Ustav* 5.2.32-33 (against fornication).
31. From Climacus 23.46; HM SMS184:114/VMCh-M:901a; not in *Ustav*.
32. From *Be gone*, slightly adapted from Mt 4:10.
33. *Depart from me*: cf. Ps 6:9/6:8; cf. above, *Ustav* 5.6.78, 6.6.
34. Cf. Gn 1:26, Wsd 2:23-24 (LXX).
35. An added play on words here: *stuzhaetъ bestudstvuia;* alt. transl.: *harasses shamelessly.*
36. [8] almost as *Ustav* 5.6.78-79 (against despondency); cf. above, *Ustav* 1.10-11, 5.3-4, 5.7.79, 8.24.

[9]   Preserve yourself from pride, and strive to travel on paths of humility. For it is said by the Fathers, that *from pride* are *born urges* of *blasphemy*.[37] They occur also from demons' envy. And if they occur from this or something else, then as fallow deer are deadly to poisonous beasts, so is humility deadly to this passion.[38] And not only to this one, but to others[39] has it been said by the holy Fathers.[40]

3rd Question

[10]   And what you are attempting, how to withdraw from the world: this ardor of yours is good, but strive in deed so to perfect this in yourself. For this is the beaten path to eternal life, by which the saintly *Fathers* went, who *came to know* by attending to *supreme wisdom*. And the withdrawal from the world is especially fitting for him who has been in the habit of intercourse with the world. For if he does not withdraw, it is as certain images and pictures of the world, that previously were in him, from the hearing and seeing of worldly things, again renewing themselves.[41] And he cannot soberly remain in prayer in meditating on God's will. He who wishes to meditate on pleasing God must withdraw from the world.

[11]   Do not desire to receive the *conversations* of the usual friends, who reason in a worldly manner and exercise themselves with the *irrational* cares entailing profits of monastic riches and the acquisition[42] of *properties,* which are reckoned to be effected in a form of goodness, and stem from misunderstanding of the Divine Writings or their own passionate attachment—*in reckoning to traverse virtue*. And you, man of God, do not commune with such people. It is not proper even to go after such people with speeches,

---

37. From Climacus 23.38; HM SMS 113:113/VMChM 900d; PG 88:969D.
38. Adapted from Climacus 25.8; HM SMS 184:119v/VMCh-M:904c; PG 88:992AB.
39. I.e., *other passions.*
40. Cf. Climacus 26.67; HM SMS 184:133v-134/VMCh-M:912d-913a; PG 88:1028A.
41. This quasi-Platonic epistemology has the earmarks of Isaac Syr., among others, for example, HTM *Discourse* 4 (Gk. 23, Slav. 56).
42. *stiazhanie*: alt. transl.: *possession.*

or revile or reproach, but leave all this to God. For God is the mighty one to right this.[43]

[12] Also preserve yourself in all ways from boldness. For boldness, as is written, is like unto a great fire, from whose face all flee, when it occurs. And turn from hearing and seeing the brothers' things and their secrets and actions. These render the soul devoid of all good and make one examine the shortcomings of one's neighbor and abandon mourning[44] for one's own sins.

[13] And do not strive to be quick of tongue *conversations* with brothers, *even if it is reckoned to be profitable.*[45] And if any brother has some information for us[46] and truly requires the word of God, and if we have, we must give him not only the word of God according to apostolic witness, but also our own soul.[47] Focus yourself *upon* such things and concord in activities with those who reason spiritually, who are *the children*[48] *of God's mysteries.*[49] With those who are not so, *conversations, even if they are brief, wither the flowers of virtue, which bloom again from the admixture of stillness and surround with softness and youth the orchard of the soul, planted by the outflowing of tears of repentance,*[50] as a most wise saint said.

4th Question.

[14] And what you seek, how not to stray from the true path: for this, I give you good counsel.

[15] Bind to yourself laws of the Divine Writings, and follow them, the true Divine Writings. *For writings are many, but not all*

---

43. Cf. above, *Ustav* 5.8.95, 10.5; below, *To German* 2.
44. *ostavliati*; var (from earliest texts): *sъstavliati* = *compose/constitute*: if not an outright error, then it must mean: *constitute grounds for mourning for one's own sins.*
45. Cf. above, *Ustav* 10.12.
46. *izvěshchenie imat k nam*: alt., idiomatic transl.: *wants to know something from us.*
47. Cf. Jn 13:15.
48. *deti* (nm, pl.): *synovъ* = sons in the original and Slavic transl.
49. Isaac Syr., Appendix B.II (*Epistle to Abba Symeon*), 439; HM SMS 179.55:252; Gk: *Epistle* 4:385.
50. In *Ustav* 10.13, applied to all untimely conversations: from Isaac Syr.—the *most wise saint* here.

are divine.[51] But you, having genuinely experienced the true from reading them and from the conversations of knowledgeable and spiritual people (insofar as not all people, just the knowledgeable know them), are to do nothing without the witness of such writings, just as I. As for myself, I inform you, *insofar as your love in God makes*[52] *witless me*[53] *speak of myself.*[54] But as it is said, I reveal my secret things to my beloved,[55] so I speak to you.

[16]   For I do nothing without witness from the Divine Writings, but I do as much as possible following the holy Writings. And if I do not find it agreeing with my knowledge at the commencement of an act I set it aside until I find. When I find *with the good grace of God*, I act genuinely *with good boldness.*[56] I do not dare do anything by myself, because *I am an ignoramus*[57] *and a rustic.*[58]

[17]   You too, if you desire, act according to the Divine Writings and by their knowledge strive to effect the divine commandments and the traditions of the holy Fathers. And if some disturbance of the things of this life move your heart, be not terrified, confirmed upon the unmovable rock of God's commandments and shielded by the traditions of the holy Fathers. And in everything be an emulator[59] of those whom you see and hear in the holy Writings containing *the witnessed life and prudence.*[60] For traveling their path is right.[61] And inscribing this in your heart, walk unbendingly along the divine path,[62] and you shall not, with the grace of God, diverge from the truth. For it is written that it

---

51. Adapted from Nikon, *Taktikon* 5:42v: this is one source of the myth of Nil's 'criticism', see above, II. 'The Best of the Bookmen', text to note 30.
52. Cf. below, *To German* 3.
53. Cf. 2 Cor 12.11.
54. Cf. below, *To German* 3.
55. Scriptural source not found; cf. *Second Apocalypse of James*, sans a substantiated link to Nil.
56. *blagoderzostno*: cf. above, *To Vassian* 10.
57. Cf. below, *Sobornik, Forew.* 2.
58. Cf. Nikon, *Taktikon,* Fwd. 8.
59. Cf. below, *Sobornik, Forew.* 4.
60. Cf. above, *Ustav,* Fwd. 14, *To Vassian* 16; below, *To German* 6.
61. Alt. transl.: *for their traveling of the path is right.*
62. Cf. above, *Ustav* 3.8.

is impossible for the him who reasons[63] rightly and lives piously to perish. But those who do God's work with corrupted knowledge, they transgress from the right path.[64]

[18] Go straight unswervingly, *having placed your hand on the Lord's plough, and not looking back,* that you be directed to *the kingdom of God.*[65] And endeavor, having received the seed of the word[66] of God, so that your heart be not found a path or a stone or a thorn, but *blessed land,* creating many *a double crop*[67] for the salvation of your soul.

[19] And let me, having examined your facility for knowledge[68] in heeding the word of God, and having found you praiseworthy in the execution of virtues, rejoice, thanking God, my having seen[69] your *heeding the word of God and preserving it.*[70] And *I pray* to you for the sake of the Lord to *pray for me, a sinner,* who is telling you *the good* but *not* in any way *doing.*[71]

[20] And may God, who effects[72] the glorious and grants every good gift to those who well effect his will, grant you the knowledge and resolve to effect his holy will by the prayers of our most pure Lady, the Mother of God, and all the saints to be blessed forever. Amen.

---

63. *mudrьstvuiushchemu* (dt. sg.), a play on *mudrovanie* = *prudence.*
64. See above, Part II, 'Once a Boyar . . .', note 118.
65. Lk 9:62.
66. *Slovo* = *logos* and hence ambiguous: may or may not be Christ.
67. Perhaps inspired by Lv 25:21, or by Mt 13:1-8/Mk 4:1-9, Lk 8:4-8.
68. *razumnoe tvoe*: literally, *your knowledgeable, intelligent,* etc., with an ellipsis.
69. *uvidevъ*—var: *uvedevъ* = *having known.*
70. Lk 11:28.
71. Cf. below, *Sobornik, Forew.* 3-4, *Postscr. 1*; and above, *Predanie* 1; *Ustav, Fwd.* 17, *To Vassian* 1, *To Gurii* 1.
72. *tvoriai:* alt. transl.: *creates.*

An Epistle of the Same Great Elder to a Brother,[1] Who Asked Him to Write for Him Something Profitable for the Soul.

[1] Your writ, Father, which you wrote to me—you ask me to write back to you something of profit and you inform me of yourself, that you reckon that I have grief towards you, due to the speeches in our conversing with you when you were here. And for this, forgive me.

[2] I advised you, reminding myself and you, as my ever beloved—as it is written: I reveal my secrets to my own and to the *sons* of my *house*[2]—that it is not proper to do anything simply and haphazardly, but by the Divine Writings and by the traditions of the holy Fathers—before exiting the monastery.[3] Wasn't that only for the sake of the soul's profit and nothing else?[4] Because now one does not see guarded the life of God's laws by the Divine Writings and by the traditions of the holy Fathers, but by peoples' own wills and human concepts. And this is found among many, that we effect perversity itself, *we reckon that we are traversing virtue*.[5] This happens from our not knowing the holy Writings, because we do not strive with fear of God and with humility to investigate them, but are heedless of them and are busied with human affairs.

[3] For this reason I conversed with you, because you truly and unpretentiously wish to hear the word of God and effect it.

---

1. German Podolnyi; see above, II. 'The Loose Cannon'.
2. Cf. 2 Enoch 36.
3. That is, when Nil and German were still together as monks in Kirillov.
4. Var. (attach to the end of the previous sentence): *only for the sake of the soul's profit and nothing else.*
5. Cf. above, *To Gurii* 11.

And I, not flattering you, nor concealing the harshness of *the narrow and afflicted path*,[6] have made a proposal to you. As for others, I converse according someone's measure.[7] As for you, you have known my meagerness from the start. As my ever spiritually beloved, on this account I write to you even now, openly doing something of myself, *insofar as your love in God compels me and makes witless me*[8] write to you *about myself*.[9]

[4] When we lived in the monastery—you know, that I withdraw far from worldly entanglements and act as much as possible by the Divine Writings, even though I cannot, due to my sloth and carelessness. Then with the departure for my pilgrimage, upon returning[10] to the monastery, I made a cell outside near the monastery, and so lived in keeping with my power. Now I have resettled far from the monastery,[11] because with the grace of God I found a place pleasing to my knowledge, since it is little traveled by children of the world, as you yourself have seen. And, especially investigating the Divine Writings, first the Lord's commandments and their interpretations and the apostolic traditions, and then the lives and teaching of the holy Fathers, I attend to them. And what is in accord with my knowledge for *the goodly-pleasing of God and for the soul's profit*,[12] I inscribe for myself and meditate on it—and therein I hold my life and breath. And I have laid my infirmity and sloth and indifference upon God and upon the most pure Mother of God. And if I happen to have something to do, and I do not find it in the holy Writings, I set it aside temporarily until I find it. Because I do not dare to do anything by my own will and my own knowledge. And if someone with spiritual love adheres to me, I counsel to do likewise, but especially you, because from the start you commended yourself to me with spiritual love.

---

6. Cf. Mt 7:14, MRIV 2.29, 3.14.
7. I.e., ability of someone to comprehend.
8. 2 Cor 12:11.
9. Cf. above, *To Gurii* 15.
10. Literally, *come*.
11. Only about twelve miles.
12. Cf. below, *Sobornik, Forew.*, 3; also above, *Predanie* 30.

On this account I also extended a word to you, counseling the good, as to my own soul: just as I endeavor to do, so I have conversed to you.

[5] Now, even if we are apart in body, yet by spiritual love are conjoined and coupled.[13] And on account of this *typikon*[14] of divine love,[15] I conversed with you then, and now I write, summoning to the salvation of the soul. And if what you have heard from me and seen written down is pleasing to you, imitate it.

[6] Desiring to be a son and heir of the holy Fathers, *effect* the Lord's *commandments*[16] and the traditions of the holy Fathers and speak to the brothers who are with you. And if your dwelling is apart, or you are in a monastery with the brothers, attend to the holy Writings and walk in the footsteps of the holy Fathers, because the Divine Writings so command. Either *submit* to such *a man*, who *is witnessed* in his practice of the word and *spiritual knowledge*, as Basil the Great writes in his discourse, whose incipit is, *'Come to me all who toil'*.[17] If you do not find such a one, then submit to God by the Divine Writings, but not irrationally, as some.

[7] And when in the monastery with the brothers, who, reckoning themselves in submission, shepherd themselves irrationally with self will, and similarly effect solitude without knowledge, leading themselves by fleshly will and undiscerning knowledge,[18] incognizant either of what they effect or of what they are convinced—of such John Climacus, discerning in the Discourse *'On*

---

13. Cf. above, *Ustav* 4.10.

14. *ustavъ*, used metaphorically, as in Iosif's Rule 4^B.13/3.13, (striving for fine clothing as a *typikon for debauchery*), or as in 13.5, a command-rule-teaching (*typikon for perfect love*, which the monks 'locks in his heart'), or, maybe, as in monastic 'academic' grammar, as a definition carrying a categorical imperative: see above, *Ustav* 2.1 and note 1.

15. *bozhestvennyia* (gn. sg.) *liubve* (dt. sg.): seeming idiomatic case shift here.

16. Cf. above, *Ustav* 10.6; below, *Sobornik, Forew.* 4.

17. *Ascetic Discourse*: used by Nil in Ustav 1.28, 5.2.25, 5.2.47, 5.8.92, 11.13, as well as the related passages in *Ustav,* Fwd. 14, *To Vassian* 16, *To Gurii* 16. On singling out the bibliographer German for an incipit, and below in [7], for a sub-title, see above under II. 'The Loose Cannon', texts to notes 37-38.

18. *razumom' nerazsudnom.*

the Differences of Stillness', says: *With self-regulation*[19] *rather than direction, they would sail by presumption,*[20] which is not for us to have.

[8]   As for you, acting according to the Divine Writings and the life of the holy Fathers,[21] with the grace of Christ, you will not sin.

[9]   And I now also am afflicted that you are afflicted Therefore I submitted to write to you, so that you would not be afflicted. *May the God of all comfort* and joy *comfort*[22] *your heart*[23] and inform of our love for you.

[10]   And if I wrote something boorishly, yet it was not to anyone else but you, my ever beloved, not wishing to scorn your request. I hope that you will receive with love and not disdain my lack of knowledge.

[11]   And concerning our affairs, I have beseeched your holiness about them, that you would endeavor to arrange them well, and for this *I bow my head.*[24] And may God grant you a reward according to your labor.

[12]   Moreover, I also beseech your holiness not to place the words which I said then as an affliction. For if externally reckoned cruel, internally they are full of profit, because I did not speak from myself, but from the holy Writings. In truth it is cruel for those, who do not wish in truth to humble themselves in fear of the Lord and withdraw from reasoning of the flesh, but rather live by their own passionate wills, and not by the holy Writings. Indeed such ones do not investigate the holy Writings with spiritual humility. Some of them even do not wish to hear now that one is

---

19. Cf. above, *Predanie* 6, *Ustav* 11.7, and below, Appendix III, Innokentii, *Zavět* 15.
20. Climacus 27.29 (with the original subtitle *On the Differences and Distinctions of Hesychasts/Solitaries*, which became in the Slavic *On the Differences of Distinction of Hesychasm/Stillness*; HM SMS 184:155/VMCh-M:925d; PG 88:1105A:VMCh-M: appears defective, having *ni* (= *not*) instead of *ini* (= ἄλλοι = *some*) before *with self-regulation* Cf. above, *Ustav* 11.9.
21. Cf. above, *Predanie*, Title; below, *Sobornik, Forew.* 4.
22. Cf. 2 Cor 1:3-4.
23. Cf. above (with a reverse), *To Vassian* 19.
24. See below, *Testament* 4.

to live by the holy Writings, as if to say: they are not written for us, and it is not incumbent upon the present generation to keep them.[25]

[13]   As for the true practitioners, in ancient times and now and until the end of time, *the words of the Lord are pure, like silver refined and purified seventy times*,[26] and his *commandments are* bright and *delightful for them more than gold* and precious stones, and they find them *sweeter than honey and combs, and keep them. And when they keep them, they receive great recompense.*[27]

[14]   Hail in the Lord, Lord Father, and pray for us sinners,[28] and we greatly bow to your holiness.

---

25. Cf. above, *Predanie* 4; *Ustav* 2.44.
26. Ps 11:7/12:6.
27. Ps 18:9, 11–12/19:8, 10-11.
28. Dionisii Zvenigorodskii's disciple Anufrii's Volokolamsk MS adds: *you and the brothers with you.*

A Little Epistle from That Same Elder to A Brother from an Eastern Country[1] Who Requested Profit for the Soul.

This, Lord, do we opine: that a profitable rule for you is to nourish yourself in physical activities, *gaging by power*,[2] but not above measure, and to meditate upon the Divine Writings, and to instruct yourself in handicrafts,[3] and to love stillness. And when, God willing, we behold each other, then the conversation will be more extensive on everything for everything.

---

1. Seen by Arkhangel'skii (*Nil Sorskii i Vassian Patrikeev*, 56) and much subsequent scholarship as Kassian of Mangup, a view disputed by Prokhorov, 'Poslaniia', 128–130; PNSIK, 215–216; in this author's view, possibly Dionisii Zvenigorodskii: see above, II. 'The Ardent Ascetic', note 60.

2. Cf. above, *Predanie* 35, 37, *Ustav* 2.23, 4.8, 5.1.9, 5.2.42.

3. Cf. above, *To Vassian* 7.

THE SOBORNIK
(HAGIOGRAPHIC CODICES)
APOLOGIAI

Foreword[1]

[1]   By God's *grace*[2] *and the most pure Mother of God's aid*,[3] I have transcribed the lives of the holy, saintly Fathers. *I have written* from various manuscripts, striving to find the correct ones. And I found in those manuscripts much uncorrected, and as much as was possible for *my meager knowledge*,[4] I *corrected*[5] them. And what was impossible, I left be, so that someone having more knowledge than we correct the uncorrected and fill in the lacunae.

[2]   As *I have written something*,[6] *and if anything be found in these not* in accord with genuine knowledge,[7] and *I beg forgiveness*[8] for

---

1. The text translated here is from SNS 2 (Sept–Dec), which starts the liturgical year. In the *Forewords of* SNS 1 (May–July) and SNS 3 (January–May) the last two sentences here are reversed. Arguments can be made for the primacy of either version.
2. Cf. Nikon, *Taktikon*, Fwd., 7.
3. Cf. above, *Predanie* 1 (and Nikon, *Taktikon*, Fwd., 1).
4. Cf. above, *Ustav* 11.19; Nikon, *Taktikon* 2:19v.
5. Cf. Nikon, *Taktikon*, Fwd., 7.
6. Cf. *Predanie* 30, *To Gurii* 1, *To Vassian* 15, *Predanie* 30, Nikon, *Taktikon* 2:19-19v.
7. *razumъ istnny*: alt. transl.: *genuine reason, knowledge of the truth*.
8. Cf. above, *Ustav* 11.19, *Testament* 3.

this. And if anyone transcribes or reads these, do not transcribe or read as such, but write and speak the truth, which is *pleasing to God and profitable for the soul,*[9] because I, a sinner, so desire. And not only what I have written here, but that which I have written and said elsewhere. *And if something be found in these not pleasing to God and not profitable for the*[10] *soul, due to my lack of knowledge and ignorance,*[11] concerning this I pray, that one not so act, but *do something better, goodly-pleasing to God and profitable for the soul.*[12]

[3]   And I[13] *rejoice in this*[14] and *thus with the grace of God I present these, taking away the cause for those seeking a cause for the harm of a soul.*[15] *I pray*[16] that those who read these and those who listen to the profit of what is read, that for the sake of the Lord they *pray for me,* so *that I* too be granted *mercy* by God,[17] because I have toiled no little amount in these things.[18]

[4]   As I reckon for the sake of the *commandment of love* of God and *neighbor,*[19] let us, attending to the *lives of* these wondrous *Fathers,*[20] be *emulators*[21] of their activity, so that with them we inherit eternal life.[22] This is true love of one's neighbor, to *elevate ones's conscience*[23] to love of God and to *effect* his *commandments*[24] according to his true Divine Writings, and as much as possible[25]

---

9. Cf. above, note 6.
10. *our* in *Ustav* 11.19.
11. Cf. above, *Ustav* 11.19; Nikon, *Taktikon,* Fwd., 7; here also above, *To Gurii* 16.
12. For [2], cf. above, *Predanie* 30, and *To German,* 4.
13. *we* in *Ustav* 11.19.
14. Cf. here also Nikon, *Taktikon,* Fwd., 2.
15. From Nikon, *Taktikon,* Fwd. 7.
16. *To Gurii* 19.
17. Closer to Nikon, *Taktikon,* Fwd. 7; cf. *Ustav* 11.19: *that I obtain mercy before the Lord.*
18. [2–3] partially related to *Ustav* 11.19.
19. Cf. above, *Ustav* 4.10; also Lv 19:8, Dt 6:5, Mt 22:37-39, *et al.*
20. Cf. above, *Ustav,* Fwd. 19.
21. Here, cf. above, *To Gurii* 17.
22. SNS 1 and 3, *Foreword,* the order of the last two sentences is reversed.
23. Cf. above, *Predanie* 1.
24. Cf. above, Ustav 10.2; To German 6.
25. *as much as possible* omitted in SNS I.

live by *the life* and teaching *of the holy Fathers*,[26] and thus be saved.[27] For if I am *sinful* and indifferent and *have done nothing good*,[28] yet I greatly desire the salvation of my neighbors.[29]

Postscript[30]

[1]   I have *angered* the all so good *God*[31] with my evil *deeds and words and thoughts*,[32] and I have not acquired *compunction* and *tears*, so that I *mourn* and *cleanse* my *filthy sins*.[33] On this account, having gathered, I have written down the words and feats and sufferings for the indictment of my soul, since *I have not done* any of these *good* things,[34] so that in the recollection of these I elevate my *darkened intellect*[35] from the darkness of passions and attain the *fruit of repentance*.[36]

[2]   *I have written from various manuscripts,* and I found dissonance in their *execution*.[37] *And as much as was possible, in accord with genuine knowledge,* I have written down. *And what is not* readily knowable,[38] this with simplicity of speech I have placed within knowledge,[39] so that all who read shall have knowledge and attain *profit.*

---

26. Cf. above, *Predanie*, Title; *To German* 8.
27. SNS 1 var.: *save.*
28. Cf. above, *Predanie* 1, *Ustav,* Fwd. 17; *To* Vassian, 1, To *Gurii* 19.
29. SNS 1 var.: *friends (iskrenimъ).*
30. Only found in Gurii Tushin's two extant SNS volumes.
31. Cf. above, *Ustav* 7.24.
32. Cf. above, *Ustav* 8.3, 24.
33. Cf. above, *Ustav* 7.15, 19.
34. Cf. above, *Predanie* 1, *Sobornik, Forew.* 4, and below, *Testament* 3.
35. Perhaps inspired by Symeon NT; cf. above, *Ustav* 8.18.
36. Cf. above, *Ustav* 8.22.
37. *ispravlenie*: literally, *correction,* and hence referring to the *uncorrected (neispravlenaia)* of *Sobornik, Forew.* 1.
38. *neudobьrazumna*: alt. transl.: *unintelligible.*
39. *na razumъ polagakh*: i.e., *have made intelligible.*

[3] And if I have not corrected something *due to* infirmity *and lack of knowledge*,[40] I beg and beseech those gaining profit from these writings to remember my wretchedness in their *prayers, so that I obtain mercy before* the Lord *God*.[41]

αμαρτολο[42] Νηλ S[43] ασυνετος[44]

---

40. *nerazumia* (gn. sg.), the fifth use the *razum-* lexeme in a few lines.

41. [2–3] partially adapted from *Sobornik, Forew.* 1–3.

42. As in KB 23/1262; αμαρτολος in KB 141/1218, Gurii's other extant SNS volume.

43. Has a rounded circumflex on top and, as seen by Prokhorov (PNSIK, 266), is almost assuredly a ligature for καὶ = *and*.

44. *Sinful and Witless Nil:* should read: Ἁμαρτωλός . . . ἀσύνετος; this is Gurii's presumed copying of Nil's Greek, photo-reproduced in Prokhorov, 'Avtografy', p. 39/PSNIK 47. The script is somewhat slavicized (especially the three-legged τ, and the η, λ, and final ς), yet uses a ligature for ετ or misspells it as ατ.

THE TESTAMENT

[1]   In the name of the Father, and of the Son, and of the Holy Spirit, I make my testament[1] to my closest lords and brothers, who are of my ethos.[2]

[2]   I beg you, cast my body in the desert,[3] so that beasts and birds consume it, since it has sinned greatly before God and is not worth a burial. If you do not *do* this, then, digging a pit in the place where we live, *bury* me in total dishonor.[4] *Fear* the word which Arsenius the Great testated to his *disciples, saying: I shall stand with you at judgment,*[5] if you give my body to anyone; my utmost exertion *was* to remain unfit for any honors and glory of this age, as *during my lifetime,* so after my death.[6]

[3]   *I beg* everyone *to pray for my sinful* soul, and *I beg forgiveness* from everyone—and from me forgiveness, that *God* may *forgive* everyone.[7]

---

1. Cf. the testaments of Kirill of Belozero and Iosif: ASEI 2.314; MRIV Int. 1-2.
2. Slightly reworded from *Predanie* 1.
3. Maybe adapted from Arsenius's *place on the mountain.*
4. Cf. Athanasius Alex., *Life of Anthony,* SNS 3:231; PG 26:972AB.
5. *Christ's judgment* in the original.
6. Freely adapted from *Life of Arsenius,* SNS 3:455 (270v); *Sayings,* Arsenius 40:15; PG 65:105BC; *Zhitie . . . Arsenii,* 32. Romanenko, after Lilienfeld, notes a similar motif in the testament ascribed to Ephrem of Syria, but no indication that Nil knew of it: NSTRM, 186. Nil's redaction of the *Life of Euthymius,* though, mentions Arsenius's 'holy tomb' as 'testimony down to today' of his 'power over filthy spirits': SNS 3:272-273; Cyril/*Kirill,* 21; Cyril Scythop., *Lives* 30—not in the Greek original: Cotelier 2:248B; Acta SS 2:675.
7. *Bogъ da prostitъ* is the formula of forgiving in God's name; cf. above, Ustav 11.19, *Sobornik, Postscr.* 1.

[4] The large cross having a stone of the Lord's passions,[8] as well as the booklets I have written—they are for my lords and brothers, who undertake to endure in this place. And if one would endeavor to perform the sanctified service for me to the 40th day,[9] for this *I greatly bow my head*.[10]

[5] The little John of Damascus booklets,[11] the Euchologion,[12] the Irmologion[13] —also here; the Psalter in octavo[14] in Ignatii's script[15] —to Kirillov Monastery;[16] the other books and objects from Kirillov Monastery, that they gave me out of love for God, whose so ever something may be, give this back to him, or to the poor; or if from some monastery or any lover-of-Christ[17] whomsoever, give it back, to the named person.

---

8. *kamenь* (nm. sg.) *strastei Gospodnikhъ* (gn. pl.): possibly a stone carving of the passion of Christ, or maybe a relic-stone from Jerusalem, placed on a large wooden crucifix.

9. That is, the full forty-day requiem process.

10. *chelomъ bьiu* (1st sg. prs.) = literally and etymologically from Chinese via the Mongols: *kow-tow* = *strike the forehead;* cf., below, *To German* 11.

11. See above, *Ustav* 7.13-14, 16-18, for Nil's use of such works.

12. *potrebnikъ* = *trĕbnikъ/trebnikъ* = prayer-book: breviary or complete *euchologion*; cf. Nikol'skii (German Podol'nyi), *Opisanie* A.8:107.

13. *irmoloi* = *irmologion/eirmologion* (from εἱρμός = the initial *troparion* of an *ode*) = hymnal with musical notation; cf. Nikol'skii (German) *Opisanie* A.12:185-189, 195; also Hannick, *Das altslavische Hirmologion*, 5-295.

14. German's Kirillov catalogue listed three such Psalters: Nikol'skii (German) *Opisanie* A.11:173-175.

15. Perhaps Ignatii Matfeev, the contemporary scribe of several miscellanies in quarto (Nikol'skii, *Opisanie* A.8:108-110), and, likely, the longstanding Kirllov leading elder and then hegumen, 1471–1475.

16. Alt. trans: *The little John of Damascus booklets, the Euchologion, the Irmologion also here, the Psalter in octavo in Ignatii's script—to Kirillov Monastery.*

17. *khristoliubьtsь* = a charitable layperson.

APPENDICES

Appendix I

THE NIL POLEV / NIL SORSKY CODEX SCETE TYPIKON[1]

The Tradition by the Typikon[2] for Monks Residing in the Outer Region,[3] that is, for Scetites,[4] on Cell Watchfulness,[5] the Quotidian Chanting, Which We Have Received from Our Fathers.

[1] It is proper to know of what we discover about the holy Fathers, who reside in the outer region, that is, in hermitages, in scetes, or in any place removed from the world on account of love of God. And this we find in the holy Writings, that such do not keep for themselves the typikon according to the synodal,[6] that is

---

1. Eparkh. 349:1-8v (Dionisii Zvenigorodskii's Eparkh. 351:173-180v version stops at the same place, without the rule for illiterate monks.). My [1–3] comprise the first, introductory division according to Beliakova ('Ustav pustyna Nila Sorskogo', 'Skitskii Ustav i ego zhachenie') and Gromilund ('Mezhdu obshel'nichestvom i obshchezhietiiem'), [4–18] the second, and [19–33] the third. According to Beliakova, this version is a combination of the first and 'Typikon' redactions of the Scete Typikon. It contains a few preferred or interesting variants from KB XII, published by Prokhorov, *Entsiklopediia*.
2. *predanie ustavomъ*.
3. *vněshněi straně* (prp.): in the context of its composition and use in the Balkans, this term most likely signifies the outskirts of a single monastery or monastery cluster, if not an isolated scete/hermitage.
4. alt. transl.: *lavriotes*.
5. that is, *watchfulness practiced in the cell*.
6. *sъbornomu* (dt. sg.): alt. transl., *katholikon*, that is, a, major church (often imprecisely translated as *cathedral*), with complete, daily services.

to say, church tradition. For the Law does not seek these, as has been stated in the Divine Writings. Especially the great apostle Paul bears witness to this, saying: 'Those who are of Christ have crucified the flesh with passions and lusts;[7] upon such there is no law',[8] and other things said by the apostle Paul about them.

[2] Moreover, the holy Fathers in the *Patericon*[9] say this: that in the outer region reside monks for whom such synodal chants are not fit, that is, Hours, canons,[10] troparia,[11] 'sessions',[12] prokeimena,[13] and so forth, that are passed down for the church, but only labor which is in God and watchfulness of intellect. Thus all of them in their cells retain watchfulness and care for themselves, that is, for their rule. Some of them established the rule of their typikon, others by the tradition and regulation of their fathers kept their typikon themselves, and, as much as they were able to include, each one struggled over his salvation according to his power.

[3] Moreover, there are many different tales about them, of which we are unworthy, of their lives and existence. But as physically infirm, therefore according to our infirmity we have received these from our father[14] to maintain in our existence, which we have set down here for those who desire and love them.[15]

[4] Concerning all-night vigils. Let it be known concerning this, that we have it so established: to do the all-night twice a week, all weeks on Sunday and Wednesday evenings.

---

7. Gal 5:24.
8. Gal 5:23.
9. *Otechestvo*: possibly the author's commentary rather than a citation from an actual patericon: no precise source identified.
10. Ritual hymns usually comprised of eight odes, numbered 1, 3, 4 . . . 9.
11. Brief hymns.
12. *sědělny* (nm./acc. pl.) = καθίσματα, (literally, *sittings, sessions*): these are divisions of the entire Psalter into twenty sets for weekly reading, during which the monks could sit—hence the name; the Slavs also used the Greek term in modified form. Each kathisma is divided into three parts. See below, note 23, also [16].
13. Special Psalter verses for festival days.
14. Perhaps Gregory the Sinaite: see above, I. 'The Northern Beacon', text to note 16.
15. Cf. above, *Predanie* 10.

[5] Concerning the Holy Forty.[16] And during a week when the festival of the Lord or any of the great saints occurs, for whom a vigilia[17] takes place, then we shall set aside the Wednesday vigil and do them on Sunday and the festival, so that we only perform two vigiliae each week, as stated earlier. This is what we have learned from our father, and we enjoin it. But as much as one may include, let him include.

The Beginning of the Exposition

[6] On the afore-mentioned festivals, when the all-night vigils occur, if our residence is near a monastery, then all will gather for the chant at the 9th Hour[18] on the eve of the festival, and thus be present in the church for the all-night vigil, completely following the church typikon, to the completion of the divine liturgy on the day of the festival. And having thus sanctified ourselves in the church according to custom, and having received forgiveness, we go with thanksgiving each to his own cell. And we always do thus, wherever there is a monastery and a church congregation, according to what has been said.

[7] If we are far, where it is impossible to come to church for vigils, and where there is something besides the community chant, which takes place in the church, then we have established this. At the time of the 9th Hour on the eve of the festival, we neighboring brothers all congregate together, where there is a community cell,[19] or a church, if there is one, and then we commence to chant the 9th Hour or Vespers according to the day it happens to be. And thus we chant Vespers, by custom. At the end is the troparion for the festival or the customary one and dismissal.

---

16. Only in Eparkh. 349 (not in Beliakova's or Prokorov's printed versions): '*O svitchetvertisia*': most likely a liturgical abbreviation.
17. *agripina* = ἀγρυπνία.
18. See *Ustav* 5.1.16.
19. *sъbornaia kelia*.

[8] If there is no fast, we shall set a table, we shall partake of a little food. He who wishes to abstain on account of the vigil, is at liberty not to eat at all, if he chooses. And after our rising from the table, we are to pass the time in spiritual discourse or reading holy books, or if someone requires again to have some sleep before the time of the chant, that is before the twilight, before the 1st hour of night or the second, according to the season—completely at the discretion of the elder.

[9] So then we commence the all-night chant, and we do the beginning: the customary verse, the Trisagion,[20] after 'Our Father', 12 'Lord, have mercy',[21] 3 'Come, let us venerate',[22] then three kathismas[23] in order, then the canon of the prayer service to the Mother of God in the 8th tone,[24] 'Distressed by many temptations'[25] or another, whatever you desire, on which we cense after the 8th ode. After the completion of this, 'It is worthy'.[26] and 'More honorable than the Cherubim'.[27]

[10] Then after these we all sit down, keeping silence and attention within ourselves, until the leader directs to read. And then, if someone needs to inquire about the readings from the Divine Writings, let him inquire. Others after the completion of the readings shall confess their thoughts,[28] whatever may have

---

20. Cf. above, *Ustav* 2.22.

21. *Gospodi/Hospodi pomilui* = *Kyrie eleison*.

22. This could be part of communion preparation in the Liturgy of either Basil the Great or John Chrysostom, or it could be the three exclamations in the Hours or Vespers services: *O come, let us worship and bow down before our king and God; O come, . . . Christ, our king and God; O come, Christ himself, our king and God.*

23. каθизмы (*kafizmy*—nm./acc. pl.): see above, note 12.

24. *glasъ* (literally, voice) = ἦχος; alt. technical transl.: *mode*. Orthodox music theory recognized and classified eight tones, and the hymnographers composed numerous hymns to the Theotokos, as in Eparkh. 76:1-225.

25. Alt. trans: *Enveloped by many temptations/dangers*; Var. KB XII: *temptations/dangers* omitted; this commences a standard supplicatory canon to the Theotokos.

26. Alt. transl.: *meet*; see below, *Predanie Addenda* 47, note 16.

27. These two lines signify a common brief hymn to the Theotokos/Mother of God, as in Eparkh. 212:129.

28. *pomyshleniia* (nm./acc. pl.); alt. transl.: *urges* (= *pomysli*).

happened to anyone, that is to say, if he was seized with hatred against a brother or an evil recollection, or if someone is controlled by any sort of passion. Such will come before the iconostasis and first make 3 bows to the holy icons with humility. Then, having turned to the father and the brothers, say a verse and fall on his face in the their midst, confessing his evils, by which he is controlled, begging forgiveness and prayer from the father and brothers—that they pray for him to be delivered from such passions with prayers. And thus, after confession and chastisement,[29] by which he has obtained forgiveness from the father, having stood up, he goes back to his place. We pass two or three hours in such rectification in God, according to the season.

[11] And then we stand, saying, 'Lord, have mercy', thrice, 'Glory and now', and we sing the second part[30] of the 3rd Kathisma[31] in order. After their completion, the Jesus Canon or whatever you wish. And we read according to what has been said before about everything, and then 'Lord, have mercy' thrice, and 'Glory, and now', as we sing the 3rd part of Kathisma Three in order. And after their completion, if it is a festival day, we sing the sticheron on the litany. If it is Sunday, we sing the Canon of the Holy Trinity,[32] during which we cense. Then the Trinity Refrain by tone in 6 verses; then the Trisagion with the usual ones. If a priest is present, he says the prayers of the litany and the dismissal, and, as much as is needed, we proceed according to the season.

[12] And then we commence singing the usual Matins: we say the Trisagion and the tropariia 'Save, O Lord, Your People',[33] and also the other 6 psalms,[34] 'God Lord', the Resurrection or festival troparii, then the 17th Kathisma, 'Blessed are the Undefiled',[35] and then the

---

29. *nakazanie;* alt. transl.: *instruction.*
30. *statie.*
31. The 3rd Kathisma contains, as its three parts, Ps 17, 18-20, 21-23/18, 19-21, 22-24.
32. See Eparkh. 292:168-175v.
33. Modern trans: *O Lord, save thy people:* Jer 31:7; cf. Ps 27:9/28:9.
34. See below [13] and note 44.
35. Ps 118/119, the entire 17th Kathisma.

Resurrection troparia, 'The Assembly of Angels[36] Marveled',[37] If it is a festival, after saying 'God Lord', then the 'Polyeleos',[38] 'Praise the name of the Lord',[39] and then the hypakoi[40] or a 'session', and then a *Stepenna*,[41] and the Gospel, and the canon, and so forth, all on order down to the first Hour, and then dismissal.

[13] Let it also be known concerning this, that the Resurrection or festival 'sessions'—we say them by each kathisma part at our sitting or at the canon after the third ode, and wherever you wish, but we do not omit them. This is what we do on a Sunday or a festival of the Lord. If it be another day, other than those mentioned, after our completion of the 10th Kathisma,[42] that is to say, the third part, as was indicated earlier, we codify[43] the 6 Psalms[44] and everything else, but we are watchful toward the reading and vigils, by the instructions. Then, having chanted through the night to dawn, we sing Psalm 50, 'Be merciful, God',[45] then complete whatever canon you choose, and with it other things down to the 1st Hour. and then dismissal.

[14] And we customarily have half of the Psalter to chant with speaking,[46] since we busy ourselves with spiritual discourses, that is, to question the father about the Divine Writings, and especially about our own passions and other corrections that occur in God, as previously said.

---

36. Heb 12:22.

37. Maybe from the 8th Kontakion of the Akathistos Hymn: Var KB XII: *marvels* omitted.

38. *polieleo* = πολυέλεος: *all-merciful*: Ps.135/136.

39. Ps. 134:1/135:1.

40. *ipakoi* = ὑπακοή: the troparion at the end of the third ode of a given canon.

41. A Sunday or chanted Matin verse composed by John of Damascus, as in his *Oktoichos Hymns*, Eparkh. 212:104-123.

42. Ps 70–71, 72–73, 74–76/71–72, 73–74, 75–77.

43. *ustavliaemъ*; Var. KB XII (and preferred): *ostavliaemъ* = omit.

44. Var. KB XII and also KB XV (Beliakova, 'Slavianskaia redaktsiia', 67): *the Hexapsalmos* (*eksapsalmy*, written as εξαψαλμы = ἐξάψαλμος): Ps 3, 37, 63, 87, 102, 142 /3, 36, 62, 86, 101, 141.

45. Ps 50:3/51:1.

46. *sъ rechenymii*: alt. transl.: with the above-mentioned.

[15]   But for these: where many brothers congregate, where it is possible, it shall be like this, as indicated: as it has been established, so it shall be.

[16]   And where it is impossible, because there be only 2 or 3, however many there be, only where the aforementioned chants be not found, or the spiritual discourses, as has been established, these shall pass the night with the Psalter and so forth, as much as possible, each shall include according to his power: chant half the Psalter as was said. If someone needs to sing the entire Psalter, for the sake of watchfulness, this we have goodly blessed, and such a one shall do the Psalter in 4 parts, 5 kathismas per part.

[17]   And again, if someone is unable to sing, and it happens to such a one to be somewhere by necessity[47] without a church, or without brothers able to sing, then he shall sing the Trisagion and the prayer, holding the prayer rope in his hand—as has been said above, each according his strength.[48] Moreover, such a one shall watchfully engage in manual work in his cell, if needed.

[18]   Everything having been said, this must be effected in every deed: pass the night only in vigils and watchfulness that is in God, and these are to be [49]according to our strength, as much as is possible to include, include.

Watchfulness for Other Days of the Daily Typikon

[19]   On the days other than the established festivals, we have received this tradition by the typikon, which is from the beginning of the month of September[50] down to April, that is, to Holy Easter, quotidianly, day and night, to chant half the Psalter, and 600 or 1000 prayers,[51] and 300 or 600 bows, and, from the community

---

47. *po nuzhi*: Var. KB XII: (defective): *ponezhe* = because.
48. *each according to his strength* not in KB XII.
49. Nil Sorskii's own handwriting commences here on Eparkh. 349, p. 6 and continues through the *Predanie,* pp. 9–14v, and then the first page of the appended articles: Prokhorov, PNSIK, 72, 81, and below, Appendix II.47.
50. The start of the Orthodox calendar year.
51. Probably Jesus Prayers.

chant, all the Hours, and communion chant, Vespers, Compline, the Midnight Office, with the kathismas in the order one chooses.

[20] And if we do not wish to chant the Midnight Office, we are then at the beginning of the Matins chant, after the saying of the start of the verse and the 'Trisagion' with the usual things, then 'Come Let Us Worship', and the kathismas, which customarily we have in order, and whatever shall have remained of them from the Vespers chant. And we shall complete half the Psalter with the readings as is the custom. Then, as the time comes, we chant Psalm 50 and whatever canon we wish. and the other usual things, that is, the daily festive, 'Praise the Lord from the Heavens',[52] 'Glory in the highest to God',[53] and then, in verse, the 'Trisagion', the 1st Hour, and dismissal, and the other Hours, which we have recollected—we who so choose shall complete each at its own time, by the tradition, every day.

[21] If someone does not desire to chant the Hours daily, then he should never miss them on Tuesday, Thursday, Saturday, Sunday, and we especially chant them daily on holy fasts. He who chooses them, and the entire Psalter is possible for him, then during Great Fast,[54] if he wishes, chant every day, except Saturday and Sunday. If not, then half the Psalter and do not omit any of the Hours, only if one is infirm. And such a one shall do what he can do according to his strength.

[22] On other days, besides those mentioned on the Great Fast, when someone chooses, as we said, to chant the Hours in their place, that is, on Monday, on Wednesday, on Friday, then such a one shall at the time of the 9th hour sing one or two kathismas in order, and with them the communion chant, and then eat bread as is customary.

[23] And without any great need, no one shall partake of any food, only as it has been said: at the 9th hour first chant, then eat.

---

52. Ps 148:1.
53. Lk 2:4: var KB XII: *to God* omitted.
54. М-цу (*40-tsu* - acc. sg.), that is, the Easter Lent: see above, [5].

Moreover, for the infirm, there is no law, but as much as one can include, include.

[24] Let it be known of this, that when we chant the entire Psalter to the end, then we read in order the Mosaic odes,[55] when we may desire, in place of the canon, only do not omit these after the completion of the Psalter.

[25] And again, whenever occurs the community chant, that is, the Psalter, the Hours and so forth, if it is possible for him, these shall always be done with bows. And besides those spoken of in the typikon and traditions,[56] only on the indicated festivals, then there will not be bending of the knees, as earlier in has been established in the Divine Canons for everything.

[26] All of the aforesaid regulations are for those who are able and read the holy Writings. What was said is necessary for everyone as much as is possible.

[27] Moreover, there are those in the toils of obedience, and for such there be no law, because they are always exercising in the cutting off of their wills within the wills of their fathers. Therefore they are praised above all.[57] And they are not slothful in doing as much as they can, but they do everything with submissiveness, and as much of what has been said they can include, they include.

[28] If one is at liberty, that is, without obedience, and still strong, with the season and place helping him, such a one shall not omit any of the aforesaid, except for bodily infirmity and permitted needs that occur, but especially force himself to do, if possible, 600 or 1000 bows, and similarly up to 1000 and 500 or 2000 prayers—let him force himself up to these.

---

55. Ex 15:1-19 and Dt 32:1-43 as canticles.
56. *predania;* var. KB XII: *propovědania* = *preaching, prophesy.*
57. Cf. MRIV 6.19, 29–30, for examples of further convergence the ideals of Iosif and and those of Nil, expressed here in the *Scete Typikon.*

[29] If[58] someone chooses more, not only with other labors that are in God—as much as one can include, include.

[30] Moreover, according to the aforesaid exposition for wintertime, this typikon is to be effected in summertime, that is, from Holy Easter, in the Sunday of the Apostle Thomas[59] down to the beginning of the month of September.

[31] We have this regulation due to the shortening of the night and day service. To chant 7 kathismas and the Hours, established earlier, and as many prayers as you wish from what has been established above, 1000 or 600: as many as one choose, let him do. Do not do bows during the Holy Pentecost.[60] During the Feast of the Holy Apostles,[61] recommence doing them, according to custom: in the cell 300 plus as many as one can and chooses. Moreover, if it happens that one of us be at the church with the brothers at the community chant, to come into the church, then he will chant the 7 kathismas in the cell, and bows and prayers as indicated above in the beginning, as many as one chooses to do, let him do. And again, no one is to go below all of these last things that have been established, except for physical infirmity or needs that arise at times.

[32] And this has been said concerning chants and bows. We chant at the proper time, at appointed hours, that it be completed each according to one's strength, as it has been said about this.

[33] And let there be other times for watchfulness, besides the established chants, prayers with bows. Then everyone shall be watchful with reading and manual work in his cell.[62] As much as one can by this, force yourself away from filthy urges, untimely exiting from the cell, and irrational idleness. Sitting in the cell, everyone shall guard himself as much as is possible by means of

---

58. In cinnabar.
59. The first Sunday after Easter.
60. Н-ци (*50-tsi* - prp. sg.): the entire fifty-day period, here.
61. The second Monday after Pentecost.
62. See above, Part II, opening citation to 'The Unexpected Bedfellow'.

the aforesaid, each confirming himself according to his power, only do not be lazy.

And this is what concerns the literate up to here.[63]

---

63. In fuller versions of the *Scete Typikon*, as in the versions printed by Prokhorov and Beliakova, provisions for the illiterate monks follow. In Eparkh. 349, Nil's *Predanie* with *addenda*, and then the *Ustav*, follow.

Appendix II

THE NIL POLEV / NIL SORSKY CODEX ADDENDA TO NIL SORSKY'S PREDANIE[1]

[43] Necessary items for sanctifying a church. Pillar decorations; two sheets of fine cotton; wax; incense; clean white sand; white fur tree gum; strong and thin rope; a high altar;[2] Greek soap with tree oil; wine; myrrh, due to scarcity mixed with tree oil; August holy water[3] with fragrant herbs; Greek sponges—four or three or two—or white cloths; on the front side of each sheet, make three crosses, on the front of each side—four nails.

[44] *The Sixth Council, Fifty-Eighth Rule. No ascetic shall administer the divine mysteries to himself, if a bishop, presbyter or deacon is present. If someone so dare as to act beyond what is commanded, he shall be excommunicated for a week. From this the foolish shall be instructed.*[4]

---

1. Eparkh. 349:15-16v. This text follows Nil's Sorsky's *Predanie*, precedes his *Ustav*, and commences in his own hand. The enumeration of paragraphs treats the text as a continuation of his *Predanie*.

2. *anaprestol*.

3. Water blessed on 1 August (in commemoration of the Holy Cross) was used, among other things, to re-sanctify a church when a dog entered it: Sreznevskii 1:5.

4. NPNF-II-Trullo 58 (last sentence adapted).

270

[45] From the great Saint Basil: *It is superfluous to demonstrate that anyone who so needs, absent a priest, shall take communion from his own hand, because by old custom and the very nature of things this is proven. All monastics in hermitages, where there be no priest, themselves keeping the communion, communicate. In Alexandria and Egypt commoners in multitudes take communion each in his own home. And when one wishes, he communicates himself, the priest having once enacted and administered it. Having accepted this, he communicates himself as he would have to take communion from a priest. For in a church the priest gives a part, and the one who takes it holds it with full authority. And so he carries it to his mouth with his hands. And it is the same in power, whether one takes one part from the priest or many parts together.*[5]

[46] And again the Lord says: 'He who eats my body and drinks my blood dwells in me and I in him'.[6]

[47] Saint Luke of Steiros asked the Metropolitan of Corinth, saying: 'Sweet Saint: I have a need to partake of the divine mysteries according to the tradition of the holy Church, and the distance of the path[7] from a church is great. I beseech you: forgive me that I partake by myself'. And he answered well: 'It is not well if one does not dispose well. Ask the local hierarch or your confessor for holy communion, and accept it with fear and trembling, and with full reverence. And when you wish to take communion, dress up a clean paten[8] and place it before holy icons and spread a smooth cloth above it, and thus place the sacred elements with the breadplate[9] and the communion spoon,[10] because the Holy, Holy Lamb is united with the life-creating blood by the priest on the holy altar. Therefore they are called holy. And having finished the canon, that is, the prostrations and the prayers of holy communion, light a candle, and having censed, kiss the holy icons and take leave and

---

5. Basil, Letter 93; PG 32:484B-485B.

6. Jn 6:56: *He . . . him* in the original.

7. Nil Sorsky's hand writing ends here (p. 15v), and Nil Polev's commences and finishes (pp. 16-16v).

8. *tschitsa/dshchitsa*: special communion tray: note the tongue-twister: *ukrasi tshchitsu chistu*.

9. *artafor* = ἀρτοφόρον, -ιον = *panarium* = communion plate; alt. transl.: *pyx*.

10. *lavida* = λαβίς.

say: "I believe in one God the Father,"[11] and "I believe in His mysteries,"[12] and then prostrate and take with your hand and partake of the divine mysteries and say thrice: 'Amen, Amen, Amen.'"[13] And take the cup with wine and water thrice and let that chalice be for the preservation of this, and likewise the above-mentioned patin. And having performed for yourself this ceremony,[14] say "It is worthy . . ." and "More honorable than the cherubim . . . ."[15] And thus do the verse and dismissal'.[16]

[48] And this is given to all who reside in hermitages, but only to the unerring and attested, who have love with all, and patience and humility.[17]

11. This may stand for the entire Nicene Creed.
12. This formula is not in the standard liturgies.
13. In the Liturgies of Sts Basil and John Chrysostom, this is said by the deacon after the consecration of the sacred elements and in unison by all the communicating congregation.
14. *akolufia* (ἀκολουθία).
15. These are two prayers to the Mother of God and follow slightly after the triple *Amen* in the Liturgy of Saint John Chrysostom.
16. Exact Slavic source extract noted in a 15th c. miscellany by Sreznevskii 1:28; greatly adapted from the original: *The Life and Miracles of Saint Luke of Steiris* (with Greek text: transl. and ed., C. L. Connor and W. R. Connor; Brookline: Hellenic College, 1994), 42.30–52:62-65.
17. The IRI type of *Ustav* follows, starting with Fwd 19–20, 1–18, and then the eleven discourses, as translated above.

Appendix III

THE ZAVĚT OF INNOKENTII OKHLIABININ

The Testament of Innokentii Okhliabinin

[1] Lo, I, the poor monk Innokentii, have written this testament.

[2] If God commands someone to live in this hermitage, I beseech you first of all to do this for the sake of the Lord: remember me, a sinner, in your prayers, and I greatly supplicate you, our fathers and brothers.

[3] And what I testate to you, that between you be no *fights* or *quarrels*,[1] but I beseech that spiritual peace in Christ be among you.

[4] And do *not accept any young or beardless monks*[2] or tonsure any such here.

This translation follows Prokhorov's publication from KB 25/1102, PNSIK, 319–322, with one variant noted from Arkhangel'skii's earlier publication from MDA (Moscow Seminary) 186, in *Nil Sorskii, Prilozhenie* III.14–16. Together they note seven copies (also Arkhangel'skii, 45, note 116), so it would have been authoritative within the northern hermitages.

1. Cf. above, *Ustav* 11.18.
2. Cf. John Tzimiskes, *Typikon* 16, BMFD, 238, and derivative Athonite regulations referenced, 243.

[5] And *do not retain any young*, beardless laymen *in service*.³

[6] And the *female* sex is in no way to *enter our* hermitage, and *no animals* of the *female* sex are to be among *us*.⁴

[7] A *drunkenness*-inducing *drink is completely improper for us* to have.⁵

[8] And concerning how to live in our hermitage—concerning prayer and chanting, how to nourish ourselves, and when it is proper to exit for necessities at a permitted time, and concerning manual work and other things—these are all arranged in the composition of our lord and my teacher, the elder Nil, in the front of this book.⁶ Therefore I have traversed quickly⁷ and written briefly, because there you will find *everything pleasing to God*.⁸

[9] Concerning the church. If our brother monks, who live in our hermitage, begin to live pleasingly to God and preserve God's commandments and wish to erect a godly church, this shall be by God's good will and their volition. And if God goodly wills it, let the church be in the name of the great Saint John the Forerunner, the Baptizer of the Lord, the third discovery of his honorable head, which is on May 25. For this great John is the mentor to all monks and dwellers in hermitages.⁹

---

3. Cf. above, *Predanie* 42; *Ustav* 5.2.43.

4. Cf. above, *Predanie* 41.

5. Cf. above, *Predanie* 36; but the prohibition is close to the other rules, such as Iosif's, not to Nil's.

6. Literally, *in this book from the upper cover*, which closely matches the mid-16th c. KB 25/1102:3-11, with the *Predanie*: for the MS description, NSPU, xxv–xxxii, and Prokhorov, PNSIK 299; in another MS (RNB/GPB Pogod. 1363), the *Zavĕt* follows the *Predanie*: Arkhangel'skii,, 45, note 116. Cf. above, *Predanie* 15-16, 26-27, 35, 37-38; also understood, possibly, *Ustav* 5.2.9-26, and probably also *Scete Typikon*.

7. Literally, *flowed across*.

8. Cf. above, *Predanie* 30.

9. Perhaps in part a response to the alleged heretical attack on monasticism as not of Evangelical or Apostolic origin: AfED, 470, 476; *Prosvetitel'*, 405-406, and esp. 409; Iosif writes:'. . . the great John, prophet and Forerunner of the coming of our Lord Jesus Christ, established for all the principle and model/form/image (*obraz*) of virginity and the monastic life.'

[10] And concerning the foundation and *adornment of the church* is written above in the words of the discourses of the writing of the elder Nil, which is in this book.[10]

[11] Concerning cells. If any of our brother monks establishes a cell for himself in our hermitage, and then if he departs from this hermitage, he is not to sell or give these cells to anyone, nor shall anyone buy the cell from him, but the superior and the brothers living there shall control those cells. If that afore-mentioned brother returns to the hermitage, he shall have no control over those cells.

[12] If the superior, after counsel with the brothers wishes to sell surplus cells, they may sell. And then, if that brother departs from this hermitage, he who purchased the cells will not have the authority to sell or give these cells, as is written above, but the superior and brothers living there will control[11] those cells. Thus, if that brother returns to this hermitage, he likewise will not have control[12] over these cells.

[13] If among the brothers, one establishes many cells or often buys cells, both after departing or coming, they will have no control over these cells. If the superior and brothers choose to give a returning brother his former cell, that is their choice.

[14] And a brother who is transiting from this life in this hermitage is not to sell or give a cell to anyone. The present brother monks, who are living in this place, shall not trade in cells or exchange among themselves. But each lives in their cells.

[15] Concerning self-regulators.[13] If any brother monk in our hermitage does not wish to govern his existence by the divine commandments, and by the writing of our lord and my[14] teacher, the elder Nil, and by this, our writ, but wishes to conduct himself

---

10. Cf. above, *Predanie* 31–34.
11. *vladěiut* (3rd pl. prs. as fut.).
12. *vlasti* (neg-acc. sg.).
13. Cf. above, *Predanie* 6; *Ustav* 11.6; *To German* 7.
14. *my* omitted in Arkhangel'skii's publication (*Prilozhenie* III:14–16) from MDA (Moscow Seminary) No. 186.

with self-regulation and self-will, the superior and brothers shall admonish[15] him.[16] If, following admonition, he does not right himself, the superior and brothers shall eject him from the hermitage, like a weed from grain, without any fear,[17] by this our testament.

[16] If that brother comes to his senses and wishes to govern his existence according to God and the traditions of the holy Fathers and according to the writing of my lord and teacher, the elder Nil, and by this our testament, the superior and brothers shall accept him into this hermitage.

[17] I, Innokentii the monk, have written these, so that after my death such shall be done.[18]

15. *nakazhutъ* (3rd. pl.): alt. transl.: chastise, instruct.
16. Not exactly as *Predanie* 5-6.
17. Cf. MRIV 13.30-31, 14.2.
18. Cf. above, *Predanie* 28; also MRIV Int. 2.

Appendix IV
INDEX OF BIBLICAL CITATIONS

Gn 1:26	*Ustav* 5.6.78	Ps 11:7/12:6	*To German* 13
	To Gurii 8	Ps 15:8/16:8	*Ustav* 4.7
Gn 2:7, 15	*Ustav* 9.3-4	Ps 16:11 (LXX)	*Ustav* 5.2.34
Gn 3:6	*Ustav* 5.1.7		*To Gurii* 3
Gn 23:4	*Predanie* 1	Ps 18:9, 11-12/	
Ex 15:1-19	*Scete Typ.* 24	9:8, 10-11	*To German* 13
Ex 15:23-25	*Ustav* 8.16	Ps 27:9/28:9	*Scete Typ.* 12
Ex 17:5-6	*Ustav* 8.16	Ps 31:7 (LXX)	*Ustav* 5.2.34
Lv 19:18	*Ustav* 4.10		*To Gurii* 3
	Sbrnk Fwd. 4	Ps 34:1/35:1	*Ustav* 6.2, 3
Lv 25:21	*To Gurii* 18		*To Gurii* 3
Nm 3:3	*Ustav* 3.3	Ps 38:7/39:6	*Ustav* 7.17
Nm 20:17	*Ustav* 11.8	Ps 38:13/39:12	*Predanie* 1
Dt 5:32/5:29	*Ustav* 11.7		*Ustav* 7.17
Dt 6:5	*Sbrnk Fwd.* 4	Ps 38:14/39:13	*Ustav* 7.28
Dt 10:20	*Ustav* 2.78	Ps 45:8, 12/	
Dt 32:1-43	*Scete Typ.* 24	46: 7, 11	*Ustav* 4.3
Jos 15:17-19	*Ustav* 8.13	Ps 50:3/51:1	*Scete Typ.* 13
Ps 1:2	*Ustav* 6.6	Ps 48:3 (LXX)	*Ustav* 7.17
Ps 1:3	*Ustav* 10.13	Ps 48:7, 17-18/	
Ps 6:3/6:2	*Ustav* 5.2.39	49:6, 16-17	*Ustav* 7.17
	To Vassian 6	Ps 50:9/51:7	*Ustav* 8.16
	To Gurii 3	Ps 50:19/51:17	*Ustav* 8.6
Ps 6:8/6:9	*Ustav* 5.6.78	Ps 52:6 (LXX)	*Ustav* 5.7.83
	Ustav 6.6	Ps 69:2/70:1	*Ustav* 5.2.35
	To Gurii 8		*To Gurii* 3

Ps 88:9/89:9	Ustav 5.2.38	Mt 4:3	Ustav 1.11
	To Vassian 6	Mt 4:4, 7, 10	Ustav 5.6.78
Ps 90:5/91:5	To Vassian 11	Mt 4:10	To Gurii 8
Ps 93:9/94:9	Ustav 4.3	Mt 5:4	Ustav 8.27
Ps 101:4,12/		Mt 5:28	Ustav 5.2.29
102:3,11	To Vassian 3	Mt 5:40	Predanie 18
Ps 102:15/		Mt 5:42	Predanie 21
103:15	To Vassian 3	Mt 5:44	To Vassian 17
Ps 104:1 (LXX)	Ustav 1.14	Mt 5:45	Ustav 5.4.59
Ps 106:1/107:1	Ustav 1.14	Mt 6:12	Ustav 5.5.56
Ps 118:1/119:1	Scete Typ. 12	Mt 6:15	Ustav 5.4.56
Ps 118:128		Mt 6:27	Predanie 1
(LXX)	Ustav 4.2	Mt 7:7-8	Ustav 8.7
Ps 134:1/135:1	Scete Typ. 12	Mt 7:14	To German 3
Ps 140:4 (LXX)	Predanie 4	Mt 8:12	Ustav 7.23
Ps 142:9/143:9	Ustav 5.6.74	Mt 11:2	Ustav 2.17
Ps 148:1	Scete Typ. 20	Mt 11:12	Ustav 5.6.78
Prv 3:34 (LXX)	Ustav 5.8.89	Mt 12:36	Ustav 7.3
Prv 4:7	Ustav 11.8	Mt 13:1-8	To Gurii 18
Prv 16:5	Ustav 5.8.89	Mt 15:18	Ustav 7.3
Prv 18:19		Mt 15:19-20	Ustav, Fwd 1
(LXX)	Ustav 11.13	Mt 15:27	Ustav, Fwd 18
Prv 10:12	Ustav 4.3	Mt 16:26	To Vassian 3
Prv 22:12	Ustav 4.7	Mt 18:8	Ustav 7.23
Eccl 1:2	Ustav 7.14	Mt 18:15	Ustav 11.5
Eccl 3:1	Ustav 11.2	Mt 18:20	Ustav 11.8
Eccl 4:9-10	Ustav 11.8	Mt 18:35	Ustav 5.4.56
Eccl 12:28	Ustav 7.14	Mt 19:19	Ustav 4.10,
Is 66:24	Ustav 7.23		Sbrnk Fwd. 4
Jer 31:7	Scete Typ. 12	Mt 19:27	Predanie 23
Dn 7:9	Ustav 7.24	Mt 22:13	Ustav 7.23
Mc 4:9	Ustav 2.16	Mt 22:29	Ustav 4.10,
Mc 7:9	Ustav 5.6.78		Sbrnk Fwd. 4
Wsd 2:5	Ustav 7.18	Mt 22:7-37	Sbrnk Fwd. 4
	To Vassian 3	Mt 23:6	Ustav 5.8.92
Wsd 2:23-24	Ustav 5.6.78	Mt 23:12	Ustav 5.7.85
	To Gurii 8	Mt 23:26	Ustav, Fwd 1
Si 7:36		Mt 24:29-31	Ustav 7.20
(Vulg.7:40)	Ustav 7.5	Mt 25:26	Ustav, Fwd 17
Mt 3:10	Ustav, Fwd 3	Mt 25:30	Ustav 7.23

Appendix IV

Mt 25:31-34, 41, 46	Ustav 7.22	Rom 12:3, 6	Ustav 8.27
Mt 25:41	Ustav 7.23	Rom 13:9	Ustav 4.10, Sbrnk Fwd. 4
Mt 26:24	Ustav 11.5	Rom 14:2	Ustav 5.1.19
Mk 4:1-9	To Gurii 18	Rom 15:4	Ustav, Fwd 15
Mk 10:24	Ustav 2.17	Rom 15.12	Ustav 5.1.7
Mk 12:31	Ustav 4.10, Sbrnk Fwd. 4	1 Cor 2:9	Ustav 2.38
Lk 2:14	Scete Typ. 20	1 Cor 10:11	Ustav, Fwd 15
Lk 4:4	Ustav 5.6.78	1 Cor 10:13	Ustav 5.6.70-71
Lk 4:30	Ustav 1.11	1 Cor 14: 14-15,19	Ustav, Fwd 2
Lk 6:27-28	Ustav 5.4.59	2 Cor 1:3-4	To Vassian 19
Lk 7:37-38	Ustav 8.19		To German 9
Lk 8:4-8	To Gurii 18	2 Cor 1:5	To Vassian 17
Lk 9:44, 46	Ustav 7.23	2 Cor 3:5	Ustav 8.14
Lk 9:62	To Gurii 18	2 Cor 7:9-10	Ustav 5.5.65
Lk 10:27	Ustav 4.10, Sbrnk Fwd. 4	2 Cor 5:10	Ustav 7.3
Lk 11:2	Ustav 11.19	2 Cor 12:2-3	Ustav 2.30
Lk 11:4	Ustav 5.4.56	2 Cor 12:11	To Gurii 15
Lk 11:9-10	Ustav 8.7		To German 3
Lk 11:28	To Gurii 19	Gal 5:14	Ustav 4.10, Sbrnk Fwd.4
Lk 12:20	Ustav 7.3		
Lk 14:11	Ustav 5.7.85	Gal 5:23-24	Scete Typicon 1
Lk 14:28-29	Ustav 11.14	Eph 5:3, 5	Ustav 5.3.49
Lk 16:15	Ustav 5.8.89	Eph 6:11	Ustav 2.11
Lk 16:26	Ustav 7.23	Eph 6:17	Ustav 11.6
Lk 21:34	Ustav 5.1.6	Phil 1:29	To Vassian 17
Lk 3:34	Ustav 5.4.59	Phil 3:13	To Vassian 4
Jn 4:23-24	Ustav, Fwd 1	Phil 3:19	Ustav 5.8.95
Jn 5:28-29	Ustav 7.21	Col 3:5	Ustav 5.3.49
Jn 5:39	Ustav, Fwd 15	Col 4:2	Ustav 2.16
Jn 5:44	Ustav 5.8.95	1 Thes 5:2	Ustav 7.3
Jn 6:56	Prdnie Add. 46	2 Thes 3:10	Predanie 15
Jn 3:15	To Gurii 13	1 Tm 2:9	Ustav 5.8.92
Acts 1:14	Ustav 2.16	1 Tm 3:2	Ustav 5.8.92
Acts 5:1-11	Ustav 5.3.49	1 Tm 6:10	Ustav 5.3.49
Acts 22:16	Ustav 1.14	Heb 4:12	Ustav 7.3
Rom 7:14	Ustav, Fwd 15	Heb 12:22	Scete Typ. 12
Rom 8:38-39	Ustav 2.43	Jas 1:12, 17	To Vassian 17

Jas 2:8	*Ustav* 4.10	1 P 5:5	*Ustav* 5.8.89
Jas 4:6	*Ustav* 5.8.89	2 P 2:1	*Predanie* 2
1 P 2:11	*Predanie* 1	2 P 3:10	*Ustav* 7.3
1 P 3:3-4	*To Gurii* 2	Jude 9	*Ustav* 6.6
1 P 3:4	*Ustav* 5.2.28	Rv 20:12	*Ustav* 7.24
1 P 4:7	*Ustav* 7.3		

BIBLIOGRAPHY

1. Works Claiming to Contain Publications and Translations of Nil Sorsky's Works
1a. Genuine Publications
1b. Faithful Translations
1bi. faithful translations of only smaller works
1c. Adaptation-Translations of Nil's *Ustav*
1d. Anthologies with Translations of Brief Extracts
2. Reference Works and Dictionaries
3. Source Publication Series or Compilations
4. Manuscript Catalogues
5. Manuscripts
6. Identified and Possible Printed and Manuscript Sources for Nil's Writings and Their Sources
7. Collective Works with Relevant Studies
8. Studies of Nil's Sources and Orthodox Spiritual Traditions
8a. General
8b. Slavic Translations
9. Primary Sources for Nil's Life, Times, and Influence
10. Studies of Nil's Life, Times, and Influence
10a. Studies Thoroughly Grounded in the Nil-vrs-Iosif Paradigm
10b. Studies Less Grounded in or Outside the Nil-vrs-Iosif Paradigm
10c. Studies Moving Beyond the Nil-vrs-Iosif Paradigm

1. Works Claiming to Contain Publications and Translations of Nil Sorsky's Works

1a. *Genuine Publications*

IRI 5 (1813): 215-336 (*Predanie, Ustav*).

Lønngren (Lënngren), Tamara Pavlovna, *Sobornik Nila Sorskogo* (The Collection of Nil Sorskii). 5 vols. (3 text, 2 *Ukazatel' Slov* [Index of Words]), *Studia philologica*. Moscow: Iazyki russkoi kul'tury, 2000–2005. (SNS)

Nil Sorsky. *Nila Sorskogo, Predanie i Ustav* (Nil Sorsky's Tradition and Typicon). Ed. M.C. Borovkova-Maikova. PDP 179. St Petersburg: 1912 (includes some spurious works). (NSPU)

Prepodobnogo otsta nashego Nila sorskogo predanie uchenikom svoim o zhitel'tsve skitskom (The Tradition of our Saintly Father Nil Sorsky to his Disciples concerning the Scete Life). Ed. Optina Pustyn Fathers. Moscow: University, 1849 / Saint Petersburg: Sinodal'naia tipographiia, 1852, 1859, 1889 (*Testament* abbreviated).

Prokhorov, G.M., 'Poslaniia Nila Sorskogo' (The Epistles of Nil Sorsky). TODRL 29 (1974) 125-143.

———. (and Elena Shevchenko). *Prepodobnyi Nil Sorskii i Innokentii Komel'skii: Sochineniia* (Saint Nil Sorsky and Innokentii Komelskii: Works). Saint Petersburg: Oleg Abyshko, 2005 (all the genuine and two doubtful works, one attributed for the first time—the genuine Epistles and the Testament also in BLDR 9: 165-183). (PNSIK)

1b. *Faithful Translations of the* **Ustav**

Grolimund, Vasileos, Monk, NSA (most genuine and four doubtful works: the non-numbered pp 213 and 215 are switched).

Lilienfeld, Fairy von, NSSS. Teil II (most genuine and five doubtful works).

Prokhorov, PNSIK (modern Russian translations accompany most of the publications).

1bi. *Faithful Translations of Only Smaller Works*

Maloney, George A. RH Appendix I (genuine Epistles, and six doubtful works, five so identified).

Under 1c, see also Bianchi, Jacamon, and Maloney.

1c. *Adaptation-Translations of Nil's* **Ustav**

Arkhimandrit/Episkop Iustin, *Prepodobnyi i bogonosnyi otets nash Nil, podvizhnik sorskii, i ego ustav o skitskoi zhizni*. (Our Saintly and God-Bearing Father Nil, the Sora Ascetic and his Typikon on the Scete Life).

2nd ed. Moscow: 1892, rpt. Montreal: Brotherhod of Saint Iov, Igumen and Wonder-Worker of Pochaev, 1976 (also Berlin: Za Tserkov', 1939); rpt. Zagorsk: Sviato-Troitskaia Sergieva Lavra, 1991; and under the honest title, *O bor'be s grekhom i strastiam po ucheniiu Prepodobnogo Nila Sorsksogo* (On the Sturggle with Sins and Passions According to the Teachings of Saint Nil Sorsky). Moscow: Novaia kniga, 1994.

Bianchi, Enzo, ed. *Nil Sorskij. Vita e Scritti*. Translation of the Communità di Bose. Turin: Piero Gribaudi, 1988 (also faithful translations of the *Predanie, Testament,* genuine Epistles, and seven doubtful works, six so identified).

Jacamon, Sophia M, OSB. *Saint Nil Sorsky (1433–1508). La Vie. Les écrits. Le skite d'un starets de Trans-Volga*. Spiritualité et vie monastique 32. Bégrolles-en-Mauges: Abbaye de Bellefontaine, 1980 (also faithful translations of the *Predanie, Testament,* genuine Epistles, and three doubtful works).

Izwolsky, Hélène. 'St Nilus Sorsky'. *A Treasury of Russian Spirituality*. Ed. George P. Fedotov. New York: Sheed and Ward, 1948, 90–133. (Abbreviated; also the *Predanie;* complete *Testament.*)

Maloney, George A., SJ. *Nil Sorsky. The Complete Writings*. Mahwah, NJ: Paulist Press, 2003 (also an adapted translation of the *Predanie*, and the faithful translations of three authentic Epistles and one of the doubtful ones found in RH).

1d. *Anthologies with Translations of Brief Extracts*

Smolitsch, Igor. *Leben und Lehre der Starzen*. Cologne: J.Hegner, 1952: 69–80.

Špidlík, Tomáš, SJ *I grandi mistici russi*. Rome: Città Nuova, 1977/1983: 129–138; Spanish transl.: *Los grandes misticos rusos*. Bartolomé Parera Galmés. Madrid: Ciudad Nueva, 1986: 129–138.

2. Reference Works and Dictionaries

Akademiia nauk SSSR/Russkia Akademiia Nauk. Institut russkogo iazyka. *Slovar' russkogo iazyka XI–XVII vv.* (Lexicon of the Rus Language, 11th–17th c.). 27 volumes to *staritsynъ*, + reference volume, through 2006. Moscow: Nauka, 1975–.

Bauer, Walter F. *A Greek-English Dictionary of the New Testament and Other Early Christian Literature*. Transl. William F. Arndt and F. Wilbur Gingrich. Chicago and London: University of Chicago. 1971.

Dictionnaire de spiritualité ascetique et mystique, doctrine et histoire. 16 vols. to date. Ed. Marcel Viller, SJ, et al. Paris: G. Beauchesne, 1932–1995.

Entsiklopedicheskii slovar' (Encyclopedic Lexicon). 41 volumes in 82. Saint Petersburg: F.A. Brokgauz (Brockhaus) and I. A. Efron, 1890–1904; 4 supplementary volumes, 1906–1907; rpt. Moscow: Terra, 1990–1994.

Lampe, G.W.H., ed. *A Patristic Greek Dictionary.* London Oxford: Clarendon, 1961–1968.

Miklosich, Franz Ritter von. *Lexicon palaeoslovenico-graeco-latinum emendatum auctum.* Vienna: G. Braumueller, 1862–65; rpt. Aalen: Scientia Verlag, 1963.

The Oxford Dictionary of Byzantium. Ed. A.P. Kazhdan. 3 volumes. New York/Oxford: Oxford University Press, 1991.

Slovar' knizhnikov i knizhnosti drevnei Rusi (Lexicon of Bookmen and Letters of Old Rus). Ed. D.S. Likhachev. 3 volumes in 7. Leningrad/Saint Petersburg: Nauka: 1987–2004 (SKKDR).

Sophocles, E.A. *Greek Lexicon of the Roman and Byzantine Periods (from B.C. 146 to A.D. 1100).* 2 volumes. New York: Scribners, 1887; rpt. Frederick Ungar, 1957.

Sreznevskii, I.I. *Materialy dlia slovaria drevnerusskogo iazyka po pis'mennym pamiatnikam* (Materials for a Dictionary of the Old Rus Language, according to Written Monuments). 3 volumes. Saint Petersburg: Imperatorskaia Akademiia nauk, 1893–1903; rpt. Graz: Akademische Verlag, 1955–1956, 1971; Moscow: Izdatel'stvo inostrannykh I natsional'nykh iazykov, 1958; 'Kniga', 1989–1993; and Znak, 2003.

Vasmer, Max (Maks Fasmer). *Russisches etymologisches Wörterbuch.* 3 volumes. Heidelberg: Carl Winter, 1953–1958; Russian: *Etimologicheskii slovar' russkogo iazyka.* 4 volumes. Moscow: Progress, 1964.

3. Source Publication Series or Compilations

Acta Sanctorum. 71 volumes. Paris: V. Palme, 1863–1940. [Acta SS].

Biblioteka literatury Drevnei Rusi [v 20-ti tomakh] (A Library of Literature of Ancient Rus [in 20 Volumes]). 15 vols. to date. Ed. D.S. Likhachev et al. Saint Petersburg: Nauka, 1997–. [BLDR]

Byzantine Monastic Foundation Documents. A Complete Translation of the Surviving Founders' Typika and Testaments. 5 volumes. Edd. John Thomas and Angela Constantinides Hero, asst. by Giles Constable. Washington, D.C.: Dumbarton Oaks, 2000 (electronically: available at http:/www.doaks.org/typ000.html). [BMFD]

Cistercian Studies Series. 1969–. [CS]
Dobrotoliubie ili slovesa i glavizny sviashchennogo trezveniia, sobrannyia ot pisanii sviatykh i bogodukhnovennykh ottsov (The Philokalia, or Discourses and Chapters of Sanctified Watchfulness, Collected from the Holy and Divinely-Inspired Fathers). Ed. and translated by Archimandrite Paisii Velichkovskii. 4 parts in 2 volumes. Moscow: Sinodal'naia tipografiia, 1857.
Drevnerusskie inocheskie ustavy. Ustavy rossiiskikh monastyre-nachal'nikov (Old Rus Monastic Typica. The Typica of the Russian Monastery-founders = expanded reissue of IRI vol. 7). modern edition, T.V. Suzdal'tseva. Moscow: Severnyi palomnik, 2001. [DRIU]
Ecclesiae Graecae Monumenta. 3 volumes. Ed. Jean Baptiste Cotelier. Paris: Francis Muguet, 1677–1686.
Fathers of the Church, The. A New Translation. New York: 1947–, Washington, 1959–. [FC]
Festugière, A.-J., OP. *Les Moines d'Orient.* 4 vols. in 7 Paris: Cerf, 1961–1965.
Hapgood, Isabel, Ed. and transl. *Service Book of the Holy Orthodox-Catholic and Apostolic Church.* Rev. ed. New York: Association, 1922.
Istoriia Rossiiskoi ierarkhii (History of the Russian Hierarchy). Compiled and ed., Metropolitan Evgeni Bolkhovitinov and Bishop Amvrosii A. Ornatskii. 6 vols in 7. Moscow: Sinodal'naia tipografiia, 1807–1815; 2nd ed.,1822. [IRI]
Makarii, Metropolitan of Moscow and All Russia. *Velikiia Minei chetii, sobrannye vserossiiskim Mitropolitom Makariem* (The Great Reading Menologies, Collected by Makarii, Metropolitan of All Russia). 22 volumes. Saint Petersburg:Arkheograficheskaia komissiia, 1868–1917. [VMCh]

———. *Velikie Minei chet'i Mitropolita Makariia. Uspenskii spisok/Die Grossen Lesemanäen des Metropoliten Makarij. Uspenskij spisok.* Ed. Eckhard Weiher, A.I. Shkurko, S.O. Shmidt. Freiburg im Breisgau: Weiher / Moscow: Historical Museum, 1–11 March, 1997; 12–25 March, 1998; 26–21 March, 2001. [VMCh-M]
Noli, Bishop Fan Stylian. *The Eastern Orthodox Prayer Book.* Boston: Albanian Orthodox Church in America, 1949.
Orientalia Christiana analecta. Rome: Pontificium Institutum Orientalum, 1923–. [OCA]
Pamiatniki drevnei pis'mennosti (i iskusstva) (Monuments of Ancient Writings [and Art]). 190 volumes. Saint Petersburg, 1878–1925. [PDP]

Patrologiae cursus completus, series graeca. Ed. Jacques-Paul Migne. 161 volumes in 166. Paris: Migne, 1857–66. [PG]

Patrologiae cursus completus, series latina. Ed. Jacques-Paul Migne. 221 volumes. in 222. Paris: Migne, 1844–80. [PL]

The Philokalia. The Complete Text Compiled by St. Nikodimos of the Holy Mountain and St.. Makarios of Corinth. Transl. and ed. G. E. H. Palmer, Philip Sherrard, and Kallistos Ware. 4 volumes. London.-Boston: Faber and Faber, 1979–1995. [PSW]

Φιλοκαλία τῶν ἱερῶν νηπτικῶν συνερανισθεῖσα παρὰ τῶν ἁγίων θεοφόρων πατέρων ἡμῶν. Ed. Nikodemos of the Holy Mountain and Makarios of Corinth. (Orig. Venice: Antonio Bortoli, 1782). 5 vols. Athens: 'Astēr', 1957. [Φκ]

Sacrorum conciliorum. Nova et amplissima collectio. 53 volumes in 58. Ed. Johannes Dominicus Mansi, microfilm: Paris-Leipzig: H. Welter, 1901–1927 (originally Florence-Venice, 1758–1798); partial English transl. of volumes 1–13: NPNF-2.14.

A Select Library of the Nicene and Post-Nicene Fathers of the Christian Church. 1st series. 14 vols. Ed. Philip Schaff. 2nd series. 14 vols. Ed. Schaff and Henry Wace. New York: Christian Literature, 1886–90, 1890–1900; rpt. Grand Rapids: Eerdmans, and New York: Scribners, 1952–56, 1974–78. [NPNF]

Sources chrétiennes. 1941–. [SC]

Trebnik (Book of Needs, Slavic *Euchologion*). 2 pts in 1. Moscow: Sinodal'naia tipografiia, 1902. rpt. Jordanville, New York: Holy Trinity Monastery, 1960.

4. Manuscript Catalogues

Abramovich, D.I. *Sofiiskaia biblioteka. Opisanie rukopisei S-Peterburgskoi Dukhovnoi akademia* (The Sofia Library. Description of the Manuscripts of the Saint Petersburg Theological Seminary). 3 volumes. Saint Petersburg: Tipografiia Imperatorskoi Akademii nauk: 1905–1910.

Arsenii and Ilarii. *Opisanie slavianskikh rukopisei biblioteki Sv. Troitskoi Sergievoi Lavry* (Description of the Slavic Manuscripts of the Library of the Trinty-Saint Sergii Laura). ChOIDR (1878) 2, 4; (1879) 2.

Bychkov, A. F. *Opisanie tserkovno-slavianskikh i russkikh rukopisnykh sbornikov Imperatorskoi Publichnoi biblioteki* (Description of the Church Slavonic and Russian Manuscript Codices of the Imperial Public Library), Pt. 1. Saint Petersburg: Tip. Imp. Ak. nauk, 1882.

Gorskii, A., and K. Nevostruev, *Opisanie slavianskikh rukopisei Moskovskoi sinodal'noi biblioteki* (Description of the Slavonic Manuscripts of the Moscow Synod Library). 5 volumes. Moscow: Sinodal'naia tipografiia, 1855–1917; rpt. Monumenta linguae slaviae dialecti veteris. Fontes et dissertationes. 2. Wiesbaden: Harrassowitz, 1964.

Gosudarstvennaia publichnaia biblioteka im. M. E. Saltykova Shchedrina [now Russkaia natsional'naia biblkioteka]. Otdel. Rukopisei (i redkikh knig) Fond No. 351. *Biblioteka Kirillo-Belozerskogo monastyria. Opis'* (The Library of Kirillov-Belozerskii Monastery. Inventory). 2 volumes. Leningrad: GPB typescript, 1985.

———. Fond No. 728. *Biblioteka Novgorodskogo Sofiiskogo sobora. Opis'* (The Library of the Novgorod Sofiiskii Sobor. Inventory). 5 volumes. Leningrad: typescript, 1984.

Iosif, Ieromonakh. *Opis' rukopisei, perenesennykh iz biblioteki Iosifova monastyria v biblioteku Moskovskoi dukhovnoi akademii* (Inventory of the Manuscripts Transferred from the Iosifov Monastery Library to the Library of the Moscow Theological Seminary). Moscow: 1882; also in ChOIDR 1881, 3.

Kagan, M. D, N.V. Ponyrko, M.V. Rozhdestvenskaia. 'Opisanie sbornikov XV v. knigopistsa Efrosina' (Description of the Codices of the Fifteenth-Century Scribe Efrosin). TODRL 35 (1980), 3–300.

Likhachev, D. S., R. P. Dmitrieva, T.V. Dianova, L. M. Kostiukhina, I.V. Pozdeeva, T. A. Kruglova, M. M. Lereman, M. D. Kagan, *Knizhnye tsentry drevnei Rusi. Iosifo-Volokolamskii monastyr'* (Book Centers of Old Rus. The Iosifo-Volokolamskii Monastery). Leningrad: Nauka, 1991. (KTsDRIVM)

Matejic, Predrag, and Hannah Thomas, *Catalog. Manuscripts on Microform of the Hilandar Research Library.* 2 volumes. Columbus: Resource Center for Medieval Slavic Studies. The Ohio State University, 1992. [CMMHRL]

Opis na slavianskite rŭkopisi v Sofiiskata narodna biblioteka (Catalogue of the Slavic Manuscripts in the National Library of Sofia: old title: *Opis na slavianskite rŭkopisi v Sofiiskata narodna biblioteka i staropechanitie knigi na Narodnata biblioteka v Sofiia*). 5 vols., Ed, Be'no Tsonev, Ma'no Stoianov, Khristo Kodov. Sofia: Durzh, pechatnitsa/Nauka i izkustvo, 1910–1996.

Opisanie rukopisei Solovetskogo monastyria nakhodiashchikhsia v biblioteke Kazanskoi dukhovnoi akademii (Description of the Manuscripts found in the Library of the Kazan Theological Seminary). 3 vols. Kazan: 1881–1889.

Titov, A.A. *Opisanie slaviano-russkikh rukopisei, nakhodiashchikhsia v sobranii A.A.Titova* (Description of the Slavonic-Russian Manuscripts found in the Collection of A.A.Titov). 2 volumes. Moscow: 1900.

———. *Rukopisi slavianskie i russkie prinadlezhashchie I.A. Vakrameevu* (Slavonic and Russian Manuscripts Belonging to I.A.Vakrameev). 5 volumes. Moscow: E. Lissner, 1888–1906.

5. Manuscripts

Hilándar Monastery (on Microfilm at HRL)
 HM SMS 179 (1390s)—Isaac the Syrian.
 HM SMS 183 (15th c.)—Basil the Great.
 HM SMS 184 (c. 1500)—John Climacus.
 HM SMS 398 (1380s)—Nikon of the Black Mountain, *Pandekty*.
 HM SMS 454 (1380s)—Peter Damaskenos (first part); Miscellany
 HM SMS 456 (1390s)—Miscellany.
 HM SMS 468 (c. 1400)—Miscellany.
 HM SMS 640 (1380s)—Scete Typikon, Gregory the Sinaite.

State Historical Museum, Moscow (GIM) (on Microfilm at HRL)
 Eparkh. 76 (end 15th-beg. 16th c.)—*Bogorodichnik* (*Theotokion*).
 Eparkh. 118 (end 15th-beg. 16th c.)—Symeon the New Theologian, Peter Damaskenos.
 Eparkh. 212 (Q4 15th c. of Iosif's Scribe-Disciple Gerasim)— Liturgical Miscellany.
 Eparkh. 292 (mid 16th c.)—Liturgical Miscellany.
 Eparkh. 317 (end 15th-beg. 16th c.)—Pope Gregory the Great.
 Eparkh. 324 (end 15th-beg. 16th c.)—Isaac the Syrian.
 Eparkh. 331 (1505)—John Climacus.
 Eparkh. 333 (end 15th-beg. 16th c. of Gelasii Sukholeny)— Symeon NT.
 Eparkh. 334 (1470s-80s)—Symeon NT.
 Eparkh. 341 (1550s-1560s)—Iosif Volotsky (Extended Rule).
 Eparkh. 342 (1540s of Dosifei Toporkov)—Miscellany with Nil Sorsky.
 Eparkh. 343 (1530: of Simeon the Hermit-Choirman)—Miscellany with Nil Sorsky.
 Eparkh. 344 (end 15th-beg. 16th c. of Tikhon Zvorykin)—Miscellany with Nil Sorsky.

Eparkh. 346 (Q4 15th c.)—Miscellany.
Eparkh. 347 (end 15th-beg. 16th c. of Tikhon Zvorykin)—Dorotheus of Gaza, Miscellany.
Eparkh. 348 (end 15th-beg 16th c. of Dionisii Zvenigorodskii)—Basil the Great with Miscellany.
Eparkh. 349 (end 15th-beg. 16th c. of Nil Polev, Nil Sorsky)— Miscellany with Nil Sorsky.
Eparkh. 350 (Q2 16th c. of Isak Sumin)—Miscellany with Nil Sorsky.
Eparkh. 351 (end 15th-beg. 16th c. of Dionisii Zvenigorodskii)— Miscellany with Nil Sorsky.
Eparkh. 355 (Q2 16th c. of Simeon Mikulinets)—Dorotheus of Gaza, Miscellany.
Eparkh. 357 (Q3 15th c. of Iosif Volotsky)—Miscellany.
Eparkh. 369 (Q1 15th c.)—Miscellany.
Eparkh. 370 (Q3 15th c.)—Miscellany.

Russian National Library (RNB), Saint Petersburg, formerly the Saltykov-Shchedrin State Public Library (GPB)
KB 3/8 Pentateuch (15th c.).
KB 85/210 (c. 1521, by Gurii Tushin)—Theodore the Studite.
KB 25/1102 (early or mid 16th c.) (of or from Innokentii Okhliabinin)—Miscellany with Nil Sorsky, Innokentii.
KB 89/1166 (pp 1–182, end 15th-early 16th c.), with Nil Sorsky.
KB 29/1196 (16th c.)—Miscellany with Nil Sorsky and a little Pseudo-Macarius.
KB 721/1198. (16th c.)—*Starchestvo* (Miscellany of Cell Regulations).
KB 8/1247 (15th c.)—*Paterik azbuchnyi* (Alphabetic Patericon).
Sof. 34 (16th c.)—*Apostol* (Acts, Epistles).
Sof. 1435 (15th c.)—Nikon Chernogorets, *Taktikon*.
Sof. 1444 (1520s)—Miscellany with Nil Sorsky.
Sof. 1468 (early 1520s, of Gurii Tushin)—Miscellany with 'Nil's' purported Prayer.
Sof. 1474 (16th c.[?]): 'Miscellany of Gennadii's Hermitage'.
Sol. 326/346 (to p 337v, by 1504, of Nil Sorsky and Nil Polev)— Iosif's Brief Rule and Brief *Prosvetitel'* (Enlightener).
Sol. 359/270 (ca. 1500)—*Izmaragd* (The Emerald—a Miscellany).
Sol. 271/793 (16th c.), 1–162—Symeon NT.
Sol. 1059/1168 (end 16th/early 17th c.): Solovetskii Monastery *Typikon* (photocopy supplied by Professor Jennifer Spock), 3–95.

Russian State Library (RGB), formerly Lenin State Library (GBL) (on line at: http://www.stsl.ru/manuscripts/index.php)

Tr-S 108—Interpreted Matthew-Mark (16th c.).
Tr-S 113—Interpreted Luke-John (1561).
Tr-S 313—Psalter (end 15th c.).

6. Identified and Possible Printed and Manuscript Sources for Nil's Writings and Their Sources (where more than one such translation is listed * indicates the English copy used in the footnotes)

Andrew of Crete. *Canon.* http://home.it.net.au/~jgrapsas/pages/canon. htm. somewhat approximates *Kanon umileniia. Tvorenie Andreiia Kritskogo* (Canon of Compunction. A Work of Andrew of Crete). Eparkh. 370: 173-203 (somewhat approximates *Magnus Canon*. PG 97: 1330C–1385C).

Athanasius of Alexandria. *The Life of Saint Anthony.* Transl. and ed., Robert T. Meyer. Ancient Christian Writers 10. Westminster, Maryland: The Newman Press, 1950. PG 26: 835–976; Nil Sorsky's Slavic: SNS 3: 147–237.

Barsanuphius of Gaza. *Barsanuphius and John. Questions and Answers. Critical Edition of the Greek Text with English Translation.* Transl. and ed., Derwas James Chitty. *Patrologia orientalis.* 31.3. Paris: Firmn-Didot et Cie., 1966, 449–616.

———. *Correspondance.* Transl., L. Regnault. Introd., notes, François Neyt, OSB, and Paula de Angelis-Noah. 3 vols. in 5. SC 426–427, 450–451, 468: 1997–2002.

———. *Glavy sviatago velikago Farsanofiia* (Chapters of the Great Saint Barsanuphius). Eparkh. 347: 205–243 (small selection).

———. *Letters from the Desert. A Selection of Questions and Responses.* Transl. and introd., John Chryssavgis. Crestwood, NY: Saint Vladimir's Seminary Press, 2003.

———. *Velikago Varsonufia* (By Barsanuphius the Great). Fragment. HM SMS 468: 72v (Abbreviation of Letter No. 119).

Basil/Pseudo-Basil of Caesarea (Basil the Great). *The Ascetic Works of Saint Basil.* Transl. and introd., W.K.L. Clarke. London: MacMillan, 1925.

———. *St Basil. Ascetical Works.* Transl. Sr Mary Monica Wagner CSC. FC 9.

———. *An Ascetical Discourse and Exhortation on the Renunciation of the World and Spiritual Perfection.* (*Sermo asceticus et exhortatio de renunciatione saeculi, et de perfectioni spirituali*). Clarke, 60–71; FC 9:15–31; PG 31: 625–48; HM SMS 183: 178v–186v.

———. *Longer Rules (Regulae fusius tractatae)*. Clarke, 125–228; FC 9: 223–338; PG 31: 889–1052; HM SMS 183:27–79 (the 55 numbered Q&As combined into 41).

———. *Shorter Rules (Regulae brevius tractatae)*. Clarke, 229–351; PG 31: 1051–1306; HM SMS 183: 79–137v (the 313 numbered Q&As not ordered as in PG 31, reduced).

———. *Constitutiones asceticae*. PG 31: 1315–1428; HM SMS 183: 137–178v.

Cercare Dio nel deserto. Vita di Caritone. Transl. and introd. Leah Campagnano Di Segni. Comunità de Bose: Qiqajon, 1990.

Clugnet, L. 'Vie et récits de l'abbé Daniel le Scétiote. I. Texte grec'. *Revue de l'Orient Chrétien* 5 (1900), 49–73, 254–271, 370–391; 6 (1901), 56–87 (introduction).

Cyril of Scythopolis. *Lives of the Monks of Palestine*. Transl. R. M. Price. Introducton and notes, John Binns. CS 114 (1991); Gk: Cyril of Scythopolis/*Kyrillos von Skythopolis*. Ed. Eduard Schwartz. Texte und Untersuchungen zur Geschichte der altchristlichen Literatur 49.2. Leipzig: Hinrichs, 1939.

Diadochus of Photice, *On Spiritual Knowledge and Discrimination (Capitula gnostica)* PSW 1: 253–296; Eparkh. 344: 276v–328v, 346: 54v–70; Φκ 1: 235–273; French transl. *Oeuvres spirituelles*. Ed. A. Piédagnel, SC 5, 84–163.

Dorotheus of Gaza. *Discourses and Sayings (Expositiones et doctrinae diversae)*. Ed. and transl. Eric P. Wheeler OSB. CS 33. Kalamazoo, 1977; PG 88: 1611–1838; Eparkh, 347: 1–203v.

———. *Oeuvres spirituelles*. Ed. and transl. L. Regnault and J. de Préville. SC 92. Paris: Cerf: 1963–65 (Greek edition, French transl.).

Drevnerusskie pateriki (The Old Rus Paterica). Ed., L.A. Ol'shevskaia, S.N. Travnikov. Moscow: Nauka, 1999.

Ephrem (Ephraim, Ephraem) the Syrian. *Paranesis. Die Altbulgarische Übersetzung von Werken Ephraims des Syrers*. Ed. and transl. (German; also Greek original). Georg Bojkovsky and Rudolph Aitzetmüller. 5 vols. Monumentae Linguae Slavicae. Fontes et Dissertationes. v 20 (1), 22 (20.2), 24 (20.3), 26 (20.4), 28 (20.5). Freiburg im Breisgau: U.W. Weiher, 1984–1990.

———. Τὰ τοῦ ὁσίοιν πατρὸς 'Εφραίμ τοῦ Σύρου πρὸς τὴν 'Ελλάδα μεταβληθέντα. Ed. E. Thwaites. Oxford: 1709.

———. *Sancti patris nostri Ephraem Syri Opera omnia quae exstant Graece, Syriace, Latine ad mss. Codices Vaticanos* (All the Extant Works in Greek, Syriac, and Latin of Our Holy Father Ephrem the Syrian, in the

Vatican Codices). 3 volumes. Ed. J.-S. Assemani. Rome: Vatican, 1732–1746.
Evagrius Ponticus. *The Praktikos. Chapters on Prayer.* Transl., introd., notes, John Eudes Bamberger OSCO. CS 4. 1970; HM SMS 468: 98–107v/Eparkh. 344: 328v-343; orig. PG 40: 1220C–1252C, 79: 1165A–1200C Φκ 1: 176-189 = Pseudo-Neilos of Sinai. *On Prayer. One Hundred Fifty-Three Texts.* PSW 1: 55-71; CS 4: 52–80; PG 79: 1165A-1200C/Φκ 1: 176-189 =

———. /Pseudo-Evagrius. *On Asceticism and Stillness.* PSW 1: 31-37; Φκ 1: 38-43.

Freshfield, Edwin Hanson, Transl. and ed. *A Manual of Eastern Roman Law. The Procheiros Nomos.* Cambridge UK: University Press, 1928.

Germanus, Patriarch of Constantinople (r. 1222–1240), *Stikhi . . . khotiaishchimъ . . . plakati* (Verses for Mourners). Eparkh. 347: 303–320v; Greek, cited in Grolimund, NSA 419, n14, from 'Einige uneditierte Stücke des Manasses und Italikos'. *Jahresbericht des K.K. Sophiengymnasiums in Wien für das Schuljahr 1901/1902.* Vienna: 1902: 13–14.

Gregorius Archiep. Thessalonicensis. *Oratio in admirabilem et angelicae parem vitam sancti ac divini patris nostri Petri qui in Sancto Monte Atho anchoretam egit.* PG 150: 996-1050; Nil's Slavic: SNS 1: 227–268.

Gregory I (the Great), Pope/Pseudo-Gregory. *Dialogues.* Transl. O. J. Zimmerman, OSB. FC 39. (PL 77: 149–432, for 1, 3–4; PL 66: 125–204 for 2: *The Life of Saint Benedict*); Eparkh. 317/VMCh-M (11): 105a–192b/203/383; cf. below, *Paterik rimskii.*

Gregory of Nyssa, *The Life of Saint Macrina.* FC 58: 163–191; PG 46: 960–1000.

Gregory Palamas, *Topics of Moral and Theological Science.* PSW 4: 346–417; PG 150: 1122B–1225C.

———. *Life of Peter of Athos.* in Lake, *Early Days of Monasticism.*

Gregory the Sinaite, *Acrostic Chapters (On Commandments and Doctrines . . . One Hundred Thirty-Seven Texts).* PSW 4:212-252; PG 150: 1240A-1300B; HM SMS 456: 3v-46 (missing mid-Ch. 112-to-mid-Ch. 115); HM SMS.640: 62–103 (missing Ch. 97–98).

———. *Further Texts.* PSW 4: 253–256; HM SMS 456: 46–47; HM SMS.640: 103–105 (both incomplete).

———. *On the Signs of Grace and Delusion.* (Short Version: Ch. 1–10): PSW 4: 256–262; PG 150: 1304D–1312C; HM SMS 456: 64v–68v (missing from mid-Ch.5 to mid- Ch.9); Eparkh. 351: 99–107v.

(continuation of Ch. 10, and 'Ch. 11–13': Greek with English transl. in Balfour, *Saint Gregory the Sinaïte,* 109–114.

(Slavic continuation of Ch. 10, with the Greek 'Ch. 11' as 'Ch. 11–12'. and a different and much longer 'Ch 13': HM SMS 456: 68v-77v; a bit different 'Ch 11–12' in Eparkh. 351: 107v–109v.

———. *On Sitting at Prayer* (*On Prayer*). PSW 4: 275–286; PG 150: 1329A–1346A; Eparkh. 351: 83–99; HM SMS 456: 59–64, and 640: 116 v–122 lack ch. 7; Φκ 4: 80–88.

———. *On Stillness and Two Ways of Prayer.* PSW 4: 263-274; PG 150:1313A-1329A; HMS 640:105–116v; HM SMS 456:47–59; Eparkh. 351:109v-127v.

Hesychius of Batos/Sinai (pseudo-Hesychius the Priest, pseudo- of Jerusalem), *On Watchfulness and Holiness.* PSW 1:162–198; PG 93:14 79D–1544D/Φκ 1:142–175; HM SMS 456: 154v–185v; Eparkh. 344: 429–472v.

Isaac of Syria (Isaac of Nineveh). **The Ascetic Homilies of Saint Isaac the Syrian.* Transl. Dana R. Miller. Boston: Holy Transfiguration Monastery, 1984) (HTM); also *Mystic Treatises by Isaac of Nineveh.* Transl. and introd. A. J. Wensinck. Amsterdam: Koninklijke akademie van wetenschappen, 1923 (transl. from the Syrian); Greek version used: *Τοῦ ὁσίου πατρὸς ἡμῶν 'Ισαὰκ ἐπισκόπου Νινευὶ τοῦ Σύρου τὰ Εὑρεθέντα 'Ασκητικὰ*. Leipzig: Joachim Spetsier, 1770/ Thessalonike: Vas. Regopoulos, 1997; modern Russian: *Tvoreniia . . . avva Isaaka Syrianina. Slova podvizhnnicheskiia* (The Works of . . . Isaac the Syrian, Ascetic Discourses. 3rd, corrected ed. Sergiev Posad: Holy Trinity Monastery, 1911. Old Slavic: HM SMS 159 (slightly defective); Eparkh. 324.

John Cassian (Slavic: Kassian Rimlianin), *Institutes of the Coenobia.* NPNF-2 11:201-90; newer edition: *De Institutis Cenobitorum Libri XII.* Ed, J. C, Guy. SC 109 (1965, with a French transl.); newer transl.: by Boniface Ramsey, *John Cassian: The Institutes*, Ancient Christian Writers, 57. New York: Paulist, 2000; *by Jerome Bertram *The Monastic Institutes, consisting of On the Training of the Monk and The Eight Deadly Sins.* London: Saint Austin Press, 1999 (Books 5-12); PL 49:34–476. Abridged: *On the Eight Vices.* PSW 1:73–93; Φκ 1:61–80; HM SMS 468:223–243v; Eparkh. 369:148–184.

John Chrysostom, *Homilies on the Gospel of Saint Matthew.* NPNF-2.10; PG 57–58.

John Climacus. **St John Climacus: The Ladder of Divine Ascent.* Transl. Archimandrite Lazarus Moore; Intro. Muriel Heppell. London: Faber & Faber—New York: Harper, 1959. New transl. (without the numbering of paragraphs), C. Luibheid and N. Russell, *The Ladder of*

Divine Ascent, New York: Paulist, 1982; PG 88:631–1164; HM SMS 184; Eparkh. 331:1–385v;VMCh-M (30): 841a–946a/1681–1891.

———. *Liber ad pastorem*. PG 88:1165–1210C; Eparkh. 331:385v-422 (with some PG *scholae*).

John of Damascus, *Philosophical Chapters [Dialectica]. Saint John of Damascus. Writings*. Transl. and ed., Frederick H. Chase Jr. FC, 1958, 7–110. PG 94:521A-5676B. Partial Slavic:VMCh Dec. 4, 141–303.

John of Damascus/Pseudo-John of Damascus. *By the Holy, Humble Monk, John the Damascene* (stgo *smirenago inoka* iωna *damaskyna*); *By the Same Monk Damaskon* (togozhe iωna damaskωn (Hymn Fragments). Eparkh. 355:207v-211.

———. *Composed by St. John of Damascus*. in *Liturgical Texts.* http://www.goarch.org/en/chapel/liturgical_texts/funeral2.asp. /*The Funeral Service/The Anthem by John, Monk of Damascus.* http://www.orthodoxinfo.com/death/funeral.aspx.

———. *Stepena na vosem' glasov"* (*Stepena* in Eight Tones). Eparkh. 212: 104-123.

Pseudo-John of Damascus, *On the Virtues and the Vices*. PSW 2:334–342; Φκ 2:232–238; PG 28:1395A–1408D (as Pseudo-Athanasius, but somewhat different) HM SMS 468:168–175; 261–262 (also attributed to Ephrem, and by Nil to Gregory the Sinaite).

John (VIII), Patriarch of Jerusalem (1106–11560), *Life of John of Damascus.* PG 94:430–489B; Nil Sorsky's Slavic redaction: SNS 2:323–358.

John Tzimiskes, Emperor, *Typikon*. Transl. George Dennis sj. BMFD 12:232–244.

Kallistos Patriarch. *Zhitie . . . Grigoriia Sinaita* (Life of Gregory the Sinaite). Ed. P.A. Syrku (Slavic text). PDP 172 (1909); Eparkh. 348:251-326; (Greek text); Ed. I. Pomialovskii. *Zapiski istoriko-filologcheskogo fakul'teta S.-Peterburgskogo universiteta* (Notes of the History-Philology Faculty of Saint Petersburg University) 35 (1896) 1–64.

Kanon molebnyi . . . pri razluchenii dushi (Prayer Service Canon . . . Upon the Separation of the Soul). *Trebnik*,109v–117v.

Karyes:Typikon of Sabbas the Serbian for the *Kellion* of Saint Sabbas at Karyes on Mount Athos. Transl. George T Dennis, sj. BMFD, 1333–1335.

Mark the Hermit, *On Those Who Think They Are Made Righteous by Works*. PSW 1:125–146; PG 65:929C–966A /Φκ 1:109–126.

Macarius/Pseudo-Macarius of Egypt, *Intoxicated With God. The Fifty Spiritual Homilies of Macarius.* Transl. and Introd., George A. Maloney, sj. Denville New Jersey: Dimension, 1978; PG 34:449A–822A. Slavic transl. of Homily 19 as *Slovo nakazatel'no k polze dushevnoi khotiashchim spasitisia* (An instructive sermon of profit to the soul for those who would be saved), KB 29/1106:111v–116v.

———. *Liber de custodia cordis.* PSW 4:194–206; PG 147:945–966/Φκ 4:18-28; Slavic. PG 34:822-842.

———. *Liber de libertate mentis* (On the Freedom of the Mind). PG 34:935C–968A. Pseudo-Pseudo-Macarius of Egypt: see Symeon Metaphrastes.

Maximus the Confessor. *Centuries on Love.* PSW 2:52-113; HM SMS 456:89v-133; PG 90:960A–1073A/Φκ 2:1-51.

Neilos of Sinai/Neilos the Ascetic. *Ascetic Discourse.* PSW 1:200–250; PG 79:719A-810D. Pseudo-Neilos of Sinai: see Evagrius Ponticus.

Nicephorus the Monk. *On Watchfulness and Guarding of the* partially under Ps-Symeon NT, *O molitvě,* HM SMS 468:79-81 (the 'Symeon NT' extract and Nicephorus's own words, but as in the longer, Latin version).

Nicetas Stethatos. *On the Practice of the Virtues* and *On the Inner Nature of Things.* PSW 4:79-138; Φκ 3:273-355; HM SMS 468:176-209 (slight modifications, different numbering: the first two 'centuria', with 82, 98 caps); Eparkh. 344:362-427.

Nikon of the Black Mountain (Nikon ho Mauroeites; Nicon Monachus, of Raithos Monastery on the Black Mountain near Antioch). *Pandekty . . . Nikona Chernogortsa.* (The Pandects of . . . Nikon of the Black Mountain—Church Slavic transl.). Spaso-Prilutskii pod Vologdoi: 1670 MS; rpt. Pochaev, 1795 (Table of contents in PG 106:1359-82); HM SMS 398.

———. *Taktikon . . . Nikon Chernogortsa.* (The Taktikon . . . of Nikon of the Black Mountain—Church Slavic translation). Pochaev: 1795; also Sof. 1435. (Original Greek, to Discourse 4: *Taktikon Nikona Chernogortsa,* Ed. V.N. Beneshevich. 1. Petrograd, 1917.). Transl. of Discourses 1–2, Robert Allison. BMFD, 377–439.

The Old Church Slavonic Translation of the Ἀνδρῶν ἁγίων βίβλος. Ed. D. Armstrong, R. Pope, and C.H. Schonveld. The Hague: Mouton, 1975.

The Order for the Burial of the Dead. in Hapgood. *Service Book,* 368–393.

O srebroliubii i liuboiměnie Sviatogo Euangelia tolkovanie (A gloss on the Holy Gospel concerning avarice and greed). Eparkh. 344:93–95v.

The Ostroh Bible 1581/Ostryzka Biblia (Facsimile reproduction). Winnipeg: College of Saint Andrew/Pisces Press, 1983).

Papacherysianthou, Denise. 'La vie ancienne de Saint Pierre l'Athonite. Date, composition, et valeur historique'. *Analecta Bollandiana* 92 (1074) 19–23.

Paterik Rimskii. Dialogi Grigoriia Velikogo v drevneslavianskogo perevode (The Roman/Italian Patericon.The Dialogues of Gregory the Great in the Ancient Slavonic Translation). Ed. K. Diddi. Moscow: Indrik, 2001 (with Greek text too); Eparkh. 317.

Percival, Henry R., Ed. *The Seven Ecumenical Councils of the Undivided Church. Their Canons and Dogmatic Decrees, together with the Canons of all Local Synods which have received Ecumenical Acceptance.* NPNF-2 14. (Original: *Sacrorum consiliorum nova, et amplissima collectio*, ed. Mansi (see above, section 3).

Peter Damaskenos *Treasury of Divine Knowledge* (Slavic Title: *Memorial for His Soul*). PSW 3:74-281; Фк 3:5-168 (no title); HM SMS 454:1-153, Eparkh. 118:144-282 (first part only).

Philotheus the Sinaite. *Forty Texts on Watchfulness*. PSW 3:16-31; Фк 2:274-286/fragment of 'Ch. 30' from Vatic. 730, 193v, Hausherr, *Méthode*, 140; Eparkh. 344:343v–362.

Predanie ustavom izhe na vneshnei strane prebyvaiushchim inokom, rekshe skitskago zhitiia (The Tradition by the Typikon for Monks Residing in the Outer Region, that is, for Scetites); HM SMS 640:1-61v (defective at the start, but with appended items); *Entsiklopediia russkogo igumena*, 158–166 (RNB KB XII version); Eparkh. 349:1-8v; KB 25/1102: 207v–283v; Russian transl. (somewhat abbreviated) of RGB Pogod. 876 version, Beliakova (assisted by N.V. Sinitsyna), 'Russkaia rukopisnaia traditsiia', 160–162; also 'Slavianskaia redaksiia' under [9] here.

Romanos Melodos, *Hymnes*. (Greek text, French transl.) Transl. and ed. José Grosdidier de Matons. Pref. Paul Lemerle. 5 volumes. SC 99, 110, 114, 128, 283. (1964–1981).

Sancti Pachomii Vita Altera. Ed. François Halkin. *Sanctae Pachomii Vitae Graecae*. Subsidia Hagiographica 19 (1932), 166–271; French: Festugière, *Moines* 4.2:159–235; Nil's Slavic: SNS 3:459–580.

The Sayings of the Desert Fathers.The Alphabetical Collection. Ed. Benedicta, Ward SLG, CS 59. Kalamazoo-Oxford, 1975; *Paterik azbuchnyi*. KB 8/1247; (*Apophthegmata patrum*. PG 65:71–440).

Scete Typikon: see above, *Predanie ustavom* . . . .

Symeon Metaphrastes, *Certamen sanctorum martyrum Eustratii, Auxentii, Evgenii, Mardari, et Orestii*. PG 116:468A-505D; Slavic:VMCh Dec. 13:944-978.

———. *Paraphrase of Macarius*. PSW 3:285-353; Фк 3:171-234; HM SMS 468:23-72v.

Symeon the New Theologian (Neotheologus, Novus Theologus,

Junior). *Catéchèses.* Intro. Basile Krivochéine. Transl. Joseph Paramelle SJ. SC 96, 104, 113. Paris: Cerf: 1963-1965. (Greek edition, French translation.); English: *The Discourses.* Preface Basil Krivochéine. Intro. George Maloney, SJ. Transl. C.J. di Catanzaro. New York: Paulist, 1980; Eparkh. 333, 334, Sol 271/793 (parts or all of 2, 4-6, 8).

———. *Hymnes.* Ed. Johannes Koder. Transl. Joseph Paramelle SJ, and Louis Neyrand SJ. SC 156, 174, 196. Paris, 1969-1971; English: *Hymns of Divine Love by St. Symeon the New Theologian.* Transl. George A. Maloney, SJ. Denville, New Jeersey: Dimension, 1976; Eparkh. 333, 334, Sol 271/793 (Intr., 3–7, 13–14, 28, 36–37, 43, 46–47, 56–57).

Pseudo-Symeon the New Theologian. 'La méthode d'oraison hesychaste'. Ed. and transl. Irinée Hausherr SJ, *Orientalia Christiana* 9.36 (Rome, 1927), 150–208 (Greek text and French transl.).

Briefer versions: *The Three Methods of Prayer.* PSW 4:64–75; Фк 5:81–89; HM SMS 456:133–144v; HM SMS 468:79–84v; Sol. 271/793.25:154–162v; also the Eparkh. 333, 334.

Pseudo(?)-Symeon the New Theologian: *O molitvě* (On Prayer), embedded in Nicephorus Monachus, *Watchfulness,* 203-204; Фк 4:25-28; PG 147:959-961; HM SMS 468:79-81; Sol. 271/793.24:149v-154; also Eparkh. 333, 334.

Combined Slavic Symeon the New Theologian and Pseudo-Symeon: Eparkh. 118:1-143v; Eparkh. 334; Sinod. 164:1-110v; Sol. 271/793.1-25:1-162v.

Symeon the Studite. *Discourse ascétique.* Ed. and introd., Hilarion Alfeyev; Transl. L Neyrand SJ. SC 460 (Greek text, French transl.).

Theodore the Studite. *The Little Catechesis = Μικρά Κατήχησις—Parva Catechesis.* Ed. Emmanuel Auvray. Paris.Victor Lecoffre, 1891. (Mainly Latin: PG 99:509-688); French transl. *Petites Catéchèses.* Transl. Anne-Marie Mohr. Introd. Marie-Helène Congourdeau. Paris: Migne, 1993; Slavic collection of 33 of these, containing the one utilized by Nil: KB 85/210.

———. *The Testament.* *Transl. Timothy Miller, BMFD 1.3:75-83/ Transl. Nicholas P. Costas. Washington, D.C.: Monastery of the Holy Cross, 1991; PG 99:1813A–1824D.

Uspenskii sbornik XI-XIII vv. (The Uspenskii Miscellany, 12th-13th c.). Ed. S.I. Kotkov. Moscow: Nauka, 1971.

Vita Graeca de S. Charitone Abbati. Acta SS 27:572F-582F; Nil's Slavic: SNS 2:41-61.

Vita S. P. N. Euthymii (Greek and Latin transl.). Ed. Jean-Baptiste Cotelier. *Ecclesiae Graecae Monumenta* 2:200-340/ *Vita S. Euthymii Magni*

Abbati. Acta SS 2:662-692; better edition in Cyril of Scythopolis/ *Kyrillos von Skythopolis,* 1-85; Nil's Slavic: SNS 3:237-306; English: CS 114:1–92; French: Festugière, *Moines* 3.1 (1962) 55–140.

Vita S. Theodoro Siciotae. (George the Presbyter and Hegumen; ex MSS Graicis a Petro Francisco Zino reddita; no Greek supplied). Acta SS 12:34A–62D; Nil's Slavic: SNS 3:385–442.

Zhitie . . .Arseniia Velikago po rukipisiam" Moskovskoi Sinodal'noi biblioteki (The Life of. . .Arsenius the Great, according to Manuscripts of the Moscow Synod Library). Ed. G. F. Tsereteli. Saint Petersburg: Imp. Ak. Nauk, 1899) (Greek text); Nil's Slavic: SNS 3:443–458.

Zhitie prepodobnago Afanasiia Afonskago po rukopisi Moskovskoi Sinodal'noi biblioteki (The Life of Saint Athanasius of Athos, according to the manuscript of the Moscow Synod Library). Saint Petersburg: Imp. Ak. Nauk. 1895 (Greek text); Nil's Slavic: SNS 1:271–389.

7. Collective Works with Relevant Studies

Amore del bello. Studii sulla Filokalia. Atti del 'Simposio internazionale sulla Filocalia,': Pontificio Collegio greco, Roma, novembre 1989. Ed. Tomás Špidlík SJ.Vatican City: Qiqajon, 1991.

Drevnerusskoe iskusstvo: Rukopisnaia kniga (Old Rus Art.The Manuscript Book). Moscow: Nauka, 1974.

Kamen' Kraeug" l'n" {The Cornerstone}. *Rhetoric of the Medieval Slavic World.* Essays Presented to Edward L. Kennan on his Sixtieth Birthday by his Colleagues and Students. Ed. N.S. Kollmann, D. Ostrowski, A. Pliguzov, D. Rowland. HUS 19 (1995 [1997]).

Knizhnye tsentry Drevnei Rusi.Raznye aspekty issledovaniia (Book Centers of Old Rus. 11th–16th c. Various Aspects of Research). Ed. D.S. Likhachev, Saint Petersburg: Nauka, 1991.[KTsDRRAI].

Medieval Russian Culture, vols.1–2. Ed. Henrik Birnbaum (1), Michael S. Flier (1–2), Daniel Rowland (2). *California Slavic Studies* 12 (1984), 19 (1994). Berkeley, Los Angeles, London: University of California Press. [MRC]

Monashestvo i monastyri v Rossii XI–XX veka. Istoricheskie ocherki (Monasteries and monasticism in Russia, 11th–20th Century. Historical Essays). Ed. N.V. Sinitsyna et al. Moscow: Nauka, 2002. [MMR]

Monastic Traditions. Selected Proceedings of the Fourth International Hilandar Conference. Ed. Charles E. Gribble and Predrag Matejic. Bloomington Indiana: Slavica, 2003.

Monastyrskaia kul'tura. Vostok i Zapad (Monastery Culture. East and West). Ed. E. D. Vodolazkin. Saint Petersburg: Institut russkoi literatury RAN, 1999. [MKVZ]

Moskovskaia Rus' (1359–1584): kul'tura i istoricheskoe samosoznanie (Culture and Identity in Muscovy, 1359–1584). Ed. Gail Lennhoff, Janet Martin. Moscow: ITZ-Garant, 1997. [MRKIS/CIM]

Mount Athos and Byzantine Monasticism. Papers from the Twenty-eighth Spring Symposium of Byzantine Studies, Birmingham, March 1994. Edd. Anthony Bryer and Mary Cunningham. Society for the Promotion of Byzantine Stydies 4. Aldershot: Variorum-Brookfield Vermont: Ashgate, 1994.

Nil Sorskij e l'esicasmo. Ed. N. Kautchtschischwili, G. M. Prokhorov (Prochorov), F. von Lilienfeld. Comunità di Bose: Edizioni Qiqajon, 1995. [NSE]

Pamiatniki kul'tury. Novye otkrytiia (Monuments of Culture. New Discoveries). Leningrad: AN SSSR, 1974– .

Rukopisnaia kniga drevnei Rusi i slavianskikh stran: ot kodikologii k tekstologii (The Manuscript Book of Old Rus and the Slavic Countries: from Codicology to Textology). Saint Petersburg: Dmitrii Bulanan, 2004.

Rukopisnoe nasledie Drevnei Rusi. Po materialam Pushkinskogo Doma. Sbornik statei. (The Manuscript Heritage of Old Rus. From the Materials of Pushkinskii Dom, Collection of Articles). Ed. A. M. Panchenko. Leningrad: Nauka, 1972.

Speculum Slaviae Orientalis: Ruthenia, Muscovy, and Their Vicinities in the Late Middle Ages. Ed. V. V. Ivanov, J. Verkholantsev. Moscow: OTZ-Garant, 2005.

8. Studies of Nil Sorsky's Sources and Orthodox Christian Spiritual Traditions

8a. *General*

Alfeyev, Hilarion (Hegumen Ilarion Alfeev). *St. Symeon the New Theologian and Orthodox Tradition.* Oxford: University Press, 2000. Russian transl. 2nd ed. Saint Petersburg: Aleteia, 2001.

———. *The Spiritual World of Isaac the Syrian.* CS 175. Kalamazoo, 2000.

Angelov, Dimitŭr, 'Isikhazmŭt—sŭshnost i rolia' (Hesychasm—Essence and Role). PB/SB 5.4 (1981) 56–78.

Balfour, David. 'Saint Gregory Sinai's Life Story and Spiritual Profile'. Θεολογία 53.1 (1982) 30–62.

———. *Saint Gregory the Sinaïte. Discourse on the Transfiguration*. Athens, 1962.

———. 'The Works of Gregory the Sinaite'. Θεολογία 53.2–4 (1982) 417–429, 696–709, 1102–1118; 54.1 (1983) 154–183.

Beck, Hans-Georg. *Kirche und theologische Literatur im Byzantinischen Reich*. Munich: C. H. Beck, 1959.

Bianchi, Enzo. 'Korni zapadnogo monashestva i vostochnogo naslediia' (The Roots of Western Monasticism and the Eastern Heritage). MKVZ, 111–121.

Bois, J. 'Les Hésychastes avant de XIV siècle. EO (1901–1902), 1:1–11.

———. 'Grégoire le Sinaïte et l'hésychasme à l'Athos au XIVe siècle. EO (1901–1902) 2:65–73.

Brock, S., 'The Prayer of the Heart in Syriac Tradition'. *Sobornost* 4/2 (1981) 131–142.

Cavarnos, Constantine. *St. Macarios of Corinth*. Belmont Massachusetts: Institute for Byzantine and Modern Greek Studies, 1972.

———. *St. Nicodemos the Hagiorite*. Belmont Massachusetts: Institute for Byzantine and Modern Greek Studies, 1974.

Chryssavgus, John. *John Climacus. From the Egyptian Desert to the Sinaite Mountain*. Aldershot /Burlington Vermont: Ashgate, 2004.

Clark, Francis, *The Pseudo-Gregorian Dialogues*, 2 volumes. Leiden: E. J. Brill, 1987.

Disdier, M.-Th. 'Une oeuvre douteuse de saint Maxime le Confesseur: Les cinq Centuries théologiques'. EO 30.162 (1931) 160–178.

Doens, Irénéé. 'Nicon de la Montagne Noire'. *Byzantion* 24.1 (1954) 131–140.

Dörries, Hermann. *Die Theologie des Makarios/Symeon*. Göttingen: Vandenhoeck & Ruprecht, 1978.

Elm, Susanna. *'Virgins of God'. The Making of Asceticism in Late Antiquity*. Oxford: Clarendon Press, 1994.

Fedwick, Paul J. 'The Translations of the Works of Basil Before 1400'. *Basil of Carsarea: Christian, Humanist, Ascetic. A Sixteenth Hundredth Anniversary Symposium*. Ed. P. J. Fedwick. Toronto: Pontifical Institute of Medieval Studies, 1981: 439–512.

Fraigneau-Julien, Bernard. *Les sens spirituels et la vision de Dieu selon Syméon, le Nouveau Théologien*. Paris: Beauchesne, 1985.

Fustigière, A.J. *Les moines d'Orient. Vol. 1. Culture ou sainteté*. Paris: Cerf, 1961.

Gouillard. Jean. 'Un auteur spirituel byzantin de XIIe siècle. Pierre Damascène'. EO 38 (1939) 257–278.

Gribomont, Jean, osb. *Histoire du texte des Ascétiques de S. Basile. Bibliothèque du Muséon* 32. Louvain: Publications Universitaires, 1953.

Guillaumont, A. 'Le vision de l'intellect par lui-même dans la mystique évagrienne'. *Mélanges de l'Université Saint-Joseph* 50 (1984) 255–62.

Halkin, F. 'Un érémite des Balkans au XIV siècle. La vie grecque inédite de St Romylos'. *Byzantion* 31 (1961) 111–147.

Hausherr, Irénée, SJ. 'Les grands courants de la spiritualité orientale'. OCP 1 (1935) 114–38.

———. 'L'hesychasme: étude de spiritualité'. OCP 22 (1956) 5–40, 247–285.

———. *Les leçons d'un contemplatif. Le traité de l'Oraison d'Evagre le Pontique.* Paris: Beauchesne, 1960.

———. *The Name of Jesus.* Transl. Charles Cumming ocso. CS 44. Kalamazoo, 1978. (Orig. *Noms de Christ et voies d'oraison.* OCA 157 [1960]).

———. 'L'origine de la théorie orientale des huit pèches capitaux'. *Orientalia Christiana* 30.86 (1933) 164–75.

———. *Penthos; la doctrine de la compunction dans l'Orient chrétien.* OCA 132 (1944); Transl. Anselm Hufstader. CS 53. Kalamazoo, 1982.

———. 'Le traité de l'Oraison d'Evagre le Pontique'. *Revue d'ascétique et de mystique* 15 (1934) 34–93, 113–70.

Jugie, Martin. 'Les origines de la méthode d'oraison des hésychastes'. EO 30.162 (1931), 179–185.

Kiselkov, Vasil Slavov, *Grigorii Sinait, Predstavitel na mistitsizma v Vizantiia prez XIV vek* (Gregory the Sinaite, A Representative of Mysticism in Byzantium in the 14th Century). Sofia: Bel Krŭst', 1928.

Krivochéine, Archbishop Basil. *In the Light of Christ. St Symeon the New Theologian (949–1022). Life—Spirituality—Doctrine.* Transl. (from French), Anthony P. Gythiel. Crestwood, New York: Saint Vladimir's Seminary Press, 1986. Russian transl. *Prepodobnyi Simeon Novyi Bogoslov (949–1022).* Paris: YMCA Press, 1980/Nizhnii Novgorod: Bratstvo Aleksandra Nevskogo, 1996.

———. 'Introduction'. Syméon le Nouveau Théologien, *Catéchèses*, v 1. SC 96:13–203.

———. 'The Writings of St. Symeon the New Theologian'. OCP 20 (1954) 298–328.

Lake, Kirsopp, *The Early Days of Monasticism on Mount Athos.* Oxford: Clarendon, 1909.

Markus, R. A. *Gregory the Great and His World.* Cambridge: Cambridge University Press, 1997.

Meyendorff, Jean, Rev. 'L'hésychasme: problèmes de sémantique'. *Mélanges d'histoire de religion offerts à Henry-Charles Puech.* Paris: Presses Universitaires de France: 1974: 543–547.

———. 'Un mauvais théologien de l'unité au XIVe siècle: Barlaam le Calabrais'. *Byzantine Hesychasm: Historical Theological and Social Problems.* London: Variorum Reprints, 1974. V:47–64 (originally published in 1954).

———. *A Study of Gregory Palamas.* (Orig. *Intoduction à l'étude de Grégoire Palamas.* Paris: Seuil,1959). Transl. George Lawrence. London: Faith Press, 1964.

Petr (Pigol'), Igumen. *Prepodobnyi Grigorii Sinait i ego dukhovnye preemniki* (Saint Gregory the Sinaite and his Spiritual Successors). Moscow: Maktsentr, 1999.

Pelikan, Jaroslav, *The Christian Tradition. A History of the Development of Doctrine.* 5 volumes. Chicago: University of Chicago Press, 1971–1989.

Plested, Marcus. *The Macarian Legacy. The Place of Macarius-Symeon in the Eastern Christian Tradition.* Oxford/New York: Oxford University Press, 2004.

Quasten, Johannes, *Patrology.* 3 volumes. Westminister, Maryland: Newman, 1950-1960 (3rd ed., 1990).

Rigo, A. 'Niceforo l'Esicasta (XIII sec.), alcune considerazione sulla vita e sull' opera. *Amore del bello*, 87–93.

Rudberg, Styg Y. *Études sur la tradition manuscrite de sainte Basile.* Lund: H Ohlssons, 1953.

Skaballanovich, Mikhail. *Tolkovyi Tipikon: Ob"iasnitel'noe izlozhenie Tipikona s istoricheskim vvedeniem* (The Explicated *Typicon*. An Exposition of the Typicon with Commentary and an Historical Introduction). 3 volumes. Kiev: N. T. Korchak-Novitsky, 1910–1915.

Solovii, Meletius OSBM. *The Byzantine Divine Liturgy: History and Commentary.* Transl. D. E. Wysochansky, OSMB. Washington, D.C.: Catholic University of America Press, 1970.

Stewart, Columba. *Cassian the Monk.* New York-Oxford: Oxford University Press, 1998.

Straw, Carole. *Gregory the Great. Perfection in Imperfection.* Berkeley-Los Angeles-London: University of California Press, 1988.

Špidlík, Tomás, SJ *The Spirituality of the Christian East. A Systematic Handbook* (with extensive bibliography). Transl. Anthony P. Gythiel. CS 79. Kalamazoo, 1986. Original: *La spiritualité de l'Orient chrétien.* OCA 206 (1978).

Völker, Walther. *Maximus Confessor als Meister des geistlichen Lebens.* Wiesbaden. F. Steiner, 1965.

———. *Praxis und Theorie bei Symeon dem neuen Theologen: Ein Beitrag zur byzantinischen Mystik.* Wiesbaden: F. Steiner, 1974.

———. *Scala Paradisi: Eine Studie zu Johannes Climacus und zugleich eine Vorstudie zu Symeon dem neuen Theologen.* Wiesbaden: F. Steiner, 1968.

Ware, Kallistos, 'The Jesus Prayer in St. Gregory of Sinai'. *Eastern Churches Review* 4.1 (1972) 3-22.

8b. *Slavic Translations*

Birkfellner, Gerhard. *Das römische Paterikon. Studien zur serbischen, bulgarischen, und russischen Überliefung der Dialoge Gregors des Grossen mit einer Textedition.* 2 volumes. Vienna: Akademie der. Wissenschaft, 1979.

Bogdanović, Dimitrije. *Jovan Lestvičnik u vizantijskoj i staroj srpskoj knijževnosti* (John Climacus in Byzantine and Old Serbian Letters); Vizantološki institut, posebna izdanja 11. Belgrade: Vizantološki . Institut, 1968.

Bulanin, D. M. '"Paranesis" Efrema Sirina'. SKKDR 1:296-99.

Diddi, Cristiano. *I Dialogi di Gregorio Magno nella versione antico-slavica.* Salderno: Europa Orientalis, 2000.

Fedotova, M.S. 'K voprosu o slavianskom perevode postnicheskikh slov Isaaka Sirina (po rukopisiam XIV-nachala XVI vv. peterburgskikh sobranii)' (The Question of the Slavic Translation of the Ascetic Discourses of Isaac the Syrian). TODRL 52 (2001) 498–511.

Granstrem, E. E., 'Ioann Zlatoust v drevnei russkoi i iuzhnoslavianskoi pis'mennosti (XI–XIV vv.)' (John Chrysostom in Old Rus and South Slavic Writings 11th–14th Centuries.). TODRL 29 (1974) 186–193.

———. 'Ioann Zlatoust v drevnei russkoi i iuzhnoslavianskoi *pis'mennosti, XIV-XV vv.*' (John Chrysostom in Old Rus and South Slavic Writings, 14th–15th Centuries). TODRL 35 (1980) 344–375.

Hannick, Christian. *Das altslavische Hirmologion. Texte und Kommentar.* Monumenta linguae slavicae dialecti veteris, t. 50. Freiberg im Breisgau: Weiher, 2006.

———. 'Die griechische Überlieferung der Dialoge des Papstes Gregorius und ihre Verbreitung bei den Slaven im Mittelalter'. *Slovo* (Zagreb) 24 (1974) 41–57.

Hemmerdinger-Iliadou. 'L'Ephrem Grec et la littérature slave'. *Actes du XIIe Congres international des études byzantines.* 2 volumes. Belgrade, 1964. 2:343–346.

Heppell, Muriel. 'Slavonic Translations of Early Byzantine Ascetical Literature', *Journal of Ecclesiastical History* 5.1 (April 1954) 86–100.

Ivanova, Klimentina and Predrag Matejic. 'An Unknown Work of St. Romil of Vidin (Ravanica) (Preliminary remarks)'. PB/SB 17 (1993) 4:3–15.

Die Pandekten des Nikon vom Schwarzen Berge (Nikon Černogorets) in der ältesten slavischen Übersetzung. 2 pts. Ed. Rumjana Pavlova, Săbka Bogdanova. Introd. R. Pavlova. Transl. of Bulgarian introducton. Renate Belentschikow. *Vergleichende Studien zu den Slavischen Sprachen und Literaturen* 6. Frankfurt am Main: Peter Lang, 2000.

Reinhart, Johann Michel. 'Die "Dialoge" Gregors des Grossen in der kirchenslavischen Literatur'. *Österreichische Osthefte* 27 (1985) 231–49.

Saenko, L.P. 'K istorii slavianskogo perevoda teksta Lestvicy Ioanna Sinaiskogo' (Towards the History of the Slavic translation of the text of the *Ladder* of John of Sinai). PB/SB 4 (1980) 4:19–24.

Syrku, Polikhronii Agapevich. *K istorii ispravleniia knig v Bolgarii v XIV veke* (The History of Correcting Books in Bulgaria in the 14th Century). 2 volumes. Saint Petersburg: Tip. Ak. Nauk,1898, 1890; rpt. London:Variorum, 1972.

Tachaios, Anthony-Emil N. 'Gregory Sinaites' Legacy to the Slavs: Preliminary Remarks. *Cyrillomethodianum* 7 (1983) 113–165.

Thomson, Francis J., 'Prolegomena to a Critical Edition of the Old BulgarianTranslation of the 'De Ascetica Disciplina'Ascribed to Basil of Caesarea, together with a Few Comments on theTextual Unreliability of the 1076 Florilegium'. *Slavica Gandensia* 13 (1986) 65–84.

Tvorogov, O.V., 'Drevnerusskie chet'i sborniki XII-XIV vv.' (Old Rus Miscellany Books of the 12th–14th Centuries). TODRL 41 (1988), 197–214; 44 (1990), 196–225; 47 (1993) 35–53.

———. 'Opisanie i klassifikatsiia spiskov sbornikov "Zlatoust"' (Description and Classification of the Manuscript Copies of the 'Chrysostom' Compilation).TODRL 39 (1985) 278–284.

Van Wijk, Nicolaas.'La traduction slave de l' '*Ανδρῶν ἁγίων βίβλος* et son prototype grec'. *Byzantion* 13 (1938) 233–244.

Vaillant, A. 'Le Saint Ephrem Slave'. *Byzantinoslavica* 19 (1958) 279–286.

Vasilii, Archbishop (Krivoshein). *Prepodobnyi Simeon Novyi Bogoslov (949–1022)* (Saint Symeon the New Theologian, 949–1022). Paris: YMCA Press, 1980.

Veder, 'Le Skitskij Paterik (Collection systématique slaves des Apophthegmata Patrum)'. *Polata knigopisnaja* 4 (1981) 51–72.

Žužek, Ivan, SJ. *Kormčaja kniga. Studies on the Chief Code of Russian Canon Law.* OCA 168. 1964.

9. Printed Primary Sources for Nil Sorsky's Background, Life, Times, and Influence

Akty feodal'nogo zemlevladeniia i khoziaistva XIV–XVI vekov (Acts of Seigniorial Landholding and Economy from the 14th–16th Centuries). 3 vols. Ed. L.V. Cherepnin and A.A. Zimin. Moscow: Nauka, 1951–1961.

Akty sotsial'no-ekonomicheskoi istorii Severo-Vostochnoi Rusi kontsa XIV-nachala XVI v. (Acts from the Social-Economic History of Northeast Rus, from the end of the 14th to the Beginning of the 16th c.). 3 volumes. Moscow: Nauka, 1952–64. [ASEI]

Ankhimiuk, Iu. B. 'Slovo na "Spisanie Iosifa"—pamiatnik rannego nestaiszhaetl'stva' (The Discourse Against the "Composition of Iosfia"—a Monument of Early Nonpossessorism). *Zapiski otdela rukopisei* GBL (Notes of the Division of Manuscripts of GBL) 49 (1990) 115–146.

Anonymous. 'Pis'mo o neliubkakh inokov Kirillova i Iosifova monastyrei' (The Writ of Emnities between the Kirillov and Iosifov Monasteries), PIV, 366–369.

Beliakova, E.V., *'Slavianskia redaktsiia Skitskogo ustava'* (The Slavic Redaction of the Scete Typikon). *Drevniaia Rus'. Voprosi medievistiki* (Ancient Rus. Questions of Medieval Studies). 2002.4 (10) 28–36; 2003.1 (11) 63–95.

Belokurov, S.A. ed. *Zhitie prep. Iosifa Volokolamskogo sostavlennoe neizvestnym* (The Anonymous Life of St Iosif Volotsky). ChOIDR 1903. 3:1–46.

Daniil, Metropolitan of Moscow. 'Danila Mitropolita Vserossiskogo o inocheskom zakone i pravile obshchogo zhitiia v sviatei obiteli'. (By the All-Russian Metropolitan Daniil concerning the Monk's Law and the Rule of Common Life in the Holy Dwelling). DRIU, 158-167.

—— (or his chancery). 'Sudnoe delo Vassiana Patrikeeva' (The Trial of Vassian Patrikeev). VPS, 285–318.

Dmitrieva, Z.V., and E.V. Krushitel'nitskaia. *Opisi Solovetskogo monastyria XVI veka* (Inventories of Solovetskii Monastery of the 16th c.). Saint Petersburg: Dmitrii Bulanin, 2003.

Dosifei Toporkov. *Nadgrobnoe slovo prepodobnomu Iosifu Volokolamskomu.* (Funeral Oration to Saint Iosif Volotsky). Ed. Kurganovskii, Arkhimandrit Gerontii. *Volokolamskii-Iosifov muzhskii monastyr' i ego sovremennoe sostoianie* (The Iosifov-Volokolamsk Monastery and its Present Condition). Saint Petersburg, 1903: 125–138.

Dukhovnye i dogovornye gramoty velikikh i udel'nykh kniazei XIV–XVI vv. (Testaments and Treaties of the Grand and Appanage Princes of the 14th–16th c.). Ed. L.V. Cherepnin and S.V. Bakhrushnin. Moscow: ANSSSR, 1950.

Efrosin of Pskov. *Prepodobnogo Efrosina Pskovskogo chudotvortsa izlozhenie obshchezhitel'nogo predaniia* (Exposition of the Coenobitic Tradition of Saint Efrosin of Pskov). DRIU, 39–56; also Serebrianskii, N. *Ocherki po istorii monastyrskoi zhizni v Pskovskoi zemle* (also ChOIDR 1908 kn 4), 508–517; German transl. NSSS, 295–313.

Entsiklopediia russkogo igumena XIV–XV vv. Sbornik Prepodobnogo Kirilla Belozerskogo. Rossiiskaia national'naia biblioteka, Kirillo-Belozerskoe sobranie, No. XII (The Encyclopedia of a Russian Superior of the 14th–15th c. The Miscellany of Saint Kirill of Beloozero. The Russian National Library, Kirillo-Belozersk Collection, No. XII). Ed. G. M. Prokhorov. Saint Petersburg: Olega Abyshko, 2003.

Epifanii Premudrii (Epiphanius the Wise). *Zhitie i zhizn' prepodobnogo ottsa nashego igumena Sergiia* (The Life and Lifestyle of our Holy Father Hegumen Sergii). Ed. N. S. Tikhonravov. *Drevnie zhitiia prepodobnogo Sergiia Radonezhskogo.* (The Old Lives of Saint Sergii of Radonezh). 2 parts. Moscow, 1892/1916; rpt. Ludolf Müller. *Die Legenden des Heiligen Sergij von Radonez.* Separate introduction and bibiliography. Slavische Propylaien 17. Munich: Wilhelm-Fink, 1967: part 1.

Innokentii Okhliabinin 'Zavet' (Testament). in Arkhangel'skii, *Nil Sorskii i Vassian Patrikeev.* 1: *Prilozhenie* (Appendix) III. 14–16; Prokhorov, PNSIK, 320–322; Modern Greek: Grolimund, NSA, 281–284.

Iosif Volotskii. 'Dukhovnaia gramota Prepodobnago Igumena Iosifa' [The Testament Rule of Saint Iosif Volotskii]. DRIU 57–155; also VMCh, Sept., 499–615; Transl., MRIV (2nd ed.) 163–308.

———. 'Kratkaia redaktsiia Ustava prp. Iosifa Volotskogo' [The Brief Redaction of The Rule of Saint Iosif Volotskii]. DRIU, 187–215; also PIV, 296–321; Transl., MRIV (2nd ed.), 117–161.

———. *Poslaniia Iosifa Volotskogo* (The Letters of Iosif Volotsky). Ed. A.A. Zimin and Ia. S. Lur'e. Moscow and Leningrad: Nauka, 1959.

———. *Prosvetitel' ili oblichenie eresi zhidovstvuiushchikh* (The Enlightener or Exposure of the Heresy of the Judaizers). 4th ed., Kazan: University, 1903; rpt. Westmead: Gregg, 1972.

———. 'To Arkhimandrit Vassian'. PIV, 141–144.

Kazakova, N.A. *Vassian Patrikeev i ego sochineniia* (Vassian Patrikeev and his Works). Moscow-Leningrad: AN SSSR, 1960. [VPS]

———, and Ia.S. Lur'e. *Antifeodal'nye ereticheskie dvizheniia na Rusi*

XIV-nachala XVI v. (Anti-feudal Heretical Movements in Rus', 14th- Beginning 16th c.). Moscow-Leningrad: AN SSSR, 1955. [AfED]
Kloss, Boris M., *Izbrannye trudy. Tom 1. Zhitie Sergiia Radonezhskogo* (Selected Works. Volume 1. The Life of Sergii of Radonezh). Moscow: Iazyki russkoi literatury, 1988.
Kormovaia kniga Iosifo-Volokolamskogo monastyria = Das Speisungsbuch von Volokolamsk. Eine Quelle zur Sozialgeschichte russischer Klöster im 16. Jahrhundert. Trans. and ed. Ludwig Steindorff *et al.* Bausteine zur slavischen Philologie und Kulturgeschichte. Neue Folge. Editionen 12. Cologne/Weimar/Vienna: Böhlau, 1998.
Kornilii Komel'skii. 'Kornilii Komel'skii, II. Ustav ili pravila' (Kornilii Komel'skii, II. Typicon or Rules). Ed. Bishop Amvrosii. IRI 4 (1812), 661–704; also DRIU, 168–186.
Kniga glagolaemaia Opisanie o rossiiskikh sviatyn', gde i v korotom grade, ili obiteli, ili monastyre i pystine pozhive i chiudesa sotvori, vsiakogo china sviatykh. Dopolnil biograficheskimi svedneiiami Graf M. V. Tolstoi (The Book Called the Description of Russian Shrines, Where and in Which City or Dwelling, or Monastery, or Hermitage They Lived and Performed Miracles, of Every Rank of Saints. Count M.V. Tolstoi Supplemented the Biographical Material). ChOIDR 1887 4 1–291.
Kniga glagolaemaia Starchestvo (The Book called the *Geronticon*). KB 721/1198: 3v–163.
Kukushkina, M.V. 'Biblioteka Solovetskogo monastyria v XVI v.'(The Solovetskii Monastery Library in the 16th Century). *Arkheograficheskii ezhegodnik za 1970 g.* (The Archeographic Annual for 1970). 1971, 357–72; . . . *za 1971 g.* (1972) 341–356.
Letopisets ellinskii i rimskii. Kommentarii, issledovanie, ukazateli. (The Hellenic and Roman Chronicle. Commentary, Study, Indices). Ed. O.V. Tvorogov and S.A. Davydova. 2 volumes. Saint Petersburg: Dmitirii Bulanin, 1999, 2001.
Nikol'skii, Nikolai Konstantinovich, 'Materialy dlia istorii drevnerusskoi pis'mennosti' (Materials for the History of Old Rus Writing). *Izvestiia Otdelenie russkogo iazyka i slovesnosti* (Transactions of the Division of Russian Language and Literature) 1897 2.1:78–79.

———. *Opisanie rukopisei Kirillo-Belozerskogo monastyria, sostavlennoe v kontse XV veka* (The Description, Compiled at the End of the 15th c. of the Kirillo-Belozerskii Monastery Manuscripts). PDP 113 (1897).
Paisii Iaroslavov. 'Skazanie izvestno o Kamenom monastyre' (The True Account of Kameny Monastery). Ed. G. M. Prokhorov, as 'Skazanie Paisiia Iaroslavova o Spaso-Kamenom monastyria'. KTsDRRAI,

136–162; also *Pravoslavnyi sobesednik* (Orthodox Interlocutor) 1 (1861) 199–214.

Pakhomii Logofet (Pachomius the Logothete). *Pachomij Logofet. Werke in Auswahl.* rpt. of the appendices to V. Iablonskii. *Pakhomii Logofet i ego agiograficheskie pisanija. Biograficheskii i bibliografichesko-literaturnyi ocherk* (Pakhomii the Logothete and his Hagiographic Writings. Biographic and Bibliograhic-Literary Essay). Saint Petersburg: Sinodal'naia tipographiia., 1908. Intro. D. Tschižewskij (Chyzhevskii). Slavische Propyläen 117. Munich: Eidos, 1963.

———. *Zhitie i zhizn' prepodobnogo i bogonosnogo ottsa nashego Sergiia* (The Life and Conduct of our Sainted and God-bearing Father Sergii). Ed. N.S. Tikhonravov; rpt. Müller, pt. 2.

Polnoe sobranie russkikh letopisei, (Complete Collection of Russian Chronicles).Vols. 1–24, St Petersburg-Petrograd-Leningrad:Archeographic Commission, 1841–1921; 2nd ed. 5 volumes. Leningrad, 1925–1929; reprints, new editions and volumes, Moscow: 1959–. [PSRL]

'Poslanie Arkhimandrita Pecherskogo Dosifeiia Sviashchenno(inoku) Pakhomiiu o sviatogorskom ustave inocheskogo keleinogo pravila (The Letter of Pecherskii Archimandrite Dosifei to the Priest[-monk] Pakhomii concerning the Holy Mountain Typikon for the Monk's Cell Rule). DRIU, 234–235.

'Povest' o Nile-Sorskom Skite' (The Tale of the Nil-Sorsky Scete). PNSIK, 393–398.

Pravila blagoustroistva monastyrskoi zhizni (Rules for the Well-Ordering of Monastery Life). Kazan:Tipo-litografiia Imperatorskogo Universiteta, 1910.

Prokhorov, 'Zhitie i chudesa Nila Sorskogo v spiske pervoi cherverti XIX v.' (The Life and Miracles of Nil Sorsky according to a Codex of the First Quarter of the 19th c.). TODRL 50 (1997), 558–567; with slight revision: PNSIK, 403–419.

Prokof'ev, N.I., ed. *Kniga khozhenii. Zapiski russkikh puteshestvennikov XI–XV vv.* (The Book of Journeys. Memoirs of Russian Travelers, 11th–15th c.). Moscow: Sovetskaia Rossiia, 1984.

Savva Chernyi. *Zhitie i prebyvanie v'krattse prepodobnogo ottsa nashego igumena Iosifa, grada Volokolamskogo* (The Life and Sojourn in Brief of our Father, Saint Iosif the Hegumen, from Volokolamsk City). VMCh, Sept., 453–499.

Shevchenko, E.E. 'Sluzhba i Zhitie prepodobnogo Nila Sorskgo, sostavlennye v seredine XIX v. ieroskimomonakhom Nilom Prikhailovym' (The Service and Life of Saint Nil Sorsky, composed by the Schema-Ieromonk Nil Prikhailov). *Rukopisnaia kniga Drevnei Rusi i Slavianskikh stran*, 166–186.

Tipik Obiteli Vsederzhitelev'—i sushche i ponta okiiana solovetskago ot oka lavry prepodobnykh i bogonosnykh otets' nashikh" Zosimy i Savatia chiudotvortsov" (The Typikon of the Pantokrator Cloister . . . of the Laura that lies by the Solovestkii Ocean Sea of our Saintly and God-Bearing Fathers Zozima and Savatii). Sol. 1059/1168:3–93.

'Ustav Pavla Vologoskogo' (The Typikon of Paul of Vologda). DRIU, 241–247.

'Ustav Prepodobnogo Kirilla Belozerskogo chudotvortsa' (The Typikon of Saint Kirill, the Belozero Wonder-worker), DRIU, 34–37.

Vassian Patrikeev. 'Slovo otvetno' (Discourse in Response). VPS, 254–271.

Pseudo-Vassian Patrikeev. 'Otvet kirillovskikh startsev' (The Response of the Kirillov Elders).VPS, 250–253.

———. 'Prenie s Iosifom' (Debate with Iosif).VPS, 275–284.

Zhitie Korniliia Komel'skgo (The Life of Kornilii Komel'skii). Ed. A.S. Gerd. Saint Petersburg: University Press, 2004; also BLDR 13:304–353.

Zhitie Korniliia Vygovskogo (The Life of Kornilii Vygovskii). Ed. E.M. Iukhimenko. *Knizhnye tsentry Drevnei Rusi. Knizhniki i rukopisi Solovetskogo monastyria* (Book Centers of Old Rus. Bookmen and Manuscripts of Solovetskii Monastery). Ed. S.A. Semiachko. Saint Petersburg: Dmitrii Bulanin, 2004: 430–435.

Zhitie Sv. Stefana Episkopa Permskogo (The Life of St Stefan of Perm [by Epifanii the Wise]). Ed.V. Druzhinin, 1897. Photomechnaic reprint and introd., Dmitrij Čiževskij.The Hague: Mouton, 1959. also: *Slovo o zhitie i uchenii . . . Stefana, byshago v Permi episkopa* (Discourse on the Life and Teaching of . . . Stefan, Who Was Bishop in Perm). BLDR 12:144–231 (VMCh version).

'Zhitie Zosimy i Savvatii Solovetskikh v redaktsii Spiridona-Savvy'(The Life of Zosima and Savvatii of Solovki in the Redaction of Spiridon-Savva). KTsDRRAI, 220–282.

Zhmakin,V.,'Nil Polev'. *Zhurnal Ministerstva narodnogo prosveshcheniia* (The Journal of the Ministry of Public Education). 1881. 216:185–199.

Zimin, A.A. 'Kratkie letopistsy XV–XVI vv.' (Brief Little Annals of the 15th–16th c.) *Istoricheskii arkhiv* (Historical Archive) 5 (1950) 2–39.

Zosima, Diakon. 'Kniga glagolaema ksenos, sirech' strannik, spisannyi Zosimom diakonom o russkom puti do Tsaria grada it ot" Tsaria grada do Ierusalima' (The Book Called *Ksenos*, that is, *The Foreigner*, written by the Deacon Zosima, concerning the Russian Route to Constantinople, and from Constantinople to Jerusalem). *Kniga khozhenii*, 126–136.

10. Studies of Nil Sorsky's Background, Life, Times, and Influence

10a. *Studies Thoroughly Grounded in the Nil-vrs-Iosif Paradigm*[1*]

Alekseev, A.I., *Pod znakom kontsa vremeni. Ocherki russkoi religioznosti* (Under the Sign of the End of Time. Essays in Russian Religiosity). Saint Petersburg: Aleteiia, 2002.

Arkhangel'skii, A.S. *Nil Sorskii i Vassian Patrikeev. Ch. 1. Prepodobnyi Nil Sorskii* (Nil Sorsky and Vassian Patrikeev. Part 1. Saint Nil Sorsky). PDP 25. St Petersburg: I. Voshchinskii, 1882; rpt. Russian Reprint Series 20. The Hague: European Printing, 1966.

Behr-Sigel, Elisabeth. 'Nil Sorskij et Joseph de Volokolamsk'. *Irénikon* 14 (1937) 362–377.

Bushkovitch, Paul, *Religion and Society in Russia. The Sixteenth and Seventeenth Centuries*. New York—Oxford: Oxford University Press, 1992.

Borovkova-Maikova, M.C. *K literaturnoi deiatel'nosti Nila Sorskogo* (The Literary Activity of Nil Sorskii). PDP 177. Saint Petersburg, 1911.

---

1. *The standard paradigm argues or assumes that beyond, or as a result of, the differences between the small, non-communal hermitage and the large coenobium and the ascetic ideals emphasized in the writings of Nil and Iosif lay open differences of opinion; that these differences, expressed at or around synods (1490, 1503, 1504), concerned the legitimacy of monastic land-holding and/or the execution of heretics, and, perhaps, overall attitudes towards Scripture and patristics; in other words, that the so-called Nonpossessor-Possessor factional rivalry within the 16th-century Russian Church went back at least to the 1490s and to Nil and Iosif themselves. The forty-six works here under '10a', which omits some of the classics of Imperial Russian scholarship not directly consulted for this book, do not take identical positions, some, such as Moiseeva's, Seebohm's, and Zimin's being fully cognizant of the high respect that Iosifov monks had for Nil. Moreover, these distinctions are not so simple, since, for example, Lur'e, the pioneer of scholarly criticism of the old paradigm, started off accepting the authenticity of the 1503 synod debates on monastic land. The division of studies here does not represent any blanket criticism of the works which accept or do not criticize the older paradigm.

Bubnova, Valeriia, *Nil Sorskii (Istoricheskoe povestvovanie)* (Nil Sorsky: A Historical Narrative). Saint Petersburg, 1992 (private printing).

Budovnits, I.U. *Monastyri na Rusi i bor'ba s nimi krestian v XIV–XVI vv.* (Monasteries in Rus and the Peasants' Struggle against Them in the 14th–16th c.). Ed. and introd. L.V. Cherepnin. Moscow: Nauka, 1966.

Fedotov, George. *The Russian Religious Mind*. 2 volumes. Cambridge, Massachusetts: Harvard University Press: 1946–1966.

Fennell, J.L.I. 'The Attitudes of the Josephians and the Trans-Volga Elders to the Heresy of the Judaisers'. *Slavonic and East European Review* 29.73 (1951) 486–509.

———. *Ivan the Great of Moscow*. London: Macmillan, 1961; New York: Saint Martin Press, 1962.

Florovsky, Georges. 'The Problem of Old Russian Culture'. *Slavic Review* 21.1 (1962) 1–15.

———. *Puti russkogo bogosloviia* (Ways of Russian Theology). Paris: YMCA Press, 1937. Transl. Robert Nichols. 2 volumes. (Volumes 5–6 of The Collected Works of Georges Florovsky, 14 volumes. 1972–1989). Belmont: Nordland, Büchervertriebsanstalt, 1979–87.

Golubinskii, E.E. *Istoriia Russkoi tserkvi* (History of the Russian Church). 2 volumes in 4. Moscow: Obshchestvo istorii i drevnostei rossiiskikh, 1900–1911; rpt. SPR 117/1–4. The Hague: Mouton, 1969.

Gonneau, Pierre. *La maison de la Sainte Trinité. Un grand-monastère russe du Moyen-Âge Tardif (1345–1533)*. Paris: Klincksieck, 1993.

———. 'The Trinity-Sergius Brotherhood in State and Society'. MRKIS/CIM, 116–145.

Grolimund, Vasileios, Monk, Ed, transl., introd., Τοῦ ἐν ὁσίοις πατρὸς ἡμῶν Νείλου Σόρσκυ ἅπαντα τὰ σωζόμενα ἀσκητικὰ (The Complete Extant Ascetica of Our Father Saint Nil Sorsky) Preface, Metropolitan Antonii Mel'nikov of Leningrad and Novgorod. Assistant, Hieromonk Athanasios Simonopetritos. Thessalonica: Orthodoksos Kypselē, 1985. [NSA]

Kazakova, N.A. 'Bor'ba protiv monastyrskogo zemlevladeniia na Rusi v kontse XV-nachale XVI v.' (The Struggle Against Monasterial Landholding in Rus at the End of the 15th and the Beginning of the 16th c.). *Ezhegodnik Muzeia istorii religii i ateizma* (The Annual of the Museum of the History of Religion and Atheism) 1958: 151–171.

———. *Ocherki po istorii russkoi obshchestvennoi mysli. Pervaia tret' XVI v.* (Essays on the History of Russian Social Thought. The First Third of the 16th Century). Leningrad: Nauka, 1970.

———. *Vassian Patrikeev i ego sochineniia* (Vassian Patrikeev and his Works). Moscow-Leningrad: Akademiia Nauk, 1960. [VPS]
Kologrivof, Ivan. *Essai sur la saintété en Russie*. Bruges: Ch. Beyaert, 1953.
Konoplev, N. 'Sviatye vologodskogo kraia' (Saints of the Vologda Region). ChOIDR 1895.4:1–131.
Lilienfeld, Fairy von, *Nil Sorskij und seine Schriften. Die Krise der Tradition im Russland Ivans III*. Berlin: Evangelische Verlagsanstalt, 1963. [NSSS]
Makarii, Metropolitan of Moscow. *Istoriia Russkoi tserkvi* (History of the Russian Church). 1st-3rd eds. 12 volumes. Saint Petersburg: I. Iu. Bokram, 1877–89; rpt. Slavica 13–14. Düsseldorf: Brucken-Europe, 1968–1969.
Maloney, George A. *Russian Hesychasm: The Spirituality of Nil Sorskij*. SPR 269. Hague-Paris: Mouton, 1973. [RH]
Meyendorff, John. 'Une controverse sue le rôle sociale de l'Église. La querelle des biens ecclésiastiques au XVIe siècle en Russie'. *Irénikon* 29 (1956) 28–46.
———. 'Forward' to Fedotov, *Russian Religious Mind* 2:vii–xiv.
Moiseeva, G.N. *Valaamskaia beseda* (The Valaamo Homily). Moscow-Leningrad: Akademiia Nauk SSSR, 1968.
Nikol'skii, Nikolai Konstantinovich. 'Obshchinnaia i keleinaia zhizn'' v Kirillo-Belozerskom monastyre v XV, XVI, i nachale XVII vekov' (Communal and Cell Life in the Kirillov-Beloozersk Monastery in the 15th, 16th, and the Beginning of the 17th Centuries). *Khristianskoe chtenie* (Christian Readings), August 1907:153–159; February 1980:267–292; June–July, 1908:880–907.
———. *Kirillo-Belozerskii monastyr' i ego ustroistvo do vtoroi chetverti XVII veka (1397–1625)* (Kirillo-Belozerskii Monastery and its Structure to the Second Quarter of the 17th Century (1397–1625).Vol. 1, part 1. *Ob osnovanii i stroeneniiakh monastyria*. (Of the Foundation and Structures of the Monastery);Vol. 1., part 2. *O sredstvakh soderzhaniia monastyria* (On the Monastery's Means of Support). Saint Petersburg: Synodal'naia typografiia, 1897, 1910; Vol 2. *Upravlenie. Obshchinaia i keleinaia zhizn'. Bogosluzhenie*. (Administration. Cell Life. Divine Service). Ed. Z.V. Dmitrieva, E.V. Krushitel'nitskaia, T.I. Shablona. Saint Petersburg: RAN/SPb Institut Istorii/SPb Filial Arkhiva-Dmitrii Bulanin, 2006.
———. 'K literaturnosti deiatel'nosti Nila Sorskogo' (The Literary Activity of Nil Sorsky). *Trudy Slavianskoi komissii Moskovskogo arkh-*

eologicheskogo obshchestva (Works of the Commission of the Moscow Archeological Society) 5 (1911). *Protokoly* (Protocols) 32–34.

Pospielovsky, Dmitry. *The Orthodox Church in the History of Russia*. Crestwood, New York: Saint Vladimir's Seminary Press, 1998

Seebohm, Thomas M. *Ratio und Charisma. Ansätze und Ausbildung eines philosophischen und wissenschaftlichen Weltverständnisses im Moskauer Russland*. Mainzer Philosophische Forschungen 17. Bonn: Bouvier, 1977.

Sinitsyna, N. V., 'Spornye voprosy istorii nestiaszhatel'stva ili o logike istoricheskogo dokazatel'stva' (Disputed Questions from the History of Nonpossession or Concerning the Logic of Historical Evidence). *Spornye voprosy otechestvennoi istorii XI–XVIII vekov* (Disputed Questions from the History of the Fatherland, 11th–18th Centuries). Ed. Iu. N. Afanasiev, A.P. Novosel'tsev. Moscow: Insitut istorii ANSSSR, 1990: 250–254.

———. 'Tipy monastyri i russkii asketicheskii ideal (XV–XVI vv.)' (Types of Monasteries and the Russian Ascetic Ideal [15th–16th c.]). MMR, 116–149.

Skrynnikov, *Gosudarstvo i tserkov' na Rusi XIV–XVI vv.* (State and Church in Russia, 14th–16th c.). Novosibirsk: Nauka, 1991.

———. *Krest i korona. Tserkov' i gosudarstvo na Rusi IX–XIII vv.* (Crucifix and Crown. Church and State in Rus, 9th–17th c.). Saint Petersburg: Iskusstvo-SPb, 2000.

———. 'Nestiazhateli i iosifliane na sobor 1503 g' (Nonpossessors and Iosifites at the Synod of 1503). *Srednevekoe pravoslavie ot prikhoda do patriarkhata. Sbornik nauchnykh statei* (Medieval Orthodoxy from its Arrival to the Patriarchate. Collection of Scholarly Articles). 2 volumes. Ed. N. B. Barabanov. Volgograd: Volggogradskaia Eparkhiia and Volgogradskii. Gosudartsvennyi Universitet, 1997–1998). 1:126–141.

Smolitsch, Igor. *Russisches Mönchtum. Entstehung, Entwicklung und Wesen, 988-1917*. Das östliche Christentum. Neue Folge 10–11. Wurzburg: Augustinus, 1953.

Špidlík, Thomas/Tomáš (Cardinal), SJ. *Joseph de Volokolamsk. Un chapitre de la spiritualité russe:* OCA 146, 1956 (also his brief references to Nil in *The Spirituality of the Christian East*).

———. 'Nil Sorskij e Iosif Volokolamskij. Le radici del loro conflitto'. NSE, 161–170.

Ware, Timothy (Bishop Kallistos of Diokleia). *The Orthodox Church*. London-New York: Penguin, 1997 (First edition: Pelican; first revised edition: 1964, and Penguin, 1991; first printing of second revised edition, 1993).

Zhmakin,V.I. *Mitropolit Daniil i ego sochineniia* (Metropolitan Daniil and His Works). Moscow: 1881 (also in ChOIDR 1881, 1–2).

Zimin, A.A. *Krupnaia feodal'naia votchina i sotsial'no-politicheskaia bor'ba v Rossii (konets XV-XVI v.)* (The Large Seigniorial Estate and the Social-Political Struggle in Russia [End 15th–16th c.]). Moscow: Nauka, 1977.

———. *Rossiia na poroge novogo vremeni* (Russia at the Threshold of a New Era). Moscow: Mysl', 1972.

———. *Rossiia na rubezhe XV-XVI stoletii.* (*Ocherki sotsial'no-politicheskoi istorii*) (Russia at the Boundary of the 15th–16th Century [Essays in Social-Political History]). Moscow: Mysl', 1982.

10b. *Studies Less Grounded in or Outside of the Nil-vrs-Iosif Paradigm*

Alef, Gustave. *The Origins of Muscovite Autocracy. The Age of Ivan III* [=] *Forschungen zur osteuropäischen Geschichte* 39 (1986).

Alekseev, Iu. G. *U kormila Rossiiskogo Gosduarstva. Ocherk razvitiia apparata upravleniia XIV–XV vv.* (At the Helm of the Russian State. An essay on the Development of the Apparatus of the Administration, 14th-15th c.). Saint Petersburg: Izdatel'stvo Sankt-Peterburgskogo Universiteta, 1998.

Begunov, Iu. K. 'Kormchaia Ivana Volka Kuritsyna' (The *Pedalion* of Ivan Volk Kuritsyn). TODRL 16 (1956) 140–159.

Beliakova, E.V. 'Russkaia rukopisnaia traditsiia Skitskogo ustava' (The Rus Manuscript Tradition of the Scete Typikon). MMR, 150–162.

———. 'Skitskii ustav i ego znachenie v istorii russkogo monashestva' (The Scete Typikon and its Significance in the History of Russian Monasticism). *Tserkov' v istorii Rossii* (The Church in the History of Russia). *Sbornik* 1 (Collection 1). Moscow: Institut russkoi istorii, RAN: 1997, 21–29.

———. 'Ustav pustyni Nila Sorskogo' (The Typikon of Nil Sorsky's Hermitage). *Literatura drevnei Rusi. Istochnikovedenie. Sbornik nauchnykh trudov* (The Literature of Old Rus. Source Study. A Collection of Scholarly Works). Ed. D. S. Likhachev. Leningrad: Nauka, 1988, 96–106.

Bushkovitch, Paul, 'The Limits of Hesychasm: Some Notes on Monastic Spirituality in Russia, 1300–1500'. *Forschungen zur osteuropäischen Geschichte* 38 (1986) 97–109.

Casey, R. P. 'Early Russian Monasticism'. OCP 19 (1953) 372–423.
Collins, Daniel E., 'Early Russian Topoi of Deathbed and Testament'. MRC 2:134–159.
Diuchev, I, 'Tsentry vizantiisko-slavianskogo obshcheniia i sotrudnichestva' (Centers of Byzantine-Slavic Collaboration). TODRL 19 (1963) 107–129.
Dmitrieva, R.P., 'Dionisii Zvenigorodskii Lupa'. SKKDR 2.1, 191–192.
———. 'Chet'i sborniki XV v. kak zhanr' (15th c. Reading Miscellanies as a Genre). TODRL 27 (1972) 150–180.
———. 'Svetskaia literatura v sostave monastyrskikh bibliotekakh XV i XVI vv. (Kirillo-Belozerskogo, Volokolamskogo monastyrei i Troitse-Sergievoi lavry)' (Secular Literature in Monastery Library Holdings of the 15th and 16th Centuries. [The Kirillov-Belozersk and Volokolamsk Monasteries and the Trinity St Sergius Laura]). TODRL 23 (1968) 143–170.
———. 'Volokolamskie cheti sborniki XVI v.' (16th-century Volokolamsk Reading Miscellanies. TODRL 28 (1974) 202–230.
Dmitrievskii, A.A. 'Bogosluzhenie v Russkoi tserkvi v pervye piati vekov' (The Divine Service in the Russian Church during First Five Centuries). *Pravoslavnyi sobesednik* (Orthodox Interlocutor) 1882, 2:138–160, 3:212–290; 9:346–373; 10:147–167; 12:372–394; 1883, 7–8: 345–374; 10:198–229; 12:420–485.
———. *Bogosluzhenie v Russkoi tserkvi v XVI veke* (The Divine Service in the Russian Church in the 16th Century). Kazan: University, 1882.
I. Duichev. 'Tsentry vizantiisko-slavianskogo obshcheniia i sotrudnichestva' (Centers of Byzantine-Slavic Communion and Collaboration). TODRL 19 (1963) 107–129.
Egorova, M.S. 'Russkie asketicheskie sborniki XIV–XVI vv. kak tip sobornika' (Russian Ascetic Miscellanies of the 14th–16th c. as a Type of Miscellany). TODRL 56 (2004) 180–234.
Fennell, J.L.I. *A History of the Russian Church to 1448*. London-New York: Longman. 1995.
Franklin, Simon, and Jonathan Shepard, *The Emergence of Rus, 750–1200*. London-New York: Longman, 1996.
Goldfrank, David, 'The *Hilandarski Tipik*, Byzantine Monastic Reform, and Late Medieval Russia'. *Love of Learning and Devotion to God in Orthodox Monasteries/Ljubav prema obrazovanju i vera u Boga u pravoslavnim manastirima*. 5th International Hilandar Conference/5. Medjunarodna hilandarska konferencija. Ed. Miroljub Joković,

Predrag Matejic. Belgrad/Columbus OH: Raška škola/Resource Center for Medieval Studies, Ohio State University, 2006: 221–228.

———. 'The Lithuanian Prince-Monk Vojšelk: A Study of Competing Legends'. HUS 11.1–2 (1987) 44–76.

———. 'Nil Sorskii.' *Modern Encyclopedia for Russian and Soviet History* 25 (1981) 11–14.

———. 'Old and New Perspectives on Iosif Volotsky's Monastic Rules'. *Slavic Review* 24 (1975) 279–301.

——— 'Theocratic Imperatives, the Transcendent, the Worldly, and Political Justice in Russia's Early Inquisitions.' *Religious and Secular Forces in Late Tsarist Russia*. (In Honor of Donald W. Treadgold). Ed. Charles Timberlake. Seattle: University of Washington Press, 1992: 30–47.

Hainsworth, Cuthbert D., O. CARM. *Staretz Paisy Velichkovsky (1722–1794): Doctrine of Spiritual Guidance*. Rome: Pontifical Oriental Institute, 1976.

Kagan, M.D. 'Istoriia biblioteki Ferapontova monastyria' (The History of the Library of Ferapontov Monastery). KTsDRRAI, 99–135.

Kagan, M.D, N.V. Ponyrko, M.V. Rozhdestvenskaia. 'Opisanie sbornikov XV v. knigopistsa Efrosina' (Description of the Codices of the Fifteenth-Century Scribe Efrosin). TODRL 35 (1980) 3-300.

Kastorskii, A.P. *Sostoianie pravoslavnogo vostochnogo monashestva so vremeni zavoevaniia Konstatinopolia turkami* (The State of Eastern Orthodox Monasticism from the Time of the Turkish Conquest of Constantinople). Kazan, 1919.

Kazakova, N.A.. 'Knigopisnaia deiatel'nost' i obshchestvenno-politicheskie vzgliady Guriia Tushina' (The Book-Copying Activities and Socio-Political Views of Gurii Tushin). TODRL 17 (1961) 170–200.

Kolycheva, E.I. 'Pravoslavnye monastyri vtoroi poloviny XV–XVI veka' (The Orthodox Monasteries in the Second Half of the 15th–16th Century). MMR, 81–115.

Kloss, B.M. 'Iosifo-Volokolamskii monastyr' i letopisanie konsta XV–pervoi poloviny XVI v.' (The Iosifov-Volokolamskii Monastery and Chronicle Writing of the End 15th-mid 16th c.). *Vspomogatel'nye istori-cheskie ditsipliny* (The Auxiliary Historical Disciplines) 6 (1974) 107–25.

———. 'Monashestvo v epokhu obrazovaniia tsentralizirovannogo gosudarstva' (Monasticism in the Era of the Formation of the Centralized State). MMR, 57–80.

Kuchumov, V. A. 'Russkoe starchestvo' (Russian Eldership). MMR, 223–244.

Lisovoi, N.N. 'Vosmnadtsatyi vek v istorii russkogo monashestva' (The Eighteenth Century in the History of Russian Monasticism). MMR, 186–222.

Likhachev, N. P. *Razriadnye d'iaki XVI veka. Opyt issledovaniia* (Chancery Secretaries of the 16th Century. An Attempt at a Study). Saint Petersburg: V. S. Balashev, 1888.

Lilienfeld, Fairy von. 'O literaturnom zhanre nekotorykh sochinenii Nila Sorskogo' (Concerning the Literary Genre of Several Works of Nil Sorsky). TODRL 18 (1962) 80–98.

Lønngren (Lënngren), Tamara Pavlovna. 'Nil Sorskii i ego "Sobornik"' (Nil Sorskii and His Collection), paper submitted to the Harvard University Early Slavic Seminar, 26 April 2002.

———. '*Sobornik* zhitii v literaturnom nasledii Nila (The Collection of Lives in the Literary Legacy of Nil Sorsky), *Palaeoslavica* 7 (1999) 334–342.

———. 'Zhitiinyi tekst v "Sobornike" Nila Sorskogo: perevod ili pereskaz' (The Vitae of Nil Sorsky's "Sobornik": Translation or Periphrasis). *Poljarnyj Vestnik* 6 (2003), 27–32.

Lur'e, Ia. S. 'Literaturnaia i kul'turno-prosvetitel'naia deiatel'nost' Efrosina v kontse XV v.' (Literary and Cultural-Educational Activity of Efrosin at the End of the 15th c.). TODRL 17 (1961) 130–168.

Meyendorff, John. *Byzantium and the Rise of Russia. A Study of Byzantine-Russian Relations in the Fourteenth Century*. Cambridge: Cambridge University Press, 1981.

Miller, David B. 'Donors to the Trinity-Sergius Monastery as a Community of Venerators: Origins, 1360s–1462'. MRKIS/CIM, 450–74.

V. Moshin. 'O periodizatsii russko-iuzhnoslavianskikh literaturnykh sviazei v X–XV vv.' (On the Periodization of Rus-South Slav Literary Ties in the 10th–15th c.). TODRL 19 (1963) 26–106.

Pliguzov, Andrei. 'Archbishop Gennadii and the Heresy of the "Judaziers"'. HUS 16 (1992) 369–388.

Prokhorov, G.M. 'Afanasii (v miru Andrei) Vysotskii' (Afanasii [as a layman, Andrei] Vystoskii'. SKKDR 2.1.79–81.

———. 'German Podol'nyi'. SKKDR 2.1:150–152.

———. 'Gurii Tushin'. SKKDR 2.1:180–182.

———. 'Innokentii Okhliabinin'. SKKDR 2.1:405–406.

———. 'Keleinaia isikhastskaia literatura (Ioann Lestvichnik, Avva Dorofei, Isaak Sirin, Simeon Novyi Bogoslov, Grigorii Sinait) v biblioteke Kirillo-Belozerskogo monastyria s XIV po XVII v'.

(Hesychastic Cell Literature [John Climacus, Abba Dorotheus, Isaac of Syria, Symeon the New Theologian, Gregory of Sinai] in the Kirillo-Belozerskii Monastery Library, 14th–17th c.). MKVZ, 44–48.

———. 'Keleinaia isikhastskaia literatura (Ioann Lestvichnik, Avva Dorofei, Isaak Sirin, Simeon Novyi Bogoslov, Grigorii Sinait) v biblioteke Troitse-Sergievoi lavry s XIV po XVII v'. (Hesychastic Cell Literature [John Climacus, Abba Dorotheus, Isaac of Syria, Symeon the New Theologian, Gregory of Sinai] in the Troitse-Sergiev Lavra Library, 14th–17th c.). TODRL 28 (1974) 317–24.

———. 'Knigi Kirilla Belozerskogo' (The Books of Kirill of Beloozero), TODRL 27 (1981) 50–70.

———. 'Nil Sorskii'. SKKDR 2.2:133–141.

———. 'Nil Sorskij nella storia della spiritualità russa'. NSE, 39–49.

———. PNSIK.

———. 'Povest' o Nil-Sorskom skite'. (The Tale of the Nil-Sorsky Scete). *Pamiatniki kul'tury. Novye otkrytiia . . . 1976* (1977) 12–20.

——— 'Zhitie i chudesa Nila Sorskogo v spiske pervoi chetverti XIX v.' (The Life and Miracles of Nil Sorsky in a Manuscript from the First Quarter of the 19th c.). TODRL 50 (1997) 558–567.

——— and N.N. Rozov, 'Perechen' knig Kirilla Belozerskogo' (The List of the Books of Kiril of Beloozero). TODRL 36 (1981) 353–78.

Romanchuk, Robert. *Byzantine Hermeneutics and Pedagogy in the Rus' North: Monks and Masters at the Kirillo-Belozerskii Monastery, 1397–1501.* Toronto: Pontifical Institute of Mediaeval Studies, 2007.

———. 'Once Again on the Greek Workbook of Timofei Veniaminov, Fifteenth-Century Novgorod Monk'. *Monastic Traditions,* 263–304.

———. 'The Reception of the Judaizer Corpus in Ruthenia and Muscovy. A Case Study of the Logic of Al-Ghazzali, the "Cipher in Squares," and the Laodicean Epistle'. *Speculum Slaviae Orientalis,* 144–165.

Romanenko, Elena V. *Povsednevnaia zhizn' russkogo srednevekogo monastyria* (The Daily Life of the Medieval Russian Monastery). Moscow: Moldaia Gvardiia, 2002.

Rozov, N.N. 'Solovetskaia biblioteka i ee osnovatel' igumen Dosifei' (The Solovki Library and its founder Dosifei). TODRL 18 (1962) 294–304.

Serebrianskii, N. *Ocherki po istorii monastyrskoi zhizni v Pskovskoi zemle* (Essays on the History of Monastic Life in the Pskov Territory). Moscow, 1908 (also ChOIDR 1908, 3–4).

Shevchenko, Elena. E. 'Knizhnik XV v. Martinian [Kirillo-Belozerski, Troitse-Sergiev, Vozheozerskii i Ferapontov monastyri]' (The Bookman of the 15th c. Martinian [Kirillo-Belozerskii,Troitse-Sergiev, Vozheozerskii and Ferapontov Monasteries). KTsDRRAI, 283–299.

——— (Elena Ševčenko).'Le raccolte librarie dello "Skit" di Nil Sorskij dalla fine del XV al XVIII secolo. Un tentativo di riconstruzione'. NSE, 143–149.

Ševčenko, Ihor.'A Neglected Byzantine Source of Muscovite Political Ideology'. *Harvard Slavic Studies* 2 (1954), 141–179; rpt. *The Structure of Russian History.* Ed. Michael Cherniavsky. New York: Random House, 1970: 80–107; Ševčenko. *Byzantium and the Slavs.* Cambridge, Massachusetts: Harvard Ukrainian Research Institute, 1991, 49–88.

Skrynnikov, Ruslan. *Tragediia Novgoroda* (The Tragedy of Novgorod). Moscow: Izdatel'stvo Sobashnikovykh, 1994.

Speake, Graham. *Mount Athos. Renewal in Paradise.* New Haven-London: Yale University Press, 2002.

Taube, Moishe. 'The Fifteenth-Century Ruthenian Translations from Hebrew and the Heresy of the Judaizers: Is There a Connection?' *Speculum Slaviae Orientalis*, 185–208.

———, 'The Kievan Jew Zacharia and the Astronomical Works of the Judaizers'. *Jews and Slavs* 3. Ed. W. Moskovich *et al.* Jerusalem: 1995: 168–198.

———, 'The "Poem on the Soul" in the *Laodicean Epistle* and the Literature of the Judaizers'. *Kamen' Kraeug"l'n"*, 671–685.

Thomson, Francis J.'The Corpus of Translations Available in Muscovy. The Cause of Old Russia's Intellectual Silence and a Contributory Factor to Muscovite Cultural Autarky'. *Christianity and the Eastern Slavs.* vol. 1: *Slavic Cultures in the Middle Ages.* Ed. Boris Gasparov and Olga Raevsky-Hughes. California Slavic Studies, 16 (1993) 179–214.

———. 'A Guide to Slavonic Translations from Greek down to the End of the XIVth Century'. *Slavianska paleografiia i diplomatika* (Sofia: 1980) 27–36.

———. *The Reception of Byzantine Culture in Mediaeval Russia.* Brookfield,Vermont: Ashgate, 1999.

———.'The Nature of the Reception of Christian Byzantine Culture in Russia in the Tenth to Thirteenth Centuries and its Implications for Russian Culture'. *Slavica Gandensa* 5 (1978) 107–39.

Veder, William R. 'Old Russia's "Intellectual Silence" Reconsidered'. MRC 2:18–28.

Vzdornov G.I. 'Rol' slavianskikh monastyrskikh masterskikh pis'ma Konstantinopolia i Afona v razvitii knigopisaniia i khudozhestvennogo oformleniia russkikh rukopisei na rubezhe XIV–XV vv.' (The Role of the Writing of Slavic Monastery Masters of Constantinople and Athos in the Development of Book-writing and the Artistic Design of Russian Manuscripts at the Turn of the 14th-15th c.). TODRL 23 (1968) 171–198.

Von Lilienfeld, 'Der athonitische Hesychasmus des 14. und 15. Jahrhunderts im Lichte der zeitgenössischen russischen Quellen'. *Jauhrbücher für Geschichte Osteuropas* 6.4 (1958) 436–448.

Zachariadu, Elizabeth A. '"A safe and holy mountain": early Ottoman Athos'. *Mount Athos and Byzantine Monasticism*, 127–134.

10c. *Studies Moving Beyond the Nil-vrs-Iosif Paradigm*[2*]

Dykstra, Tom E. *Russian Monastic Culture. 'Josephism' and the Iosifo-Volokolamsk Monastery 1479–1607* = Slavistische Beiträge 450. Munich: Otto Sanger, 2006.

Goleizovskii, N.K. '"Poslanie ikonopistsu" i otgoloski isikhazma v russkoi zhivopisi na rubezhe XV–XVI vv.' ('The Epistle to the Icon Painter' and Echoes of Hesychasm in Russian Painting at the Juncture of the 15th and 16th Centuries). *Vizantiiskii Vremennik* (Byzanitine Periodical) 26 (1965) 219–238.

Goldfrank, David. 'The Deep Origins of *Tsar'-Muchitel'*: A Nagging Problem of Muscovite Political Theory.' RH/HR 31.3-4 (Fall-Winter 2005) 341–354.

———. 'The Literary Nil Sorskii.' HUS 28.1-4 (Forthcoming).

———. *The Monastic Rule of Iosif Volotsky*. Transl. and ed. David Goldfrank. CS 36. Kalamazoo, 1983; 2nd rev. ed., Kalamazoo, 2000. [MRIV]

———. 'Nil Sorskii and Nikon of the Black Mountain'. RH/HR, 33:2-3-4 (2006) 365–405.

———. 'Nil Sorskii's Share of *Prosvetitiel'*. *Rude and Barbarous Kingdom Revisited*. Festschrift for Robert Crummey. Bloomington, Indiana: Slavica, forthcoming.

2. **These works emphasize, variously, the degrees to which a) Nil shared ascetic and ecclesiological ideals with Iosif and collaborated with him; b) Iosifov monks assisted as well as honored Nil; and c) the more reliable paper trail sheds doubts upon the 1503 synod raising the issue of monastic lands or, at least, upon Nil's supporting confiscation by the state.

———. 'Nila Sorskogo priverzhentsy sredi startsev Iosifo-Volokolamskogo monastyria' (Nil Sorsky's Devotees among the Monks of the Iosifov-Volokolamsk Monastery). *Slavistiches'kyi almanakh*. Kiev (forthcoming).

———. 'Recentering Nil Sorskii'. *Russian Review* 58.2 (2007) 2–19.

———. 'The Role and Image of Athos in Muscovite Monastic Life of the Late 15th and Early 16th Centuries'. *Monastic Traditions*, 114–128.

———. 'Sisterhood Just Might Be Powerful: The Testament-Rule of Elena Devochkina.' RH/HR 34 (2007) 189–206.

———. 'Who Put the Snake on the Icon and the Tollbooths on the Snake? A Study in Last Judgment Iconography'. *Kamen' Kraeug"l'n"*, 180–199.

Grolimund, Vasilii. 'Mezhdu otshel'nichstvom i obshchezhitiem: skitskii ustav i keleinye pravila. Ikh voznikovenie, razvitie, i rasprostranenie do XVI veka' (Between Anchoritism and the Coenobium: the Scete Typikon and Cell Rules. Their Rise, Development, and Spread up to the 16th c). MKVZ, 122–135.

Kloss, B.M. *Nikonovskii svod i russkie letopisi XVI–XVII vekov* (The Nikon Chronicle Compilation and Russian Chronicles of the 16th and 17th Centuries). Moscow: Nauka, 1980.

———. 'Nil Sorskii i Nil Polev-"spisateli knig"' (Nil Sorsky and Nil Polev—"Book Copyists"). *Drevnerusskoe iskusstvo: Rukopisnaia kniga* (Old Rus Art. The Manuscript Book). Moscow: Nauka, 1974: 150–167.

Kolkutina, Elena Vl. See Romanenko, Elena.

Lilienfeld, Fairy von, 'A proposito della ricerche sulla figura e il ruolo storico di Nil Sorskij. Una problema di metodo'. NSE, 53–70.

Lur'e, Ia. S. *Dve istorii Rusi XV veka. Rannye i pozdnie, nezavisimye i ofitsial'nye letopisi ob obrazovanii Moskovskogo gosudarstva* (Two Histories of Rus, 15th Century. Early and Late, Independent and Official Chronicles concerning the Formation of the Muscovite State) = *Collections historiques de l'Institut d'études slaves* 35. Paris: Institut d'études slaves—Saint Petersburg: Dmitrii Bulanin, 1994.

———. *Ideologicheskaia bor'ba v russkoi publitsistike kontsa XV-nachala XVI veka* (The Ideological Struggle in Russian Public Controversy in the End of the 15th-Beginning of the 16th Century). Moscow-Leningrad: Nauka, 1960.

———. 'K voprosu ob ideologii Nila Sorskogo' (The Question of Nil Sorskii's Ideology). TODRL 13 (1957), 182–213.

———. 'Kogda byla napisana «Kniga na novgorodskikh eretikov»?' (When Was the 'Book Against the Novgorod Heretics' Written?) TODRL 49 (1996) 78–88.

———. 'Kratkaia redaktsiia "Ustava" Iosifa Volotskogo. Pamiatnik ideologii rannego iosiflianstva' (The Brief Redaction of Iosif Volotsky's Rule. A Monument of Early Iosifite Ideology). TODRL 12 (1956) 116–38.

———. 'Nil Sorskij e la composizione dell' 'Illuminatore" di Iosif di Volokolamsk'. NSE, 97–110.

———. 'Unresolved Issues in the History of the Ideological Movements of the Late Fifteenth Century'. MRC 1:150–171.

———. 'Ustav Kornilii Komel'skogo v sbornike pervoi polovine XVI v.' (The Rule of Kornilii Komel'skii in a Codex from the First Half of the 16th c.). *Rukopisnoe nasledie Drevnei Rusi*, 253–259.

———. 'Zametki k istorii publitsistichekoi literatury kontsa XV-pervoi poloviny XVI v. (Notes to the History of Promotional Literature of the End 15th—First Half 16th C.). TODRL 16 (1960) 457–465.

Ostrowski, Donald. 'Church Polemics and Monastic Land Acquisition in Sixteenth-Century Muscovy'. *Slavonic and East European Review* 64 (1986) 355–379.

———. *A 'Fontological' Investigation of the Muscovite Church Council of 1503* (Ph. D. Thesis, Pennsylvania State University, 1977).

———. 'Loving Silence and Avoiding Pleasant Conversations. The Political Views of Nil Sorskii'. *Kamen' Kraeug"l'n"*, 476–96.

———. '500 let spustia: Tserkovnyi Sobor 1503 g.' (500 Years Later: The Church Council of 1503). *Palaeoslavica* 11 (2003), 214–239.

———. 'Toward Establishing the Canon of Nil Sorsky's Works'. *Oxford Slavonic Papers* 31 (1998) 35–50.

Pliguzov, A.I 'La dottrina dei primi "Nestjazhateli" in una prospettiva storica: dall' "Insegnamento" di Nil Sorskij al programma di secolarizzazione di Ivan IV'. NSE, 123–142.

———. '"Kniga na eretikov" Iosifa Volotskogo' (Iosif Volotsky's 'Book Against the Heretics'). *Istoriia i paleografiia* (History and Paleography) 1–2 (1993) 93–138.

———. 'O khronologii poslanii Iosifa Volotskogo' (The Chronology of Iosif Volotsky's Epistles). *Russkii feodal'nyi arkhiv* (Russian Feudal Archive) 5 (1992) 1043–1061.

———. *Polemika v russkoi tserkvi pervoi treti XVI stoletii* (Polemics in the Russian Church of the First Third of the XVI Century). Moscow: Indrik, 2002.

Prokhorov, G.M. 'Avtografy Nila Sorskogo'(Nil Sorsky's Autographs). *Pamiatniki kul'tury. Novye otkrytiia. 1974 g.* (1975) 37–54.
Romanenko, Elena V. *Nil Sorskii i traditsii russkogo monashestva* (Nil Sorsky and the Traditions of Russian Monasticism). Moscow: Pamiatniki istoricheskoi mysli, 2003. [NSTRM]
────── (= Kolkutina, Elena V.). 'Nil Sorski e il suo "skit"'. NSE, 111–119.
Shevchenko, Elena E. 'Neizvestnyi avtograf Nila Sorskogo' (An Unknown Autograph of Nil Sorskii). TODRL 58 (forthcoming).
Toucas-Bouteau, Michèle. *Le monastère Saint Cyrille du lac Blanc, centre spirituel, économique, culturel et social de la fin de XIVème siècle au début du XVIème.* (Ph.D. dissertation). 3 volumes. Bordeaux: Université Michel de Montaigne, 1995.
──────. 'Nil Sorskij e il monastero di Kirill di Belozero'. NSE, 71–95.

INDEX

ABRAMOVICH, D (scholar), 41.
ACHSAH AND CALEB (OT), 77, 205.
ACCOUNTABILITY (ultimate), for asceticism according to one's power, 159; of the superior, 116.
ADAM, 163-64, 196, 211.
ADAPTING (sources) (*See also*, LITERARY DEVICES, NIL SORSKY, metaphrasis), 80–83.
ADORNMENTS (*See also* ALMS), prohibition of in all respects, 21, 78, 98, 275; unseemly to admire, 98, 121–22.
AEGEAN SEA, 14.
AFFLICTIONS, 175n; as means of acquiring tears, 207n; consolation over as spiritual alms, 119; during spiritual struggles, 142; endurance of as participating in Christ's passion, 236–37, required of neophytes, 81, 120; grant tears, 207–08; in Nil's relationship with German, 248; intellect must transpose the worthless, 208; labor with prayer as antidote, 153; monasticism as 'narrow and afflicted path', 246; not feared by adepts, 150; ought be discounted, 151; praying for those who afflict, 236; results from avarice, 172.
AGATHON (Desert Father), 90, 138n; as named, indirect source, 127; as unnamed, 69, 77, 80, 174.
AITZETMÜLLER, RUDOLPH (scholar), 79n.
AKATHISTOS HYMN, 264n.
ALEKSEEV, A. I. (scholar), 31n–32n.
ALEKSEI (archpriest, accused heretic, d. pre-1490), 60n.
ALEXANDER OF KAMENNYI (hermit), 35-36.
ALEXANDER, GRAND PRINCE OF LITHUANIA, KING OF POLAND (r. 1492–, 1501–1506), 37.
ALEXANDER THE GREAT (Tale), 11.
ALEXANDRIA, 271.
ALLELUIA (prayer segment), 144.
ALMS (*See also* CHARITY), better than adorning a church, 97–98, 121; blessing of bread,

324

gift of, 120; cedes to nonpossession, 97, 119; charity of the soul, applied to the neophyte's patience, as better, 97, 120; giving as monastic practice, 57; incumbent upon (?wicked) possessors, 97, 119; monk's giving requirement is verbal, spiritual, 119–20; monk's restricted receiving, 58n, 118, 225–26.
ALPHABETIC PATERICON, 16.
ANASTASIUS OF SINAI (ascetic Father, 7th c.), writings on the soul, urges, and thoughts, 66n.
ANATHEMA, of heretics, eternal, 50–51; in *Enlightener/ Prosvetitel'*, in *Predanie,*115.
ANCHORITIC MONASTICISM (*See also* HERMITS, SOLITUDE), 25, 48, 75; hermitages for solitiude, 128.
ANDREI-IOASAF (young prince-monk of Kamennyi, early 15th c.), 35–36.
ANDREI MAIKO (state secretary, Nil's presumed brother, d. 1502/3), 5, 31n, 34, 36–37, 43, 55, 60n.
ANDREI RUBLEV (iconographer, late 14th-early 15th c.), 49.
ANDREW OF CRETE (hymnographer-martyr-archbishop, c. 660–740), *Canons*, 16; as source, 69, 79; texts mixed with other authors by Nil, 81, 199n–200n.
ANGEL(S), 191; 'and men', as formula, 200–01; comparison to humans, 95, 149; as image, form, and rank of monk, 168; as radiant, 200; as recipients of dying person's futile prayer, 195; as witnesses of monk's vow, 167; at the second coming, 197–98; at the terrible judgment, 198; command to Anthony, 153, 234; demons as the devil's, 197.
ANGER (*See* EIGHT . . . URGES).
ANKHIMIUK, IU.V. (scholar), 60n.
ANTHONY THE GREAT (251–356, anchorite), Life, 25, 28, 31, 227n; as source, 69, 77, 153, 192, 234n, 255n; text mixed with another author by Nil, 83, 176n.
ANTICHRIST, PRECURSOR OF, as pejorative, 28n.
ANTIOCH, 28.
ANTIOCHUS, (7th c. author of *Pandects*), 205n.
ANTIQUITY (Classical), astronomical notions of, 197n.
ANUFRII ISAKOV (Iosifov disciple of Dionisii Zvenigorodskii), 47n, 48, 63n, 249n.
APHTHARODOCETISM (ancient heresy), 61.
APOCALYPTICISM, 48, 52.
APOCRYPHA, as source, 245n.
APOLOGETICS (theological), 12.
APOPHTHEGMATA, 83, 126; unidentified, 190.
APOSTLES, 54; as source of Divine Writings, 113; as universal teachers, 113; on the terrible judgement, 191–92; witness of, as guide to our advice, 242.
—feast of, 268.

ARABS, 28.
ARIANISM (heresy), 28.
ARISTOTELIANISM, 9, 87.
ARKHANGEL'SKII, A. S. (scholar), 5, 33n, 40n, 250n, 273n, 275n..
ARSENIUS THE GREAT (c. 354–c. 450, anchorite), Life, 25, 29n, 62n; as source, 69, 77, 224n, 255n; as 'perfect at stillness', 224.
ASTROLOGY, 28, 54.
ASCETIC PRINCIPLES, 122, 159; subordinated to self-preservation, 166.
ATHANASIUS OF ATHOS (Byzantine pedagogue, coenobiarch, c. 9920–c. 1000), 15; Life, 27, 119n.
ATHANASIUS THE GREAT (Patriarch of Alexandria, r. 328–373), 25, 28; anti-Arian writings (*A. of Alexandria*), 30; as unnamed source, 70.
—Ps-Athanasius, 73n.
ATHENS (Ancient), ACADEMY, 21.
ATHOS (*See* MOUNT ATHOS).
AVARICE (*See* EIGHT . . . URGES).
AZOV, SEA, 15.

BALKANS (region), 4, 16, 17.
BALTIC SEA (region), 4.
BARGAINING, prohibition of, 21, 65, 119.
BARLAAM OF CALABRIA (1290–1348, anti-Hesychast, then Catholic bishop), 18.
BARSANUPHIUS OF GAZA (ascetic Father, d. *c.* 540), 78, 124n, 126n, 144; as direct and/or named source, 68–69, 119,
127, 179, 230–31; as guarded, recommended reading in 1852, 104; as model glosser, 80; Nikon as transmitter, 71, 78; nonpossession over alms, 97; problem of Slavic texts, 78; text combined with Jesus Prayer by Nil, 179.
BASIL THE GREAT OF CAESAREA IN CAPPADOCIA (bishop, ascetic Father, c. 330–379), 34; 'Ascetic Discourse', 92, 247; *Asceticon*, Slavic (*Postnicheskie slova*), 75–76; as named or direct source, 69–70, 75–76, 97, 118n, 119, 120, 122, 136n, 166–67, 185n, 185, 219, 247; as possible source, 163n, 172n–73n, 186n, 225n, 235n–236n; as recommended reading in 1852, 104; as source via Isaac or Peter Damaskenos, 214n; Epistle No 93, as source, 271; manuscripts, 48; on therapy for despondency, 94, 181; 'Shorter Rules', enumeration, 76.
—γνῶσις, as *razumъ*, 90; φρόνησις as *mudrovanie*, 91.
BASILIAN ORDER (Uniate monastic), 70.
BEARDLESS YOUTHS, BOYS: avoidance of, 171; prohibition, 65, 123, 272–74.
BELIAKOVA, E.V. (scholar), 259n, 269.
BELARUS (*See also* WESTERN RUS), 6.
BELOOZERO (town, district, also appanage principality, 1238–1486), xxiii, 20, 33n, 34, 44, 47; 'Hermits', 32n.

'BELOVED', as term of epistolary address, 231, 243, 245–46, 248.
BERTRAM, JEROME (scholar), 94n.
BETTLEHEIM, BRUNO (psychologist), *The Informed Heart*, 96.
BEZMOLV- (hesychasm/stillness lexeme), 55n.
BIANCHI, ENZO (Prior of Boze), 63n, 68, 107–08, 164.
BIBLE (*See also* DAVID, GOSPELS, NEW TESTAMENT, OLD TESTAMENT, PAUL, SCRIPTURE), 54, 91; Septuagint, 85.
—Gospel διαλογισμός, Hebrews' ἐνθύμημα as *pomyshlenie*, 88–89.
BIBLIOGRAPHIC TECHNIQUE, 42.
BLACK SEA, 15.
BLASPHEMY, urge of, 40, 53, 240–41; as related to despondency, 23, 64, 167; befell Fathers and Martyrs, 240; caused by 'unclean demon', 240, pride and demon's envy, 241; humility as remedy, 241; repulsed with incantations against despondency, 180, 240; urge-transposition as remedy, 240.
BOJKOVSKY, GEORG (scholar), 79n.
BOLDNESS: goodly, 235, 243; negative, of pretensions 221, impedes mourning for sins, 242.
BOLSHAKOV, SERGEI (scholar), 13n.
BOOK(s), at terrible judgment, 198; for meditative reading, 50, 203, and/or services, 215; owned or copied by individuals, 12, 22, 30, 33–50, *passim*; service, 102–03; single-authored ascetic, 70–73.

BOROVKOVA-MAIKOVA, M. C. (scholar), 63n, 65, 124n.
BOYAR(S) (Russian secular magnates), 4, 5n, 27, 34, 37, 39, 58–59.
BREATH CONTROL, concentrates intellect, 139.
'BROTHERS', all due the respect of 'saints', 235; as lords, 113, 255–56.
BULGARIA, 14, 15, 71, 73n, 227n.
BYZANTIUM, 4, 38, 52.

CALENDAR, ORTHODOX, 25n, 30, 35, 52, 54.
CALLING, monasticism as, 59.
CANDLE, as metaphor, 46–47, 49.
CANON, as cell rule for singing, etc., 153; as specific hymn, 207, 260: in *Scete Typikon*, 264, 276: to Holy Trinity, Jesus, 263; ode of, 264n.
CANONS (Church law) (*See also* KORMCHAIA KNIGA), 43n, 44, 47, 50–52, 59, 267; Slavic manuscripts, 45.
CANONARCH, 215n.
CAPITAL PUNISHMENT, 50–52.
CAPPADOCIA, 26.
CAREFREENESS, 116, 213–16, 221.
CARELESSNESS: in conversing with urges leads to passion, 136; to be avoided, 157.
CASSIAN (*See* JOHN CASSIAN).
CELL: hosting only like-minded, 215; restrictions on advising within, 120–21; simplicity of buildings and objects, 122; transgressions to be confessed, 117.

CELL RULE, (for chanting, etc.), 11n.
—in *Scete Typikon* for non Vigil days: bows, numbers 265, 267; exceptions, 267–68; food, 266, fasting exception for the infirm, 276; Hours, 266; liturgical choice, 265–66; Mosaic canticles, 276; Psalter, 265–68, during Lent, 266.
CHANTING (*See also* PSALMODY, SINGING), 50, 226.
CHARITON OF ICONIUM (ascetic, mid 3rd–mid 4th c.), Life, 26, 165n, 221n.
CHARITY (*See also* ALMS), as general obligation, 53; love and c. as forgiveness, 174–75; material as superior to adorning churches, 78, 121; of the soul, 65, 97, 120; unacceptability of ill-gotten gains, 21, 118.
CHASTITY, 53; as vow, 167–68; strugglers to be summoned for aid, 169.
CHRIST (*See also* GRACE, JESUS PRAYER, LORD, SECOND COMING), birth, 53n; defiance of Herod Antipas, 53; disciples, 142n; passion, 237, 256; persecution by Judaean elite, 33n; scourging, 53n.
—as bearer of human talent, xxiii; final human destination, xxiii; universal teacher via the Divine Writings, 113.
—as 'Holy, Holy, Lamb', 271; 'King', 197; 'Lord God Jesus Christ', 240; 'our Lord', 225; redeemer, 171; Savior, 199; 'Son of God'; 'Son of Man', 197; uni-essential with God, 114n; Word of God, 192.
—authority to forgive, 200, to judge, 255n.
—'brothers in', as formulation, 58.
—commandments, 118; forgiveness, 85.
—dual nature of, 114; 'perfect God, perfect man' source, 114n.
—grace: as recipient of the self-weakener's soul, 166; preserves us in virtue, 225, 248; as redeeming agent, 160.
—invoked as God, 201; Immortal King, 201; King of all, 206; Lord, 189, 199–200; Lord and Savior, 113; Lord of glory, 201; 'Lover of Man', 199; Master, 199; Most Gracious One, 200–01; Righteous Judge, 201; Savior, 199, and intercessor, 200; Terrible Judge, 201; Trinity, 255, 'clement', 201.
—omnificence, 113.
—perfected human, soul as 'dwelling' of, 213, 214n.
—summoning to our aid as type of mental activity = watchfulness, 92, 173.
CHURCH, Greek Orthodox (Byzantine), 7; Russian Orthodox, 7–8, 14, 59; property management of, 59; 'Synodal Apostolic', in Nil's credo, 115; Union, 7, 48.
CHURCHES (Shrines), as God's, 50; items needed for sanctifying, 270.

CIVIL (STATE) LAW, 52, 52n.
CIVIL WAR, Muscovy (mid-15th c.), 6, 36.
CLIMACUS (*See* JOHN CLIMACUS).
COENOBITIC (COMMUNAL) MONASTICISM, 16, 25, 54, 57–58; as acceptable to Nil, 24, 27; as clamour, 223; compromised by secular customs, 19; contrasted with solitude, stillness, 145; entrance gifts, 39; entrepreneurship and private property, 39; rules not excessive, 225; stillness, in, 48, 128.
COLLECTIVE SELF-CHARACTERIZATIONS: capable of following the Fathers, 115–16; disinformed by the intellect, 122; infirm, 115, 118, 122, 260; passionate, 118, 122, 139; unknowledgeable neophytes, 224; unworthy, 117, of the Fathers, 260.
COMMEMORATIONS, xii, 36, 37n, 46, 47, 253, 257.
COMMANDMENTS (*See* CHRIST, DIVINE WRITINGS, GOD, GRACE, GRATITUDE, LORD, LOVE).
COMMONERS: heroics, 154–55; babble, 217.
COMMUNAL PRAYER, 58n.
COMMUNION: liturgical linked to the mystical, 95–96.
—self-administering, 22, 96, 123n; justification, 272; restricted to adepts in hermitages, absent a priest, 271, 273; ritual, 272–73.
COMPLINE, 11, 48, 266.

COMPLAINING, avoidance of, 159, 176.
COMPUNCTION, 143n, 205–07, 211; and weeping as 'king' and 'general' of an army of virtues, 208.
CONCEIT, to be avoided, 166.
CONDEMNING, avoidance of, 159.
CONFESSION, private, to the Lord, of all transgressions, 48, 83, 116, 155, 158, 182, 200, 205, 208; to the group, of passions, evil feelings, at Vigils under *Scete Typikon*: procedure, 262–64, corrrections 'in God', 264; to the superior, 24, 57, 65, 117.
CONSTANTINOPLE, 7, 10, 14–15, 19, 128, 165, 224.
CONTENTION, contentiousness, etc., avoidance of, 159, 215.
CONTRITION, 91, 156, 203; as offering to God, 203.
CONTRIVED EXCUSES, 115.
CONTROL (of entire life), 158–61.
CONVERSATIONS: 'godly', proper, 'spiritual', 159, 215, 224; ideal of humble eloquence, 236; good, avoidance of, 215–16; create turmoil of the soul, negate tears of repentance, 216, 242; idle, worldly, avoidance of, 159, 215–17, 241; improper, as inciting passions, 172, unclean urges, 234; lead to 'captivation', 135; proper as requiring extreme circumspection, 242; with the knowledgeable impart the Divine Writings, 243.
CONVERSOS, relapsed, 31n.

COUNCILS, ECUMENICAL, LOCAL: teachings and stipulations in Nil's credo, 115; in Trullo (6th Ecumenical), 270.
COUNCIL (*Sobor*), monastic, elder, 45n, 47, 121n.
COUNSELING: need for, 43; restricted to the competent, 120–21; urged on German, 247.
CHINA, 256n.
CHRONICLES, Russian monastic, 40.
CORINTH, 271.
CREMASCHI, LISA (translator), xi.
CRIMEAN KHANATE, 15.
CROSS, Nil's with stone of Lord's passions, 256.
CROSS OVER, as metaphor, 158, 204.
CROSS, SIGN OF, to accompany self-fortifying prayer, 235.
CYRIACUS THE RECLUSE (Palestinian, 447/9–554/6), Life, 26, 28.
CYRIL OF ALEXANDRIA (theologian, Patriarch, r. 412–35), 114n.
CYRIL OF JERUSALEM (theologian, Bishop, r. 350–1386), 63n.

DAILY ROUTINE, 158–59.
DAVID (*See also* PSALMS), 69, 78, 159, 168, 189, 239; as named source, 203; as 'The Prophet', 142; 'Second', as metaphor, 29.
DAMASCUS, 77.
DAMNATION (as 'judgment'), 197.
DANIEL OF SCETIS (abbot, 6th c.), Life, as source, 69, 169, 224.
DANIIL CHERNY (iconographer, late 14th–early 15th c.), 49.
DEADNESS (mortification), total, 213, 216, 220, 221n.

DEATH, as corruption, 196; as mystery, 195; as result of Adam's transgression, 163, 196; as soul separating from body, 195, 199–200; 'hour' of, 193-95; suddenness of, 193–95, 232.
'DEBATE BETWEEN LIFE AND DEATH', 48.
DEMON(S) (*See also* EVIL BEINGS, PASSION, SPIRIT, URGE), 185; aim for our destruction, 172; arrogance of 170n; artifices to impede prayer via anger or lust, 210–11; as mortal danger for active hesychast, 221; as purveyors of grief, 177, as the devil's angels, 197; attack with lust when we cannot pray, 170; dark gaze of, 200; entrance impeded by intellect placed in Scripture, 234; of idleness, 37; prayers against, 28, 189; saintly disguises, 35; 'unclean' causes blasphemy, 240.
DENIS (accused heretic, d. post-1490), 60n.
DERGACHEVA, IRINA (scholar), 13n.
DESERT FATHERS, 9, 71; as source, 77.
DESPONDENCY (*See* EIGHT . . . URGES).
DETACHMENT (*See also* RENUNCIATION/ WITHDRAWAL), 68, 72, 213–18.
DEVIL (*See also* ENEMY, SATAN, SERPENT): among the eternally anathematized, 51, destined for 'eternal fire', 197; art/cunning and evil linked, 85, 154; artifices, 122; as 'evil seducer', causes recollections of soft

faces, 171; as partial origin of our bad living, 114; as 'prince of this world', 200; envies and impedes those praying, 210.

DIADOCHUS OF PHOTICE (Bishop, ascetic Father, 5th c.), 69, 144.

DIMITUR KANTAKUZENI (b. 1435), 16.

DIONISII (Greek hegumen of Kamennyi, 14th c.), 35–36; tomb, 36.

DIONISII GLUSHITSKY (Vologda coenobiarch, d. 1437), 35.

DIONISII ZVENIGORODSKII (Iosifov prince-monk, d. 1530s), 46–48, 47n, 50, 124n, 249n, 250n; copy of *Ustav*, 225n, PDP type, 65; manuscripts, 47–48; *Scete Typikon*, 259n.

DIONYSIUS THE AREOPAGITE (corpus of Ps-Dionyseus, 5th c.), 30.

DISBELIEF, as passion, 53.

DISCIPLESHIP, as obligation, 53; as real or metaphorical 'rank' (order), 62, 226, 231.

DISCOURSE AGAINST IOSIF'S COMPOSITION, 60n.

DISHONOR (*beschestie*), 220n.

DISOBEDIENCE, when required, toward impious rulers, 53–54.

DISPASSION, as necessarily imperfect, 136; attained, 128.

DISSIDENCE, struggle against (*See also* HERESY, 'Judaizers', NOVGOROD, 'Heretics'), xi, 28n, 30, 33n, 54.

DIVINE LIGHT, 49.

DIVINE (or HOLY) WRITING(S) (*See also* NIL SORSKY, and the 'Divine Writings'), 'Holy' likely as Scripture, 164; as attributed source, 69, 126, 130, 151, 154, 160, 162, 164, 169, 172, 193, 205, 207, 224–26, 239, 243; as contrasted with other writings, 40, 242–43; as mastered by 'reliable teacher', 129, 247; as mirror of weaknesses, 151; as opposed to human will and concepts, 245; as Scripture, 260; as substance of Nil's teaching, 114, 116–17, 130, 236, 248; as substitute for 'reliable teacher', 129, 247, for the will of God, 225; as ultimate, limiting authority and guide, 8, 42, 43, 48, 124, 156, 190, 242, 245–46, 248, to be fervently heeded, 236, studied with fear of God and humility, 245, 248; command imitating the Fathers, 247; continued validity affirmed, 115, 248–49; differentiate liturgies for coenobia and scetes, 259–60; elucidate commandments, 252; encompassed by Gregory the Sinaite, 141; errors from ignorance, misconstruing of, 241, 245, 248; instruct in true knowledge and quench searing passions, 81, 130; laws of, to be followed, 242; literacy of assumed in *Scete Typikon*, 267; metaphor of living waters, 80–81, 130, 236; object of meditation, 37, 54, 100, 250; our 'sufficiency', 205; read and discussed at services under *Scete Typikon*, 262, 264; remain vaild, 248–249; sources of, 113;

submission to God via, 247;
subset of all writings, 40; witness of, as total *sine qua non*,
243, 245.
DMITRII SHEMIAKA (Prince of
Galich, d. 1455), 6, 9.
DMYTRO TUPTALO (1651–1709,
Metropolitan of Rostov,
1702–1709), menologies, 1–2.
DON, RIVER, 15.
DOROTHEUS OF GAZA (ascetic
Father, early 6th c.), Slavic texts,
40, 77; as source, 69, 77, 120,
174, 186, unnamed, 80, 176n;
as recommended reading in
1852, 104; principle of
endurance applied by Nil to
neophytes, 81, 120; texts
mixed with other authors and
texts by Nil, 82–83, 176n,
187n.
DOSIFEI (Archimandrite of
Pecherskii, early 15th c.), 138n.
DOSIFEI TOPORKOV (Iosif's
nephew-writer, d. post-1547),
47.
DOXOLOGY, 208.
DRACULA TALE, Slavic, 11.
DREAMS, avoidance of, 143.
DRUNKENNESS: beverages causing
prohibited, 57n, 274; dishonors
rank of nobleman, 217; to be
avoided, 65, 122, 163.

EATING AND DRINKING,
—in accord with strength, needs,
122, 159, 164; in fear of God,
159; requires non-selectivity,
166; with thanksgiving and
self-contempt, 164.

ECCLESIASTES, 219n.
EDEN, 196.
EFFEMINATE FACES, guarding
against, 123, 171.
EFROSIN (Kirillov ieromonk,
master-copyist, -teacher, d. c.
1511–1514), 11, 16, 19, 40.
EFROSIN (Pskov-Elizarov coenobiarch, d. 1479), Rule: as possible source, 118n, 123n.;
official imprimatur, 99.
EGOROVA, M. S. (scholar), 9n.
EGYPT: Desert monasticism,
25–26; OT bondage, 218n;
self-administration of communion, 271.
EIGHT PRINCIPAL URGES, THE (*See
also* EVAGRIUS OF PONTUS,
JOHN CASSIAN, *LOGISMOS*,
URGE), 5, 53, 76, 88, 93–94,
162–63.
—AVARICE (No. 3), 10, 53, 57, 67,
97, 172-73; as idolatry, 172,
and root of all evil, 97, 172; as
unnatural disease arising from
want of faith and intelligence,
172; self-justification of willfulness as greed/usury, 117;
suffices for destruction, 172.
—DESPONDENCY (dejection, despair, depression, No. 6), 67,
76, 85, 88, 153–54, 156,
175-78; abject prayer as remedy, 179; ἀκηδία, original
meaning, 94; arises from act of
fornication, 168; as brutal, 179;
as fierce struggle for hesychasts, 177; as if suspension of
Providence, 177; Basil on
therapy, 94, 181; danger from

solitude, 222–23; 'Enemy' active in, 177–80; God's testing, 177–81; leads to ingratitude, blasphemy, and even worse urges, 23, 40, 53, 178–80; manual labor as remedy, 179; mediates for a crown, 178; patience and trust required, but enduring in stillness as best, 180–81; prayers against, 179–80; reading as remedy, 179.

—FORNICATION/LUST (No. 2), 10, 28, 54n, 64, 67, 74, 77, 85, 167–72, 188, 238–40; abstinence from food as remedy, 166; as befitting animals, 171; as brutal, 179; attacks all who struggle in God, 238; avoidance of passion-inciting faces and voices as remedy, 240; danger of at gatherings, 167; dual nature of struggle, 167, 238; fear of God as remedy, 167, 238; generates tears, 207n; memory of angelic rank or of shame before men as remedy, 168; neophytes must completely sever, 171; prayer for aid as remedy, 168–70, 239–40; relation to sadness, 175–77; remembrance of vow as remedy, 238; the 'strong' may engage and regulate, 171; 'unnatural' class, as unbefitting animals, 171.

—GLUTTONY (No. 1), 10, 54n, 65, 67, 120, 163-167, 187n; as Adam's transgression and origin of death, 163; control as gateway to virtues, 167; defeated by timely, measured eating, 164; promotes fornication; 163, 166, and death, 167.

—PRIDE (arrogance, No. 8), 10, 53, 67, 170n, 184-88; as abomination, 184; caused by deceitful ardor, 219; as summary, destruction-bearing evil, 184; glory as shame, 187; humility in practice as remedy, 185–87; of talents or inherited or acquired worldly success, 98–99, 187; of the worldy regarding possessions, villages, 97–98, 186–87; suffices for destruction, 172; prayer as remedy, 187; recollection of God as remedy; self-reproach as remedy, 186, 188; the virtuous as vulnerable, 186–87.

—SADNESS (grief, melancholy, No. 5), 54n, 67, 94; contemplation of Providence as remedy, 175; contrast of the 'beneficial'' . . . 'over sins,' with the pernicious over the worldly, 94, 175–75; gratitude and repentance as salvatory remedies, 176; link to despondency, 175; prayer, reading, spiritual conversations as remedies, 177.

—'seven deadly sins' analogy, 88.

—VAINGLORY (No. 7), 54n, 67, 158, 182–84; as a clever spirit, 182; as a stillness-perverting 'passion of the soul', 223; consciousness of pleasing God over humans as remedy, 182; generates pride, 184, tears,

207n; humility as remedy, 187; memory of death, mourning, and humility or recall of transgressions as remedies, 182–84; prayer as remedy, 187; self-reproach as remedy, 186, 188; the virtuous as vulnerable, 186–87.
—WRATH (anger: hence avoidance of malice, No. 4), 10, 53, 67, 77; compels memory of evil, 173; guarding against after tears, 210; one's miracles cannot compensate for, 174; overall forgiveness as remedy, 173; praying for or summoning prayers of offender as remedy, 174.
'EIGHTH COUNCIL', as pejorative, 7.
'ELDER', an, as attributed source, 80, 190, 220,
'ELEVENTH RUNG', as metaphor, 79, 150.
ENCLOSURE (of monks), 57, 57n; permission required for even necessary leaves, 120.
ENSLAVEMENT, to God as opposed to the world, 158.
EMANCIPATION PROCLAMATION (Russia's, 1861).
ENEMY, ADVERSARY (*See also* DEVIL, SATAN), 166–67, 170n, 185; as chief of an army, 208; as in temptation of Christ, 131; as jailor of the sinful, 200; as of our souls, 233; as source of evil and mistakes, 114; as unavoidable source of assault, to be combated, of an urge, 131–35, 137, 160, 189; attacks the despondent with mounting despair, 177, the lustful, 170, presenting the good as abominable, 171; confuses the precipitous, 221; due to the Fall, gained entrance into all humans, 132; evil artifices, 180; mocks the fallen, 185; operates at God's sufferance, 178; tears from his thoughts to be transplanted, 208; uses inner urges to disrupt the mourning, 210.
EPHREM (EPHRAIM) OF SYRIA (ascetic Father, hymnographer, 4th c.), 17, 142; *Paranesis* and the problem of the Greek 'Ephraim', 79; Slavic texts, 50: as direct and/or named source, 69, 79, 187n, 206, 225; as possible source, 197n, 201n, (less likely) 255n; as recommended reading in 1852, 104; on the heart, 91–92.
—Ps-Ephrem, 73n, 142n.
EPIFANII LENKOV (Iosifov elder), 46n.
EPIFANII THE WISE (hagiographer, later 14th-early 15th c.), 4.
EPISTEMOLOGY, 52.
EPISTLES (of Nil), 23, 41, 76; consciously as sermon, 231; dates, 63; manuscripts, 45, 62n–63n, 63–64, 66n; structures, 64.
—'LITTLE', 47, 62–63, 63n, 100, 229n, 250.
—'TO GERMAN', 42–43, 62–63, 64, 76, 245–49.
—'TO GURII', 39, 62–63, 238–44.
—'TO VASSIAN', 58–59, 60n, 60–63, 86, 231–37.

ETERNAL LIFE, 114; found in Scripture, 130; goal of God's trials, 237.
ETHICS, 52–53, 87, 98.
EUCHOLOGION, 256.
EUGENIA THE MARTYR (at Rome, 3rd c.), Life as source, 69.
EUSTRATIUS THE MARTYR (Sebasteia, late 3nd c.) (*See also* SYMEON METAPHRASTES), Life, prayer as source, 79.
EUTHYMIUS THE GREAT (377/8–473, ascetic), 26; Life, 26, 28n, 31, maybe contradicting Nil, 255n.
EVAGRIUS OF PONTUS/PS-NEILOS THE SINAITE (ascetic Father, 346–97), 176, 138n: as author of *Chapters on Prayer*, 12–13; as possible indirect source, 119n; *Praktikos*, 65n: on the 'Eight Urges', 67, 76; as unnamed source, 68–70, 138, 205.
—νοῦς as *umъ*, 90, 142n; νοήματα as *pomyshlenie*, 89, 140n–41n; σκοπός as *razumъ*, 91.
EVIL BEINGS (*See also* DEMONS), operation of, 127.
EXEGESIS, parabolic, 77.
EXPULSION FROM CLOISTER, 117.
EXTERIOR ACTIVITY, as futile without the interior, 127.

FALL (of humanity), 164; as metonymy for fornication, 168.
FASTING, 122; cuts off urges, 221n.
FATEI (FOTII) THE OLD (Iosifov writer, 1st half 16th c.), 46n.

FATHERS, EXEMPLARY (?Kirillov's equivalent of the Council Elders), respect due to their authority, 236.
FATHERS, REVERENTIAL, to be emulated within the cloister, 236.
FATHERS, THE' (or THE HOLY'; *See also* TRADITIONS), as attributed source, 69, 80, 86, 117, 118, 124, 126–38, 162–65, 168, 170–72, 174, 181, 184, 186, 188, 190, 193, 199, 204, 207, 220, 223–24, 233–34, 238–41, 243; as guide, 42, 246; as model glossers, 80; as models to imitate, 102, 130, 247–48, 253; as practitioner-teachers, 150–51; as sources of the Divine Writings, 113, 226; as 'the thoughtful', 165; as 'the wise', 143, 163; enlightened by knowledge, 226; grasp of supreme wisdom, 213; life of in *Predanie* title, 113; Lives, in *Sobornik*, 251; of the 'outer region' (*Scete Typikon*), 259–60; traditions to be followed, 115–16.
FEAR (*See* GOD, TERROR).
FËDOR KURITSYN (state secretary, accused heretic, d. c. 1500), 37, 60n.
FEMALES (human, animal): avoidance, 171; prohibition, 65, 123, 274.
FERAPONTOV MONASTERY (Beloozero), 20, 30, 33n, 35.
FILARET DROZDOV (Metropolitan of Moscow, reformer, r. 1821–1867), 103–04; 1852 guidelines for monastics, 104.

FILOFEI (Hegumen of Kirillov, 1464/5–1465/6), 10n.
FILTH, FILTHY (usually referring to sex; *See also* UNCLEAN), 166, 168, 207; flesh, 205; lusts, 171; self, 185, 201; sins, 253; soul, 206; spirits, 253n; urges, 154–55, 168, 170, 180, 239, 268.
FIRE METAPHORS, SIMILES, negative: 130, 136, 140, 211, 242; positive: 147, 178, 209.
FLORENCE, UNION OF (1439), 7.
FOOD AND EATING REGULATIONS, 58n, 164–67; as proportional to strength, 122, 165: varied rule for, 164; fasts, 165; tasty, recollection of, 163; turn to stench, 164.
FORCES, DEMONIC, EVIL, 87.
FORGIVENESS (human), 53, 85, 173, 175; Nil's, 255; of heart, 174.
FORNICATION (*See* EIGHT . . . URGES).
'FOUR WINDS', 197.
FOX, as metonym for tyrant, 53.
FREEDOM, monastic sense of, 218n.
FRIENDS, 'usual,' with worldly conversations, to be shunned, not reproached, 241–42.
FREUDIAN PSYCHOLOGY, 96.
FUNERAL SERVICE, Orthodox, 206n.
FURY, as passion, 53.

GALMOZZI, MARUSJA (translator), xi.
GENNADII (Archbishop of Novgorod, r. 1484-1504), 30-31, 33n, 34, 51-52, 54, 56.

GENTRY, 5, 44, 55.
GEORGE, SAINT, cult of, 28.
GERMAN PODOL'NYI (d. 1533, devotee of Nil, erstwhile Kirillov teacher, bibliographer), 20, 34, 36, 36n, 42–46, 76, 78; manuscript catalogue, 43, 78n, 256n; student or kinsman of, 42–44, 44n.
GERMANUS (Hymnographer-Patriarch of Constantinople, r. 715–730), *Verses*, Slavic texts, 50; as source, 69, 79, 206.
—τῶν φρενῶν as *smyslъ*, 89.
GERMANY, 48.
GERONTII (Metropolitan of Moscow, r. 1463–1479), 35.
GIFT(S) (of God), 128, 137, 147, 151, 156n, 174, 193, 207; granted followers of God's will, 244; patience in afflictions as, 127; require timing, 219; tears as, 203–05, 207.
GLUTTONY (*See* EIGHT . . . URGES).
GOD (*See also* CHRIST, GRACE, GIFT, LORD), all that displeases to be avoided, 225–26; conversation with as result of meditative reading, 37; covenant with precludes intercourse with laity, 218; enlightenment from, 43, in prayer, 49; fear of, as positive, 59, 167–68, regarding assigned work, 120; effect of abandonment by, 185; good deeds with, as help at time of death, 195; goodness of, 208, as provider, 226; joy of, 148; knowledge of, 148; life in, 158; 'man of',

as metaphor, 39; miracles (humans), as result of granted divine powers, 156; monasticism as service to, 58, 233; redemption of Hebrews as servitude to, 218n; role at the terrible judgment, 198; role in driving off urges, 133; services of labor partake of, 226; solace of, as aid for stillness, 220; 'spiritual rod', 177–78; trust (human) in, 158; vision of, 148; work (human) of, 144, 150–51, 156; ('the Lord's'), 158, 213, 225.

—adopts those who love enemies, etc., 174; alleviates fears, 235; attends to praying intellect, 127; benefits humans via misfortunes, 58; condemns, punishes for goading an urge, 188; drives away urges, 169, 234, 239; enlightens, instills knowledge, understanding, 161, 225; forgives the determined and the confessing infirm, 134, the practitioners of love, 160; grants to humans awards according one's labor, 248, divine powers, 156, tears, 207n, the 'word', 133, 140; imparts skill in stillness to the most active and faithful, 129; judges toil favorably over results, 202; leads pious sufferers to eternal life, 237; limits (human) time in ecstasy to allow for teaching, 149; manipulates *theoria*-producing grace, 23; never abandons the faithful, 180; renders to each according to his deeds, 114; sees to the needs of the patient, 236; spares the contrite and humble, 203; takes those he loves from the 'world' into monasticism, 232.

—aid of, 133–34, 140, 170, 185, 189, 193, 205, 213, 220, 235, to those who avoid improper intercourse with others, 234; invoked in prayer of repentance 205; summoned, 140, 169, 179, 189–90, 208, 230.

—as Creator, Maker, 205–06, 211, 'good judge', 202; inquisitor and judge, 167, 'joy of mine,' 168, 239; Master, 206, 'mighty', and the proper one to reproach others, 241–42; 'most gracious', 198, 'Most High', 59, 233–35; omni-observing, 158, 167, 176, 'Omnipotent One', 239, omnipresent, 158, omniscient, 158, perfect tranquility, 145, recipient of gratitude, 55, 191, 'of all joy and comfort,' 59, 237, 248; responsible for all human fortune and achievements, 187, sufficient judge of shortcomings, 39, total practitioner of his created human capacities, 158, ultimate aid to be summoned against evil urges, 189, ultimate master-pedagogue, 23.

—as 'Father', 114, 126, heavenly, 173–74, the righteous as 'blessed of, 198.

—commandments to be followed, 115, 158, 160n, 225,

contemplated, 190; role in origin of death, 196; to 'work' and 'guard', 211.
—creation of to be appreciated, 166; proper approach to, 213–14, 221; righteousness, to be followed, 158; will as goodly, combined with monk's preserving his commandments will effect the erection of a church, 274; will, as perfect, 227, to be followed, 158, 221.
—design (*oikonomia*) of (*See also* Providence), 145, 203, 207.
—love (for humans) of, 148, 160n, 206; applying self to, 157; as prayer of the intellect, 221; as 'sweeter than life', 148; creates beneficial afflictions, 237; experienced, 148; mysteries of designs of grant tears, 207; no sin defeats, 176; required for repentance, 206; 'spiritual rod' from, 177–78; takes one from the world into monasticism, 58, 233, as a grace, 237; 'typikon' of divine, 247.
—to be gazed upon, 151, 159, glorified, 158; pleased (as opposed to humans), 158.
—Trinitarian theology of, 114.
—word of: as fundamental message, must be spoken, 116; as ascetic's sword, 221; heeding as facility in knowledge, 244; 'seed' of: triple metaphor with heart as 'blessed land.' and 'double crop', 244; sought in epistle, 231.
'GOD IS WITH US', 158n.

GOLDEN HORDE (*See* QIPCHAK KHANATE).
GOLDFRANK, DAVID (scholar), and Iosif, xii, 49; and Nikon, 70; previous mistakes noted, 9n, 32n, 38n, 59n, 74n.
GOLEIZOVSKII, N. K. (scholar), 49.
GOSPEL(S): adaptations, 81; as book, 35; as rhetorical model, 84–85; as source, 84n, 86n, 91, 114n., 118, 119n, 126, 129–30, 130n, 131n, 142, 168n, 173–75, 180n, 183n, 187n, 191, 196–98, 203n, 206n–07n, 209, 221n, 232n, 244n, 246n, 266n, 271; language, 88; Old Slavic, 174n; texts blended, 85.
GRAND COMPLINE, 158n, 207n.
GRACE (OF GOD; *See also* CHRIST): abandons the non-humble, 156; as acquirable, 128, 160; of the Spirit by following the commandments, 128; credited for a successful outcome, 20, 23, 116, 160, 246; directs to good deeds, 225; enlightens, instills knowledge, 151; grants the soul compunction and tears, 208–09; helps direct to good deeds, 225; hope placed in, 68; helps to keep one on the 'divine path', 243; instructed the ascetic masters with the same knowledge, 86, 126; invoked as responsible for *Sobornik*, 251–52; needed even by adepts for spiritual success, 233; one becomes worthy of, 50; operation of in prayer, 139, 141, of Spirit of in prayer, 209; perfects the saints, 142;

persists to today, 152; promotes good boldness to the trusting, 235; protects from enemies, 156; tears as from, 193, or as result of, 202; visitation should prompt humble, grateful confession, 155.
GRAMMAR (pedagogical-curricular), 9, 54, 215n, 247n.
GRATITUDE (thankfulness), as commandment, 55.
GREECE, 25, 27.
GREEK LANGUAGE (and texts), 7, 15, 18, 103.
GREGORY, "COMRADE' (recipient of Epistle from Basil), 75.
GREGORY HAMARTOLUS (9th c.), *Chronicle*, 16.
GREGORY OF NYSSA (bishop-theologian, c. 335–c. 385–395), as unnamed source, 70; Life of Macrina (4th c.), prayer as source, 79; text mixed with other authors by Nil, 83.
GREGORY PALAMAS (1296–1359, Hesychastic Theologian, Metropolitan of Thessalonika, 1347–1359), 18, 93, 95; on the heart and intellect, 96n; Taboric Light theory, 95.
GREGORY THE GREAT, POPE OF ROME (r. 590–604), *Dialogues* ('*Italian Patericon*') attributed to, as source, 69, 77, 193, 204–05.
GREGORY THE SINAITE (ascetic Father, c. 1263–1346), 9, 24, 71, 95, 105; Life, 48, as source, 128n; and coenobitism, 128; *Acrostic Chapters* (discourses on prayer), 73; as source, 43, 48, 66–69, 73, 127n, 128, 129, 138–46, 155–56, 163–64, 169, 185n, 186, 221: must be the Slavic, 139n; un-attributed, 151–52, 234n, 236n, 239n; as model adapter, 81, employer of Aristotelian conceptual world, 87, glosser, 80, reverser of word order, 85; possible 'father' in *Scete Typikon*, 260–61; possible source, 163n, un-attributing user of Climacus, 140n–41n., 170n, of Isaac, 143, transmitter of Basil/Ps-Basil, 76, 129n, 240n, Ephrem/Ps-Ephrem, 79, 142, utilizer of Barsanuphius, Diadochus of Photice, Mark the Ascetic, 144, of Ps-Symeon, 138n–39n; on breath control, 139n; on the heart, 91, 138–39; and the intellect, 96; Slavic texts, 40, 72–73; system-*typikon*, 143–46; texts blended and adapted by Nil, 82, 131, 138, 179; texts mixed with other authors by Nil, 82, 141.
—Ps-Gregory (*See also* Ps-John of Damascus), 73n, 131, 134; text mixed with other authors by Nil, 83.
—ἐνέργεια as *děistvo,* 92; νοῦς as *umъ,* 90.
GRIBOMONT, JEAN OSB (scholar), 75–76.
GRIEF OF THE MIND, as substitute for failed tears as physical deeds, 202–03.
GROLIMUND, VASILEIOS (monk-scholar), xi, 62n–63n, 65, 68,

78, 106, 124n, 164n, 189n, 214n, 218n, 230n, 259n.

GUARDING (of gains, against assaults; *See also* INTELLECT), 68 210–12; as type of mental activity = watchfulness, 92, 153; 'of the intellect', 86; corrupted by conversation, 216–18, within the heart seen as metaphorical, 96n; soul forgets due to intercourse with laity, 218.

GURII TUSHIN (1452/1455–1526, devotee of Nil, Kirillov master-copyist, also hegumen, 1484), 19, 39–41, 63n; Greek letters, 254; manuscripts, 17, 22, 23n, 39–41, 45, 64, 253n–254n; spiritual love claimed to edify Nil, 238.

HABITATION/COMMUNITY of two or three as ideal (*See also* 'ROYAL ROAD'), 222–25.

HAGIOGRAPHY, 16, 24–30, 35, 54; Slavic texts, 40, 50.

HANDICRAFTS, 11, 48; to be mastered, 100, 250.

HARLOT (NT), as model of tears, 189.

HATRED, of heretics, as duty, 52.

HAUSHERR, IRÉNÉE SJ (scholar), 75.

HEART: abducted in 'captivation', 134; 'action', 'activity' of,' 86, 126; adultery of, from entertaining lustful urge, 91, 168; as containing sin, 213; as locus of implanted words, 193; as source of evil, defiling thoughts, 86, 126; as vulnerable to lust, 167–68; 'blessed land' as triple metaphor with 'seed' of word of God and 'double crop', 244; depth of,· 207; guarding of, 191, attentiveness as, 209; images of, 91–92, 95–96; prayer of, as wellspring of all good, 140; pain of creates cheer, 152; relation to the intellect, 95–96: in guarding by gazing into, 138, in the assault of an urge, 131, urge confined within, 139–42; silent prayer of, as type of mental activity = watchfulness, 93; 'secret man of,' 91, 167–68, 238–39; should contemplate the terrible judgment, 199; 'thoughts of', 91; vineyard of, as metaphor, 80, 130.

HEAVEN(S) (*See also* KINGDOM): at time of Second Coming, 197; h. fatherland for ascetics as metaphor, 59, 233; palace of, 198.

HEBREWS (ancient), 218n.

HEDONISM, 122.

HELL: as Satan's goal for humanity, 200; vision of in model self-deprecation, 186.

HELLAND, T (scholar).

HERACLITUS (Hellenic philosopher, late 6th c.), 81.

HERESY, HERETICS, (*See also* DISSIDENCE. 'JUDAIZERS,' NOVGOROD, ancient, obscure, 28, 52n, 61; issue of condemnation or execution of, 43n, 46n, 59, 60n, 310n; opposition to, 50; Spanish, 31n.

HERMIT(S), 25–28, 35–36, 50.

HERMITAGE (as type of monastic community), 8, 21–23, 32n, 35-36, 47, 50, 56, 58, 128, 259, 271–72.
HEROD ANTIPAS (tetrarch), 53n.
HEROD THE GREAT (King of Judaea, r. 37–34, BCE), 53n.
HESYCHASM (*See also* BEZMOLV-, STILLNESS), 54, 95–96.
HESYCHIUS OF JERUSALEM (presbyter-exegete, 5th c.), 76.
HESYCHIUS OF SINAI (ascetic Father, 7th–9th c.), *On Watchfulness*, 65n, 76; as source, 76, 86, 126n, 128. 138; four types of, 92; text mixed with other authors by Nil, 82, 129n.
—νοῦς as *umъ*, 90; διαλογισμός, of Gospel, ἔννοια as *pomyshlenie*, 88–89.
HILANDAR MONASTERY (Mount Athos), 15; manuscripts, xiii–xiv, 73n, 78.
HILANDAR RESEARCH LIBRARY, xiv, 14, 17, 69.
HILARION (anchorite, 291–371/372), Life, 25.
HISTORY, SACRED, 54.
'HOLY FATHERS' (*See* Fathers).
HOLY FOOLS, 217n.
'HOLY FORTY' (Lent), 261.
HOLY LAND (*See also* PALESTINE), 11.
HOLY SPIRIT: ancient denial of hypostatic equality of, 28; consolation of, 181; fruits of, 213; operation of aided hesychasts, 223, in prayer, 147; the 'perfect' in, 143; the perfected as filled with, 213; visitation of, 220n.

HOURS, 11n, 260, 262n; Book of, 17, 35.
HUMANISM, BYZANTINE, 11.
HUMILITY, 91, 145n; accompanies love of neighbor, 160; as means of self-strengthening, 67; as summoning an enemy's prayers, 174; 'contrite and humble heart', 91, 203; defeats vainglory and pride, 186, 241; from expulsion, 117; from Providence, 156; Gregory the Sinaite on, 73; in rituals, 263; model self-reproach, 186; of one's reasoning, 155; prayer for, 187, in 162, words of, 169, 239; required for investigating the Divine Writings, 245, 248, proper conversations, 235–36, self-administration of communion, 272; stillness, 220–21; total regarding one's self, 156, 185.
HUNGARY, 48.
HYMNOGRAPHER(S) (*See also* JOHN OF DAMASCUS); as source, 69, 194, 206; texts adapted, combined by Nil, 82, 189–90.
—νοῦς as *umъ*, 90.
HYSSOP, 206.

ICONOCLASM, 50; controversy (Byzantine), 26–27, 28.
ICONOGRAPHY, 49.
ICONOSTASIS, 263.
ICONS: terrible judgment, 201n; miraculous, 36.
IDIORRHYTHMA (*See also* LAURA, SELF-REGULATION), 16n, 116; as acceptable to Nil Sorsky, 27.

IDLENESS, as demon, 37.
IERONYMOS OF AEGINA (monk, 1883–1966), 71n.
IGNATII MATFEEV (Kirillov igumen, 1471–1475), 256n.
ILLITERATE MONKS, 39n, 50, 64n, 259n, 269n.
ILLUMINATION, (higher), 146.
IMMORTALITY, tasting, 140.
IMMUNITY CHARTER, Kornilii's, 58.
IMPASSIVITY (See DISPASSION).
IMPIETY, 54.
INCARNATION, doctrine, 52.
INDIFFERENCE, opposed, 116; towards assigned tasks, 120.
INFERIOR RANKS (See COMMONERS).
INFIRMITY (of body), as legitimate hindrance, limit, with concessions, 118, 122, 133–34, 141, 159, 162, 182, 203–04; as 'true', 204; of faith or soul, 166, of 'urge', 211.
INNOKENTII OKHLIABININ (Nil Sorsky's disciple-hermitage founder, d. c. 1511–1514), 13–14, 22, 37–39, 55; and Kornilii, 57n; as 'poor monk', 'sinner', 273; IRI type of Ustav, 65; requests prayers, 273.
—Zavĕt (Testament), 38, 273–76; and Kornilii, 58n; and Predanie, 38, 65, 123–24, 224n, 274n; and Ustav and Scete Typikon, 274n; as authoritative, 276; beardless males banned, 273–74; cell ownership, 275; female gender banned, 274; future church, 274: adornments banned, 275; intoxicating beverages banned, 274;
Nil's writings as authoritative, 274–76; quarrels to be avoided, 273; self-regulators to be admonished, then expelled, but allowed back if reformed, 275–76; superior and brothers govern, 275.
INQUISITION: debate over, 43, 43n, 59–60; Russia, xi, 31, 50–52, 54; Spain, 31n.
INTELLECT (*umъ*) (See also HEART), 83; as agent of prayer, 90, 126; God attends to, 127; as 'optic' of the soul, 109, 127; focused by breath control, 139; deceivable by 'artful praises,' 122; disinforms, 122; requires cleansing, at night, 127; requires compunction, 211; should preview the second coming, etc., 196, 199; to be united in love, near or far, 160; vulnerability to destructive dissipation, 211.
—guarding (preserving) of, 124, 261; as watchfulness, 128; keep deaf and mute at time of prayer, 138; maintain in piety, 159: failure results in 'the fire', 127; suspend in reverence, 158.
IOANNIKIOS THE GREAT (anchorite, 752–846), Life, 28, 29.
IONA, METROPOLITAN OF MOSCOW (r. 1448–1461), 7, 10.
IOASAF (Obolensky, Archbishop of Rostov, r. 1481–1489), 30, 33n.
IOSIF VOLOTSKY (coenobiarch, 1439/40–1515), xii, 8, 41, 43n, 44–55, 45n; and charitable labor, 78n; and Kornilii

Komel'skii; and nonpossession, 78n; and Ps-Macarius, 78n; and stillness, 48–50, 54; and the Desert traditions, 78n; attacks against, 29, 43n, 44, 59–61; effects execution of 'heretics', 51–52, 59–60; excommunication of, 44–45; Life by Savva Cherny, 115n; rhetorically addressed by Ps-Vassian, 29, 101; Testament, 255n.

—*Enlightener* (*Prosvetitel'*), 43n, 59: adaptation of the eight urges, 53; manuscripts, 51; political doctrine, 53; on John the Forerunner and monasticism, 274n; on prayer, 52-53; 'Tale of the . . . Novgorod Heretics', 52; theology within, 52; use of *razumъ*, 124n.

—Rule(s), xii, 11n, 21n, 48–50, 56–58, 121n, 153n, Brief and Extended versions, 57n; enforcement, 121n; Goldfrank translation of, 68; official imprimatur, 99; 'Rule in Brief', 64n; use of John Cassian and Nikon, 70n; similar to *Scete Typikon* on cutting off will, 267n; 'typikon,' metaphorically, 247n.

IOSIFITES (Josephites), xii; attacks against, 44, 46, 61.

IOSIFOV-VOLOKOLAMSKII MONASTERY (*See also* VOLOKOLAMSK PATERICON), 35, 40, 45–47, 50, 61, 66n; manuscripts, 45–48, 64, 73n, 124n, 249n; patronizes Nil, 45.

IRMOLOGION, 256.

IRRATIONAL, THE, 237; concerns of monastic properties and profits, as, 39, 99, 205, 214–15, 241, or of the world, 97, 237; freedom from as spiritual prerequisite, 215; movements of the flesh as, 205; lust as, 209; self-will as, 42; sinfulness in general, 206; vrs rational, 214–16, 247.

ISAAC OF DALMATIA (anchorite, d. 383), Life, 27–28.

ISAAC THE SYRIAN (of Nineveh, 7th c. [Nestorian] ascetic-mystic Father and bishop), 19, 120n, 133n.

—ascetic homilies and letters, 75; as guarded recommended reading in 1852, 104, 108; characterizations of, 71; *Epistle to Abba Symeon*, 242n; Greek versions, 71–72; modern translations and printing, 72n.

—Slavic texts, 26n, 40, 49n, 71–72, 103: as source, 67–69, 71–72, 105, 119, 127, 129n, 132, 146–49, 151–55, 162, 169, 176, 185n, 188–89, 192–93, 202–04, 207, 209, 216–18, 224–25, 233n, 241n; as model glosser, 80; as possible source, 185n, 209, unnamed, 80, 234n, 236n, 239n, 242n; for alliteration, 86; on poverty over alms, 97; on the heart, 91, 95, and the intellect, 96; texts blended and adapted by Nil, 82; texts mixed with other authors by Nil, 82–83, 143a, 192–93.

—γνῶσις, as *razumъ*, 90; διάνοια as *myslь*, *smyslь*, 89–90; ἐνέργεια as *děistvo*, 92; ἔννοια as *myslь*, 89; νοῦς as *umъ*, 90; σύνεσις, as *razumъ*, 91.

ISAAK SUMIN (Iosifov elder), 46n.

ISAIAH THE SOLITARY (of Scetis and Palestine, d. post-431), 126n, 174n.

ISIDOR (Metropolitan of all Rus, r. in Moscow, 1436–1441), 7.

ISIDORE THE PRIEST (Desert Father), as possible source, 163n.

ITALY, 7, 48; Renaissance, 41.

IUSTIN (Archimandrite, later bishop: translator-modernizer), xi, 107–08, 202n.

IVAN IUREVICH PATRIKEEV (prince-boyar, 15th c.), 37.

IVAN III VASILEVICH, GRAND PRINCE OF MOSCOW (r. 1462–1505), 6–7, 33–35, 33n, 37, 54; and church lands, 30–31, 54.

IVAN VOLK KURITSYN (state secretary, burned as heretic, 1504), 51, 60, 60n.

IVAN GAVRILOV (a Prince Zabolotskii, friend of Andrei Maiko), 33n, 36n.

IZMARAGD ('The Emerald', 14th miscellany, 114n.

IZWOLSKY, HÉLÈNE (scholar), xi, 93n, 94n, 107, 202n.

JACAMON, SOPHIA OSB (scholar), xi, 62n–63n, 68, 107–08.

JACOB'S LADDER, as inspiration, 73.

JERUSALEM, PATRIARCHS, 26, 28.

JESUS PRAYER, 21, 21n, 52–53, 55, 78, 83, 174n, 191n, 207; combined with other prayers by Barsanuphius, Nil, 174, 179; in *Scete Typikon*, 266–67; Jesus's name as weapon against urges, 170, 233, 240; types, 138.

'JEWISH-REASONING' (JUDAIZING), as pejorative, 28.

JEWS, 31n, 175n; 'Judaica' (Hebrew or Hebrew-origin texts), 30, 54.

JOHN (correspondent of Barsanuphius), 78.

JOHN CASSIAN (ascetic Father, c. 360–423/5), *Institutes*, on the 'Eight Urges', 67, 71, 126n; abridged Slavic 'Kassian Rimlianin' texts, 40, 71, 94: as possible source, 163n, 165n, 171n, 173n, 185n; as unnamed source for *Slovo* 5, 71, 80, 167–68, 175–77, 182, and 'To Gurii', 238n–240n; (?) inspiration from non-abridged version, 71, on avarice, 97, 173n; Nil privileges over Slavic NT wording, 176n; texts mixed with other authors by Nil, 82–83, 175; use of *cogitatio* vrs Nil's *pomyslъ*, 89n.

JOHN CHRYSOSTOM (Patriarch of Constantinople, r. 398–407); as named or source, 69, 78, 195; on community prayer, 49n, 52, 78n.

JOHN CLIMACUS (of Sinai, ascetic Father, 579–649), 16, 42, 76, 155n, 226n; *Ladder*, 65n,

73–74, section 'On the Differences of Stillness', 247; *Treatise for the Pastor*, 74; *scholia*, 73.
–Slavic texts, 50, 214n, 248n; as source, 66-70, 74, 83, 116, 117n, 130n, 152-53, 159, 163n, 169-70, 178, 182, 192, 202-03, 203n, 208-10, 214-16, 219, 222-25, 233-34; unnamed, 80, 184, 193, 234-35, 239n–241n; adaption by Symeon flagged by Nil, 82; analysis of lust as archetypical for urges, 93, 136; as model employer of 'differences,' 87n, of figures of speech, 83-84, 188; as model glosser, 80; as possible source, 163n, 172n; as recommended reading in 1852, 104; on detachment, 97; stages of struggle against *logismoi* (See also PHILOTHEUS), 66, 70n, 93; texts blended and adapted by Nil, 82, 85; texts mixed with other authors by Nil, 82–83, 131, 132n–37n, 143n–46n, 182n–83n, 187n, 192n–93n.
—ἐνέργεια as *děistvo*, 92; ἐνθύμημα as *pomyshlenie*, 89; ἔννοια as *myslъ*, 89n; νοῦς as *umъ*, 90; σκοπός as *razumъ*, 91.
JOHN COLUBUS ('the Dwarf', 339–?405, ascetic), Life, 26.
JOHN OF DAMASCUS (hymnographer, theologian, c. 675–750), 9, 12, 29; booklets, 256; *Dialectica*, 87; Hymns as source, 79; as unnamed Hymnographer, 194–96; Life, 16, 26, 192n.

—Ps-John of Damascus, 73n; text mixed with other authors by Nil, 83, 131n–34n.
JOHN THE EVANGELIST ('disciple of the Lord'), as named source, 197.
JOHN THE HESYCHAST (Palestinian bishop, 454–559), Life, 26, 28.
JOHN THE FORERUNNER (BAPTIST): as founder/mentor of all monks, 274; third discovery of his head as dedication of Innokentii's hermitage church, 274.
JOHN TZIMISKES (Byzantine Emperor, r. 969–76), *Typikon* for Athos Laura, 123n, 273n.
JUDAEANS (Ancient), and Christ/Crucifixion, 33n, 51, 175; curse on descendants, 51.
'JUDAIZERS' ('Jewish-reasoning', See also DISSIDENTS, HERETICS, NOVGOROD), 28n, 54.
JUDGING OTHERS (negatively), avoidance of, 43.
JUDGMENT, TERRIBLE (LAST), 47, 67, 183n, 191, 196–20, 208; as locus of post-mortal suit, 255; as spectacle, 197–98.

KALLISTOS (author of *Life* of Gregory the Sinaite), 128n.
KALYVY (Mount Athos), 15n.
KAMENNYI (*See* SPASO-KAMENNYI MONASTERY).
KARYES KELLION (Mount Athos), 15.
KASSIAN BOSOI (Iosif's comrade, ascetic, d. 1531), 46n.

KASSIAN (Kirillov hegumen, r. 1448–1464/5, 1465/6–70), 9–10, 35.
KASSIAN (Novgorod-Iurev archimandrite, burned as heretic, 1505), 50.
KASSIAN (orig. Constantine, Prince of Mangup, d. 1504), 33n, 63n; Nil's likely spurious epistle to, 33n, 250n.
KATHISMA (*See also* SESSION, PSALTER), 260n, 262–66.
KAZAKOVA, N. A. (scholar), 32n.
KHRISTOFOR (Kirillov hegumen, r. 1428–1434), 8–9.
KHVOROSTININ FAMILY, 38.
KELLION, KELLIA (*See also* KARYES; NIL SORSKY, CELL, Athonite, 15, 15n; German's, 43, Kornilii's, 56).
KIEV, 4, 7n.
KING, HEAVENLY, and earthly, analogy, 50–51.
KING vrs TYRANT, dichotomy, 53–54.
KINGDOM: of God, 176n; of heaven, 148, 174, 181, 204, as 'violent', 142; of the Lord, 198; prepared for the 'blessed', 197.
KIPRIAN (Bulgarian Metropolitan of Lithunian Rus, 1382–1389, of all Rus, 1389–1408), 73n.
KIPRIAN (Kirillov hagiographic compiler), 12.
KIRILL OF BELOOZERO (coenobiarch, d. 1427), 8–9, 21, 50, 60; Life, 10, 11n; Testament, 255n; Traditions', 41.

KIRILLOV-BELOZERSK MONASTERY (*See also* NIL SORSKY), 6, 8–9, 19, 20, 22, 30, 34, 35, 37–40, 44–47, 55-56, 59, 66n; abandonment by "Major Elders', 1483–1484, 19; in Nil's Testament, 256; manuscripts, xiii, xiv, 39, 43, 77, 101n, 124n.
KIRILL OF TUROV (bishop-writer, 12th c.), 180n.
KLOSS, B. M. (scholar), 55, 66n.
KNOWLEDGE (*razumъ* = *gnosis*), 135n; 151, 161n; according to God, 148; approached only with mental (noetic) activity, 127; as same for all the ascetic masters, 238, instructed by God's grace, 86, 126; as sin to a sinner, 231; as true, taught by Divine Writings, 81, 130; chanting with, 215; corrupted leads to transgressions, 244; divine, of the Lord, 154; enlightened the Fathers, 226; for worldly profit, 232; genuine as discriminating, 232, as principle of editing saints' lives, 251, 253; God's, 180–81; Nil's alleged limits, 226, lack of 231; of Divine Writings as basis for all action, 243; praying with, 208; spiritual acquired by the saints, 130; undiscerning, also fleshly will, as lack of, 247.
KNOWLEDGEABLE, as knowing the Divine Writings, 243.
KOZELSK (region), 103.
KOMEL (forest, lake region), 38, 56.

KONOPLEV, N. (scholar), 56, 57n, 58
KONTAKION, 264n.
KORMCHAIA KNIGA (*Pedalion*, collection of Church canons), 60–61.
KORNILII KOMEL'SKII (coenobiarch, 1452/5–1537): and non-possession, 56–58; disciples, 56; Life, 55, 56n, 58; monastery structures, 56; Rule, 55–58, 236n.
KVASHNIN (boyar family), 39.

LABOR (service), as coenobitic requirement, 55, 57n; as general requirement, 118, 225–26; as if for Christ, 235; as remedy for: all urges, 234, despondency, 153, scattered intellect; as specific advice, 234; assigned, 11, 235; as virtue, 37, 53; exploitation, prohibited, 21, 98, 118–19; outdoor prohibited, 58, 118.
LADDER *(See also* JOHN CLIMACUS), 116–17.
LAITY, pernicious effects on monk attempting stillness, 217–18.
LATIN LANGUAGE (and Western texts), 7, 48, 54.
LAURA, as type of monasticism *(See also* IDIORRHYTHMA), 27.
LAURA (Jerusalem, Saint Sabbas), 26.
LAURA/LAVRA (Mount Athos), 15.
'LAST TIMES,' as apocalyptic image of the present, 102.

LAW *(See also* CANONS), 54; OT as metaphor or synecdoche for standard rituals, 260, 267.
LAZINESS *(See* SLOTH).
LËNNGREN, TAMARA (scholar), 25, 29, 35, 46n.
LENNON, JOHN (composer-singer), 105.
LENT ('Great Fast'), 164n, 187n.
LIBRARY: monastery's, 40; early catalogues, 42–43; personal, 35, 48.
LILIENFELD, FAIRY VON (scholar), xi, xii–xiii, 5n, 13n, 32n, 40n, 54–55, 62n, 65, 68, 87, 95, 106, 124n, 145n, 164n, 189n, 255n.
LITERARY-RHETORICAL DEVICES: allegory/parable, 84, 150, 204–05, 211, 220n; alliteration, 86, 136, 203n, 235n; antimetabole, 85n, 173; anacolouthon, 183n; analogy, 84, 230n; anaphora, 84, 219n; aphorism, dictum, gnome, 67, 70, 73, 84, 163, 203n; breviloquence, 86, 144, 219n; categorization, 84, 214–15; ellipse, 84–85, 105, 214n, 237n; enigma, 85, 154, 180; epistrophe, 84, 162, 168, 219n; homoiophony, 84, 135, 162; hypallage, 85, 154n., 180; hyperbole, 84, extended avoided by Nil, 41n; indirect speech, 83–84, 188; internal rhyme, 85, 153n; isocolism, 235n; kerygma, 84, 192; metaphors, 73, 79, 83, 108, and metonym so identified by Nil's text, 84, 127n, 147, 184, 197,

211; neologism, 232n; onomatopoea, 218; oraculum, 84; paradox, 83; parallelism, 86, 168; pathos, 84; personification, 83–84, 188; play on words, 138n, 142, 159n, 160n, 162n, 244n; pleonasm, avoided by Nil, 41n.; polyptoton, 84, 142n, 158, 213, 224n, 227n; proverb, 220n; recourse to authority, 84, 203, 218; repetition in general, 219; reversal of source's word order, 85–86, 117n, 127n, 132n, 135n, 136n, 178n, 185n, 198n, 214n, 217n, 223n, 237n, 248n, 251n, 252n; rhetorical *taxis/dispositio*: *exordium*, 63, 64, *narratio*, 63, *peroratio*, 65; shift of address, 84, 148–49; specification: by differences, 84, 131, 162, by type, 84, 161, 215–16; summary paragraphing, 84, 160–61; synecdoche, 84, 215–16; tongue-twister, 77, 79, 86, 136, 271n; topic sentence, 84, 216.
—artful words to be avoided in summoning divine aid against urges, 169.

LITHUANIA (*See also* WESTERN RUS), 4, 6.

LITURGICAL PRAYER, as source, 67–69.

LITURGY, 11; of Basil, Chrystostom, 262n, 272n; Slavic texts, 16, 40.

LIUBHEID, COLM (scholar), 93n.

LOGIC, THE (*Logika*, of Al-Ghazali, d. 1111, Jewish-Slavic translation), 30.

LOGISMOS, 23, 59, 88 (*See also* EIGHT . . . URGES, POMYSLЪ, URGE); 23, 59, 88; the good to be employed against the evil, 88; struggle against, 66, 70–71, 74, 76; unclean, 64.

LORD, LORD FATHER, as forms of polite address, 100, 249, 250.

LORD, THE (*See also* CHRIST, GOD, SECOND COMING), 86; as dwelling of the perfected soul, 214; as if at David's right hand, 159; as merciful, 205; as mighty in battle on our behalf, 169–70, 234, 239; as model of endurance and forgiveness, 174–75; as recipient of prayers for tears, 205, 207; as skilled and faithful in our trials, 178; attaining, as achievement of stillness, 80, 130; calls to account for welcoming, feeling/acting on an urge, 189; commandment to forgive, 173, Lord's Prayer, 173n; commandment to love, 160, enemies, 174–75; commandments in general, 213–14, 246, as path to future bliss, 237, lauded, 249; commands study of Scripture, 129–30; 'day of', 191; direct experience of, 148–49; harrowing of Hell (descent to Hades), 196; humanity as slaves of, 196; invoked for personal prayers from Nil's addressees, 237; kingdom of, 198; likeness of, in forbearance, 20; 'Lord Jesus', as name, 139–40, 142, 233, 235; love of humans as underlying Providence, 207; makes one worthy of tears, 209–10; 'Master' as address, 95, 149, 187; mercy before as personal goal, 227; obedience in (assigned work), 120; on death and the judgment, 191; on evil, defiling thoughts, 86, 126 191; opposes the proud, 184; provides, 118; rewards the penitent, 151; settles in the perfected, 213; to be summoned to drive off an urge, 133–34, 142, 163, 189–90, 233; visitation of, 208, 211, 213; word(s) of, as source or basis of instruction, 126, 163, 191, 196, 209, 222–23, 271.

LOVE (*See also* GOD): after recovery from despondency, 178; as begotten by God, 148, from 'operation of the Spirit,' 209; as commandment, 55, 159–60: of neighbor and God effect the other commandments, 252; essential for approaching God, 214; how practiced, 160, in receiving an admonition, 248; toward enemies, 174–75; 'in God', 243, 246; Nil's for German, 248; of a passion, urge, 136; of God: in vision, 148, steadfastness from, 150; of God yields charity, 256, the scete life, 259; of humility, 185; of silence, 185; of stillness and its traditions, 100, 117, 150, 260; of the Lord, 151; of the heavenly kingdom, 204; of the Mother of God and the Church's teachings in Nil's credo, 114–15; of 'the natural', 208; of the world, etc., 151, 185n, 194, 218, 237, evil results from, 231, foolishness of, 232; of visions of God, 149; qualifies for self-administration of communion, 272; spirit of, 187n; spiritual, 42, 236, 238, 246–47; tears of, 206; 'typikon' of perfect, 247n; yields beneficial afflictions from God, 237, tears, 207n.

LOVER-OF-CHRIST, as charitable layperson, 256.

LUKE (Evangelist), 138n; as author of Acts, implied, 141–42.

LUKE OF STEIRIS (near Delphi; Greek ascetic and healer, d. 953), 271; Life, 272n.

LUR'E. IA. S. (scholar), 32n, 51n.

MACARIUS (4th c. ascetic Father) / Ps-MACARIUS, 23; actual sources utilized in Slavic version, 78–79; as direct and/or named source, 68–69, 78, 149–50, 180, 199n; 213–14; as recommended reading in 1852, 104; Syriac tradition, 132n.

—Ps-Ps-Macarius (*See* SYMEON METAPHRASTES.

—νοῦς as *umъ*, 90; σκοπός as *razumъ*, 91.

MACRINA (nun, sister of Gregory of Nyssa, Basil the Great, 4th c.; *See also* GREGORY OF NYSSA), Life, prayer as source, 79, 199n.

MAIKO/MAIKOV (family) (*See also* ANDREI MAIKO), 5.
MAKARII (Archbishop of Novgorod, 1526–1542, Metropolitan of Moscow, 1542–1563), 102.
MAKSIM THE GREEK (Michael Trivolis, theologian-writer in Russia, c. 1470–1556), 41, 48.
MALONEY, GEORGE SJ (scholar), xi, xii–xiii, 40n, 56, 63n, 68, 71n, 78, 81–82, 93n, 94n, 95, 108, 202n.
MANICHEANISM (as Christian heresy), 28.
MANUSCRIPT PRODUCTION, 39, 41.
MARIA IAROSLAVNA (princess wife of Vasilii II, d. 1485), 36, 37, 55.
MARK THE ASCETIC (or Hermit, Desert Father, 5th c.), 126n; as source, 69.
MARTINIAN (Palestinian anchorite, d. c. 400), Life, 26, 28, 189n.
MARTYRDOM, 89n, 150n, 200n; of 'secular' philosophers, 192n.
MARTYRS, 28, 53–54, 69, 79, 98, 121, 169, 199–200; confessing faith at time of death, 240.
MATEJIĆ, MATEJA (Serbian Orthodox priest, scholar), 14.
MATERIAL LIFE (*See also* ADORNMENTS; INNOKENTII, *Zavět*; *PREDANIE*,), 21, 30–32, 65, 75–76, 97–99, 118–22, 173, 186–87, 226, 270–72, 274–75.
MATINS, 11, 164n, 263.
MATTHEW, EVANGELIST, as unnamed source, 80, 196–97.
MAXIMUS CONFESSOR (ascetic Father, c. 580–662); as source, 69, 77, 116, 168, unnamed, 80, 239n; as possible source, 172n–73n; combines psalms, 85, 168n; Slavic manuscripts, 77.
MEASURE, as proportionally notioned requirement (*See also* MIDDLE), 83, 87, 202; applied to cell activities according to needs, 145, to conversations, 215; to urges as enemy, 162; as limit of abilities, 100, 144, 162, 226n, 231, 238, 246; 250; lack of turns good to evil, 219; of food requirements, 164–65; paradox of, 83, 145; the 'perfect' envisioned for adepts, 150.
MEDITERRANEAN SEA (region), 165.
MEDITATION (*See also* PRAYER, READING), mystical, corrupted by conversation, 216; on God's will, 241; on the spiritual, 226.
MEHMET II THE CONQUEROR, OTTOMAN SULTAN (r. 1444–1446, 1451–1482), 7.
MELANTHIA, MOTHER (purported disciple of Eugenia), 121n.
MEMORY, nature of: assault of an urge as recollection, 131; heart as organ of, 92, 148.
MEMORY (REMEMBRANCE) of: another, in prayers (*See also* COMMEMORATIONS), 253, 273; cell chants, 266; commandments of forgiveness, 173, moderation, 163; disgrace, 168; evil, 224n: brought by urge of wrath, 173, to be confessed, 263, expelled, 160; objects of lust, 171; passions, by Clima-

cus, in crafting words, 224; prayers for mourning, 182; Psalm, by Symeon, in crafting words, 203; saints' lives, by Nil, to inspire repentance, 253; Scripture, as beneficial, 234; sin, 155, 183: for tears, 207; the world and its things, 163: as 'dung and ashes' during ecstasy, 148; things, as demon's incitement, 210; virtues, 'defrauds' passions, 162n; vows, against lust, 167, 238.

MEMORY (REMEMBRANCE) of death, 57, 67, 74, 76, 84, 88, 97, 182n, 191–202, 237; as good urge, 88; as remedy for vainglory, 182–83; as type of mental activity = watchfulness, 92, 153; for tears, 207; of concrete deaths, 77, 193–94; protocol for, 190.

MEMORY OF GOD, THE LORD, 95, 137, 146, 214; as God's love and prayer of the intellect, 221, as 'pain of the heart,' 144n.

'MENTAL ACTIVITY', 76; contrasted with bodily, 127.

'MENTAL PRESERVATION', 86, 126.

MENTAL WAR, v, 59, 70, 131, 154, 160–61, 211, 233; combat, single, as metaphor, 220–21; as equipotent force, 137, differentiated by nature of enemy, 162 ; defeats, 127, 154, 155, 170, 182, 184, caused by carelessness, 136; stages, 66, 70n, 83, 93, 131; summary statement, 188; victories, 127, 155, 160–61, 163, 233.

—ASSAULT (No. 1), as urge, image, recollection, random thought, 131–32, 231, 233.

—CAPTIVATION (No. 4), 93, as involuntary abduction of the soul, most dangerous at time of prayer, 134–35; prayer frees from, 141.

—CONSENT (No. 3), as the soul's welcoming the urge and potentially penitential, 133–34.

—COUPLING (No. 2), 93, as willful conversation, meditation with the urge, 132–33, 135–36, 155.

—PASSION (No. 5), as voluntary and habitual requiring penance, 135–36.

MENTOR (See PEDAGOGY).

MERCY, divine: beneficially punitive, to be thanked, 233; prompts forgiveness, 143–44; visitation to all ranks, 154; saves from despondence, 177.

METROPOLITAN OF MOSCOW, office of, 4, 5–7, 33–34, 35.

MEYENDORFF, JOHN (scholar), 32n.

MICAH, as unnamed 'Prophet,' 142.

MIDDLE (See also MEASURE), 135n; as norm, 221–22; 'path', 222.

MIDNIGHT OFFICE, 266.

MILLER, DANA (scholar), 72n.

MIND (*smysh*), 83; delusion of, 206.

MINDLESSNESS, in seeking wealth, fame, etc., 32, 151.

MIRACLES (See also NIL SORSKY, Hagiography), 36.

MISCELLANY (*Sbornik*), ascetic: Dionisii's, 48; Efrosin's, 11; German's (with the Kirillov bibliographies), 43, 78n;

Gurii's, 41, 101; Innokentii's, 37–38; Iosif's, 50; (?) Paisii's, 35n; Tikhon Zvorykhin's, 47–48.
Mochos (Egypt, location of Pachomius's monastery), 121.
Moiseeva, G. N. (scholar), 32n.
Monasticism: as calling apart from the world, 151, of 'the Most High,' as honor, 233; as 'rank of service' to God, 233.
Monasteries, as fitting for stillness, including urban, 128.
Money, 40.
Mongols, 256n.
Monophysitism ('heresy'), 28, 28n.
Moore, Lazarus (archimandrite, scholar), 93n.
Moscow, 4–8; kremlin, 4, 7, 9; regime, 4, 5, 14, 15, 54, 59, 103; synods: of 1490, 31, 37, 51, of 1503, 31–32, 32n, 97, of 1504, 51–52, of 1509 (not identified), 44, 45.
Moses (OT), 218n.
Moskva (river), 5.
Mother of God, 'most pure Lady/Mistress' (*See also* Theotokos), 13; as genuinely so, 114; assistance of to Christ invoked as responsible for *Predanie*, 113, to God's grace for *Sobornik*, 251; prayer service to, in *Scete Typikon*, 262; prayers of, as intercessionary, invoked, 59, 225, 235, 244, 246; prayers to at self-communion, 272n; provides, 118.

Mount Athos (*See also* Stillness), 13–18, 27, 35, 37, 103; and Basilian *Asceticon*, 75; as model for stillness in twos or threes, 17, 224; regulations, 123n, 273n; Slavic codices, 16; Slavic Monks; 14–16.
Mount Sinai, 15n, 76, 95.
Mourning (*See also* Tears), 67, 72; as purgative and protection from sins, 207–08; generates solace, 209; to be maintained as remedy against vainglory, 182–83.
Mutual edification and support, 151, 224–25, 238.
Myslь, myslen-, translation, 89–90.
Mysticism, 95.

Negative example, as positive, 116.
Negligence, in fighting urges as sinful, 133.
Neilos the Sinaite (ascetic Father, d. *c.* 430; *See also* Evagrius of Pontus), 12, 69, 76; as named source, 138, 189, 204, 210–11, 224; as possible source, 211n.
Neophytes: agony of confining intellect, 141; inner person conforms to the outer, 185; labor, service as means to repel urges, 153; mocked when pretentious, 221; must avoid speaking, 185, confess and summon the Lord against urges, 13–34, endure afflictions, 81, 120, completely

sever, 171; need God's restraint to repulse urges, 139; paradigmatic advice to Vassian, 235–36; prayer and use of good urges against bad ones, 162; recommended Jesus Prayer 138; sing "without measure', 83, 145; use hunger to fight gluttony, 165.
NESTORIANISM ('heresy'), 28, 28n.
'NEW CONSTANTINOPLE', 8.
'NEW ISRAEL', JERUSALEM', 8.
NEW TESTAMENT (excluding Gospels, Paul), as source, 115n, 134n, 142n, 160n, 168n, 172n, 184n, 190n, 191, 198n.
NICENE CREED, 272n.
NICEPHORUS MONACHUS (ascetic Father, 13th c.); as Ps-Symeon, 74, 126, 132; as transmtter for Desert Father (Agathon), 77, 127n; as unnamed source, 70, 126n.
NICETAS STETHATOS (11th c., disciple of Symeon the New Theologian), 19, 128; as source, 69, 183–84, unnamed, 80, 172; text mixed with other authors by Nil, 82, 182.
NICHOLAS BULEV (German physician-astrologer, active 1490s–1520s), 48.
NICOLA (d. 847–850, Studite abbot, militant iconodule), Life, 27.
NIFONT (hegumen of Kirillov, r. 1475–1482, of Simonov, 1482–1484; Bishop of Suzdal, 1484–1508), 37, 47n.

NIFONT KORMILITSYN (hegumen of Iosifov, 1522–1543, not so identified), 47.
NIGHTTIME, 152–53.
NIKEPHOROS THEOTOKIS (1731–1800, polymath educator; Archbishop of Astrakhan and Poltava, r. 1786–1792), 72n.
NIKOL'SKII, N. K. (scholar), 20n, 32n.
NIKON (Patriarch of Moscow, r. 1652–1666), 102.
NIKON OF THE BLACK MOUNTAIN (Slavic 'Chernogorets', near Antioch, 11th c. coenobiarch-renovator, encyclopedist), 20, 26, 40; *Pandekty* and *Taktikon* (Slavic), 68–71, 153n, and Greek originals, 113n; as adapter, 116n; as possible model, 71; as possible source, 172; as unnamed source transmitter, 68, 70: for Anthony and the angel, 153, 234, for Barsanuphius, 70, 119, 220n, Basil, 119, Climacus, 74, 116, Chrysostom, 121, Maximus, adapted, 116; as unnamed source, 69–71, 113n–23n, 129n–30n, 226n–27n, 238n, 243n, 251n–52n; for the stages of struggle against *logismoi*, 70, 131n–33n, 135n–36n; manuscripts, 70n; text mixed with other authors by Nil, 83, 131n–33n, 135n–37n.
NIL POLEV (Iosifov Monastery elder, d. post-1514), xxiii, 22, 42, 44–47, 47n, 50, 59;

manuscripts, donations of, 45–46, 46n; inscription, 92n, 259, writing, 271n; IRI type of *Ustav*, 66, 123; *Scete Typikon*, 259n.

NIL SORSKY (1433/4–1508, *See also* EPISTLES, LITERARY DEVICES, PREDANIE, TESTAMENT, USTAV), xii, xxiii; alters thrust of a source, 220; and 'academic' pedagogy, 12; and conversations, 235n; and Dionisii Zvenigorodskii, 47–48; and the 'Divine Writings' as ultimate guide, 13, 20, 113–16; and Gennadii, 30–31, 33n, 34, 51–52; and German Podol'nyi, 42–44, 76, 245–49; (?) and Gregory Palamas, 18, 93; and Gurii Tushin, 39–40, 238–44; and heart-mind dichotomy, 92n; and Innokentii, 13–14, 22, 38–39, 57, 65–66, 71n, 122n–23n, 224n, 274–76; and Iosif, 48–55, 78n, 267n: *Enlightener (Prosvetitel')*, finest, earliest full, brief redaction copy, 51–55, 60; and Kirillov's landholding, 11–12; and Kornilii Komel'skii, 55–58, 122n; and monastic lands and wealth, 31–32, 39: purported stance at 1503 Synod, 32n; and Nil Polev, 44–46; and repression of heretics, 50–52; and stillness, 12, 18; and Vassian Patrikeev, 58–61, 231–37; alleged 'criticism', 40, 243n; apologizes for possible offenses, 248; as editor, 24, 27, 29–30; as governed completely by the Divine Writings, 116, 243, 246: speaks from them, 130, 248; as 'great elder,' 231n; as harassed by would-be disciples, 115–16; as if under compulsion, 116, 231, 246; as master-teacher, 19, 22, 23, 29, 87; as pedagogic glosser, 69, 127, 132–34, 137–39, 141–42, 145–46, 148–52, 156–57, 162–64, 167–68, 173–74, 215–16, 221–23, 248; as possible disciple of Paisii Iaroslavov, 34–36; as recommended reading (in 1852), 104; associated with both types of *Ustav*, 66; as theological-calendrical consultant, 30; as the superior: by word of God, 116, of the like-minded, 113–14, reluctance, 115–16; autograph manuscripts, 44–46, *Scete Typikon* and *Predanie* addenda, 259n, 265n, 271n; becomes a monk, 5, 10–11, 10n; book-copying, 12, 29, 55; burial request, 3, 255; canonization, 3; 104; cell outside Kirillov, 18–20, 38, 246; converses critically according to the listener's 'measure', 146; counsels as he lives, 243, 246–47; critical of institutional pride, 36n, 186–87; death, 3, 22, 38, 43, 44, 45, 59, 66; disciples as like-minded collectivity, 38–39, 113; hymnography, 12, 22; Kirillov period, 10–14, 245n; knowledge of Greek, 18, 27, 38, 83: copied signature,

254; literacy requirement, 50; literary-rhetorical devices, 12, 83–86; logic, 85; metaphrasis (editing), 12, 81–86; modesty, 64; originality, analytical, 87n; origins, 5; prayer, 10, 12, 22, 41; *Prayer and Thanksgiving* (doubtful, purported work), 33n, 41, 63n; rejects personal honors, 255; requests personal prayers, 237, 244, 249, 252, 254, and forgiveness in general, 227, and specifically, 245, for poor editing of Lives, 252, and grants forgiveness, 255; scete/hermitage activities, 23: Sora founding, 20–21, structure, 21–22; (?) secular experience as chancery official, 5, 11–12; signature of, 18n, 115n, 130n, 231n, 254; source selection, consciousness thereof, 68; spiritual conversations, 12; struggle against genuine demons, in the eyes of eulogists, xxiii, 102, as public service, 102; stylistics, 41n; waives responsibility for self-regulators, 116.
—collective characterizations: in rank of disciples, 226; infirm, 154, 190, 192, 233; mindless strugglers over worldly concerns, 151; passionate, 151, 154, 192, 233; sinful, 150; unable to defeat urges, 188; unworthy, 260.
—hagiography, 12, 18, 22, 24–30: (?) corrections, 24, 30, 101; demons in, 28; miracles in, 28-30, 101.

—Ps-Nil, 63, 103.
—self-effacement: as filthy and prodigal, 201, boorish, 247; carelessness, 246; evil in word, thought, deed, 253; ignoramus, 243; indifferent, lazy, 130, 246; infirm (in soul and body), 115, 246; 'meagerness', 238, 246; non-doer of good, 113–14, 116, 130, 231, 253; of 'darkened', passion-ridden intellect', 253; rustic, 243; 'sinful', sinner 57, 64, 115, 130, 151, 200, 231, 238, 252, 254; 'foremost' among, 198, in such a 'swamp', 237; slave to passions, 130, so deluged, 237; unknowledgeable, 62, 64, 115, 130, 226, 231, 238, 248, 252, witless, 243, 254; wretched, 253.
—writings, xxiii, 29, 38; as 'classroom', 109; as reminder to self, 113, 130, 226; authenticity issue, 62–63.
NIL vrs IOSIF, paradigm and its problems, xi–xiii, 30–32, 58, 310n; 320n.
NONPOSSESSION (Poverty), 28, 39, 97–99, 10; absolute, 50, 57, 78n; and detachment, 97; and memory of death, 97; and prayer, 97; and purity of soul, 98; avoidance of excess, 117, 119, 173, of silver objects, 98, 173.
NONPOSSESSORS (*See also* VASSIAN PATRIKEEV), xii, 36; claim Nil for themselves, 99, 101.
NOVGOROD (Great Novgorod), 4, 6, 30, 35, 126n; 'Heretics', (or

'Judiazers'), 28, 30–31, 37, 51, 53-54, 60n. 126n, 274n; Sofiia, library, 40: PDP type of *Ustav,* 66.

OBEDIENCE, 47, 53, 55; assigned work as 'in the Lord', 120; to mentor, other and 'exemplary' 'fathers', the superior, and the lived, knowledgeable in the Divine Writings, 235–36.
OLDER MONKS (*See* INFIRMITY).
OLD TESTAMENT (excluding Psalms), 11; as source, 142, 160n, 164n, 180n, 184, 196n, 198n, 205n–06n, 211, 219n, 222n–23n, 244n, 263n, 267.
ONOUPHRIUS THE HERMIT (d. 400), Life, 26.
OPTIMA HERMITAGE, 103.
ORIGENISM ('heresy'), 28.
OSOBOZHITIE (*See also* IDIORHYTHMA, LAURA), 16n.
OSTROWSKI, DONALD (scholar), 31n, 32n, 33n, 62, 99.
OTTOMAN EMPIRE, 15–16.
OTTOMAN TURKS, 7.

PACHOMIUS THE GREAT (coenobiarch, 290/292–346/348), Life, 25–26, 29n; as source, 69; tilts columns of his church to avoid exulting in beauty, 121–22.
PAISII IAROSLAVOV (possible mentor of Nil, d. 1501), 11, 30, 31, 32n, 33–36, 33n, 36n, 51.
PAISII VELICHKOVSKII (1722–1792, neo-hesychast), 38, 72n, 103.
PAISIUS THE GREAT (ascetic master, d. 400), Life, 25, 26, 28.

PAKHOMII LOGOFET ('the Serb', Hagiographer, d. after 1484), 10, 11n.
PALESTINE (*See also* HOLY LAND), 15, 25, 26, 95, 165.
PANOV, I. (scholar), 51n.
PANTALEIMON MONASTERY (Mount Athos), 15.
PAPHNUTIUS THE RECLUSE (abbot of Scetis, hagiographer, 4th-early 5th c.), Life, 26.
PARADISE, 163, 167, 211.
PARTNER, NANCY (scholar), 87.
PASSIONS (*See also* DEMON, SPIRIT, URGE), in general, 53; all to be opposed, 136; cleansing intellect of, 80; of the soul test and school the monk, 220; quenched by Divine Writings, 81; sexual: avoidance of physical or sensory contact with object of desire 136.
PATERICA, ancient: as source of a question, 230, of the varied cell rules of Scetites, 260; Slavic manuscripts, 45.
PATIENCE (endurance), 47, 81, 120, 225n.
PATRIARCHATE OF CONSTANTINOPLE, 7.
PATRISTICS, authority of, as issue, 52, 310n.
PATRIKEEV FAMILY, 59, 233n.
PAUL, APOSTLE: as source, 118n, 126–27, 130, 142n, 147, 150, 160n, 163n, 166, 172, 179n, 191, 205n, 209n, 221n, 237, 237n, 248n, 260; on avarice, 97, 172; on labor, 118; on Scripture, 130; on spiritual ec-

stasy, 147; on suffering for
Christ, 237; on waiving the
(OT) Law, 260; prays in spirit
and intellect, 90, 126–27.
PAUL OF THEBAID (anchorite,
?228-341), Life, 25.
PEDAGOGY, MONASTIC, 59; as absolute requirement, 222; aca-
demic', 10, 12, 16, 37, 38n, 40;
Apostles and Fathers as models, 113; 'desert', 9, 37; for stillness, 129; Divine Writings as
substitute, 129; German
Podol'nyi, 42–43; in virtues,
sermon as vehicle for, 231;
mentor, role of, 223, 235: 'reliable teacher', traits, 129, 247;
Neoplatonic influence, 162n;
specializations at Nil's time, 19,
20, 54; texts, 9–11, 23–24, 29.
PENTHOS (See also TEARS), 67, 94.
PENTECOST, feast of, 268.
PENITENCE (See REPENTANCE).
PETER, APOSTLE (See also NEW
TESTAMENT), 91, 189.
PETER OF ATHOS (hermit, early
10th c.), Life, 18, 27.
PETER DAMASKENOS (ascetic
Father, maybe *nom de plume*,
12th c.), 75, 224n; Slavic texts,
40, 50; as source, 69, 86,
136-37, 162, unnamed, 80; as
possible source, 173, 204n,
208n, 219n; *myslъ*, etc., useful
against a po*myslъ*, 89, 162;
texts mixed with other authors
by Nil, 82–83, 132n–37n;
translation, 89n.
PETER THE GREAT (Tsar, Emperor,
r. 1682–1725), 5n.

PHARAN MONASTERY (Palestine),
26.
PHARISEE, 53n.
PHILANTHROPY, false, 117.
PHILOKALIA, 71, 75, 76, 87, 90, 92,
93n, 94n, 103.
PHILOSOPHY (formal, secular), 7,
52, 54, 192; grammatical-
epistemological-ontological
categories: apparent vrs
genuine, 232; automatic, 209;
categories in visionary speculation, 95; cause, 138, 148, effects, 230; definition, 87, 192n,
247n; establish/decree (verb),
137; distinctions, differences,
87, 131, 160–61, 164; elements, 195; essence, 149; force,
power, 87, 116, 144, 146, 189,
195, 204, 211, 217, 246, 250,
260: natural, 202, used for relics, 255n; linkages, 87; measure,
middle (See also MEASURE;
MIDDLE); nature, 149, 155, 164,
166, 204, 215: grants tears,
207n, 'of things', 172; natural
union, 195; operation, 92–93,
128, 141, 144, 147, 160, 175n,
209, 223; particularity, 140;
power, 271; quality-quantity,
185; reason 215, (?) scientific,
215n; sensible-mental dichotomy, 128, 158; state, 133–35;
system/ procedure/ method,
143–45, 153, 163, 207, 218n.
PHILOTHEUS THE SINAITE (ascetic
Father, 9th–10th c.), v, 126n, *On
Watchfulness*, 65n; as source, 69,
76, 83, 127, 152, 158, 191; stages
of struggle against *logismoi* (See

also JOHN CLIMACUS), 66, 70n; on the heart and intellect, 96; text mixed with other authors by Nil, 83, 131, 132n–34n.

—ἐνέργεια as *děistvo*, 92; νοῦς as *umъ*, 90; ὀπτικόν as *zritelnoe*, 109.

PHOCAS (East Roman/Byzantine Emperor, r. 602–610), 29.

PHOTIUS/FOTII (Metropolitan of all Rus, r. 1410–1431), 6.

PHYSICAL ACTIVITIES, to be measured, 250.

PHYSIOLOGUS (bestiary), 16.

PILGRIMAGE, to the Holy Land, 15n; (?) also Nil, 15, 247.

PILLLAR (STYLITE) MONASTICISM, 26, 28.

PLATO, 21n, 241n.

PLEASING TO GOD AND PROFITABLE FOR THE SOUL (or the inverse), as formula, 111, 121, 225–26, 238, 246, 252; modified, 236; defects to be corrected, 111, 121, 227, 252.

—pleasing to God (by itself), 127, 132, 219, 274; contrasted with pleasing humans, 158; used regarding Nil, 100.

PLESHKOV, IVAN (lay writer, 1660s), 5n, 102.

PLIGUZOV, ANDREI (scholar), 31n, 32n, 60n.

POKROVSKII, KONSTANTIN (scholar), 29.

POLITICAL THEORY, 53–54.

'POLYELEOS' (psalm, -hymn), 264.

POMIALOVSKII, IVAN (Scholar), 27.

POMYSLъ, translation issue (*See also* LOGISMOS, URGE), 88; Nil's use vrs John Cassian's *cogitatio*, 89n; distinct from *pomyshlenie*, 89–90.

POSEIDON/NEPTUNE, 13n.

PONTIUS PILATE, 53n.

POVERTY (*See* NONPOSSESSION).

PORPHYRY (Aristotelian Neoplatonist, c. 234–c.305), *Eisagoge*, 87.

PRAYER (*See also* HEART, JESUS PRAYER, NIL SORSKY), 28; against urges, 140, 154, 162; all thoughts to be avoided during, 135; as effective on behalf of another's correction or salvation, 227, 237, 252, 254; as essential cell activity, 48, 50; as gazing upon the Lord, 159; as guarding of the heart, 191; as homily, 79; as penitential plea, 79: model of, 199–201; as remedy, 79; as wellspring of virtues, 91, 140; endurance of pains in, 141–42; for tears, 204–07; for those who offend, afflict, 174, 236; formulaic, 83; hesychastic, 72, 75–76, Ps-Symeon on, 74–75; intellective; as memory of God and God's love, 221; as required, constant meditation, 159; in 'spirit' and 'intellect', 90; liturgical and other in *Ustav*, 67–69; neglect of results in prayer 'to the air', 127; nighttime, 83; of beneficiaries, 116; of the wrathful as unacceptable, 77, 174; operation of, 141, in the heart, 144; requires abundant feeling, 210; silent, of

heart as type of mental activity, watchfulness, 92, 153; to be recited from the depth of the heart, 207; transcended, 146; true, as stillness of intellect, 160–61; verbosity to be avoided, 153.
—rope, in *Scete Typikon*, 265.
PRECISION in attentiveness, as required, 156.
PREDANIE (of Nil), 24, 25, 41, 62; addenda, 22; adornments in buildings and clothing rejected, 98, 121–22; advising outsiders, qualifications for, 65, 120–21; and alms, 57, 65, 118–20; and poverty, 32; bargaining prohibited, 65, 98, 119; boys prohibited, 65, 123; 'charity of the soul', 65, 120; composition, 63, 64–65; confession, 57, 65, 117; credo, 65, 114–15; enclosure, 57, 65, 120; expulsion, 57, 116; females (human and animals), prohibited, 65, 123; food, 65, requirements proportional to ascetic power, 122; hired labor to be paid, 98, 119; ill-gotten gains as gifts prohibited, 65, 118; Innokentii and, 38, 65, 123–24; intoxication prohibited, 65, 122; Kornilii and, 55–58; labor and self-support, 75, 98, 118; lacks official imprimatur, 99, 102; lawsuits rejected, 98, 118; manuscripts, 45–46, 62n–63n, 65, 66n; obedience, 57, 65, 75, 116–17, 120; perpetual validity, 120–21; poverty (nonpossession) as major theme, 32, 76, 97, 118–22; silence, 57, 120; simplicity in material things, 65; stratification, 58.
—sources: Barsanuphius, 119; Basil; 118n, 119–20, 122; Chrysostom, 78, 121; Climacus, 74, 116–17; Dorotheus, 120; Eugenia, Life, 121; Isaac, 119; Maximus, 116; Nikon, 70, 74, 78, 113–23; Pachomius, Life, 121; proportion of text, 69.
PRESENTATION (CANDLEMAS), FEAST OF, 21–22.
PRESENTATION OF THE THEOTOKOS, 56.
PRESUMPTION, as a stillness-perverting 'passion of the soul,' 223.
PRIDE (*See* EIGHT . . . URGES).
PROFIT (to soul): authority of Nil's writings subordinated to, 227; characterization of writings, 111, 113; from simple rule, 100, 250; to others as well as self from assigned work, 120; sought in epistle, 245; verbal, despite lack of deeds, 116; within a seemingly harsh message, 248.
PROKEIMENA (*See also* PSALTER), 260.
PROKHOROV, GELIAN (scholar), xi, 25, 31–33n, 38n, 63n, 64, 66n, 106, 124n, 164n, 183n, 250n, 259n, 269n, 273n.
PROPHETS, 54.
PROPORTIONALITY TO THE INDIVIDUAL, 100, 115–16, 122, 133, 140, 144–45, 159, 162,

164–67, 170, 178–79, 202, 204, 219, 221, 226, 231, 233, 238, 246, 250, 260–61, 265, 267, 269.

PROSTRATIONS, 11 11, 46, 55.

PROVERBS (*See also* OLD TESTAMENT), 91.

PROVIDENCE (*See also* WISDOM); as design (*oikonomia*), 145, 156, 226n, 235n, not to be opposed, 235; orchestrates humbling assaults of urges, 155; overall operation, 197; underlies beneficial afflictions, 175–76, 233.

PRUDENCE, 212; as general principle, 243, 244n; establishes good time and measure, 219.

PSALMODY (chanting, singing), 142–43; as remedy for fatigued intellect, 153; effected by disciple-assistant, 143; euchotherapeutic, 144n.

PSALMS (*See also* DAVID), 153, 239; adaptations flagged by Nil, 81, 189, 203; as source, 69, 77–78, 91, 114–15n, 134n, 158n–59n, 168, 169n–70n, 180n, 189n–90n, 195n, 200n, 203, 206n, 217n, 219, 222n, 222–23, 225n, 234n–35n, 239n–40n, 249n, 262–66; combined by Maximus, 85, Nil, 195.

PSALTER (*See also* KATHISMA, PROKEIMENA, SESSION), 21n, 256n, 260n.

PSKOV, 4.

PUBLICAN, (NT) as model of sighs, 189.

PURITY (PURIFY): aid of successful strugglers to be summoned, 169, 239; as beloved by God, 168; as inner as well as outer, 167–68, 238–39; as state, 214, of true practitioners, 249; effecting the commandments in, 213–14; mental, 127n; model prayers for, 189, 206–07; not for the prideful, 184; of conscience, 53; of heart, 128, 189; of intellect, 19, 152, 206, 216; of prayer, 206; of soul, 75, 98, 128, 173, 207, 214; of the Lord's words, 249; prayer in, 210; rank of, 132n, high, 154; tears as purifying waters, 206.

PUSILLANIMINITY, shunning of, 202.

QIPCHAK KHANATE (Golden Horde), 4, 6.

QUARRELS, suits, to be avoided, 226.

RAZUMЪ, translation, 30n, 90–91, 124n, 126n; distinction from modern, 90.

READING, MEDITATIVE, 37, 48, 50, 104, 207, 215, 226; as remedy for wandering intellect, 153; hermeneutic, 203n; of saints' lives, 145, for tears 207; Scripture, for 'life', 129–30.

REASONING (positive and negative) (*See also* 'Jewish-Reasoning') 60n; 'rightly,' 244.

REFECTORY, 11–12, 56.

RELICS, 36, 255n.

RENUNCIATION/ WITHDRAWAL (of/ from world and worldly concerns), 8, 32, 39, 58, 6, 152, 213, 241–42; as joyful, 64, 237; re-

quired for meditation on God's will, 241; requires suppressing images of the world, 241.
REPENTANCE, 47, 48, 53, 92, 151; in course of mental warfare, 155; goal of *Sobornik,* 253; model prayers of, 199–201; required to avoid torments, 137.
REPROACHING, of others, avoidance of 39, 60–61; of self, 133, 155, 164, 186, 188, converts a fall into a victory, 165.
REQUIEM, forty-day, 256.
RESURRECTION, human, 196; of 'life' or 'judgment' dichotomy, 197.
REVERENCE, 158.
REVERENTIAL FATHERS, as model, 60.
RIGHTEOUSNESS, as bearing afflictions, characteristic of the 'saints', 237; God's as human aim, 158.
ROMANIA, 14.
ROMANCHUK, ROBERT (scholar), 8–10, *passim,* 11n, 87n, 162n, 203n.
ROMAN PERSECUTION OF CHRISTIANS, 25, 26.
ROMANENKO, ELENA (scholar), 3n, 12n, 27n, 31n, 32n, 37n, 255n.
ROMANOS MELODOS (Byzantine Hymnographer, d. c. 556), as possible source, 198n, 201n.
ROSTOV (town, region), 55.
'ROYAL ROAD' ('King's Highway' of two or three monks), 24.
RUS (land of all Eastern Slavs), 4, 5.

RUSSELL, NORMAN (scholar), 93n.
RUSSIAN NATIONAL LIBRARY (Manuscript Division), 66n, 69–70.

SABBAS THE SANCTIFIED (abbot of Jerusalem Laura, 439–532), Life, 26–28, 31.
SACRAMENTS, 167.
SADNESS (*See* EIGHT . . . URGES).
SAENKO, L. P. (scholar), 73n.
SAINTS, collectively, as attributed source, 69, 80, 129, 192, 193, 205, 207, 218, 239; anonymous one as named source, 232; as combatants, 155, forgivers, 175; as glossers, 80; as God's, 50; model bearers of afflictions, 237; ecstasy limited by God to enable teaching, 149–50, prayers of, invoked, 59, 225, 235, 244; remain appropriate models, 151–52; thrones granted to, 147.
SAINTS' LIVES, as recommended reading, 145; in 1852, 104.
SALLUST (Patriarch of Jerusalem, r. 486–494), 26.
SALVATION (*See also* SOUL), 85, 113–14, 116, 253, 260; despondency's ploy against, 179; grief and, 176; memory of death and, 193; possible for all, 136n; requires submitting to abuses, 220; tears and, 207; the willing, 157, 172, Nil's writings as directed toward, 114, 124.
SATAN (*See also* DEVIL, ENEMY), 102, 175n, 180, 240.

SAVA OF SERBIA (renovator of Hilandar, archbishop, 1168–1237), 17; Life, 17, 41.
SAVVA·CHERNYI (Bishop of Krutitsa in Moscow, 1544–1554, Iosif's biographer, not so named), 41.
Scete: at Mount Athos, 15; in *Scete Typikon*, 259; Sora Hermitage so termed by Nil, 123; traditional, 22.
SCETE TYPIKON (*See also* CELL RULE, VIGILS), 9, 21, 39n, 50, 259–269; assumed literacy, 267; illiterate monks, 21, 39n, 50, 259n, 269n; other modes of watchfulness, manual work, reading, guarding, enclosure, 268–69; principle of doing as much as possible, 261, 265, 267–68; itself, 267; seasonal variance, 262, 265, 268; Slavic manuscripts, 21n, 259n; 'toils of obedience', will severance, allow for exceptions, 267; specified portion for the literate, 269.
SCRIPTORIA, MONASTIC, 15, 22, 45.
SCRIPTURE (Biblical, Holy Writ; *see also* BIBLE, NEW TESTAMENT, OLD TESTAMENT); as named or purported source, 146, 158, 184, 203, 205, 219, 222–23; as recommended reading, 129–30, in 1852, 104; authority of, as issue, 52, 310n; intellect placed within impedes demons, 234; Slavic manuscripts, 16, 40, 45.

SCHOLASTICISM, 7, 11n.
SEA FIGURES OF SPEECH, 15, 42, 44, 63, 134, 145, 177, 189–90, 223.
SECOND APOCALYPSE OF JAMES, 243n.
SECOND COMING, 52, 196–97, 199–201.
SECRETS, revealing of, as sign of personal love, 243, 245.
SELF-ABASEMENT (*See also*, under NIL SORSKY): Andrew of Crete's model prayer of repentance, 205; as recommended attitude, 61; Gregory the Sinaite's model declamation, 186; hyperbolic expressions of, 68.
SELF-COMPULSION (-force, required), 129, 140, 178–79, 199, 202, 204; in *Scete Typikon*, 267; limits of, 166, 204.
SELF-REGULATION: as negative, 42, 221, 247, 276.
SELF WILL, 42, 117, 246–48, 275–76.
SERAPION (Hegumen of Kirillov, 1482–1484), 19.
SERAPION (Archbishop of Novgorod, 1507–1509), 44, 45.
SERBIA, 9, 15, 16, 29, 41, 73n; manuscripts, xiv.
'SERIOUS ENTERTAINMENT,' 87.
SERPENT (*See also* DEVIL, ENEMY, SATAN), 196.
SERVICE (Church and individual; *See also* LABOR), 217n.
SESSION (*See also* KATHISMA), 260, 264.
ŠEVČENKO, IHOR (scholar), 68.
SEVERANCE (from the world): and stillness, 19–20, 213–18, as im-

mediate requirement, 233; coupled with prayer-thought, 137–38; from one's will, 117, 267; initial, of assault of urge, as key, 133.

SHAMAN (Finnic, named Pam, 14th c., not so identified), 4.

SHEVCHENKO, ELENA (scholar), 21n, 45n, 66, 66n, 124n.

SIGHS (GROANS): with tears accompany prayer-summons for aid against urges, 189; as means of acquiring tears, 205; as substitute, 202–03.

SILENCE: after Compline 48; at services, *Scete Typikon*, 263; at work, 57; of the intellect, 96; kept by adepts, 146, secular martyrs, 192n; vrs stillness, source issue, 214n; when meeting people, 185.

SIMEON THE HERMIT/CHOIRMAN (Iosifov master-scribe, d. ?1530s), 46n.

SIMON (Metropolitan of Moscow, r. 1495–1511), 56.

SIMONOV MONASTERY (Moscow), 60.

SINITSYNA, N.V. (scholar), 31n, 32n.

SINS, in general, 53; 'known and unknown', as formula, 200.

SKRYNNIKOV, RUSLAN (scholar), 31n.

SLAVIA ORTHODOXA, 15.

SLEEP, 158; as image of death, 159.

SLOTH, SLOTHFUL (lazy, -iness): as cause of ' bad living, 114, claim that Fathers' model no longer applies, 151, consent' to an assaulting urge, 133, defeat by a transgression, 117, an urge, 170; is avoided by those in genuine obedience, 129; Nil as, 130, 246, but his words can compensate, 114; stillness is prayer without, 99, 214, requiring detachment, 217; to be avoided in conversation, 236, in cell activities, 259.

SMYSLЪ, translation, 89.

SOBORNIK O BOZE (Nil's edited hagiographic collection), 25–30; claimed editorial principles, 251, 253; goal of recollection of the good, 253; heresy combated, 26–28, 53; labor entailed, 62, 252; lacks official imprimatur, 102; manuscripts, 44–45, 62n; miracles within, 29–30; nonpossession (poverty) within, 31.

—*Apologiai: Foreword*, 25, 62–63, 251–53; *Postscript*, 62–63, 253–54; textual questions, 152n, 253n–254n.

SOLITUDE (*See also* STILLNESS), 24, 28, 42, 48); danger of despondency, 222–23; requires 'angelic strength', 223.

SOLOVETSKII (SOLOVKI) MONASTERY, 38; library, 40.

SOFIA (ZOE), PALAIOLOGA (second wife of Ivan III, 1455–1503), 33n, 34.

SORA HERMITAGE (or Scete), xii, xiii, xxiii, 44, 47, 54, 63, 102, 246; and Kirllov, 103; and new service books (17th c.), 102–103; becomes wealthy coenobium after 1830, 103; cells and ownership, 38, 38n; church(es), 22; of the Presentation, 21–22; confession, 22; court patronage and entrance gifts, 102; cult of Nil, 102; German Podol'nyi and, 42; guard, 22; ieromonk-superior, 22; Innokentii (and his *Zavĕt*) and, 38; log cabin cells, 21; manuscripts, IRI type of *Ustav,* 65–66; mill, pond, 21; poverty, 32; role of *Predanie,* 24; *Scete Typikon* and, 48; Tale of (*See also* 'Tale of the Arrival of Nil Sorskii'), 5.

Sora, Lake and River, 20.

Soul (*See also* Salvation): aims to attain the spiritual, 129; and body as the whole person, 158; as better than the body, 120; as locus of the urge-passion, 133, 135; chastity of muddied by human contact, 218; departure/separation from the body at death, 195, 199–200; directly addressed regarding the terrible judgment, 199; ideal enslavement to a ascetic body, 159; liable to confusion from overexertion, 204, to destruction from precipitous action, 222; purity of, 128; salvation of, 58, 92, 175, 215, 232–33, 236, 244, 247; speaks for the entire person, including the soul, 199–201; the unprofitable for to be avoided, 226.

Soviet Union, 7n.

Spaso-Kamennyi Monastery, 9, 11, 30, 34, 35–36; *Genuine Account of the Foundation of Kamennyi Monastery* (post–1476), 35.

Špidlík, Thomas SJ (Cardinal, scholar), 32n.

Spirit, Holy, 114; borne on words of hesychastic masters, 151; fruits of, 213–14; operation moves the soul, 147.

Spirit, human, as agent of voiced prayer, 126.

Spirits, wicked, as unclean and identical with urges, 139.

Starchestvo (as adept-disciple relationship), 103.

State Secretary (*diak*), 5, 36–37, 51.

Steadfastness (strengthening), 64, 72, 154–57, 160.

Sticheron (verse), 164n.

Stillness (Hesychasm; *See also* Bezmolv-), 50n; abode of, 225; as coenobitic cell routine, 11, 48; as deponing of speculations, 141; as light-generating activity, 129; at Athos, 17–18; can cause arrogance, 220; cell literature, Slavic texts, 14, 16, 17, 35, 45; Climacus definition, 99; conclaves, periodic, among the dispersed, 224; discourse of, 59; from vigor of activity, heat of faith, God grants, 129; in hagiography, 55; instruction in usually needed, 129; perfect, as elevation on the cross and mortification, 220; severance from the worldly, 19–20, 213–18; struggle for, combined with

struggle against *logismoi*, 66, 95; to be avoided by those governed by passions of the soul, 223–24.
STOUDION MONASTERY (Constantinople), 19, 28; and Basilian *Asceticon*, 75; stillness practiced, 128.
SUPERIOR, MONASTIC, authority of, 55; Kirillov's as directing with aid of 'Exemplary Fathers,' 236; assigns work, 120; authorizes leaves, 120; corrects transgressions, 117.
SURIUS, LAURENTIUS, O. Cart. (hagiologist, 1522–1578), 102.
SUZDAL, 6.
SWEETNESS (as feeling), 91, 141, 144, 147–49, 152, 206, 209; in conversation, 236; in the Lord's commandments, 249; worldly as false, 231.
SYLVESTER (Pope, r. 314–35), *Pope Sylvester of Rome* (Life), 30.
SYMEON METAPHRASTES (later 10th c., Byzantine hagiographer, writer); Life of Eustratius the Martyr, prayer as source, 79, text mixed with other authors by Nil, 83, 199n–200n; *Paraphrase of* (Ps-) *Macarius*, as unnamed source, 23n, 70, 149-50, 178n, 181n; text mixed with other authors by Nil, 82, 175.
SYMEON THE NEW THEOLOGIAN (949–1032, ascetic-mystic Father, hymnographer), 17, 19, 115n, 128; on David, 203; didactic use of hymns, 75.

—Ps-Symeon, 17, 70, 80, 74–75, 126n, 132, 138, 152n; and breath-control method of prayer, 74–75.
—Slavic corpus (including Ps-Symeon) and texts, 40, 50, 74–75; and the heart-mind dichotomy, 86, 92n, 95; as source, 67–69, 75, 86, 129, 132, 136n, 138n–40n, 141, 179, 203–04, 206; 208; as model glosser, 80; as possible source, 164n, 234n, 253n; explains Gregory Sinaite, 141n; texts blended and adapted by Nil, 82, 126n, 129n; texts mixed with other authors by Nil, 82, 126n, 129n, 138n, 203n, 213n, unnamed, 114n–115n, 126n, 138n, 213n, 234n–35n, 253n.
SYMEON THE STUDITE (mentor of Symeon NT, fl. 975), 19, 128, 203n; named as authority, 69.
SYMEON THE STYLITE AND THAUMATURGE OF THE WONDROUS MOUNTAIN (521/2–592), Life, 26, 27.
SYMEON STYLITE THE ELDER (390–459), Life, 26, 28.
SYRIA, 25, 26.

'TALE OF THE ARRIVAL OF NIL SORSKII' (1660s), 21.
TEARS (*See also* MOURNING), 48, 67–68, 75; accompany prayer-summons for aid against urges, 189; as gift, role of grace in acquisition, 202, 204; as greatest solace, 209; as purifying,

206–07; calm urges, cheer the intellect, 209; means of acquisition, 207; model prayers for, 205–07; rein in anger, 210 spontaneous from grace, as the most effective, 208.
TERROR, as juvenile, opposed by prayer, hope in God's goodness, 234–35.
TESTAMENT (OF NIL), 3, 69, 255–56; disposition of goods, 62n, 63, 256; manuscripts, 62n–63n; structure, 63.
THEODORE OF SYKEON (anchorite, d. 613), Life, 28–29; as possible source, 234n.
THEODORE THE STUDITE (coenobiarch, iconodule, 759–826), 29; Life, 27; Slavic texts of *Little Catechisms*, 40, 77: as source, 69, 77–78, 189, unnamed, 239; Kirillov recension as likely, 77; *Testament*, 114n, 115n, 123n.
THEODOSIUS THE GREAT (Palestinian Coenobiarch, 423–529), Life, 26, 28, 31.
THEOLOGY, dogmatic, 54.
THEORIA (Mystical contemplation; *See also* VISION), 23, 32, 146–50, 153n, 159n, 217.
THEOTOKOS (*See also* MOTHER OF GOD), 142n; hymns to, 262n; metaphorically imagined role in the foundation of Mt. Athos, 13.
'THIRD ROME', 8.
THOMAIS THE MARTYR (Alexandria, 6th c.), as source, 69, 169.
THOMAS, APOSTLE, 35; feast of, 268.

THOUGHT(S), as used in this translation, 88–89; the evil to be prevented, 153; the good to be ignored during prayer, 140.
TIME, seasonal and latitudinal reckoning, 165.
TIMING, 68, 219–27; lack of turns good to evil, 219.
TITHING, 53.
TIKHON ZVORYKIN (Iosifov treasurer, bibliophile), 47.
TONE (Orthodox musical system), eight-, 262–63.
TORTURE/TORMENTS, 6, 50, 52, 54; future, 114, 137, 179, 197–98, 202, 208; crown(s) differentiated, as polar opposite, 137; fear of as deterrent of sin, 129; non-repentance, not failed combat as cause, 136–37; welcomed by martyrs, 83, 200n.
TRADITION(S) (rules combined with teachings): apostolic, 246; general, in the *Scete Typikon*, heretical, 115; of the angel to Anthony, 224; of the holy Fathers, 115, 243, 245, 247; mandated outside of cloister too, 117; of the monks' individual 'fathers', 260; of the saints, 115, 229; of the 'synodal'/church, 259–60; of 'the wicked and vain', 114.
TRANCE, in negative sense, resulting from the passionate engaging in stillness, 224.
TRANSLATION PRINCIPLES, xii, 105–09; true and pseudo-translations, xi, 33, 68, 105–09, 124n.

TRANSVOLGANS (*See also*
  'BELOOZERO HERMITS',
  GERMAN PODOL'NYI, GURII
  TUSHIN, NONPOSSESSORS,
  VASSIAN PATRIKEEV), xii, 32n,
  46; anti-inquisitional stance in
  their name, 46n.
TRIALS, as necessary for crowns,
  176.
TRIFON (Kirillov hegumen,
  1435–1448, Archbishop of
  Rostov, 1462–1467), 9, 10n.
TRINITY: as analogy, 223; doctrine,
  52, invoked as 'thearchic', 190.
TRISAGION, 140, 262–63, 266.
TROITSA-SERGIEV MONASTERY, 6,
  9, 35n, 37; opposition to Paisii
  Iaroslavov, 34–35.
TROPARION (-IA), 153, 207, 260,
  263; hypakoi, 264; of repen-
  tance, 143; of the Resurrec-
  tion, 264.
TROPES, in sources, 5, 20.
TYPIKON (for effecting stillness),
  144.
TYRANT (*See also* KING), 126n.

UKRAINE (*See also* WESTERN RUS),
  6, 7n, 103.
Umъ, translation, 90.
UNCLEAN, IMPURE: demon, 240;
  pride, 188; quality, 189; urges,
  64, 155, 189, 233–34, 240,
  wicked spirits, 139.
UNIAT CHURCH, 7.
UNION, of saint with God,
  147–48.
UNRIGHTEOUSNESS, 158.
URGE(S) (*logismos, cogitatio, pomysl'*;
  See also DEMON, PASSION,

SPIRIT, EIGHT . . . URGES), 23;
  active in intellect, 139–40; by
  nature, some derive from others, 172; chaste and gentle,
  154; contradicting them, 162;
  contrast of 'pious' intellection
  over an urge and a wicked
  urge, 135; defrauding the
  wicked by means of the good,
  162; filthy, attacks of, befall
  even the successful, 233; create
  despair, 155, formulaic rebukes
  against, 190; from worldly life
  assail, 231; infirmity of, 205;
  neutral 'captivation' by while
  handling everyday needs, 135;
  scorning and driving them off,
  by the 'perfect', 162; summoning (praying for) divine help
  against, 140, 154, 163, 168–70,
  172, 188–90, 234, for neophytes and the infirm, 162:
  model prayers against, 189–90;
  summoning specific saints,
  169; the bad follow the good,
  138; the good as virtues, 162;
  terror regarding, 59, 234;
  transposing wicked into good,
  133, 208, away from vainglory,
  182; unclean, incited by improper conversations, etc., 234;
  wicked to be severed, 233.
USTAV (of Nil), xi, 25, 41, 62; and
  Predanie principles, 68; as
  source- and textbook, 23–24;
  Innokentii and, 38; lacks official
  imprimatur, 99, 102; manuscripts, 45–48, 62n, 63n, 65–66,
  66n; prayer, diverse and heavy
  role of, 79; structures, 65–68:

types (PDP, IRI), 65–66, 123n–24n, 272n; sources, 66–80, proportion of texts, 69; technical translation issues, 86–94, 109; translations and adaptations of, xi, 33, 65–66.

VAINGLORY (See EIGHT . . . URGES).
VALENS (Roman Emperor of the East, r. 364–378), 28.
VANITY: of conversations, 218; of the world, 152, 158; life as, 194.
VARSANOFII (Tverian hermit, 15th c.), 50.
VASILII II VASILEVICH, GRAND PRINCE OF MOSCOW (r. 1425–1461, with interruptions), 6–7, 9, 36.
VASILII III IVANOVICH, GRAND PRINCE OF MOSCOW (r. 1505–1533), 34, 44, 56, 58, 60.
VASSIAN (VASILII) PATRIKEEV, (prince-monk, devotee of Nil, d. post–1531), 37, 41, 58–61, 231n, 236; as distinct from Nil, 59–61; fears (spiritual) addressed, 59, 64, 233–34; polemics against Iosif, 59–61.
—Ps-Vassian, 29; writings, 61.
VATOPEDI MONASTERY (Mount Athos), 15.
VESSELS, SACRED, requirement of simplicity, 121.
VESPERS, 11, 261–62, 266.
VIGILS, 22; not required of everyone, 145–46.
—in *Scete Typikon*: as proper for the healthy, 159; bi-weekly formal gatherings, 260; commencing at 9th Hour or Vespers, 261; community cell as substitute for church, 261; discretion at the meal, 262; elder's authority, 262; group confessions and discussions, 262, 264; liturgy according to the church typikon, 261; priest's role if present, 263; Psalter, *Trisagion* and prayer substitutions for just two or three monks, 265; regular days, 265–68; Resurrection and festival seasons, 264; special festivals of the Lord, 261, 264; specifics of the service, 262–64; spiritual discourse (sermon) or reading, 262, care over latter 264; Sundays, 263–64.
VILLAGES, lands, monastic 97–98, 186–87, 215.
VIRTUE(s): abstinence of stomach as gateway to, 167; accomplished and knowledgeable in, as epistolary compliment, 244; all as necessary to combat the anger arising from prayer with watchfulness, 210; as an army led by compunction, 208; as no guarantee that the snares of the world will not prevail, 232; 'defraud' passions, 162, via recollection, 162n; epistle as sermon for edification of, 231; God's chastisements aim for advancement in, 168; malice endured over can lead to pride, 186; path of, as perfect life, 237, keeping to it defeats despondency, 178; prayer of the heart as wellspring

of, 140n, 145; remembrance of death as the most necessary, 193, in God/prayer of the intellect as the premier, 221; require grace, 106-08, 156; self-will and concern for riches as false, 241, 245; stillness as life of, 102, as promoter of, 217; wither from non-spiritual conversations, 242; witness of as mark of one to emulate, 236.

VISION, of future bliss, 147, 150.

VISITATION, of God, 155; Holy Spirit, 220n; the Lord, 208, 211; mercy, 154.

VISITORS: discouraged, 216, by Isaac the Syrian, 19–20; only experienced elders to converse with them, 21.

VOLOGDA (region), 9, 44, 55.

VOLOKOLAMSK (region), 44.

VOLOKOLAMSK PATERICON (1540s), 35.

WATERMARKS, 25.

WATER METAPHORS, SIMILES (as life-bearing and/or flame quenching: 80–81, 130, 140, 145, 205–06, 217, 236.

WATCHFULNESS, 48, 76; as identical to mental activity, 153; as required mental activity: Hesychius's four types 92; of the intellect, 260; regarding assigned work, 120.

WESTERN RUS (*See also* BELARUS, LITHUANIA, UKRAINE), 10.

WICKEDNESS, 54; as passion, 53, of the soul, stillness-perverting, 223.

WILLFULNESS, prohibition of, 55, 117.

WITHDRAWAL, from the world (*See* RENUNCIATION).

WISDOM, God's (*See also* PROVIDENCE), as Divine Providence, 196; supreme (*premudrost'*), linked to full renunciation 108, 213, 241.

'WOMAN-SINNER'; (presumed Gospel harlot), 207.

WORD, DEED, AND THOUGHT, as formula for all activity, 158, 192, 198, 200, 253; modified use of, 160, 174, 208, 211.

WORD, OF GOD (*See* GOD, word of).

WORK TERMS, 92.

WORLD: as transient, grief- and evil-ridden, 231–32; entanglements in, to be shunned, 97–99, 151, 158, 215, 246; merry-making as basic of, 237; snares of, as super-seductive, 232; vanity of, 158.

'WRIT OF EMNITIES' (*Pismo o neliubkakh*, 1550s–60s), 32n, 45.

'YOUR HOLINESS,' as term of epistolary address, 248–49.

YOUTHS, to be avoided, 63, 123, 171.

ZEAL, graceful, as ideal, 235.

ZHMAKIN, V (scholar), 40n.

ZIMIN, A. A. (scholar), 32n.

ZOGRAF MONASTERY (Mount Athos), 15.

www.ingramcontent.com/pod-product-compliance
Lightning Source LLC
Chambersburg PA
CBHW031229290426
44109CB00012B/224